European Union and its Neighbours in a Globalized World

Volume 15

The series publishes monographs and edited volumes in the field of European and international law and policy. A special focus is put on the European neighbourhood policy, current problems in European and international law and policy as well as the role of the European Union as a global actor. The series supports the publishing and distribution of research results of cross-border research consortia. Besides renowned scientists the series is also open for publication projects of young academics. The series emphasizes the interplay of the European Union and its neighbouring countries as well as the important role of the European Union as a key player in the international context of law, economics and politics.

Dušan V. Popović • Rainer Kulms
Editors

Repositioning Platforms in Digital Market Law

Springer

Editors
Dušan V. Popović
University of Belgrade, Faculty of Law
Belgrade, Serbia

Rainer Kulms
Max Planck Institute for Comparative and International Private Law
Hamburg, Germany

ISSN 2524-8928 ISSN 2524-8936 (electronic)
European Union and its Neighbours in a Globalized World
ISBN 978-3-031-69680-0 ISBN 978-3-031-69678-7 (eBook)
https://doi.org/10.1007/978-3-031-69678-7

This Springer imprint is published by the registered company Springer Nature Switzerland AG
The registered company address is: Gewerbestrasse 11, 6330 Cham, Switzerland

Preface

Online platforms and their ecosystems are the cornerstone of the digital economy. They have brought forth positive network effects. But they are also known for their information asymmetries, their potential for market failures, and their problematic relationship with data protection law. This volume provides a detailed analysis of the current process of repositioning online platforms in the digital economy as regulators express concerns about the evolution from mere intermediaries to gatekeepers. This includes an assessment of regulatory choices from an economic policy perspective. The exclusive reliance on competition law instruments has proven to be incapable of coping with cases of platforms abusing their market power. Therefore, the book explores the European Union's new approach towards digital markets, as new legislative instruments (such as the Digital Markets Act, the Digital Services Act, the Proposal of AI Act, the Data Act, and the Data Governance Act) have been enacted or are proposed. The EU's emphasis on new regulatory *ex ante* instruments (as in the Digital Markets Act) calls for an assessment of their overlap or their interface with existing supranational and national competition rules. The message of this volume is intended to reach beyond academics and researchers. It also recognises the crucial needs of practitioners in the digital sector who stand to benefit from the analysis of the law of online platforms, undertaken by a working group of renowned authors from different jurisdictions.

The book starts with a comparison of the risk-based regulatory approaches adopted in the Digital Markets Act and the Digital Services Act. These are complex and polycentric regulatory regimes that shift the regulatory role towards non-state actors such as surrogate regulators which are required to develop their own systems of internal control and risk management. This chapter, authored by Tatjana Jovanić (University of Belgrade, Serbia), argues that the internalisation of the platforms' responsibility for management of systemic risks and compliance with due diligence obligations call for more substantive rules to provide benchmark for measuring performance. The following chapter, authored by Matija Damjan (University of Ljubljana, Slovenia), focuses on the interoperability requirements introduced by the Digital Markets Act. The chapter discusses the implications of interoperability requirements for gatekeepers, including the need to ensure user data portability and the provision of technical interfaces for interoperability. The chapter argues that, while promoting competition and innovation, interoperability requirements also raise questions about the optimal balance between standardisation and diversity in the digital economy.

The territoriality of copyright norms is challenged by technological advances. While the Internet allows for cross-border content delivery, the free movement of goods and services also appears to be incompatible with territorial copyright regimes. The chapter, authored by István Harkai and Péter Mezei (University of Szeged, Hungary), argues that this contradiction may be resolved by use of legal geography, a research method combining the interfaces of geography and law. This chapter takes a new approach to comparing the internal market and territorial fragmentation rules of EU copyright law and the contractual practices of platform providers, in order to answer the question of how geography determines the development of a legal area. The following chapter, authored by Dušan V. Popović (University of Belgrade), assesses content moderation mechanisms from the freedom of expression perspective. The author identifies three concerns. First, content moderation activities may lead to excessive filtering of users' content, in contradiction with the formal absence of general monitoring and filtering duty in EU law. Another concern stems from the use of recommender systems. Moreover, further freedom of expression concerns are reflected in the use of content demotion mechanisms by online platforms in addressing 'borderline content'.

The chapter authored by Magdalena Knapp (University of Warsaw, Poland) and Anna Piszcz (University of Bialystok, Poland) assesses the transparency obligations stemming from the Digital Services Act. The authors conclude that, though the layered structure of the obligations and self-assessment model puts the burden of enforcement on providers of online platforms, it also invites more actors to the process. Therefore, third parties, such as consumers or the civil society, will play a crucial role in enforcing the transparency obligations set out in Digital Services Act. The authors argue that the Digital Services Act applies its own logic, different from that of EU consumer law, resting predominantly on *ex ante* primary fairness obligations, while the consumer law relies upon *ex post* prohibition of unfair practices. The following chapter, authored by Giulia Schneider (Università Cattolica del Sacro Cuore, Italy), explores stakeholder engagement in EU digital platform regulations. The chapter tests two different hypotheses: (i) to which extent EU digital platform regulation addresses corporate digital sustainability interests; and (ii) whether the considered regulations employ, as a regulatory technique, co-regulation mechanisms building on stakeholder engagement capacities for the attainment of the relevant interests.

The Digital Markets Act is silent on data access to platforms or *de facto* owners of data that do not qualify as gatekeepers. The chapter authored by Rainer Kulms (Max Planck Institute for Comparative and International Private Law, Germany) evaluates the regulatory strategies for data access below the DMA's gatekeeper threshold. The chapter explores the data access scenarios under the P2B-Regulation, the EU's new Data Act, the GDPR and German competition law. The chapter also examines the potential of unfair trading law for developing access standards, given that fairness has become a crucial element of digital market policy. The following chapter authored by Giacomo Tagiuri (University of Amsterdam, The Netherlands) analyses self-preferencing practices and their future after the adoption of the Digital Markets Act. The chapter argues that Art. 6.5 of the DMA is unlikely to work as a *per se*, form-based, rule for the *ex ante* identification of prohibited conduct. Most likely, this provision will work as a form of quality standard for the design and presentation of rankings by vertically integrated platforms, to be enforced collaboratively with the undertakings. The privacy concerns are at the heart of the chapter co-authored by Thomas Papadopoulos and Louiza Kofina (University of Cyprus, Cyprus), which assesses the Digital Markets Act and its complex relation with the provisions of the EU's General Data Protection Regulation. The authors conclude that the Digital Markets Act is nevertheless a conservative legal instrument which proper application is restricted due to the reliance on highly debatable concepts, including GDPR-compliance consent and data portability.

The final chapter in the book provides a much-needed global perspective to the issue of digital platforms' regulation. The chapter authored by Yane Svetiev (University of Sydney, Australia) assesses the platform regulation in the USA and Australia, which allows for comparisons with the more advanced and more interventionist EU approach. The chapter argues that the initiatives to control platform power in these jurisdictions follow a common emergent template of measures, focused on identifying conduct violations for specifically designated platforms on the basis of structural criteria of size and concentration. The author concludes that this approach is unlikely to provide a satisfactory solution for addressing the problem of the economic or political power concentration by the 'digital giants'.

The editors are immensely grateful to the contributors for their dedication to repositioning online platforms. Special thanks are also due for the research facilities which the editors have experienced at to their home institutions, the University of Belgrade Faculty of Law, and the Max Planck Institute for Comparative and International Private Law.

Belgrade, Serbia — Dušan V. Popović
Hamburg, Germany — Rainer Kulms

Contents

Platform Regulation: Ex Ante Tools and Strategies in the Regulatory Toolkit

Tatjana Jovanić

Abstract This Chapter provides a brief comparison of the risk-based regulatory approaches adopted in the Digital Markets Act and the Digital Services Act. One of the main characteristics of both legislative instruments is the normative choice to tie compliance duties proportionately to the type of risks and severity of impact that online platforms create. The DSA and the DMA are examples of complex and polycentric regulatory regimes that shift the regulatory role towards non-state actors as surrogate regulators which are required to develop their own systems of internal control and risk management. In addition to specifying social outputs, the enforcement of the DMA and the DSA reflects a primary characteristic of meta-regulation: the regulated platforms are obliged to improve their internal management in order to achieve public goals. The requirement that platforms develop effective risk management strategies and compliance schemes on their own entails the possibility of undesired risk-enhancing effects of the risk-based regulation and the mechanisms it mandates. This Chapter argues that the internalisation of the platforms' responsibility for management of systemic risks and compliance with due diligence obligations call for more substantive rules to provide benchmark against which to measure performance.

1 Introduction

Digital markets have become a necessity in modern life. Understood as the core infrastructure of the twenty-first century economy and public sphere and being integral to economic and social activity, their infrastructural powers have the key attributes of public utilities. At the same time, technological development is positively correlated with the development of digital markets. This, on the other hand, raises

T. Jovanić (✉)
University of Belgrade, Faculty of Law, Belgrade, Serbia
e-mail: tanja@ius.bg.ac.rs

D. V. Popović, R. Kulms (eds.), *Repositioning Platforms in Digital Market Law*, European Union and its Neighbours in a Globalized World 15,
https://doi.org/10.1007/978-3-031-69678-7_1

the issue of the impact of technology-related and other risks on competition, consumer choice and the fundamental rights of users of digital platforms. For this reason, some countries have already adopted a legal framework that aims to regulate the functioning of digital markets, and many initiatives are currently in the pipeline. The issue of the economic power of platforms and the protection of users of their services is one of the legislative priorities in the European Union.

It is not only the services provided through platforms that are subject to regulation, but also the risks that may arise due to their intermediary function. In addition to the specific type of service provided, risk regulation also takes into account the size and importance of the platform itself. The object of regulation is protection against defined risks, which also shape the approach to regulatory enforcement. Regulatory strategy is largely based on risk. In this sense, the regulation of platforms is not based only on one specific ex ante 'regulatory antitrust' approach, but rather the regulatory strategy is largely based on risk. The regulation of digital markets and especially digital services in the EU, together with new regulatory regimes related to personal data and artificial intelligence, mark a new approach to EU regulatory governance of digital technologies. Since digital markets are developing markets, excessive restrictions could slow down innovation and threaten their economic potential and thus social benefits. In this sense, the regulation does not only introduce new rules and standards of behaviour, but also new regulatory strategies that incorporate the role of regulated entities and the wider community.

The Digital Services Act (DSA)[1] and the Digital Markets Act (DMA)[2] are legislative acts that are asymmetric by design. The asymmetry reflects the rising importance of the largest digital services providers in the digital economy. As regulatory intermediaries, such providers are expected to take an active role in curbing illegal content and address issues of societal risks posed by their intermediary role. Substantially addressing anti-competitive practices and liability for content, a number of hybrid ex ante rules on business conduct and procedural due diligence obligations of the largest online platforms reflect a shift towards a new regulatory approach to digital markets. Such new obligations, related to market conduct and the new layers of procedural requirements, oblige service providers to put mechanisms in place to monitor compliance. Albeit it departs from the traditional methodology of competition policy and introduces ex ante tools to provide legal certainty of what platforms (especially larger and hence riskier ones) can or cannot do, the Digital Markets Act aims at designing contestable and fair markets. Changing the role of service providers, notably online platforms, and focusing on how platforms behave as content moderators, the DSA moves the responsibility of intermediaries away from the area of liability and deeper into the realm of regulation.[3] Although the DSA

[1] *Regulation (EU) 2022/2065* of the European Parliament and of the Council of 19 October 2022 on a Single Market For Digital Services and amending Directive 2000/31/EC, O.J. L 277 (2022).

[2] *Regulation (EU) 2022/1925* of the European Parliament and of the Council of 14 September 2022 on contestable and fair markets in the digital sector and amending Directives (EU) 2019/137 and (EU) 2020/1828, O.J. L. 265 (2022).

[3] Buiten (2021), p. 23.

is based on a more extensive risk based framework, both acts pose significant questions regarding the clarity of the platform's duties and due diligence obligations, and raise a number of questions related to the compliance of platforms and their business and individual users. In this sense, not only are platforms regulated entities (as causes of risk and risk bearers), but the regulatory strategy requires them to establish appropriate risk self-control mechanisms.

Since the entire emerging toolbox of platform regulation is so extensive that a description of it would go far beyond the scope of a single chapter, this chapter provides a brief comparison of the regulatory approaches adopted in the DMA and the DSA. It portrays a general overview of the toolbox and scope of compliance obligations, from the regulatory strategy perspective. Therefore, the contribution focuses on the nature and main features of new proactive and risk-based regulatory regimes established by the DMA and the DSA, as meta-regulatory frameworks that incorporate rules on the behaviour, the mechanisms of decision-making and the networks of actors involved in regulation.

2 Futility of Competition vs. Regulation 'Dichotomy' in Regulating Digital Services

Digital markets have significantly transformed the way of living and play a fundamental role in modern societies, delivering substantial benefits for consumers and businesses, the economy and society. They have opened new markets, lowered prices, spurred innovation, created jobs and boosted the economy. Digital markets and services can play an important role in supporting societal values, such as non-discrimination, free speech and democracy. This is especially true for platforms. In short, a platform is a service holding an intermediary function in access to information, content, goods or services, as a rule published or provided by third parties. As online multilateral markets, platforms are data-driven (data is often user-generated), automated, based on algorithms, formalised by ownership, and monetised (depending on the selected business model).[4]

From former startups, through strategic acquisitions to the most powerful global players, the accumulation of market power has created network effects, economies of scale, and unequal access to data as some of the key resources in a modern world. The lack of effective competition in such ecosystems can cause harm to their non-professional and business users and competitors, and conversely can have a negative effect on the development of the digital economy. The real and potential harms caused by powerful digital enterprises and the inadequacy of existing competition policy tools have been recognised in many official reports.[5] The emerging

[4] Van Dijck (2021), p. 323.

[5] Cabral et al. (2021); Cremer et al. (2019); Competition and Markets Authority (2020); Stigler Committee (2019).

legislation across the globe, establishing the substantive legal norms of digital markets and digital services, is predominantly based on rules introducing tools of an ex ante nature, with important procedural norms related to the supervision, control and enforcement powers of the designated supervisors. A dominant sentiment is that antitrust enforcement can have a negative impact on the dynamic nature of digital markets and may ultimately lead to the breakup of dominant intermediaries. Even less disruptive ex post measures require ongoing monitoring, which would be an easier task for regulators than for antitrust authorities. When carefully crafted, regulation is said to be able to provide legal certainty and restrain the potential harmful effects of the digital markets and services.[6] Differences between ex ante and ex post approaches have almost decisively delineated competition protection and sector specific regulation.[7] In contrast to backward looking and fact specific competition legislation, sector specific ex ante rules are forward looking insofar as their role is to follow public policy priorities and prescribe types of market behaviour regardless of particular circumstances. Applied to a wide range of operators satisfying certain criteria, ex ante rules aim to address the market failures of industry structures.[8] Both competition and sector specific regulation aim to address market power. The choice between ex ante or ex post instruments should be based on significant benefits with respect to the applicability and enforcement of the existing general competition policies and risks posed by intermediation in digital markets. Whereas antitrust enforcement, apart from merger enforcement, proceeds on a case-by-case basis, regulators could look forward by constraining future conduct before infringements of competition occur. Considering the fact that digital markets are in constant change and are too innovative to be supervised ex post, it seems that the primary motive for establishing a specific ex ante regime for digital markets and providers of intermediary services is the ability to proactively shape the behaviour of supervised intermediaries before harm occurs. The proactive regulatory approach assumes monitoring the fulfilment of ex ante rules, setting pro-competitive and pro-consumer due diligence obligations, and establishing open and productive relationships in order to take swift proactive action where the supervisor identifies risks of potential problems occurring or risks that have materialised.

In the domain of economic regulation, aimed at addressing and deterring harmful practices, ex ante intervention is based on prescriptive rules and specific, predominantly positive obligations as requirements on firms to take or not take certain actions. On the other side, one of the main characteristics of competition legislation is the dominance of negative obligations, i.e. prohibitions of certain actions and conducts.[9] In contrast and despite the fact that competition law rules are often

---

[6] Stigler Committee (2019), pp. 99–100.

[7] See, for instance, Alexiadis (2012), pp. 139–140; Monti (2008); Dunne (2015); Competition Law and Economic Regulation: Making and Managing Markets (CUP, 2015); de Streel (2008); OECD (2021a, b).

[8] Compared to remedies in competition legislation (with the exception of merger control), ex ante intervention is better at resolving structural issues. OECD (2021b), pp. 12–14.

[9] OECD (2021a), p. 8.

enforced in a lengthy procedure, rules of an ex post nature are broader in scope and could address a wider range of misbehaviours. In addition to directly or indirectly promoting competition, the adoption of ex ante regulation provides the legislator leeway to consider a broader set of societal objectives and policy goals than traditionally attributed to competition law. In digital markets, ex ante rules are intended to ensure fairness, contestability, transparency and innovation, as well as to safeguard social goals beyond purely economic considerations. However, markets, actors, services and technologies, whether or not subject to ex ante regulation, are constantly evolving and the risks of obsolete or non-existing rule-based ex ante approach can be compensated by competition law as a fall-back mechanism. As will be specifically pointed out in this chapter, the new European legal framework on digital markets, especially the Digital Markets Act, represents an overhaul of the tools of antitrust and fills the gap caused by the traditional dichotomy between economic regulation and antitrust. The new EU digital markets regulatory regimes represent a paradigmatic shift from ex post enforcement of competition rules toward an ex ante regulatory regime of regulation of competition, labelled as 'precautionary antitrust'[10] or 'a more regulatory approach to antitrust law'.[11]

The regulation of digital markets means the integration of two forms of economic regulation, as well as the integration of different aspects of social regulation. A new pro-competition framework to promote competition and protect consumers and businesses in the digital world can only bring the expected outcome incorporated into the wider normative framework, in particular sectoral regulations, fair business trading rules, consumer protection, as well as data protection. The pro-competitive approach to digital services providers can also address market failures that other regulators may also be considering. As an example, data protection law enforcement, with a view to protect consumers, may reduce barriers to entry and allow for more competition. Conduct such as the acquisition of personal data may infringe data protection law, consumer and competition law. The issue of market failures related to the operation of digital services, especially platforms, should therefore be considered as the broader concept of a wider regulatory space, which assumes a range of regulatory options addressing interconnected market failures in attention markets.[12]

[10] Porteuse (2022).

[11] Cappai and Colangelo (2021).

[12] Monti (2020), p. 2.

3 The Role of the Digital Markets Act and the Digital Services Act in European Digital Constitutionalism

Over the past three decades, the evolution of EU policy on digital technologies has faced a paradigm shift, which may be explained as 'European digital constitutionalism'.[13] Initially driven by the purpose of fostering the development of digital services in the internal market, the rise of risk regulation and risk governance have largely increased the role of constitutionalism.[14] Digital constitutionalism assumes limits on platforms in exercising powers, especially through the protection of fundamental rights and the rule of law. One of the key contributions of the Digital Single Market Strategy is the shift from fostering internal markets towards balancing the promotion of innovations, legal instruments protecting rights and core values, and mandating the transparency, fairness and accountability of platforms.[15]

Since the establishment of the first EU legislative framework for digital services in the E-Commerce Directive (ECD) of 2000[16] remained outdated, pending the legislative initiative to draft the Digital Services Act, the European Commission identified the need to promote fairness and responsibility of online platforms and to modernise the liability regime through the introduction of new tools.[17] The Platform to Business (P2B) Regulation was introduced in 2019,[18] with the aim of promoting better trading, combatting unfair practices and supporting the transparency for business users of online platforms. This paved the ground for the Digital Markets Act and the Digital Services Act. The main motive for the shift from ex post policing of the platforms' market behaviours to introducing and enforcing constraints on their behaviour ex ante was mainly the inadequacy of Articles 101 and 102 of the TFEU.[19] In fact, in a drafting phase the DMA was detached from the DSA due to conceptual differences between competitive ex ante remedies for platforms as gatekeepers, which was the subject matter of the DMA, and platform liability rules and

---

[13] For a more detailed overview see: De Gregorio (2021) and Suzor (2018).

[14] De Gregorio and Dunn (2022), p. 478.

[15] Communication from the Commission to the European Parliament, the Council, the European Economic and Social Committee and the Committee of the Regions, A Digital Single Market Strategy for Europe, COM(2015) 192 final.

[16] Directive 2000/31/EC of the European Parliament and of the Council of 8 June 2000 on certain legal aspects of information society services, in particular electronic commerce, in the Internal Market, O.J. L 178/1 (2000).

[17] European Commission, Accompanying the Document Communication from the Commission to the European Parliament, the Council, the European Economic and Social Committee and the Committee of the Regions on the Mid-Term Review on the implementation of the Digital Single Market Strategy A Connected Digital Single Market for All' (Staff Working Document), SWD (2017) 155 final.

[18] Regulation (EU) 2019/1150 of the European Parliament and of the Council of 20 June 2019 on promoting fairness and transparency for business users of online intermediation services, O.J. L 186/57 (2019).

[19] Turillazzi et al. (2023), p. 102.

guarantees to fundamental rights protection and societal risks.[20] The early 2010s were marked by intensive legislative activities of developed countries regarding the regulation of platforms.[21] It remains to be seen whether new European legislation will further instantiate the 'Brussels Effect', whereby European legislation, similar to the GDPR, influences how social media platforms exercise their powers and moderate content.[22]

3.1 *Digital Markets Act: A Competition–Regulatory Hybrid*

The goal of the DMA is to ensure a contestable and fair market across the digital sector, by promulgating ex ante rules that oblige large online platforms which act as 'gatekeepers' between business users and final users. The specific regime introduced by the DMA is wider since it is encompasses a broader set of objectives, going beyond the protection of undistorted competition and efficiency grounds, and the need to detect the anticompetitive object or effect. As explicitly stated in Recital 11 of the Preamble, 'this Regulation therefore aims to protect a different legal interest from that protected by those rules and it should apply without prejudice to their application'. Instead of it, the DMA identifies a category of obligations to be implemented by gatekeepers in performing core platform services. From the standpoint of the enforcement strategy, this is actually the reversal of intervening in markets: the regulated gatekeepers are expected to demonstrate compliance in practice. They are expected to comply not only with all obligations related to gatekeeper practices that limit contestability or are unfair, as explicitly defined in Articles 5, 6 and 7 of the DMA, but also data protection regulation (GDPR), legislation on cyber security, consumer protection, and product safety, as well as with accessibility requirements.[23]

Even during the legislative drafting phase, the Digital Markets Act spurred academic debates on its nature. Commentators discussed whether it is a special competition regime or an instrument distinct from competition law. Some characterised it as 'a competition hand in a regulatory glove',[24] 'precautionary antitrust',[25]

---

[20] Savin (2021), p. 3.

[21] For example, United States: Bills introduced in the House of Representatives on 11 June 2021 - H.R. 3816 ('American Choice and Innovation Online Act'); H.R. 3825 ('Ending Platform Monopolies Act'); H.R. 3826 ('Platform Competition and Opportunity Act of 2021'); H.R. 3849 ('Augmenting Compatibility and Competition by Enabling Service Switching Act of 2021'. United Kingdom, Online Safety Act 2023; Digital Markets, Competition and Consumers Bill 2023 (Originated in the House of Commons). Germany: Act against Restraints of Competition (Competition Act – GWB), 10th amendment, January 2021. Japan: Act on Improving Transparency and Fairness of Digital Platforms, May 2020. Australia: News Media and Digital Platforms Mandatory Bargaining Code 2021.

[22] For more details see Nunziato (2023).

[23] Article 8 DSA.

[24] Moreno Belloso and Petit (2023).

[25] Porteuse (2022).

'sector-specific competition law',[26] 'a revolution grounded on traditions',[27] 'more regulatory approach to competition law',[28] an inherent novelty of pro-competitive economic regulation in a 'difficult epistemological position'.[29]

Competition enforcement becomes regulatory in nature when it is based on ex ante regulatory-type remedies, which introduce detailed positive obligations requiring continuous monitoring and exceed the prevention of anticompetitive behaviour, which is the main goal of competition policy.[30] The provisions of the DMA can also be presented as a line of business restrictions—a type of competition remedy that includes requirements ranging from structural separation to behavioural restrictions. The latter include restrictions such as mandated access, non-discrimination obligations, and mandatory standards on portability and interoperability.[31]

The DMA differs from traditional ex ante regulation for a number of reasons. For example, it does not apply to the whole sector, but rather to platforms as entities, based on the size and prescribed characteristics that qualify them as gatekeepers. However, contrary to traditional ex ante economic regulation, the DMA is applicable to entities that are also not in a commercial relation. This means that the DMA is not a sectoral regulation but an asymmetric entity regulation. Since it focuses on gatekeeping, it differs from traditional entity-based regulation, and thus its regulatory approach may be defined as sui generis.[32] The two forms of economic regulation, competition law and sectoral regulation are sometimes labelled as ex post and ex ante. Whether precautionary antitrust or regulation of competition, the Digital Markets Act is the representation of varying manifestations of the same phenomenon, market intervention.[33]

To use Commissioner Margrethe Vestager's words, the enforcement of the DMA, as 'a hybrid approach', is based on both ex ante regulation and traditional competition tools.[34] As a hybrid, the DMA combines the characteristics of both types. Its nature is more prescriptive, as are sector specific regulations, while its goals are indispensably linked to the competition policy aims. Namely, contestability may be explained as 'inter-platform competition', while fairness implies a concern for intra-platform exclusion and exploitation.[35] Competition law clearly serves as a reference point, as the DMA is based on the idea that the enforcement of the abuse of dominance rules is ineffective both procedurally (lengthy investigation and

[26] Petit (2021).

[27] Larouche and de Streel (2021), pp. 543–545.

[28] Cappai and Colangelo (2021).

[29] Larouche and de Streel (2021), p. 545.

[30] Dunne (2015), pp. 79–87.

[31] OECD (2020), pp. 25–27; OECD (2021a), p. 42.

[32] Pinar (2022), p. 19.

[33] Dunne (2015), p. 48.

[34] Vestager (2022).

[35] Bostoen (2023), pp. 6–7; Moreno Belloso and Petit (2023), p. 13.

remedial issues) and substantively (difficulty to prove dominance and abuse).[36] Recognising that a traditional cease-and-desist order may be insufficient to preserve the competition in digital markets, influential competition law scholars suggested remedies with restitutive elements ('restorative remedies').[37] In EU competition law, such remedies have been imposed in exceptional circumstances and defined by the Court, with the aim of reviving previously existing competition.[38] They are based on the assumption that competitors should take efforts to re-establish previous conditions. Making uncompetitive practices, such as self-preferencing prima facie, unlawful has turned the exception into the rule: enforcement on a regular basis, as opposed to a one-off, would be difficult. It would require continuous identification of deviations from the prescriptive obligations and could lead to the over-enforcement of competition law. From the standpoint of the regulated gatekeepers, the reversal of the burden of proof means that they are required to provide evidence that the undertaken practices and transactions do not have anticompetitive effects, or that the efficiency gains outweighed such effects.[39]

To conclude, the regulatory regime established by the DMA is based on the premise that the gatekeeper must fulfil its regulatory compliance obligations and bear the burden of implementing effective compliance. This applies even in situations when they are expected to provide 'sufficiently sustained argument' to reverse the presumption that they fulfil the main designation criteria.[40]

3.2 *Digital Services Act: A Shift from Liability Regimes to Regulatory Compliance*

The DSA has a broader scope and aims to upgrade the existing rules on platform responsibility for the provision of digital services. It seeks to improve the protection of consumers in the online area and to create a uniform legal framework for the liability of online service providers for illegal content. The impact of the DSA is threefold: (1) it sets out general rules on the liability of providers of intermediary services; (2) it introduces a regime of due diligence obligations, especially for online platforms; and (3) it strengthens the cooperation between national enforcement authorities.[41]

The liability rules, set out in Chapter II of the DSA, determine under which circumstances providers of online intermediary services are legally obliged to monitor the online content. The rules avoid drawing the line between legal and illegal

[36] Bostoen (2023), p. 1.

[37] Cremer et al. (2019), p. 68.

[38] Bronner case is one example. Oscar Bronner and Mediaprint, Case C-7/97, ECLI:EU:C:1998:569.

[39] Ibáñez Colomo (2020), pp. 26–29.

[40] Article 3.5 DMA.

[41] Eifert et al. (2021).

content and defining a number of liability exemptions based on the intermediary's functions: mere conduit, caching and hosting.[42] The DSA has preserved the ECD approach to platform liability, removing liability for user generated content, but it introduced the obligation to remove potentially illegal content promptly or to disable access to it.[43]

The liability rules are complemented by due diligence obligations. The new legislative framework on user protection shifted from the ECD's mandatory disclosures to transparency obligations, while making a shift in the protection of citizens' fundamental rights, from the ex post approach of the ECD to an ex ante risk-based approach. Striving to encompass the broad range of intermediary services, the due diligence obligations are not drafted in a one-size-fits-all way, but through a layered (asymmetric) risk-based approach. In contrast to the ECD, which mainly relied on self-regulatory initiatives and sanctioning discretion of Member States, the DSA provides much stronger enforcement mechanisms and procedures, based on different regulatory methods.

Whereas the DMA codified ex ante regulation, the DSA reaffirmed ex post liability rules from E-Commerce Directive Chapter II. The final section of Chapter III 'Other provisions concerning due diligence obligations' introduced the elements of the mixed regulatory regime: standards, codes of conduct (including codes of conduct for advertising and accessibility), and crisis protocols. The nature of the public enforcement model of this regulation and the role of platforms and other non-state actors are further elaborated below, from the perspective of regulatory strategy and the risk-based approach.

4 Transcending the Traditional Divide Between Social and Economic, Public and Private Regulation

Regulation in itself is a wide and ambiguous concept. It is often reduced to denote the exercise of public control and command over private activity. More broadly, it refers to any state action aimed at influencing business or social behaviour.[44] Modern governments have undergone changes, from direct intervention to a regulatory state, where the state increasingly aims to achieve a range of social and economic goals through third parties, controlled and influenced by the state through a mix of contractual arrangements and rules. As complexities of modern societies urged the reassessment of old and the creation of new areas of regulatory concern ('regulatory arenas'), some authors observed that we now live in an age of 'regulatory governance' or 'regulatory capitalism'.[45]

[42] Articles 4, 5 and 6 DSA.

[43] EDRi (2020).

[44] Baldwin et al. (2011), p. 3.

[45] Levi-Faur (2011a); Braithwaite (2008).

It follows from the previous discussion that the emerging European digital markets framework cannot clearly fit into the traditional division into two forms of economic regulation: ex post competition protection and ex ante sectoral regulation. This does not resonate as well with the strong ideological distinction between 'economic' and 'social' regulation. In contemporary economies, markets are meant to serve society and the tools of economic regulation are not employed to support only the goals of achieving competitive markets or correcting externalities. Even if they do, the external effects of such tools are often socially preferable. Conversely, using the tools of social regulation to achieve only socially desirable goals may result in regulatory regimes that unnecessarily burden businesses, reduce choice for consumers, or deploy excessive public resources. Modern economies feature interconnectedness and interdependence of both economic and social values. In this context the distinction between social and economic regulation is based on the primacy of values and the purpose it is designed to achieve.[46] Although the core values of economic regulation are efficiency, competition and correction of market failures, a balance must be struck between economic and social values, such as fairness, transparency, equity and protection of fundamental rights. In different policy areas and depending on the circumstances, modern regulators have to be aware of the fact that a regulatory regime can serve more than one purpose. In fact, many regulatory regimes governing industries where business activities may result in social harms represent a mixture of regulation tools, which is based on economic and social demands.[47]

The DSA and the DMA are perfect examples of complex regulatory regimes that seek to enhance efficiency, market contestability and consumer choice, while at the same time achieving socially desirable outcomes. Complex regulatory regimes, such as the regulation of technology, which balance economic and social goals, are often presented through the debate on the innovation principle vs. the precautionary principle.[48] To level the playing field and face the dichotomy between social and economic, i.e. the innovation principle versus the precautionary principle, regulatory strategy should be based on aligning risks rather than values. Therefore, modern regulatory regimes should not address conflicting values through black and white choice suitable for traditional dichotomies, but through the design of regulatory processes and collaborative approaches to regulation. This is one of the main premises of the concepts of regulatory governance and the regulatory state. To shape market behaviour and achieve welfare (as a sum of both economic and non-economic goals), the modern regulatory state recognises and allows for alternative regulatory techniques, as well as deploying direct regulatory tools.[49] This means that, in addition to traditional command and control tools, incentives and disincentives, the state is willing to shift the regulatory role towards non-state actors, often based on

[46] Windholz and Hodge (2012), pp. 225–226.

[47] Braithwaite (2008), p. 197.

[48] For a detailed analysis see: Portuese and Pillot (2018).

[49] Morgan and Yeung (2007), p. 5.

co-regulation and/or meta-regulation strategies centred around risk and regulatory compliance.

From a regulatory governance perspective, a number of regulatory intermediaries—whether regulated subjects, beneficiaries of rules, or independent third parties—could serve as formal or informal regulatory intermediaries.[50] In fact, one of the main areas of research in regulatory governance relates to the functions of intermediaries and their strategies and governance technologies.[51] Regulatory intermediaries have become indispensable participants in many regulatory regimes. Many regulatory systems rely on chains of intermediaries. Such complex forms of governance are usually labelled 'polycentric' governance arrangements.[52] Regulators rely on intermediaries in all stages of the regulatory process due to their capacities, effectiveness and facilitatory role in public policy implementation and law enforcement. Through the rules, as coordination devices, regulatory intermediaries are formally involved in regulatory regimes with the aim of resolving conflicts and decreasing transaction costs. Regulatory regimes are frameworks that encompass norms, mechanisms of decision-making, institutions, and networks of actors involved in regulation.[53] Regulatory regimes exist in Europe in many policy fields of social regulation, such as public health, food safety, product safety and consumer protection. They also exist in the field of market regulation, for example, in financial services and sector specific areas, covering utilities such as gas, electricity, transport, etc. In this sense, as large platforms represent modern utilities, the DMA and the DSA formally establish a European platform economy regulatory regime.

Legal theory has recognised the role of platforms as private regulators, notably in regulation of access and interactions between existing users.[54] Such powers of platforms seem to be one of the key reasons for adopting the Digital Markets Act and the Digital Services Act. As private regulators, platforms take care of their ecosystem not only in terms of the technical infrastructure, but also the rule-setting function in social interactions that occur through platforms. The power of platforms to dictate and influence competition in the relevant market has been recognised in official reports preceding the adoption of the DMA.[55] While the DMA mostly focuses on gatekeepers as regulated intermediaries, the DSA puts in place a larger procedural framework for private enforcement of its goals and endorses certain regulatory roles of platforms and other non-state actors. Subject to duty of care, the due diligence obligations focus on risks related to market contestability, transparency and fairness. The perspective of platforms-as-regulators is inverted through the substitution of their private regulatory powers with top-down public regulation.[56]

[50] Abbott et al. (2017), p. 15.

[51] For a broader overview see Levi-Faur (2011a).

[52] See, for instance, Black (2008).

[53] Levi-Faur (2011b).

[54] See, for instance, Busch (2020) and Dunne (2021).

[55] Cremer et al. (2019), pp. 60–63.

[56] Dunne (2021), pp. 252–255.

5 Risk Governance of Platforms in Digital Markets

5.1 Towards a Risk-Based Approach to Regulation

Regulatory governance has faced several paradigm shifts over the past several decades. The focus of regulation have shifted from market failures and provision of public goods, to balancing risk and harm. Risk has become a public good, a reason for government regulation, and the object of control. Risk regulation is therefore the intervention of the government in markets or social processes, aimed at controlling potential adverse consequences.[57] Moreover, risk has transcended from public good to a measure used to determine the scope of risk regulatory systems.[58] In risk-based regulatory governance, risk has become an approach to regulatory governance.[59] The risk-based approach denotes that the legal requirements establishing the duties of the regulated are related to risk. This process is often confused with risk-based regulation or a risk-based approach to regulation.[60] In a nutshell, risk-based regulation is a strategy of prioritising oversight and enforcement authorities, based on the risky profile of certain actors and behaviours, allowing them to streamline compliance assessment and enforcement activity, wisely and effectively, in areas of greatest risk.[61] Risk governance and the risk-based approach to regulation are based on the belief that risks can be anticipated and controlled.[62] However, regulatory approaches centred around risks can never guarantee the expected outcome. This means that risk-based regulation assumes that regulators who base their strategy on this approach take risks.[63]

Risk-based regulatory frameworks often include risk assessment, risk management and risk communication and often contain preventive, ex ante risk mitigation measures, incentives and sanctions for noncompliance, to deter risk-enhancing behaviours. Risk analysis, as a broader concept, encompasses risk assessment and risk management. It is based on a set of methodologies and processes used to detect and quantify risks and make decisions based on the probability and potential outcome of the materialisation of risk.[64] While risk-based regulation is a public strategy for standards setting, oversight and enforcement, the risk-based approach could be applied to businesses as regulated subjects. It may also be denoted as the risk-based compliance.

Risk regulation and risk-based regulation involve normative choices to solve normative ambiguities, which include the definition of goals, determination of the

[57] Hood et al. (2001), p. 3.

[58] On evolution and development of risk regulatory systems see: Wiener (2003), pp. 207–215.

[59] For a risk regulation perspective from a governance perspective see: Hutter (2017).

[60] Black (2010), pp. 187–188.

[61] Baldwin et al. (2011), pp. 281–283.

[62] Hutter (2017), p. 102.

[63] Black (2010), p. 193.

[64] Hutter (2006), pp. 202–215.

scope of risks and acceptable levels of risk imposed on society.[65] In determining the sources of risk and acceptable risk levels or the acceptable extent of risks, regulators engage in normative and political decision making.[66] Namely, acceptable levels of risk may be imposed in the form of threshold values, principles, or more detailed criteria. In some areas of risk regulation, such as environmental protection, food safety and health, decisions on acceptable risk levels are supported by science and empirical knowledge. This is especially the case in countries with the Anglo-Saxon legal system, which prefer a rational–instrumental form of risk governance. In the European approach to risk governance is mainly deliberative–constitutive, as public administration plays a big role in complexities of technological risk evaluation before harm arises.[67] The risks of modern societies are often subject to uncertainties. In the absence of scientific knowledge and the probability and impact of a risk, one of the main characteristics of the European approach to risk governance is the application of precautionary measures.[68]

Precautionary measures originate in a fear of a future risk and may specify actions to control activities that can cause or augment risks, establish certain limits to activities or events, define criteria for activities or products, and prohibit certain activities presumed to be risky. Likewise, precautionary antitrust has emerged in Europe following the introduction of European enforcement of interim measures. The European Commission has gradually abandoned effects-based analysis, focusing on reversed burdens of proofs rather than evidentiary rules, and hypothetical risks rather than evidence of actual harm. As an example of precautionary antitrust, the Digital Markets Act inverted the presumption of dominance, lowered the standard of proof for hypothetical harm and shifted the burden of proof regarding platform business conduct.[69]

The main characteristics of the DSA, as a risk-based regulation, is the normative choice to tie compliance duties proportionately to the type of risks and severity of impact that online platforms create.[70] Similarly to the DMA, the European legislator imposed more stringent due diligence obligations to larger platforms, considering that the bigger the platform is, the higher the risk posed to platform users and the society. As is the case with the DMA, the DSA's asymmetric design is based on the definition of risk coming from both the size of the platforms and especially the impact of content dissemination on fundamental rights. Moreover, the DSA applies the concept of systemic risk, which very large online platforms (VLOPs) can create, and mandates risk management obligations to mitigate systemic risks.

---

[65] For further discussion on normative choices in risk-based regulation see: Baldwin and Black (2016).

[66] Renn (2008), p. 56.

[67] For more on European approach to risk governance see: Alemanno (2013).

[68] Wiener (2003), pp. 209–248.

[69] For the genesis of precautionary antitrust in Europe and the characteristics of competition enforcement in digital markets see, in particular: Porteuse (2022).

[70] Efroni (2021).

5.2 *Risk-Based Approach to Designating Large Platforms as Systemically Important Regulatory Intermediaries*

As an important step in the development of the concept of the platform as a legal construct, the Digital Markets Act introduced two criteria: functional (i.e. the definition of the core platform services) and size, which is actually the presumption that functional criteria have been met if specified thresholds have been reached (financial criteria, a defined number of the Member states and/or of platform users). A gatekeeper is 'an undertaking providing core platform services, designated pursuant to Article 3',[71] which defines both the functional criteria and the presumption based on size. Providers of core platform services are entitled to rebut the presumption by submitting 'sufficiently substantiated arguments', demonstrating that, despite meeting the thresholds, the core platform service in question fails to meet the three functional criteria test and 'manifestly call into question the presumptions'.[72] As ex ante regulation, the DMA obliges companies to self-assess whether they meet the qualitative and quantitative criteria, and to notify the Commission. That means that regulated subjects bear the evidential and legal burden of having a strategic market status, while the European Commission is not prevented from designating a platform as a gatekeeper. In situations when thresholds are not met, following a market investigation, the Commission may designate a provider of core platform services as gatekeeper. The decision may be based on a number of elements, such as the size of the provider, the number of users depending on access to the platform, network effects and data driven advantages, barriers to entry, or other structural factors.[73]

Article 3 of the Digital Markets Act seems to lack clarity regarding the underlaying rationale and logic, and it is unclear whether it regulates large platforms as digital markets or as actors. It may be concluded that the 'strategic market status' concept, as a source of risk, is the main objective. The Explanatory Memorandum of this act uses risk terminology in explaining its fundamental 'core platform services' concepts where a limited number of large platforms 'serve as gateways'.[74]

Although the provisions of the DSA specifying that the due diligence obligations and enforcement may be qualified as more risk-based compliance requirements, systemically important platforms are defined quantitatively, which is opposed to the definition of gatekeepers under the DMA, where they are defined based on their gatekeeping function and impact on the internal market (albeit the financial criteria

[71] Article 2(1) DMA.

[72] Article 3(5) DMA.

[73] Article 3(8) DMA.

[74] In particular the following: Recital 14 'In particular, online intermediation services ... all have the capacity to affect a large number of end users and businesses, which entails a risk of unfair business practices'; Recital 15 'It is only when a core platform service constitutes an important gateway and is operated by an undertaking with a significant impact in the internal market'; Recital 31 'Such rules are needed to address the risk of harmful effects of practices by gatekeepers, to the benefit of the business environment in the services concerned, of users and ultimately of society as a whole'.

are considered a presumption for designating platforms as gatekeepers). VLOPs are platforms that provide services to an average of at least 45 million active users within the Union, or 10% of the Union's population.[75]

VLOPs are systemically relevant as they 'can be used in a way that strongly influences safety online, the shaping of public opinion and discourse, as well as online trade … Effective regulation and enforcement is necessary in order to effectively identify and mitigate the risks and the societal and economic harm that may arise. Under this Regulation, providers of very large online platforms and of very large online search engines (VLOSEs) should therefore assess the systemic risks … and should take appropriate mitigating measures in observance of fundamental rights'.[76] The risk-based approach played a role in defining VLOPs, as can be inferred from the Commission's Impact Assessment.[77] It appears that one of the main reasons for setting the quantitative criteria is the scarce financial and human resources of the digital services supervisors. The rationale to focus on entities exposing the largest number of consumers to risk, regardless of their (relative) severity, may be unnecessary and counterproductive from a pure risk assessment perspective. The focus on detecting risks only if they occur within big platforms creates a regulatory blind spot.[78]

5.3 DSA: 'Hybrid' Risk-Based Approach in European Governance of Digital Technologies

Compared to other EU regulatory regimes related to the impact of digital technologies on fundamental rights, notably data protection and artificial intelligence, the DSA's risk-based approach may be described as median. The principled risk-based approach of the GDPR relies on regulated subjects:[79] it does not set risk thresholds and does not define mitigating measures, but rather entitles controllers and processors to evaluate risks and choose measures in managing risk. That is why it is labelled as the bottom-up approach, opposed to the Artificial Intelligence Act, which represents a top-down approach.[80] The AI Act imposes differentiated obligations on the basis of prescribed risk scores for regulated AI systems, but does not leave targets the possibility to evaluate such risk scores. The top-down approach means that the AI Act prescribes various categories of risks and leaves a relatively limited margin of discretion to providers.

[75] Article 33.1 DSA.

[76] Preamble, Recital 79 DSA.

[77] European Commission (2020), para 167.

[78] Laux et al. (2021).

[79] For a broader explanation of the nature of risk-based regulation in European data protection regulation, see in particular: Quelle (2018).

[80] De Gregorio and Dunn (2022), pp. 476–478.

The DSA represents a hybrid system, mixing the two above perspectives.[81] Based on legally prescribed objective criteria, it identifies four risk categories of intermediary service providers (top-down) and enables them to choose the measures to reduce the risks related to online content (bottom-up). The duties of intermediaries of digital services are defined in order of ascending burden, proportionally to the defined risks stemming from the provision of their services. This means that the preliminary risk assessment is made from the top. Very large online platforms, as a high-risk category, are further required to make frequent impact assessments of systemic risks, to put in place reasonable, proportional and effective mitigation measures, and to develop internal control systems. Regulatory compliance obligations for different risk categories of intermediaries, imposed by the DSA, will be presented further in this chapter. They are predominantly top-down, mandating compliance-based discipline, while the risk management obligations of very large online platforms are of a bottom-up nature, making them accountable for their policies and the harms and dangers arising from their infrastructures. Therefore, compared to the GDPR which, delegates risk assessment and mitigation duties to data controllers, the DSA mandates a first risk assessment and assigns to the regulated entity the possibility for a double evaluation, allowing for different degrees of discretion. On the other hand, the AI Act directly regulates the functioning of AI systems.[82]

5.4 *DMA: Precautionary Approach to Duties and Risk-Related Obligations of the Gatekeepers*

Substantive issues in regulatory compliance, related to market contestability and fairness, are stipulated in Articles 5 and 6 of the DMA and are fully applicable to each of the core platform services.[83] Article 5 identifies gatekeepers' duties imposed without qualification, i.e. not dependent on any form of specification or implementing acts. These are some frequent practices commonly faced by users of online markets, which are also recognised by legislators and market conduct regulators outside of the EU. Due to their transformative potential, another group of gatekeeper duties, listed in Article 6 DMA, requires further specification. This article empowers the Commission to alter gatekeepers' business systems and influence the design of products, setting requirements to alter their business model where core monetisation strategies are declared to go against the goals of the DMA regime. Its rationale is to prevent the exploitation of market power and contribute to redistributing rents across the integrated chain of users. The obligations prescribed in Article

[81] Ibid, pp. 484–488.

[82] Ibid, p. 488.

[83] Core platform services are defined in Article 2(2) DMA.

6 seek to prevent a) strengthening, b) leveraging and c) exploitation of market power by gatekeepers.[84]

Although the analysis of the selective regulatory instruments foreseen in the DMA is beyond the scope of this paper, it would be useful to classify the scope of obligations introduced by the DMA in the domain of gatekeeper regulatory compliance. Whether blacklisted (Article 5) or greylisted (Article 6), the regulatory compliance obligations prescribed in Articles 5 and 6 may be classified under four theories of harm: (1) addressing a lack of transparency in the advertising market; (2) preventing platform envelopment through bundling or self-preferencing, including access to platforms and data; (3) facilitating the mobility of business users and clients, including obligations related to neutrality, interoperability and portability; (4) preventing unfair practices.[85]

In terms of their nature, the obligations related to gatekeeper business conduct take the form of prohibitions and prescriptions. These range, for instance, from prohibitions related to personal data linked to the opt-in obligation for the use of personal data, to obligations ensuring price transparency in advertising intermediation. Proscriptive obligations, which are typical for competition law as reactive remedies (cease-and-desist orders and injunctions), are dominant in Article 5. These prohibitions tend to relate to the DMA's fairness goal as their objective is to prevent gatekeeper conduct that would result in the exclusion or exploitation of the platform's service users. On the other hand, prescriptive rules, as positive obligations, tend to relate to contestability as the DMA's goal—notably the promotion of interplatform competition.[86] Positive obligations presuppose more complex enforcement strategies, as opposed to prohibitions, where the Commission has to initiate noncompliance proceedings and undertake a factual investigation, similar to competition law enforcement. Positive remedies are more typical features of sector-specific regulations, rather than of competition enforcement.

5.5 The DSA: Risk-Based Approach in Defining Asymmetric Due Diligence Obligations and the Concept of Systemic Risk

As pointed out above, the DSA is a hybrid system of risk-based regulation. From the top-down perspective, it identifies four risk categories of providers, whereas from the bottom-up perspective it provides opportunities for intermediaries to be actively involved in reducing the risks. The DSA implements a layered approach to setting due diligence obligations (Table 1). In addition to general due diligence obligations, which apply to a broad group of online intermediary services, the DSA has foreseen

[84] This is a relative short and concise classification by Ibáñez Colomo (2021), p. 10.

[85] De Streel et al. (2021), p. 19.

[86] Bostoen (2023), pp. 22–23.

Table 1 DSA—Four layers of due diligence obligations

Intermediary services	Layered due diligence obligations
VLOPs	Risk management Duties arising from crisis response mechanisms Compliance function and independent audit Additional transparency obligations Data access
Online platforms	Internal complaint handling mechanisms Out-of-court dispute settlement Trusted flaggers and measures against misuse Additional transparency obligations Specific obligations for online platforms allowing consumers to conclude distance contracts with traders
Hosting services	Notice and action mechanisms Duties to provide information
General obligations for all intermediary services	Designation of single points of contact and legal representatives Provision of information on the terms and conditions Transparency obligations—periodical reports on content moderation

additional obligations for the relevant activities and relevant service providers, which apply cumulatively. The DSA makes a distinction between the following activities: intermediary services, hosting providers, online platforms, and very large online platforms. This means that a VLOP is not only required to comply with the provisions related specifically to this category, but also the obligations related to 'ordinary' online platforms, in addition to the general due diligence obligations.

The general due diligence obligations for all intermediary services include: establishing a single point of contact for regulatory authorities and recipients of services, designation of legal representatives for providers of intermediary services that do not have an establishment in the Union, incorporating certain information in the provider's terms and conditions, and compliance with the transparency reporting duties related to content moderation.[87] In addition to these obligations, hosting services (including providers of online platforms) are required to implement an accessible notice and action procedure to allow third parties to notify the provider of illegal content, provide the statement of reasons for restrictions, and information giving rise to a suspicion of a criminal offence.[88]

While hosting activity is about storing information, online platforms are conduits of information to the public. The DSA introduces a number of information and due diligence obligations for platforms, which impose new administrative duties. Carving out the exception for micro and small enterprises, the DSA strengthens requirements for online platforms, related to complaint management and reporting

[87] Section 1 Chapter 3 DSA.

[88] Section 2 Chapter 4 DSA.

obligations.[89] In addition to requirements related to internal complaint handling mechanisms, recipients of their services are entitled to select certified out-of-court dispute settlement bodies for resolving disputes. For the purpose of detecting, identifying and notifying illegal content, the DSA has authorised Digital Services Coordinators to award a status of trusted flaggers to independent entities, which are given priority in the handling of complaints and provided precautions against the misuse of complaints in relation to users who frequently report manifestly illegal content or make unfounded complaints. In addition to the general transparency obligations, the DSA requires online platforms to enable users to lodge complaints and publish information on out-of-court disputes, suspensions and the main parameters used in their recommender systems. Last but not least, providers of online platforms should put in place appropriate measures to ensure online protection of minors, identify traders and inform the public about advertisements on their online interfaces.[90] The top layer of obligations specifies the strictest requirements for the limited subcategory of systemically important platforms, with regard to risk management, data access, compliance function, transparency, and implementation of independent audits.[91] Further transparency obligations are imposed in relation to online advertising[92] and reporting.

Moreover, the DSA applies the novel concept of 'systemic risks' to digital markets. Systemically important platforms have to address three specific systemic risks that can materialise due to the design or functioning of their services and related systems or from the use made of their services.[93] These systemic risks are the following: (a) dissemination of illegal content; (b) negative effects on certain fundamental rights (i.e. privacy, freedom of expression and media, the rights of a child, prohibition of discrimination); (c) negative effects on civic discourse, electoral process and public security; and (d) negative effects related to gender-based violence, public health, protection of minors, and physical and mental well-being. The DSA mandates the assessment of systemic risks, enumerating a number of factors for assessing the influence of the listed systemic risks.[94] Moreover, it obliges the VLOPs to pay attention to the potential intentional manipulation of their services as a source of systemic risks. In addition to the systemic risks that are the object of regulation and the risk-based approach utilised in defining the VLOPs and the layered due diligence obligations, the DSA formally established risk management requirements to be fulfilled by systemic platforms through both business and compliance strategies.[95]

[89] Section 3 Chapter 4 DSA.

[90] Section 4 Chapter 5 DSA.

[91] Section 4 Chapter 6 DSA.

[92] Article 39 DSA.

[93] Article 34.1 DSA.

[94] Article 34.2 DSA.

[95] Articles 34 and 35 DSA.

6 The Nature of Enforcement and Strategic Compliance Management

6.1 Risk-Based Compliance Enforcement Strategies: A Meta-regulatory Approach

In complex regulatory regimes, regulatory compliance is not defined only by norms. As each of the involved stakeholders may have their own interpretation of what compliance means, the interaction between the state, corporations and other participants in decentred regulatory regimes contributes to the better understanding of compliance obligations and better enforcement of rules. From the perspective of regulation and regulatory governance, compliance also represents an enforcement strategy based on cooperation (described as 'advise and persuade'), as opposed to deterrence. This strategy is more focused on prevention then punishment and its main focus is on fulfilling the goals of legislation, rather than sanctioning its violation. Compliance-oriented enforcement strategies are incorporated in various approaches to enforcement, where regulated entities and third parties bear a greater part of the regulatory burden compared to direct state intervention.[96]

Due to the complexities of modern regulatory regimes and risks, the fulfilment of statutory requirements and strategic compliance-oriented enforcement strategies heavily depend on compliance expertise in the corporative world.[97] This is especially the case with risk-based regulation, where the regulated subject not only must understand the regulator's goals and the choice of tools, but must also know how to respond to them. This is one of the underlaying rationales of meta-regulation, an enforcement strategy that is based on a surrogate role of the regulated subjects, who are required to develop their own systems of internal control and risk management.[98] Avoiding direct intervention and prescriptive obligations, meta-regulation assumes that businesses, as surrogate regulators, apply self-regulation through internal rules and oversight mechanisms and report on the results. Public authorities, alone or through the involvement of selected private actors, oversee the process, scrutinise risk management measures and check whether the ultimate regulatory objectives are being met. Both systemic and 'individual' risks have rapidly grown in complexity and uncertainty in the past several decades. To improve the legitimacy of risk governance, governments have been increasing the openness of their risk governance regimes.[99] They rely on third parties for scientific knowledge and technical risk assessment, while mandating a high level of risk communication in risk assessment and management.

[96] Gunningham (2010), pp. 121–125.

[97] Parker (1999), pp. 135–140.

[98] Gunningham (2010), pp. 135–139; Hutter (2006), pp. 202–227.

[99] For an overview of the role of the government in risk governance regimes, see notably: Hood et al. (2001).

As risk-based regimes, the DMA and especially the DSA are based on the underlying idea that complex issues of the role and risks related to the power of large online platforms cannot be solved only by rules and they therefore introduce specific risk measures and processes. The EU sector-specific regime is based on non-individualised rules. To make it capable of providing regulatory flexibility for dynamic and innovative digital markets and to fill the gaps, the European legislator has provided a number of modalities of updating and interpreting the rules. The European Commission and, to a certain extent, national authorities and public society are entitled to risk-manage (or at least to oversee) the risk management of the platforms. Similarly to the risk-based obligations of data controllers adopted in the GDPR, platforms are mandated to operate in a way that is tailored to respect fundamental freedoms and public interest. The risk-based approach can be interpreted as a special compliance approach, holding platforms accountable for calibrating their obligations beyond so called 'tick-box' compliance,[100] especially with regards to systemic risks.

'Tick-box' compliance favours regulatory regimes based on prescriptive rules. This is especially the case with the DMA, which represents sector-specific and predominantly rules-based regulation. On the other hand, principles-based regulation is often firm-specific. In this regard, it would be useful to compare the main traits of the EU and the UK approaches. Contrary to the European style of designating large platforms, based on numerical parameters of risk setting, the Digital Markets Task force proposed that the Digital Markets, Consumer and Competition Bill be based on the idea that designation of regulated platforms in the UK should be a result of an evidence-based economic assessment. If the assessment shows that a firm has a strategic market status, it will be subject to legally binding firm-specific regulation.[101] Rather than the European rules-based 'one size fits all' requirements, the UK approach, if adopted, will be based on enforceable codes of conduct that are tailored to the specific business model and activities of a strategic platform. The code is based on broad ex ante high level principles providing a dose of flexibility, such that platforms have a level of discretion as to how they comply. One of the main rationales for avoiding prescriptive rules is to strike the right balance between providing clarity and flexibility, diminishing the risks of over-intervention and its negative effect on innovation. The broad principles that set the standards as to how the platform should behave would be flexible enough to address changing business models and technological developments, and would not hamper innovation and other benefits. Avoiding stipulating specific positive and negative obligations applicable to the designated platform does, however, require intervention from the supervisor, in the form of specific guidance on the interpretation of the principles. When risk-based strategy is based on principles, supervisors are expected to provide more guidance on the meaning of the principles. However, when the object of regulation

[100] Quelle (2018), pp. 506–507.

[101] Competition and Markets Authority (2020), pp. 32–33.

is complex, changing and involves large economic interests, the regulatory strategy should be based on a 'prudent mix of rules and principles'.[102]

Regardless of the choice between strict rules and broader principles, compliance with hard law and codes should not be diminished and linked only to a function, but rather should be embedded as compliance culture throughout the regulated digital services provider. Similarly to the case of the GDPR regime, where the success of meta-regulatory tools relies on the relationship with supervisors and their guidance,[103] fostering a compliance culture is considered crucial to its overall success. However, credible deterrence, which requires firms to change their behaviour, the supervisor's prompt actions and substantial sanctions, is necessary when harm does occur. Although the obligation to comply with the requirements of the regime rests with the regulated firm, the regulatory skills of the digital market regulator/supervisor can be a decisive factor.[104] Therefore, the establishment of a strong compliance culture in risk-based compliance strategies of regulated digital services providers is dependent on the clarity of the expectations by the supervisory authority, who should provide clear guidance.

6.2 *The Nature of the European Digital Markets' Public Enforcement Model*

The DMA requires all gatekeepers, with few exceptions,[105] to comply with all obligations regarding each of the core platform services listed in their designation decision. One of the reasons for the ambiguity in defining the practical elements of effective compliance is illustrated in its Preamble: 'The gatekeepers should ensure the compliance with this Regulation by design. Therefore, the necessary measures should be integrated as much as possible into the technological design used by the gatekeepers'.[106] Another example of prohibiting gatekeepers to undermine effective compliance with regulatory obligations is the anti-circumvention clause, preventing gatekeepers from engaging 'in any behaviour that undermines effective compliance' with the set regulatory compliance obligations, regardless of whether that behaviour 'is of a contractual, commercial or technical nature, or of any other nature'.[107]

---

[102] Braithwaite (2002), p. 65.

[103] Binns (2017), p. 34.

[104] As the Digital Markets Taskforce concluded, the supervisor's approach '*will be important in encouraging and supporting compliance. Getting this right will be essential to the success of the regime*'. Competition and Markets Authority (2020), p. 40.

[105] A possibility for limited suspension or exemption to 'facilitate compliance' is defined in Articles 9 and 10 DMA.

[106] Preamble, Recital 65 DMA.

[107] Article 13(4) DMA.

Meta-regulatory approaches are based on provisions that entitle the gatekeepers to be free to choose implementing measures as long as they contribute to achieving the objectives of the DMA. As previously explained, the EU regulatory regime on digital markets is based on the premise that the gatekeeper must bear the burden of implementation and demonstrate effective regulatory compliance. Given the nature of the gatekeepers' obligations listed in Article 6, Article 8 DMA entitled the Commission to specify, by means of a decision, how those obligations are to be implemented. As a mean of assisting the compliance efforts by gatekeepers, the Commission may decide (but is not obliged) to engage in a process initiated by a gatekeeper, based on a reasoned request, to determine whether the measures implemented or to be implemented by the gatekeeper, with a view to ensure compliance, meet the objectives in the specific circumstances of the gatekeeper.[108] Although the Commission has the discretionary right to engage in this process, if it decides to specify the measures it is required to 'ensure that the measures are effective in achieving the objectives of this Regulation and the relevant obligation, and proportionate in the specific circumstances of the gatekeeper and the relevant service'.[109] It seems that in this way the European legislator tried to allow flexibility for applying the rule-based approach. Similarly, if the gatekeeper demonstrates in its reasoned request that compliance with a specific regulatory obligation from the designation decision would endanger the economic viability of its operations, due to exceptional circumstances beyond its control, the Commission may adopt a 'suspension decision' related to the whole obligation or its part.[110]

The Digital Market Act provides several mechanisms for addressing non-compliance, including measures in cases of systematic non-compliance with its provisions. When a gatekeeper has engaged in systematic non-compliance, the Commission may investigate whether a gatekeeper has systematically infringed one or more of the regulatory compliance duties and has maintained, strengthened or extended its gatekeeper position in relation to the designation criteria set out in Article 3(1).[111] Should this be the case, the Commission may impose any behavioural or structural remedies that are proportionate and necessary. Finally, if the gatekeeper fails to comply with one or more of the above decisions, the Commission is authorised to adopt a non-compliance decision.[112] Although it resembles competition enforcement, the European Commission enforces the DMA provisions mostly as a sector-specific regulator. Enforcement of the DMA, and the DMA compliance process in general, is based more on a continuing dialogue with the gatekeepers, compared to 'the more one-off procedure under competition law'.[113] Therefore, it

[108] Article 8(3) DMA.

[109] Article 8(7) DMA.

[110] DMA, Article 9(1). Paragraph 3 of this Article entitles the Commission to provisionally suspend the application of specific obligations already prior to the decision.

[111] DMA, Article 18.

[112] DMA, Article 29 (1).

[113] Bostoen (2023), p. 35.

can be expected that the Commission's diligence and proactive approach to defining obligations (while respecting the specificity of each individual core platform services provider) and its contribution to promoting the compliance process and compliance culture would largely contribute to better implementation of the DMA. In the absence of clear-cut indications for evaluating compliance with the duties imposed under the DMA's regulatory compliance requirements, the transfer of responsibility to gatekeepers has placed focus on the internal control systems.

To summarise, the European Commission plays a dominant role in the enforcement of the DMA. It enjoys exclusive jurisdiction to conduct market investigations related to gatekeeper designations and other issues, and has extensive powers with respect to monitoring and remedies. The Commission is empowered to adopt delegating and implementing acts related to the methodology and procedures for the implementation of the DMA. Opposed to the DSA, in the DMA enforcement Member States play a marginal role.[114]

Unlike the Electronic Commerce Directive, the DSA strongly focuses on enforcement, which is evident from the fact that its Chapter IV 'Implementation, cooperation, penalties and enforcement' contains 39 articles, out of the total of 93 articles in the text. The DSA also establishes national Digital Services Coordinators (DSC), as the designated independent authorities of the Member States responsible for platform and other intermediary services supervision in their Member States, as well as assistance mechanisms between DSCs and the Commission. The European Board for Digital Services has been established with the aim of facilitating mutual cooperation. The Board's role is to assist in coordinating enforcement activities, including joint investigations. Furthermore, the Commission has been granted far reaching monitoring and enforcement powers regarding VLOPs and VLOSEs, introducing a centralised regulatory model resembling antitrust enforcement.[115]

In addition to national and European public institutions and supervisory networks, the European legal framework for digital services authorised a number of external entities to oversee the platforms' obligations. This, once again, confirms the meta-regulatory character of the enforcement strategy, especially with regard to the implementation of due diligence obligations of the platforms, as stipulated in the DSA. While the scope of external entities foreseen in the DMA is mainly related to the independent audit of consumer profiling techniques,[116] the DSA introduced several categories of entities expected to contribute to the fulfilment of the DSA regulatory goals. Compared to the DMA, the DSA has put forward more detailed rules on independent audits for organisations authorised to perform the mandatory yearly audits for very large online platforms.[117] To provide protection against illegal content, platforms are required to process notices submitted by 'trusted flaggers', the status of which is awarded by the Digital Services Coordinators, upon fulfilment of

[114] See Article 38 DMA.

[115] Buiten (2021), p. 23.

[116] DMA, Article 15.

[117] DSA, Article 37.

all specified conditions with respect to expertise, competence and independence.[118] Also, the DSA authorises 'vetted researchers', academics with proven expertise in the relevant field, specifying the criteria for the award of this status and granting them access to data for the purpose of investigating systemic risks.[119]

6.3 Co-regulation, 'Private' Regulatory Tools and Strategic Compliance Management

Platform regulation is a paradigm of polycentric regulation. The European digital services framework has created a specific framework, involving platforms as intermediaries and other actors in a regulatory regime that has assigned different roles to private parties. Since the 2000s there have been many examples of standard setting and other forms of co-regulation in areas such as audiovisual media, data privacy, domain names, Internet security, network neutrality, etc. The trend towards co-regulation may be explained as a shift away from the evidently dysfunctional neo-liberal agenda for self-regulation, towards greater transparency, democracy and fundamental rights, through greater representation in co-regulatory bodies.[120] A goal-oriented and reflexive meta-regulation framework can better accommodate the instruments of self-regulation and co-regulation, as well as the processes and instruments that are available to regulated entities, in achieving public policy goals. The tools of self-regulation and co-regulation are diverse, ranging from codes of conduct and best practices, to industry standards and contracts.[121]

The DSA promotes the development of voluntary codes of conduct, especially for risk mitigation concerning specific types of illegal content, disinformation, manipulative and abusive activities, and activities with adverse effects on minors. The Commission and the Digital Services Coordinators encourage and facilitate the drawing up of voluntary codes of conduct by platforms, civil society organisations, and other relevant stakeholders (co-regulation). They also monitor their objectives, content and enforcement, and even mandate reporting measures and outcomes.[122] This mode of governance could also be described as supervised self-regulation. Adherence to and compliance with a given code may be considered an appropriate risk mitigating measure. Consequently, the refusal to participate in the application

[118] DSA, Article 22.

[119] DSA, Article 40.

[120] Marsden (2011), p. 47.

[121] For more details see Cantero Gamito (2020), pp. 6–14.

[122] Article 45.3 and 45.4 DSA. See also Article 46.2. and Article 47.2. introducing minimal requirements for code of conduct for digital advertising) and codes of conduct for accessibility, addressing the particular needs of persons with disabilities.

of a code may be taken into account when determining whether the online platform has violated due diligence obligations.[123]

Another form of co-regulation, aimed at facilitating the application of obligations dependent on technological means, are standards related to certain technical procedures. The DSA authorises the Commission to support and promote the creation and adoption of international and European voluntary industry standards. Although it may seem that standardisation delegates law-making to the private actor, it does encourage the involvement of new actors into the regulatory process in areas where the legislator lacks resources and understanding of complex technological issues. However, standardisation by non-governmental bodies in the field information and communication technology is often contested,[124] notably in cases where standards intersect with fundamental rights. Although the DSA, while setting requirements for voluntary codes, does not stipulate procedural rules ensuring better representation and legitimacy of standard setting, the current proposal amending the EU Regulation on Standardisation aims to constitutionalise private standard-setting by reinforcing accountability and modernising the governance of European standardisation bodies.[125]

Finally, the terms and conditions of platforms (as regulatory intermediaries) represent a necessary private tool in the enforcement of regulation. The DSA has recognised the capacity of platforms to police online behaviour and enforce rules, especially those embedded in algorithms. As this meta-regulatory approach poses risks of censorship, it obliges platforms to act in a diligent, objective and proportionate manner in applying and enforcing terms and conditions, to respect legitimate interests and fundamental rights, as well as to ensure that their policies and procedures, resulting in removal of media content, should be publicly accessible.[126]

The DSA features both external and internal audits and risk assessments. To assess the compliance with all layers of due diligence obligations, as well as the commitments undertaken pursuant to the codes of conduct and crisis protocols, VLOPs and VLOSEs are independently audited at least once a year.[127] The DSA specifies the criteria for professional organisations performing audits as well as the minimal content of the audit report. It also empowered the Commission to adopt the Delegated Regulation, including rules on independent audits, which has been transmitted to the European Parliament and Council. Although the DSA will stimulate the growth of audits and risk assessments as an industry, the practical problems are clear. One issue is the choice of instrument, since research practices, approaches and methods are still emerging and many of the existing approaches are not ready for implementation. Another problem is the lack of substantive rules that would

[123] Preamble, Recital 104 DSA.

[124] Kanevskaia (2020), pp. 572–573.

[125] Proposal for a Regulation amending Regulation (EU) No 1025/2012 as regards the decisions of European standardisation organisations concerning European standards and European standardisation deliverable, COM(2022) 32 final.

[126] Article 14.4 and Article 14.6. DSA.

[127] Article 37 DSA.

serve as a benchmark against which external auditors will provide measurements and assessments.[128]

The issue of the substantive rules on how to interpret the systemic risks that are subject matter of risk assessments is also evident at the internal level. Due to the encouragement of deliberate efforts to induce the regulated systemically important platforms to create their own internal regulations and manage internal processes of control, meta-regulation is sometimes referred to as 'management-based regulation'. In addition to specifying social outputs that must or must not be reached (performance-based regulation), the enforcement of the DMA and especially the DSA reflects a primary characteristic of management-based approaches, which compel regulated organisations to improve their internal management in order to achieve public goals.[129] The DSA mandates internal self-assessment, organisational structures and risk management requirements as a way to internalise the costs of accessing information. Very large online platforms are required to carry out risk assessments themselves as they have full access to the user data 'and they are often best placed to know the problems caused by their users and how to remedy them in the most cost-efficient way'.[130] The DSA, as a risk-based regulation, interferes in the platforms' risk management approaches by introducing factors that may influence the materialisation of systemic risks.[131] Moreover, it sets requirement with regard to risk mitigation measures. The DSA provides some examples of such measures, such as adapting content moderation and recommendation systems, strengthening internal supervision, enhancing cooperation with trusted flaggers, implementation of codes of conduct and crisis protocols, etc.[132]

The requirement that platforms develop effective risk management strategies and compliance schemes on their own entails the possibility of undesired risk-enhancing effects of the risk-based regulation and the mechanisms it mandates.[133] A notable feature of modern corporate governance is the emphasis on risk culture as a behavioural aspect of risk management. Risk governance, emphasising internal structures and risk culture, assumes a link between risk culture and risk compliance. Compliance, as a process and a business function, has become an important pillar in risk management.[134] Contrary to traditional compliance, which entailed conforming to clear cut rules backed by sanctions, compliance based on risk requires a risk-assessment process to precede the definition of the compliance risks and priorities. Risk-based compliance requires the platform's management to identify the specific

[128] On the risks related to independent audits created by the DMA and DSA, see Laux et al. (2021).

[129] Coglianese and Lazer (2003), p. 694.

[130] Cauffman and Goanta (2021), pp. 770–771.

[131] Article 34.2 DSA.

[132] Article 35.1 DSA.

[133] See Efroni (2021).

[134] On the relationship between internal systems of control, risk management and compliance see Miller (2019), Chapters 4, pp. 18–20.

risks, to assess the magnitude and likelihood of those risks, and to implement measures to manage and mitigate the identified risks.[135]

Finally, both the DMA and the DSA require systemically important platforms to establish the compliance function and appoint a compliance officer.[136] Both regulations stipulate the requirements for institutional and operational independence of the compliance function and authorise the head of the compliance function to report directly to the platform management. The requirements for compliance officers have been set, including the necessary qualifications, knowledge, experience and ability to operationalise measures and monitor compliance within the platforms. Both regulations feature the explicit requirement for the management body to approve and review the internal compliance strategies, programmes and policies, at least once a year. As the more risk-based regulation, the DSA mandates the compliance function to be involved, appropriately and in a timely manner, in all issues related to legal requirements set out in regulations, including the risk assessment and mitigation strategy. The DMA extends the tasks of the compliance function to include monitoring compliance with the Commission's implementing act, imposing binding commitments to ensure compliance with the obligations under the DMA.[137] Among the tasks typical for regulated compliance functions and references to specific commitments, the wording of the articles related to the compliance function in both regulations suggest that compliance professionals in systemically important platforms will be responsible for the education of employees, the definition of compliance risks and internal monitoring and supervision of the regulatory compliance obligations. Among the tasks of the compliance function, the DSA stipulates monitoring the compliance of the VLOPs 'with its obligations under this Regulation'.[138] Similarly, the DMA introduces the tasks of 'organising, monitoring and supervising the measures and activities of the gatekeepers that aim to ensure compliance with this Regulation'.[139] With regard to this, it is noteworthy that the European Commission has recently adopted the Template Form for reporting, pursuant to Article 11 of the DMA (Compliance Report). This form specifies that the gatekeepers are obliged to provide, inter alia, a detailed explanation of the assessment of compliance with obligations set out in the DMA, any reports prepared by the head of the compliance function for the management body, in particular on risks of non-compliance with this regulation and the description of all the measures taken in response to those reports.[140]

This level of detail in the legislation shows that the compliance function is assigned not only a large and important role, but also the responsibility for

[135] Savin and Bagley (2023), pp. 3–4.

[136] Article 41 DSA and Article 28 DMA.

[137] In connection with Article 18 DMA (Market investigation into systematic non-compliance). Commitments for obligations laid down in Articles 5, 6, and 7 are introduced under Article 25 DMA.

[138] Article 41.3 (e) DSA.

[139] Article 28.5 (a) DMA.

[140] European Commission (2023), Section 2, paras. 2.1.3–2.1.4.

detecting, preventing and correcting breaches of conduct requirements.[141] While the methodologies for evaluating corporate compliance management in the transnational legal order are sufficiently defined and moderately developed, the internalisation of the platforms' responsibility for management of systemic risks and compliance with due diligence obligations presuppose more substantive rules. Without such rules, audits, risk assessments and compliance management lack a benchmark against which to measure performance. Consequently, the DMA and especially the DSA mandate the development of processes for strategic compliance management that are designed to reduce risks of non-compliance with these regulations and to reinforce ethical conduct and the platform's reputation. Risk-based compliance transcends the traditional concept of compliance risks and requires constant involvement of the management and all corporate departments, as well as the active cooperation with supervisors.

7 Conclusion

From a comparative law perspective, the European digital services legal framework seems to be the most extensive attempt so far to make large platforms responsible. By introducing graduated due diligence obligations as an egregious example of prescriptive risk regulation, with a special focus on the subcategory of systemically important platforms, the DSA has introduced obligations that mostly belong to the realm of social regulation. On the other hand, inspired by the competition protection legislation instruments and modifying the orientation towards restorative remedies, the DMA has envisaged the instruments of pro-competitive economic regulation, in the form of both proscriptive and prescriptive rules.

This approach in formulating pro-competitive supervisory expectations and regulatory obligations—in a situation where classical competition law protection would not be able to effectively address market failures—requires continuous monitoring of the behaviour of the market participants. The multitude of extensive compliance requirements implies not only clearly defined requirements and supervisory expectations regarding the behaviour of intermediaries in digital markets, but also the capacity of the European Commission and national authorities to encourage compliance. By promulgating due diligence obligations and pro-competitive regulation measures, both acts impose a series of obligations on the platforms and expect them to develop internal business compliance risk management systems. Effective risk mitigation by platforms, as regulatory intermediaries, assumes that both the regulated and the regulators have to understand and develop a more systematic understanding of the new risks stemming from the operation of systemically important online platforms and to develop evidence-based tools and methodologies for

[141] This corresponds to the general sentiment of supervisory authorities, which has contributed to enhancing the profile of the compliance function and tracing the compliance organisation's increase in importance. Gadinis and Miazad (2019), p. 2146.

risk identification, risk management and compliance in general. Research on this topic has started to emerge, and the main idea of this Chapter was to point to the fact that the risk-based regulation of systemically important platforms introduced by the DSA and the DMA is to a large extent based on risk-based compliance enforcement strategy and calls for strategic compliance management.

References

Abbott KW, Levi-Faur D, Snidal D (2017) Theorizing regulatory intermediaries: the RIT model. Ann Am Acad Pol Soc Sci 670:14–35
Alemanno A (2013) Regulating the European risk society. In: Alemanno et al (eds) Better business regulation in a risk society. Springer, Berlin, pp 37–56
Alexiadis P (2012) Balancing the application of ex post and ex ante disciplines under community law in electronic communications markets: square pegs in round holes? In: Buttigieg E (ed) Rights and remedies in a liberalised and competitive internal market. Gutenberg Press, Malta, pp 137–164
Baldwin R, Black J (2016) Driving priorities in risk-based regulation: what's the problem? J Law Soc 43:565–595
Baldwin R, Cave M, Lodge M (2011) Understanding regulation: theory, strategy, and practice, 2nd edn. Oxford University Press, Oxford
Binns R (2017) Data protection impact assessments: a meta-regulatory approach. Int Data Priv Law 7:22–35
Black J (2008) Constructing and contesting legitimacy and accountability in polycentric regulatory regimes. Regul Gov 2:137–164
Black J (2010) Risk-based regulation: choices, practices and lessons being learnt. In: OECD (ed) Risk and regulatory policy: improving the governance of risk, OECD Reviews of Regulatory Reform. OECD, Paris, pp 185–236. https://doi.org/10.1787/9789264082939-11-en
Bostoen F (2023) Understanding the Digital Markets Act. Antitrust Bull 68:263–306. Tilburg Law School Research Paper. https://doi.org/10.2139/ssrn.4440819
Braithwaite J (2002) Rules and principles: a theory of legal certainty. Aust J Leg Philos 27:47–82
Braithwaite J (2008) Regulatory capitalism: how it works, ideas for making it work better. Edward Elgar, Cheltenham
Buiten M (2021) The Digital Services Act: from intermediary liability to platform regulation. https://doi.org/10.2139/ssrn.3876328
Busch C (2020) Self-regulation and regulatory intermediation in the platform economy. In: Cantero Gamito M, Micklitz H-W (eds) The role of the EU in transnational legal ordering. Edward Elgar, Cheltenham, pp 115–134
Cabral L, Haucap J, Parker G, Petropoulos G, Valletti T, Van Alstyne M (2021) The EU Digital Markets Act. Publications Office of the European Union, Luxembourg. https://doi.org/10.2760/139337
Cantero Gamito M (2020) The role of the EU in the transnational governance of standards, contracts and codes. In: Cantero Gamito M, Micklitz H-W (eds) The role of the EU in transnational legal ordering. Edward Elgar, Cheltenham, pp 2–25
Cappai M, Colangelo G (2021) Taming digital gatekeepers: the 'more regulatory approach' to antitrust law. Comput Law Secur Rev 41:105559
Cauffman C, Goanta C (2021) A new order: the Digital Services Act and consumer protection. Eur J Risk Regul 12:758–774
Coglianese C, Lazer D (2003) Management-based regulation: prescribing private management to achieve public goals. Law Soc Rev 37:691–730

Competition and Markets Authority (2020) A new pro-competition regime for digital markets – Advice of the Digital Markets Taskforce, CMA 135, CMA London. https://assets.publishing.service.gov.uk/media/5fce7567e90e07562f98286c/Digital_Taskforce_-_Advice.pdf
Cremer J, de Montjoye Y-A, Schweitzer H (2019) Competition for the digital era. Final report for the European Commission. https://ec.europa.eu/competition/publications/reports/kd0419345enn.pdf
de Gregorio G (2021) The rise of digital constitutionalism in European Union. Int J Const Law 19:41–70
de Gregorio G, Dunn P (2022) The European risk-based approaches: connecting constitutional dots in the digital age. Common Mark Law Rev 59:473–500
de Streel A (2008) The relationship between competition law and sector specific regulation: the case of electronic communications. Reflets et perspectives de la Vie Economique 47:55–72
de Streel A, Liebhaberg B, Fletcher A, Feasey R, Krämer J, Monti G (2021) The European Proposal for a Digital Markets Act: a first assessment. CERRE Assessment Paper. https://cerre.eu/wp--content/uploads/2021/01/CERRE_Digital-Markets-Act_a-first-assessment_January2021.pdf
Dunne N (2015) Competition law and economic regulation: making and managing markets. CUP, Cambridge
Dunne N (2021) Platforms as regulators. J Antitrust Enforc 9:244–269
Efroni Z (2021) The Digital Services Act: risk-based regulation of online platforms. Internet Policy Review (16 November 2021). https://policyreview.info/articles/news/digital-services-act-risk-based-regulation-online-platforms/1606
Eifert M, Metzger A, Schweitzer H, Wagner G (2021) Taming the Giants, The DMA/DSA Package. Common Mark Law Rev 58:987–1028
European Commission (2020) Commission Staff Working Document, Impact Assessment, accompanying the document Proposal for a Regulation of the European Parliament and of the Council on a Single Market For Digital Services (Digital Services Act) and amending Directive 2000/31/EC DSA, SWD (2020) 348 final, 15.12.2020, Part 1/2
European Commission (2023) Template Form for Reporting Pursuant to Article 11 of Regulation (EU) 2022/1925 (Compliance Report). https://digital-markets-act.ec.europa.eu/system/files/2023-10/Article%2011%20DMA%20-%20Compliance%20Report%20Template%20Form.pdf
European Digital Rights (EDRi) (2020) The EU's attempt to regulate Big Tech: What it brings and what is missing' (EDRi, 2020). https://edri.org/our-work/eu-attempt-to-regulate-big-tech
Gadinis S, Miazad A (2019) The hidden power of compliance. Minn Law Rev 103:2135–2209
Gunningham N (2010) Enforcement and compliance strategies. In: Baldwin R, Cave M, Lodge M (eds) The Oxford handbook of regulation. Oxford University Press, Oxford, pp 120–145
Hood C, Rothstein H, Baldwin R (2001) The government of risk: understanding risk regulation regimes. Oxford University Press, Oxford
Hutter B (2006) Risk, regulation, and management. In: Taylor-Gooby P, Zinn J (eds) Risk in social science. Oxford University Press, Oxford, pp 202–227
Hutter B (2017) A risk regulation perspective on regulatory excellence. In: Coglianese C (ed) Achieving regulatory excellence. Brookings Institution Press, Washington, pp 101–114
Ibáñez Colomo P (2020) What can competition law achieve in digital markets? An analysis of the reforms proposed. https://doi.org/10.2139/ssrn.3723188
Ibáñez Colomo P (2021) The Draft Digital Markets Act: a legal and institutional analysis (February 22, 2021). https://doi.org/10.2139/ssrn.3790276
Kanevskaia O (2020) Governance of ICT standardization: due process in technocratic decision-making. N C J Int Law 45:549–618
Larouche P, de Streel A (2021) The European Digital Markets Act: a revolution grounded on traditions. J Eur Compet Law Pract 12:542–560
Laux J, Wachter S, Mittelstadt B (2021) Taming the few: platform regulation, independent audits, and the risks of capture created by the DMA and DSA. Comput Law Secur Rev 105613. https://doi.org/10.1016/j.clsr.2021.105613

Levi-Faur D (2011a) Regulation & regulatory governance. In: Levi-Faur D (ed) Handbook on the politics of regulation. Edward Elgar, Cheltenham, pp 31–21
Levi-Faur D (2011b) Regulatory networks and regulatory agencification: towards a single European regulatory space. J Eur Public Policy 18:810–829
Marsden CT (2011) Internet co-regulation: European law, regulatory governance and legitimacy in cyberspace. Cambridge University Press, Cambridge
Miller G (2019) The law of governance, risk management, and compliance, 3rd edn. Aspen Publishers
Monti G (2008) Managing the intersection of utilities regulation and EC competition law. Compet Law Rev 4:123–145
Monti (2020) Attention intermediaries: regulatory options and their institutional implications, TILEC Discussion Paper DP 2020-018. https://doi.org/10.2139/ssrn.3646264
Moreno Belloso N, Petit N (2023) The EU Digital Markets Act (DMA): a competition hand in a regulatory glove. Eur Law Rev 48:391. https://ssrn.com/abstract=4411743
Morgan B, Yeung K (2007) An introduction to law and regulation: text and materials. Cambridge University Press, Cambridge
Nunziato DC (2023) The Digital Services Act and the Brussels Effect on Platform Content Moderation. GWU Legal Studies Research Paper No. 2023-28. https://ssrn.com/abstract=4425793
OECD (2020) Line of Business Restrictions. DAF/COMP/WP2(2020). https://one.oecd.org/document/DAF/COMP/WP2(2020)1/en/pdf
OECD (2021a) Competition Enforcement and Regulatory Alternatives. OECD Competition Committee Discussion Paper. OECD, Paris
OECD (2021b) Ex ante regulation of digital markets. OECD Competition Committee Discussion Paper. OECD, Paris
Parker (1999) Compliance professionalism and regulatory community: the Australian trade practices regime. J Law Soc 26:215–239
Petit N (2021) The proposed Digital Markets Act (DMA): a legal and policy review. J Eur Compet Law Pract 12:529–541
Pinar A (2022) Regulating competition in digital platform markets: a critical assessment of the framework and approach of the EU Digital Markets Act. Eur Lar Rev 47:85. https://doi.org/10.2139/ssrn.3978625
Porteuse A (2022) Precautionary antitrust: the changing nature of competition law. J Law Econ Policy 17:548–634
Portuese A, Pillot J (2018) The case for an innovation principle: a comparative law & economics analysis. Manchester J Int Econ Law 15:214–237
Quelle C (2018) Enhancing compliance under the General Data Protection Regulation. The risky upshot of the accountability- and risk-based approach. Eur J Risk Regul 9:502–526
Renn O (2008) Risk governance. Coping with uncertainty in a complex world. Earthscan, London
Savin A (2021) The EU Digital Services Act: towards a more responsible internet. J Internet Law 24:1–25
Savin A, Bagley C (2023) On a strategic management approach to the new EU risk-based compliance regulations. IICJ 16:1–12
Stigler Committee on Digital Platforms (2019) Final Report. https://research.chicagobooth.edu/stigler/media/news/committee-on-digital-platforms-final-report.
Suzor N (2018) Digital constitutionalism: using the rule of law to evaluate the legitimacy of governance by platforms. Social Media + Society 4. https://doi.org/10.1177/2056305118787812
Turillazzi A, Taddeo M, Floridi L, Casolari F (2023) The digital services act: an analysis of its ethical, legal, and social implications. Law Innov Technol 15:83–106. https://doi.org/10.1080/17579961.2023.2184136
van Dijck J (2021) Governing trust in European platform societies: introduction to the EJC Special Issue. Eur J Commun 36:323–333

Vestager M (2022) A new age of international cooperation in competition policy. Speech at ICN Annual Conference. https://ec.europa.eu/commission/presscorner/detail/en/SPEECH_22_2822
Wiener JB (2003) Whose precaution after all? A comment on the comparison and evolution of risk regulatory systems. Duke J Comp Int Law 13:207–262
Windholz E, Hodge G (2012) Conceptualising social and economic regulation: implications for modern regulators and regulatory activity. Monash Univ Law Rev 38:212–237

The Interoperability Requirements for Digital Gatekeepers

Matija Damjan

Abstract The paper examines the new regulatory framework for digital gatekeepers in the EU, specifically focusing on the interoperability requirements introduced by the Digital Markets Act (DMA). It delves into the definition and designation of digital gatekeepers, highlighting the criteria that classify certain large online companies as gatekeepers due to their significant market impact, user base, and entrenched market positions. The paper's core analyses the DMA's provisions regarding interoperability, distinguishing between vertical and horizontal interoperability. Vertical interoperability concerns the integration of different levels of the value chain, such as hardware and software compatibility, while horizontal interoperability focuses on the interoperability of substitutable products and services, like messaging apps. The paper discusses the implications of these requirements for gatekeepers, including the need to ensure user data portability and the provision of technical interfaces for interoperability. The paper reflects on the broader legal and economic implications of the DMA's interoperability requirements, arguing that while promoting competition and innovation, these also raise questions about the optimal balance between standardisation and diversity in the digital economy.

1 Introduction

When the European Union (EU) started devising its regulatory framework for the Internet around the year 2000, most online companies were startups, the success of whose business models was unsure, particularly in light of the ongoing implosion of the dot-com bubble. The legislators felt that fledgling tech businesses should be shielded from excessive legal risks to encourage the development of the new

M. Damjan (✉)
University of Ljubljana, Faculty of Law, Ljubljana, Slovenia
e-mail: matija.damjan@pf.uni-lj.si

D. V. Popović, R. Kulms (eds.), *Repositioning Platforms in Digital Market Law*, European Union and its Neighbours in a Globalized World 15,
https://doi.org/10.1007/978-3-031-69678-7_2

technological environment.[1] Consequently, the E-Commerce Directive[2] laid down standard rules for providing online services in the EU. To provide legal certainty for online business, it established the freedom to provide online services across the Single Market without prior authorisation requirements and subject to regulation only in the Member State of the services provider's registered headquarters.

The economic literature at the time expected that online markets would remain highly competitive as consumers could easily access many competitors' offerings. However, quite early on, a limited number of major 'gateways' between businesses and consumers emerged. Today's web is marked by the dominant position of tech giants, which hold significant market shares in search engines, social media, online retail and cloud computing.[3] Consumers and businesses depend on their platform services, and the economy of scale makes it difficult for new entrants to compete. Tech giants' dominance is supported by the vast collection of user data, which they use for targeted advertising, personalisation of services, and market analysis. Their platforms can influence public opinion, disseminate information and affect political processes.

Whereas fragile online businesses once had to be relieved of superfluous legal burdens, consumers and businesses now need protection against big tech's potential abuse of market power. The European Commission launched investigations into possible abuses of a dominant market position against several tech giants, such as Microsoft,[4] Google,[5] Amazon[6] and Apple,[7] which have been referred to as having a 'superdominant' market position.[8] However, antitrust actions based on Article 102 of the Treaty on the Functioning of the European Union (TFEU)[9] are a relatively slow response to ongoing abuses of market power.[10] The tech giants' increasing economic, cultural and political influence has led to calls for their stricter *ex ante* regulation.[11] The common thrust of the recent EU legislation concerning the digital sector has been to impose additional responsibilities on the largest online players.

---

[1] Rowland et al. (2012), pp. 72–73.

[2] Directive 2000/31/EC of the European Parliament and of the Council of 8 June 2000 on certain legal aspects of information society services, in particular electronic commerce, in the Internal Market, OJ L 178, 17.7.2000, pp. 1–16.

[3] Crémer et al. (2019), p. 12.

[4] Commission decision of 24 March 2004 in case C-3/37.792 – Microsoft.

[5] Commission decisions of 27 June 2017 in case AT.39740 – Google Search (Shopping) and of 18 July 2018 in case AT.40099 – Google Android.

[6] Commission decision of 20 December 2022 in cases AT.40462 – Amazon Marketplace and AT.40703 – Amazon Buy Box.

[7] Commission antitrust proceedings in cases AT.40452 – Mobile Payments and AT.40716 – App Store Practices.

[8] Case T-612/17 Google and Alphabet v Commission, para. 182–183. See Crémer et al. (2019), p. 125.

[9] Consolidated version, OJ C 326, 26.10.2012, pp. 47–390.

[10] Jackson (2022), p. 7.

[11] Jackwerth (2022), pp. 200–201.

The first step in this direction was taken by the Directive on Copyright in the Digital Single Market[12] adopted in April 2019, which excluded the largest social networks and video platforms[13] from the safe haven provision concerning copyright law violations, which remains in power for other intermediaries. A more comprehensive and generally applicable legislative effort to prevent the abuse of big tech's market power was taken in 2022 by adopting the Digital Services Act (DSA)[14] and the Digital Markets Act (DMA).[15] The legislative package aims to protect the users' fundamental rights and establish a level playing field for businesses to foster innovation, growth, and competitiveness.[16] The DSA introduced asymmetric regulation of online services: stricter rules apply to very large online platforms and very large online search engines. The DMA presented new sector-specific *ex ante* competition rules for the largest online businesses to prevent anticompetitive market behaviour before it occurred[17] and thus overcome the slowness of antitrust cases.[18] The regulation complements rather than replaces the rules protecting undistorted competition and sets other objectives distinct from those of EU competition law.[19]

This paper will focus on the DMA's requirement that the dominant online players make their services and products interoperable, thus enabling end users to interact with users of alternative services. This provision aims at reducing problematic network effects, where the value of a service increases with the number of its users, creating a positive feedback loop that attracts more users and entrenches the service provider's position. Digital ecosystems typically integrate various services and products to make users reliant on their platforms for diverse digital needs, making it extremely difficult for new market operators to challenge, regardless of how innovative and efficient they may be.[20] Interoperability should enable users of digital services to switch between different apps and thus avoid user lock-in. The paper will first look at the definition of digital gatekeepers, which are bound by the new interoperability requirements and the notion of interoperability. This will be fol-

---

[12] Directive (EU) 2019/790 of the European Parliament and of the Council of 17 April 2019 on copyright and related rights in the Digital Single Market and amending Directives 96/9/EC and 2001/29/EC, OJ L 130, 17.5.2019, pp. 92–125.

[13] Referred to in the Directive as 'online content-sharing service providers'.

[14] Regulation (EU) 2022/2065 of the European Parliament and of the Council of 19 October 2022 on a Single Market for Digital Services and amending Directive 2000/31/EC, OJ L 277, 27.10.2022, pp. 1–102.

[15] Regulation (EU) 2022/1925 of the European Parliament and of the Council of 14 September 2022 on contestable and fair markets in the digital sector and amending Directives (EU) 2019/1937 and (EU) 2020/1828, OJ L 265, 12.10.2022, pp. 1–66.

[16] Recital 107 of the DMA. Proposal for a Regulation of the European Parliament and of the Council on contestable and fair markets in the digital sector (Digital Markets Act), COM/2020/842 final, Brussels, 15.12.2020, pp. 2–3. Akman (2022), p. 89.

[17] Most of the legal obligations in the DMA can be traced back to competition law cases. Moreno Belloso and Petit (2023), pp. 391, 394.

[18] Monti (2021), p. 90.

[19] Recital 11 of the DMA.

[20] Recital 3 of the DMA.

lowed by analysing the DMA's provisions concerning vertical and horizontal interoperability. The functioning of the new rules will be examined in the broader legal context and from the perspective of achieving the set goals.

2 Digital Gatekeepers

When speaking of big tech, internet giants, digital titans and similar terms, people usually have in mind the names of concrete companies providing ubiquitous online services, such as Google, Facebook, Apple, Microsoft, Amazon and TikTok.[21] These are the dominant market players clearly targeted by the DMA. Yet, defining them in abstract terms is more challenging. The DMA dubs these businesses 'gatekeepers' and defines them based on the type of service they provide and their economic power. Gatekeeper status is not synonymous with dominance as understood in EU competition law. Yet, it is a similarly structural concept that focuses the application of the DMA on the largest online companies.[22]

To be considered a gatekeeper, an undertaking must provide one or more of the 'core platform services' listed in Article 2 of the DMA: online intermediation services (as defined in the Platform-to-Business Regulation[23]), online search engines,[24] social networks, video-sharing platforms, number-independent interpersonal communication services (i.e., instant messaging), operating systems, web browsers, virtual assistants, cloud computing services or online advertising services, including advertising intermediation services.[25] These services are listed out as they can affect a large number of end users and businesses[26] and have characteristics that their providers can exploit to reduce market competition, such as extreme scale economies

[21] Google, Amazon, Facebook, Apple and Microsoft are collectively also referred to as GAFAM or the Big Five. Huckova and Semanova (2023), p. 301.

[22] Moreno Belloso and Petit (2023), p. 395. Gatekeeper is arguably a legislative definition of a (quasi) dominant position in a particular sector (online platforms) for a particular activity (core platform services). Desai (2021), p. 15. Cf. Unver (2022), pp. 236–239.

[23] Regulation (EU) 2019/1150 of the European Parliament and of the Council of 20 June 2019 on promoting fairness and transparency for business users of online intermediation services, OJ L 186, 11.7.2019, pp. 57–79. The definition covers services intended to facilitate the initiating of direct transactions between business users and consumers, allowing the former to offer goods or services to the latter. Moreno Belloso and Petit (2023), p. 397.

[24] Defined in the Platform-to-Business Regulation as a digital service that allows users to input queries in order to perform searches of, in principle, all websites, or all websites in a particular language, on the basis of a query on any subject in the form of a keyword, voice request, phrase or other input, and returns results in any format in which information related to the requested content can be found.

[25] The Commission's initial proposal for the DMA did not include virtual assistants or web browsers; these were added during the legislative process due to their significant role in accessing digital markets. Turner (2022), p. 43.

[26] Recital 14 of the DMA.

resulting from nearly zero marginal costs of adding users, strong network effects, multisidedness of services, lock-in effect, a lack of multi-homing for the same purpose by end users, vertical integration, and data driven-advantages.[27]

Yet the fact that a digital service qualifies as a core platform service does not suffice to designate its provider as a gatekeeper. Under Article 3 of the DMA, an undertaking can be designated as a gatekeeper if it meets three objective economic criteria proving its market position:

a) it has a significant impact on the internal market, which occurs if it provides the same core platform service in at least three Member States, reaching an annual turnover in the EU of at least EUR 7.5 billion in the previous three financial years, or a market valuation of at least EUR 75 billion;
b) it provides a core platform service that is an important gateway for business users to reach end users,[28] meaning that the service must have at least 45 million monthly active end users and at least 10,000 yearly active business users in the EU;[29] and
c) it enjoys an entrenched and durable position in its operations, or it is foreseeable that it will enjoy such a position soon, as demonstrated by the fact that the active end-user and business-user thresholds have been consistently met in the last three financial years.

The recitals to the DMA explain that a high group turnover realised in the Union in conjunction with the threshold number of users of core platform services reflects a relatively strong ability to monetise those users. A high market capitalisation relative to the number of users reflects a significant potential to monetise those users in the near future.[30] A high number of business users depending on a core platform service to reach an increased number of monthly active end users enables the service provider to influence the business users' operations to its advantage. The fact that the high numbers of end users and business users were met in at least three Member States over at least three years demonstrates the service provider's entrenched and durable position or the foreseeability of enjoying such a position in the future.[31]

The Commission makes an official designation of an undertaking as a gatekeeper upon the undertaking's notification that it meets the above criteria, which must be made without delay. The undertaking can present substantiated arguments that its core platform service does not satisfy the requirements for the designation as a gatekeeper, although it meets all the thresholds in Article 3(2) due to the circumstances in which the core platform service operates. Conversely, even if a core platform

[27] Recital 2 of the DMA. See also Jackson (2022), pp. 8–9.

[28] Such a platform service can also intermediate between end users themselves, e.g., in the case of instant messaging services. See Recital 15 of the DMA.

[29] The methodology for calculating active user numbers is set out in the Annex to the DMA.

[30] Recital 17 of the DMA.

[31] Recitals 20 and 21 of the DMA.

service does not satisfy the quantitative thresholds, the Commission may still designate it as a gatekeeper based on a qualitative assessment considering the size, operations and position of the company, network effects and data-driven advantages, scale and scope effects and user lock-in (Article 3(8) of the DMA).[32]

In September 2023, the Commission designated, for the first time, six gatekeepers—Alphabet (provider of Google and YouTube services), Amazon, Apple, ByteDance (provider of TikTok), Meta (provider of Facebook and Instagram) and Microsoft. In total, 22 core platform services provided by gatekeepers have been designated. The gatekeepers have six months to fully comply with the DMA obligations for each designated core platform service.[33] Most of the gatekeepers are US companies, except ByteDance, which is headquartered in China and incorporated in the Cayman Islands. The designation does not allay the claims that the EU is ready to act only against foreign service providers based outside the Union.[34] On the other hand, this confirms that Europe has failed to create digital undertakings successful enough to reach the gatekeeper status.

3 Gatekeepers' Obligations

Gatekeepers are market players that are so strong that their anti-competitive behaviour can be anticipated and pre-empted by *ex ante* rules. The DMA comprises a number of obligations and prohibitions (dos and don'ts), which apply to undertakings designated as gatekeepers, but only for those of their core platform services that individually constitute an important gateway for business users to reach the end users and were listed as such in the designation decision concerning the respective gatekeeper (Article 6.1 of the DMA). The rules are based on the Commission's experience dealing with anti-competitive behaviour in digital markets.[35]

The DMA expressly prohibits several types of unfair business practices typical for online platforms; it introduces specific rules for users' data protection in an online environment[36] and requires increased transparency for business users concerning the pricing, performance and general conditions of access to the store.[37]

[32] Hutchinson and Treščáková (2022), p. 572.

[33] The Commission's press release IP/23/4328, 6 September 2023.

[34] Cf. Huckova and Semanova (2023), p. 302. Turner (2022), p. 42.

[35] Desai (2021), p. 14.

[36] Without the user's express consent, gatekeepers may not collect, store or process end user personal data collected through third-party services, track end users outside the core platform service or process users' personal data for targeted advertising (Article 5(2)). Online interfaces must not use "dark patterns" to obtain users' consent for collecting personal data (Article 13(4) and 13(6).

[37] Search engines must explain their pricing and fee systems to advertisers and publishers (Articles 5.9 and 5.10), search engines must give them access to their marketing and advertising performance data (Article 6.8), software application stores must publish general conditions of access to the store by third parties (Article 6.12).

Hence, they aim to ensure fair, reasonable, and non-discriminatory competitors' access to the platform, avoiding user lock-in and allowing genuine consumer choice.[38] These rules complement and elaborate existing EU laws on unfair business practices, data protection[39] and platform-to-business relations[40] to consider the specifics of gatekeeper services as well as the case law concerning the abuse of dominant market position.[41] DMA's interoperability requirements for online businesses, however, are a relative novelty in legislation. Nevertheless, case law in the field of antitrust has long recognised interoperability as crucial to healthy competition, particularly in the software market, as a means of reducing user lock-in and network effects.[42] Compatibility requirements can be imposed on incumbent firms to lower entry barriers for actual and potential competitors without dictating market outcomes arbitrarily.[43]

Interoperability is defined in Article 2(29) of the DMA as the ability to exchange information and mutually use the information which has been exchanged through interfaces or other solutions so that all elements of hardware or software work with different hardware and software and with users in all the ways in which they are intended to function.[44] Interoperability can function in two directions. The so-called vertical interoperability refers to the interoperability of products and services at different levels of the value chain or product or protocol stack, for example, the interoperability between hardware and software, between operating systems and multiple app stores or between platforms and payment systems. Vertical interoperability gives business users access to essential functionalities of the system, allowing the development of their services to complement those provided by the system.[45] Horizontal interoperability, on the other hand, means exchanging and using information between substitutable products and services, which operate at the same level of the chain or stack. For example, interoperability between different email services or, under DMA, between gatekeepers' messaging services.[46]

---

[38] Turner (2022), p. 43. Cf. Jackson (2022), p. 11.

[39] Huckova and Semanova (2023), p. 299.

[40] Proposal for a Digital Markets Act, p. 3.

[41] In case T-612/17 Google and Alphabet v Commission, the General Court upheld the Commission's finding that Google violated Article 102 TFEU by self-preferential treatment of their Google Shopping service, which hindered the ability of competitors to access the market. Jackson (2022), pp. 13–14.

[42] See case COMP/C-3/37.792 – Microsoft. The Commission's press release 'Antitrust: Commission welcomes new Microsoft proposals on Microsoft Internet Explorer and Interoperability', MEMO/09/352, Brussels, 24 July 2009.

[43] Moreno Belloso and Petit (2023), p. 405. Unver (2022), pp. 228–229.

[44] The definition of interoperability in the DMA differs from the narrower definition of the same term in the Digital Content Directive (Directive (EU) 2019/770 of the European Parliament and of the Council of 20 May 2019 on certain aspects concerning contracts for the supply of digital content and digital services, OJ L 136, 22.5.2019, pp. 1–27.).

[45] BEREC (2023), p. 16.

[46] Ibidem.

4 Vertical Interoperability

4.1 The Relevance of Vertical Interoperability

A dominant platform in one market can leverage its market power to restrict competition in adjacent markets by hindering the interoperability of its services with complementary products and services offered by third parties.[47] If a gatekeeper imposes technical restrictions on the installation and operation of third-party apps on the gatekeeper's platform, the situation is very similar to the one examined by the Commission in the Microsoft case concerning Windows Media Player.[48] The Commission found that Microsoft had abused its position in the operating systems market by preinstalling Windows Media Player and by hindering the interoperability between Windows and alternative media players offered by Microsoft's rivals. As a remedy, Microsoft was ordered to provide interoperability information and to propose a version of its operating system without Windows Media Player.[49]

Similarly, the gatekeeper's rules for the distribution of apps can restrict the end user's ability to install and effectively use third-party apps or app stores on hardware or operating systems provided by the gatekeeper and access such apps or app stores outside the gatekeeper's core platform services. This prevents software developers from using alternative distribution channels, and limits end users' choice between different apps from different distribution channels.[50] The DMA contains several provisions aimed at preventing gatekeepers from self-preferencing, that is, favouring their own services or products, for example, by reserving a better ranking and related indexing and crawling for their own offering than that of the products or services of third parties also operating on that core platform service.[51] Horizontal interoperability requirements add to that by preventing gatekeepers from designing their core platform services in a way that would technically hinder third-party apps and app stores from effectively competing with the gatekeepers' own offerings.

Interoperability can encourage the development of complementary products and services and boost competition regarding them, giving consumers greater choice by reducing lock-in. Interoperability allows competitors to share the same network effects the gatekeeper enjoys. While maintaining access to the gatekeeper's user base, they can compete on features that users of complementary products or services might value, such as additional functionalities, privacy, security or lower price.[52] Interoperability also allows interconnectedness and free data flow, which are crucial in a data-based economy. Vertical interoperability was among the Internet's founding principles, whose access layers (protocol stack) interoperate through

---

[47] Kerber and Schweitzer (2017), p. 52.

[48] Case COMP/C-3/37.792. See Hutchinson and Treščáková (2022), p. 585.

[49] Hutchinson and Treščáková (2022), pp. 577–588. Bourreau et al. (2022), p. 36.

[50] Recital 50 of the DMA.

[51] Recital 51 of the DMA.

[52] Morton et al. (2023), p. 1019.

standard interfaces. The functionalities of each layer can be replaced without affecting the system's functioning.[53] Similarly, vertical interoperability under the DMA is supposed to encourage innovation in today's complex platform economy. However, if interoperability is achieved through uniform standards and interfaces, this may also limit the scope of innovation concerning the standards and interfaces and lead to a greater degree of homogeneity of complementary products and services. Consequently, an optimal level of interoperability should be found that balances benefits and costs.[54]

4.2 *Third-Party Apps and App Stores*

Article 6(4) of the DMA concerns the interoperability between a gatekeeper's operating system and third-party software applications. The gatekeeper must allow and technically enable the installation and effective use of competing apps and app stores on its operating system as well as make them accessible by other means than the gatekeeper's core platform services. This provision prohibits contractual and technical barriers to interoperability that a gatekeeper might use to restrict competing apps on its operating system. This is particularly important for the competition to reach single-homing consumers using only the gatekeeper's platform.[55]

Interoperability in the narrow technical sense is insufficient to address the competition concerns connected with the gatekeeper's dominant position. Therefore, this basic technical provision is underpinned by additional requirements that the gatekeepers must follow. First, gatekeepers must ensure that end users can set third-party apps or app stores as defaults instead of the gatekeeper's own apps or services. The downloaded software must be allowed to prompt the end users to decide whether they want to set that app or app store as their default, and the gatekeeper must technically enable end users to change the default settings easily. Additionally, the gatekeeper must allow and technically enable end users to easily uninstall any gatekeeper's or other apps except those that are essential for the functioning of the operating system or of the device and which cannot technically be offered on a standalone basis by third parties (Article 6(3) of the DMA).

The gatekeeper must not restrict the end users' ability to switch between or subscribe to different apps and services accessed through the gatekeeper's core platform services (Article 6(6) of the DMA). This prohibition should allow more undertakings to offer their services, ultimately providing greater choice to the end users. Gatekeepers should ensure a free choice irrespective of whether they manufacture hardware through which such apps or services are accessed. They should not raise artificial technical or other barriers to make switching impossible or

[53] Bourreau et al. (2022), p. 26.

[54] Kerber and Schweitzer (2017), p. 42.

[55] Morton et al. (2023), p. 1050.

ineffective. However, merely offering a pre-installed app to consumers and promoting it via discounts and special offerings should not be considered a prohibited barrier to switching.[56] These provisions of the DMA address some of the Commission's findings in its investigation into Apple's App Store rules. The Commission concluded in its statement of objections that Apple abused its dominant position by imposing its in-app payment system on rival app developers and by restricting app developers' ability to inform iPhone and iPad users of alternative services ('anti-steering obligations').[57]

The end users' ability to switch is supported by data portability requirements concerning the vast amounts of data the gatekeepers collect while providing the core platform services and other digital services. Switching from one app to another is unappealing for the end user if they have to manually re-enter or recreate all the data they have already generated in the gatekeeper's app (data-induced lock-in effect).[58] To prevent the gatekeepers from using the control over data to restrict end users from switching or multi-homing, end users should be able to take their data and identifying information from one platform to another, including by authorising the new service provider to port their data from the gatekeeper's platform.[59] Accordingly, the DMA requires the gatekeeper to enable effective portability of data provided by the end user or generated through the end user's activity on the gatekeeper's platform. Effective and immediate access should be provided both to end users directly as well as third parties authorised by the end user whose data is concerned, and they should receive the data in a standard format that can be immediately and effectively accessed and used. Gatekeepers must also provide, free of charge, the necessary tools and technical means, such as application programming interfaces (APIs), for effective data portability, including the option of continuous and real-time access to such data (Article 6(9) of the DMA). Free real-time data portability should help alternative providers compete with integrated platform services.[60]

This provision complements the data portability right under the General Data Protection Regulation (GDPR). It aims at facilitating switching or multi-homing, which should, in turn, lead to an increased choice for end users and act as an incentive for gatekeepers and business users to innovate.[61] Business users should also benefit from similarly worded data portability requirements for the data provided and generated by themselves and their end users when using the gatekeeper's core platform services (Article 6(10) of the DMA). Compared to the GDPR, which limits

---

[56] Recital 53 of the DMA.

[57] Cases AT.40437 Apple - App Store Practices (music streaming), AT.40716 Apple - App Store Practices and AT.40652 Apple – App Store Practices (e-books/audiobooks).

[58] Kerber and Schweitzer (2017), p. 52.

[59] Data portability is not a new concept. Telephone operators have long been required to enable their consumers to retain their telephone numbers when switching to new providers. OECD (2021), p. 15.

[60] Morton et al. (2023), p. 1050.

[61] Recital 59 of the DMA.

the data portability right to specific processing activities, the DMA extends this requirement to non-personal data processed on core platform services provided by gatekeepers, irrespective of the grounds and nature of the processing.[62]

It is important to note that the interoperability requirements must be implemented in a way that does not compromise the integrity of the gatekeeper's systems. The gatekeeper is allowed to take the strictly necessary and proportionate technical or contractual measures to ensure that third-party apps and app stores do not endanger the integrity of the hardware or operating system provided by the gatekeeper. The integrity of the hardware or the operating system includes any design options that need to be implemented and maintained for the hardware or the operating system to be protected against unauthorised access by ensuring that security controls specified for the hardware or the operating system concerned cannot be compromised.[63] Furthermore, the gatekeeper can implement similar measures to enable end users to effectively protect their security in relation to third-party apps or app stores. However, such security measures should not be implemented as a default setting or pre-installation (Article 6(4) of the DMA).

4.3 *Hardware and Software Features*

Gatekeepers often act in dual roles as developers of operating systems and manufacturers of devices, such as mobile phones, tablets and wearable devices. They can misuse such dual roles to prevent alternative service and hardware providers from accessing their devices' operating system or other (hardware or software) features under equal conditions as the gatekeeper's own devices or services. For example, a gatekeeper can restrict access to some of the functionalities in its device, such as near-field communication (NFC) technology, secure elements and processors, authentication mechanisms and the associated software, where such access is necessary to provide the alternative service effectively. Such limitations can significantly undermine innovation by alternative providers and choices for end users.[64] The Commission investigated this type of restrictions in the Apple Pay case,[65] where Apple Pay is the only mobile wallet that may access the NFC 'tap and go' technology embedded on Apple mobile devices for contactless payments in stores, whereas Apple does not make the NFC input available to third-party app developers of mobile wallets on its operating system iOS.[66]

---

[62] Etteldorf (2022), p. 258.

[63] Recital 50 of the DMA.

[64] Recitals 56 and 57 of the DMA.

[65] AT. 40452— Apple-Mobile payments.

[66] The Commission's press release IP/22/2764 'Antitrust: Commission sends Statement of Objections to Apple over practices regarding Apple Pay', Brussels, 2 May 2022. See Moreno Belloso and Petit (2023), p. 394.

Under Article 6(7) of the DMA, the gatekeeper must ensure, free of charge, that any alternative providers of ancillary services or hardware have effective access to and interoperability with the same operating system, hardware or software features that are available or used in the provision of its ancillary services and hardware. This only applies when the gatekeeper's operating system or virtual assistant that controls the hardware and software features is listed in the Commission's designation decision as the relevant core platform services. Such access and interoperability can equally be required by apps related to the gatekeeper's relevant services, together with, or in support of, the core platform service. The obligations aim to allow competing ancillary service providers to interconnect through interfaces or similar solutions to the respective features as effectively as the gatekeeper's own services or hardware.[67] For example, end-users should be able to create a social media account using an existing profile from another provider, such as the familiar "sign in with Google" feature, or to use a third-party payment system, such as Google Pay instead of Apple Pay.[68]

Again, the gatekeeper can take strictly necessary and proportionate measures to ensure that interoperability does not compromise the integrity of the operating system, virtual assistant, hardware or software features provided by the gatekeeper.

5 Horizontal Interoperability

5.1 Number-Independent Interpersonal Communications Services

The Commission's proposal of the DMA initially contained only provisions on vertical interoperability. However, The European Parliament amended the text to mandate horizontal interoperability for instant messaging services and social networks operated by gatekeepers.[69] Horizontal interoperability works between platforms by opening the network to entry so that both platforms' users can connect.[70] Forcing interoperability to break network effects has occurred in the past, for instance, in the telephone system, where users of different wireless and wired networks can call each other. Similarly, various email providers connect. So, it was argued that the same could be done to social media platforms.[71] In the negotiations between the Parliament and the Council moderated by the Commission, the final text of Article 7 of the DMA was formulated, which only requires horizontal interoperability of

[67] Akman (2022), p. 96.

[68] Bourreau et al. (2022), p. 38.

[69] Ibidem, p. 39.

[70] Morton et al. (2023), p. 1024.

[71] Desai (2021), p. 18.

instant messaging services, which compete with the regulated telephone services, including short message services (SMS).[72]

Instant messaging enables users to exchange text messages and other forms of digital content in real time, with the option of creating chat groups, allowing multiple users to communicate in a single conversation thread. Some services also offer voice and video calling capabilities, adding another interaction layer. These services are usually accessible across various platforms, including smartphones, tablets, and computers, enabling users to stay connected regardless of the device they are using. For security, many modern instant messaging services have implemented end-to-end encryption to ensure that only the communicating users can read the messages.[73]

Due to these advantages, the use of instant messaging has drastically increased in recent years, replacing, to some extent, emails and SMS.[74] However, unlike these traditional communication methods, instant messaging services are not based on common standards and are mutually incompatible, meaning that the users of one such service cannot communicate with the users of another. The lack of interoperability allows gatekeepers that provide instant messaging services to benefit from strong network effects. Providing instant messaging as part of their platform ecosystem, gatekeepers can increase entry barriers for alternative providers of such services.[75] To reduce these adverse effects on competition, DMA requires that gatekeepers ensure interoperability of certain basic functionalities of their instant messaging services with third-party instant messaging services. This means users should be able to send and receive messages without regard to the messaging app used.

The DMA refers to instant messaging services as 'number-independent interpersonal communications services' (NIICS). The term is defined in Article 2 (7) of the European Electronic Communications Code (EECC)[76] as "means an interpersonal communications service which does not connect with publicly assigned numbering resources, namely, a number or numbers in national or international numbering plans, or which does not enable communication with a number or numbers in national or international numbering plans." The term NIICS is actually broader than instant messaging as it can also include video-conferencing, voice calls and email services corresponding to the definition. The DMA's interoperability requirements can apply to all types of NIICS, although the legislative discussions revolved mainly around instant messaging services.[77]

In September 2023, the Commission designated Meta's WhatsApp and Messenger services as NIICS subject to interoperability requirements· This means that in the future, users should be able to text these NIICS from smaller messenger

---

[72] Etteldorf (2022), p. 259. Moreno Belloso and Petit (2023), pp. 405–406.

[73] BEREC (2023), pp. 6–7.

[74] BEREC (2023), p. 4.

[75] Recital 64 of the DMA.

[76] Directive (EU) 2018/1972 of the European Parliament and of the Council of 11 December 2018 establishing the European Electronic Communications Code (Recast), OJ L 321, 17.12.2018, pp. 36–214.

[77] BEREC (2023), p. 4.

services, such as Signal, Telegram and Viber. In parallel, the Commission opened a market investigation to assess Apple's submissions, arguing that, despite meeting the thresholds, iMessage service does not qualify as a gateway under the DMA.[78]

5.2 *Interoperability Requirements for NIICS*

NIICS are generally not subject to the same kind of regulation as other categories of electronic communications networks and services as they do not use public numbering resources or participate in a publicly assured interoperable ecosystem.[79] However, the preamble to the EECC notes that increased use of NIICS could entail a lack of sufficient interoperability between communications services, which could hinder end-to-end connectivity and access to emergency services as well as significant barriers to market entry and obstacles to further onward innovation.[80]

The DMA addresses some of these concerns in Article 7 by requiring gatekeepers whose NIICS are designated as their core platform services to make the basic functionalities of their services interoperable with another provider's NIICS offered in the EU. This should be done by providing the necessary technical interfaces or similar solutions that facilitate interoperability upon request and free of charge. Interoperability should be implemented according to the following timeline:

a) end-to-end text messaging, sharing of images, voice messages, videos and other attached files between two individual end users should be made interoperable within six months after the NIICS has been listed in the designation decision;[81]
b) group chats and group sharing of mages, voice messages, videos, and other attached files should be interoperable within two years from the designation; and
c) end-to-end voice calls and video calls between individuals and within groups should be interoperable within four years from the designation.[82]

To enable such interoperability in practice, the gatekeepers concerned will have to publish a reference offer laying down the technical details and general terms and conditions of interoperability with their NIICS, including the necessary details on the level of security and end-to-end encryption. The Commission reserves the right to consult the Body of European Regulators for Electronic Communications

[78] The Commission's press release IP/23/4328, 6 September 2023.

[79] Recitals 11 and 44 of the EECC.

[80] Recital 149 of the EECC.

[81] Article 3(10) of the DMA sets a general deadline for complying with the obligations under the Regulation.

[82] Upon a gatekeeper's reasoned request, the Commission may extend the time limits for compliance where this is necessary to ensure effective interoperability and to maintain the necessary level of security, including end-to-end encryption (Article 7(6) of the DMA).

(BEREC) to determine whether a gatekeeper's reference offer is suitable in technical and legal terms[83] to ensure compliance with this obligation.[84]

Regulated reference offers are a common instrument for promoting transparency and preventing discriminatory terms in electronic communications markets. BEREC Report concludes that minimum requirements for an interoperability reference offer could include a description of the service and specification of the relevant basic functionalities and their features; technical definition and documentation of relevant interfaces and standards to be used; data protection and data security rules; rules on dynamic adjustments; rules on dispute resolution between providers; spam and abuse protections; details on necessary interoperability tests; service level agreements and service level guarantees; key performance indicators; charges, terms of payment and billing procedures; rules for obtaining users' consent to use the interoperable basic functions; duration, renegotiation and causes of termination of agreements; limitation of liability and indemnity; the gatekeeper's single point of contact for requesting and implementing interoperability for providers of NIICS; technical support by the gatekeeper regarding implementation.[85]

Following the publication of the reference offer, any alternative provider of NIICS may request interoperability with the gatekeeper's service, covering some or all of the basic functionalities, and the gatekeeper will have to render the requested functionalities interoperable within three months after receiving the request. Both providers' end users will be free to choose which of these services they will use. In all cases, the gatekeeper and the requesting provider should ensure that interoperability does not undermine a high level of security and data protection.

The DMA does not specify how the interoperability between NIICS should be implemented in technical terms but leaves this to reference offers. Thus, the gatekeepers will be able to set the technical terms that competing messaging service providers will have to follow. This risk is that the gatekeeper defines and manages a de facto standard.[86] One way of ensuring communication between NIICS is by using APIs to exchange data, removing the need for identical technical solutions. Yet, APIs must specify which functions are available, which format data are transmitted in, and who can communicate using the interfaces. So, by providing APIs, the gatekeeper will also set the conditions for interoperability. For example, suppose the specified means of identifying the NIICS end users are telephone numbers. In that case, this can limit the alternative providers who wish to use pseudonymised identifiers to protect the end users' privacy.[87] Open APIs allow service providers to

[83] Particularly, the gatekeepers' licensing schemes for proprietary APIs require independent oversight due to their potential for imposing unnecessary restrictions.

[84] Recital 64 of the DMA.

[85] BEREC (2023), pp. 33–34.

[86] Crémer et al. (2019), p. 59.

[87] BEREC (2023), pp. 18–19.

build their systems around a standard interoperable with multiple platforms, yet may still limit the space for innovative solutions.[88]

Article 46(1)(c) of the DMA authorises the Commission to adopt implementing acts laying down detailed arrangements for the application of the operational and technical arrangements for executing interoperability of NIICS Recital 96 and Article 48 of the DMA mention that interoperability obligations could be facilitated by using technical standards and that, where appropriate and necessary, the Commission may request European standardisation bodies to develop them.[89] Prescribing common standards would reduce the risk of the gatekeepers setting too restrictive technical conditions for interoperability. However, such standards would also limit alternative NIICS providers' technological innovation opportunities.[90]

5.3 Critical Views

Ex ante requirements for interoperability between communication services can benefit market competition since network effects no longer work in favour of the dominant player alone but benefit all service providers.[91] Network effects are shared among all providers and are aggregated into market-wide network effects. This should increase consumers' choices as providers will have to compete with the quality and additional functionalities of their services.[92] Yet, critics point out that horizontal interoperability may reduce the incentive for users to use multiple services (multi-homing), potentially entrenching existing technologies and business models and thus reducing competition in developing new features.[93] Mandated interoperability can also limit innovation potential by adding new technical standards as barriers to entry for new communication technologies. The need for coordination between the gatekeepers could also provide opportunities for their collusive behaviour to restrict competition.[94]

Recital 64 of the DMA provides that in all cases, the gatekeeper and the requesting provider should ensure that interoperability of NIICS does not undermine a high level of security and data protection. Yet, significant concerns exist regarding the technical feasibility of implementing interoperability, especially for end-to-end encrypted messaging services. Opening platforms to third-party data flows may cause privacy and security risks.[95] Some experts argue that lacking a global standard

---

[88] Cf. OECD (2021), p. 13.

[89] BEREC (2023), p. 32.

[90] Crémer et al. (2019), p. 59.

[91] Kerber and Schweitzer (2017), p. 51. Bourreau et al. (2022), p. 19.

[92] BEREC (2023), pp. 16–17.

[93] OECD (2021), p. 22. Bourreau et al. (2022), p. 21.

[94] Crémer et al. (2019), p. 59.

[95] Bourreau et al. (2022), p. 40.

for encryption, making end-to-end encrypted services interoperable is virtually impossible without compromising security and on the other hand, using open API libraries with API keys risks creating entry points for cyber-attacks. This could be prevented by reviewing APIs to eliminate privacy and cyber-security risk. Access to APIs could also be limited to licensed third parties.[96] The DMA leaves the resolution of these issues to gatekeepers themselves and the possible implementing acts adopted by the Commission in the future.

6 Conclusion

Interoperability measures, first developed in antitrust case law, have been legislated in the DMA as *ex ante* requirements for digital gatekeepers. Together with other DMA and DSA rules, they position the gatekeepers in the role of information infrastructure operators rather than regular competitors in the digital market. The legal regime for the gatekeepers' core platform services is akin to incorporating the essential facilities doctrine in legislation.[97] Interoperability rules for core platform services operate as a framework to facilitate smaller market players, which can increase competition in online markets, encourage innovation and boost consumer choices. However, ensuring interoperability and data portability can also pursue other policy goals apart from economic efficiency and consumer choice, for example, promoting end users' privacy and control over their data.[98] Treating core platform service as a universal service can provide electronic communication infrastructure crucial for the functioning of the modern economy and the political, cultural and social development.[99]

Boosting interoperability seems to be a trend in EU policies on the digital economy. In its Digital Agenda, the Commission identified a lack of interoperability as one of the most significant obstacles to digitalisation and declared effective interoperability between networks, devices, applications, data repositories, and services as one of the primary goals.[100] Apart from the DMA, this is reflected in the proposed Data Act, which contains measures to promote the development of interoperability standards for data sharing and processing in line with the EU Standardisation

[96] Ibidem.

[97] Jackson (2022), p. 17.

[98] OECD (2021), pp. 37–38.

[99] Kerber and Schweitzer (2017), p. 48.

[100] A Digital Agenda for Europe, COM(2010)245 final, Brussels, 19.5.2010, p. 3. Digital Single Market Strategy for Europe, COM(2015)192 final, Brussels, 6.5.2015, pp. 15–16.

Strategy.[101] The proposed Interoperable Europe Act includes measures for a high level of public sector interoperability across the EU.[102]

The Digital Agenda called for standard-setting by the industry, supported by public policy, to promote greater interoperability.[103] Considering the recent legislative activity, it seems that the public policy element in defining the interoperability parameters will be significant. Due to the concerns about the gatekeepers' increasing economic, political and cultural influence, it is unlikely that they will be left to decide themselves what the legal and technical terms of interoperability will be. Interoperability as a legal term and the technical manner of its implementation in the EU can be expected to develop rapidly.

References

Akman P (2022) Regulating competition in digital platform markets: a critical assessment of the framework and approach of the EU Digital Markets Act. Eur Law Rev 47(1):85–114

BEREC (2023) BEREC Report on Interoperability of Number-Independent Interpersonal Communication Services (NI-ICS), BoR (23) 92, 8

Bourreau M et al (2022) Interoperability in digital markets – report. Centre on Regulation in Europe, Brussels

Crémer J et al (2019) Competition policy for the digital era – final report. Publications Office of the European Union, Luxembourg

Desai K (2021) Changing competition law for the digital sector. Eur Compet Regul Law Rev 5(1):11–23

Etteldorf C (2022) DMA – Digital Markets Act or Data Markets Act? Eur Data Prot Law Rev 8(2):255–261

Huckova R, Semanova M (2023) Various consequences of Digital Markets Act on gatekeepers. EU Comp Law Issues Chall Ser 7:295–314

Hutchinson CS, Treščáková D (2022) Tackling gatekeepers' self-preferencing practices. Eur Compet J 18(3):567–590. https://doi.org/10.1080/17441056.2022.2034332

Jackson E (2022) Upping the (ex) ante digital competition reform in the era of Google Shopping. Plassey Law Rev 2:7–19

Jackwerth K (2022) Great expectations: the Facebook case and subsequent legislative approaches to regulate large online platforms and digital markets. J Intell Prop Inf Technol Electron Commerce Law 13(3):200–223

Kerber W, Schweitzer H (2017) Interoperability in the digital economy. J Intell Prop Inf Technol Electron Commerce Law 8(1):39–58

Monti G (2021) The Digital Markets Act: improving its institutional design. Eur Compet Regul Law Rev 5(2):90–101

Moreno Belloso N, Petit N (2023) The EU Digital Markets Act (DMA): a competition hand in a regulatory glove. Eur Law Rev 48(4):391–421

[101] The Commission's press release IP/23/3491 'Data Act: Commission welcomes political agreement on rules for a fair and innovative data economy', Brussels, 28 June 2023.

[102] Council of the EU press release 854/23 'Interoperable Europe act: Council and Parliament strike a deal for more efficient digital public services across the EU', Brussels, 13 November 2023.

[103] Bourreau et al. (2022), p. 36.

Morton F et al (2023) Equitable interoperability: the "supertool" of digital platform governance. Yale J Regul 40(3):1013–1055

OECD (2021) Data portability, interoperability and digital platform competition. OECD Competition Committee Discussion Paper, http://oe.cd/dpic

Rowland D, Kohl U, Charlesworth A (2012) Information technology law, 4th edn. Routledge, London

Turner V (2022) The EU Digital Markets Act – a new dawn for digital markets? Antitrust ABA 37:42–48

Unver MB (2022) Threading the needle from 'interoperability' to 'gatekeeping': quest for a layered model. Int Rev Law Comput Technol 36(2):223–250. https://doi.org/10.1080/13600869.2021.1964916

Recalibrating Territoriality in Platform End-User License Agreements

István Harkai and Péter Mezei

Abstract The issue of territoriality in copyright law has long been an area of in-depth and thorough research. The territoriality of copyright norms is an established fact, but it is also challenged by technological advances and a long-standing political process. Geographical determinacy is a crucial determinant of the cross-border flow of content enabled by various communication technologies. This is also reflected in the overall legal norms governing the issue. On the one hand, the digital space created by the emergence of the Internet allows for cross-border content delivery, while on the other hand, the free movement of goods and services, one of the four fundamental freedoms of the European Union, also appears to be incompatible with territorial copyright regimes. There have been many attempts to resolve these contradictions in the European Union, and legal geography, a research method combining the interfaces of geography and law, can help to find a solution. Using this research method, this paper takes a new approach to comparing the internal market and territorial fragmentation rules of EU copyright law and the contractual practices of platform providers, in order to answer the question of how geography determines the development of a legal area and how far these geographical and political boundaries can be crossed.

The research was carried out in the framework of the Interdisciplinary Centre for Research Development and Innovation Excellence (ICRC) Human and Social Sciences Cluster, ICT and Social Sciences Challenges Competence Centre, Research Group Legal and Policy Aspects of Digital Public Spheres.

I. Harkai (✉) · P. Mezei
University of Szeged, Szeged, Hungary
e-mail: harkai.istvan@juris.u-szeged.hu; mezei.peter@szte.hu

D. V. Popović, R. Kulms (eds.), *Repositioning Platforms in Digital Market Law*, European Union and its Neighbours in a Globalized World 15,
https://doi.org/10.1007/978-3-031-69678-7_3

1 Introduction

In recent years, the advent and expansion of platforms have added a new, complex layer to the European Union's copyright legal system, highlighting the specificities of the separate territorial development of copyright and the contradictory interpretation of the rules on licensing digital content.[1] In our study, we examine the layering of contractual practices for the use of digital content by predominantly US-based platform operators and its effects on end-users with EU nationality. These private ordering mechanisms contain either only partial or no reference to EU law rules. Indeed, as will be seen from the analysis of end-user contracts, they often rely on US copyright law and the Digital Millennium Copyright Act (DMCA)[2] instead of, or in addition to, EU law.

Member States' copyright rules are governed at EU level by a number of directives and regulations. In practice, however, the implementation and enforcement of these norms might vary considerably from one Member State to another, exacerbating the disadvantages of the territorial fragmentation of the digital single market. Territorial fragmentation is of particular relevance in the platform economy, where the content and formal requirements of contracts of use for the distribution of content to the public are determined by national copyright law, while respecting the principle of contractual freedom.[3] This will create uncertainty for the content industry, intermediary service providers and users, who will be less able to rely on the EU copyright framework.

An important step in this framework is the Digital Single Market Strategy,[4] which aims to create a digital single market, where the free movement of digital goods and services can be achieved, in particular through cross-border licensing and access to content. Platforms' contractual practices in this area are only partially compliant with EU copyright rules, with operators often relying on the US legal framework to limit their liability and ensure access to content. In addition to the territorial fragmentation of the EU digital single market, this phenomenon highlights two other important aspects. On the one hand, the role of geography as an

---

[1] Schwemer (2019), p. ix.

[2] Public Law 105-304 – Oct. 28, 1998 Digital Millenium Copyright Act (chrome-extension://efaidnbmnnnibpcajpcglclefindmkaj/https://www.congress.gov/105/plaws/publ304/PLAW-105publ304.pdf).

[3] Schwemer (2019), p. 30.

[4] Communication from the Commission to the European Parliament, the Council, the European Economic and Social Committee and the Committee of the Regions – A Digital Single Market Strategy for Europe. SWD (2015) 100 final, Brussels, 6.5.2015, COM(2015) 192 final (chrome-extension://efaidnbmnnnibpcajpcglclefindmkaj/https://eur-lex.europa.eu/legal-content/EN/TXT/PDF/?uri=CELEX:52015DC0192&from=FI).

analytical tool in jurisprudence and, on the other hand, the way legal colonialism is manifested in the digital environment. Indeed, platforms, through their contractual practices, bring with them foreign legal institutions to the continental European copyright system, which has its roots in civil law.

The intersection of foreign copyright elements in the contractual practices of platforms, the nationality of the platforms' mother company and the Digital Single Market Strategy provide an excellent reason to analyse the contractual practices of platform operators, which have a major impact on the possibilities and flexibility of access to content, using the geographical and comparative law method.[5] First, we introduce the copyright-relevant, multi-layered EU regulatory sources on platforms. Second, the paper presents the nature of legal geography as a research methodological tool. Third, we examine the contractual practices of platforms providing services in Europe that bring Anglo-Saxon copyright elements not familiar in the European copyright system into civil law-based authors rights system. Finally, we present the results of a comparison of the contractual practices of platform providers. Extracts from EULAs relevant to our topic are included in the appendix at the end of the paper.

2 The Multi-Layered Platform Regulation of the EU

In the European Union, it was the Junkcer Commission (2014–2019) that unfolded the first bundle of regulations on platforms; which was then followed further norms introduced during the tenure of the von der Leyen Commission (2019–2024). Sooner or later, these norms will form a compact, holistic, "one-size-fits-all" collection of rules. This graduate and granular development might be summarized as follows.

The first important sources of law were closely connected to data protection law. In 2016, the GDPR was introduced,[6] representing a pattern for the rest of the world—something that later triggered the birth of the term "Brussels-effect".[7] The GDPR was later followed by multiple other regulations (some in draft yet) related

[5] Schwemer highlights the transformative nature of the internet and digitalisation, which has transformed content consumption patterns, shifting the status quo towards access-based business models that define how content is consumed and the framework for access through their contractual practices. Schwemer (2019) p. 38.

[6] Regulation (EU) 2016/679 of the European Parliament and of the Council of 27 April 2016 on the protection of natural persons with regard to the processing of personal data and on the free movement of such data, and repealing Directive 95/46/EC (General Data Protection Regulation) (Text with EEA relevance).

[7] Bradford (2020).

to the concept of data: the Open Data Directive,[8] the draft Data Governance Act,[9] and the draft Data Act[10]—all encompassed by the EU's Data Strategy.[11]

A nice bunch of other sources of law might come into play when it is about platforms. These include the AVSM Directive on video sharing platforms;[12] the CDSM Directive on the copyright aspects;[13] the Digital Services Act on e-commerce and digital services;[14] the Digital Markets Act on digital competition law;[15] the directive on the supply of digital content and digital services related to consumer protection law;[16] the P2B regulation on transparency of business uses of platforms;[17] or the most recent—currently negotiated in the trilogue—AI Act.[18]

Although all of these norms work with special, vertical norms, they ultimately form parts of a bigger picture: a horizontal set of rules regarding the digital single market. This means (for the purposes of the present paper) that any service provider

[8] Directive (EU) 2019/1024 of the European Parliament and of the Council of 20 June 2019 on open data and the re-use of public sector information (recast).

[9] Proposal for a Regulation of the European Parliament and of the Council on European data governance (Data Governance Act), Brussels, 25.11.2020., COM(2020) 767 final, 2020/0340(COD).

[10] Proposal for a Regulation of the European Parliament and of the Council on harmonised rules on fair access to and use of data (Data Act), Brussels, 23.2.2022., COM(2022) 68 final, 2022/0047(COD).

[11] Compare to https://commission.europa.eu/strategy-and-policy/priorities-2019-2024/europe-fit-digital-age/european-data-strategy_en.

[12] Directive 2010/13/EU of the European Parliament and of the Council of 10 March 2010 on the coordination of certain provisions laid down by law, regulation or administrative action in Member States concerning the provision of audiovisual media services (Audiovisual Media Services Directive) (Codified version) (Text with EEA relevance).

[13] Directive (EU) 2019/790 of the European Parliament and of the Council of 17 April 2019 on copyright and related rights in the Digital Single Market and amending Directives 96/9/EC and 2001/29/EC (Text with EEA relevance).

[14] Regulation (EU) 2022/2065 of the European Parliament and of the Council of 19 October 2022 on a Single Market For Digital Services and amending Directive 2000/31/EC (Digital Services Act) (Text with EEA relevance).

[15] Regulation (EU) 2022/1925 of the European Parliament and of the Council of 14 September 2022 on contestable and fair markets in the digital sector and amending Directives (EU) 2019/1937 and (EU) 2020/1828 (Digital Markets Act) (Text with EEA relevance).

[16] Directive (EU) 2019/770 of the European Parliament and of the Council of 20 May 2019 on certain aspects concerning contracts for the supply of digital content and digital services (Text with EEA relevance).

[17] Regulation (EU) 2019/1150 of the European Parliament and of the Council of 20 June 2019 on promoting fairness and transparency for business users of online intermediation services (Text with EEA relevance).

[18] DRAFT Compromise Amendments on the Draft Report Proposal for a regulation of the European Parliament and of the Council on harmonised rules on Artificial Intelligence (Artificial Intelligence Act) and amending certain Union Legislative Acts (COM(2021)0206 –C9 0146/2021 – 2021/0106(COD)).

offering access to copyright protected contents might need to comply with all—relevant—pieces of these rules to ultimately fit into the EU's Digital Single Market Strategy.

In fact, this means two things for platforms willing to operate within the EU. On the one hand, their business models and internal regulations shall also be "holistic". Viewed from this perspective, the copyright concerns remain minor compared to data protection, competition or some transparency requirements. On the other hand, not even this argument of ours minimize the crucial (quite frequently central) nature of copyright norms. The business model of numerous platforms is primarily based on the sharing of copyright protected contents (by the platforms or by their users). These platforms—especially "online content-sharing service providers" under the CDSM Directive—shall predominantly focus on the copyright-relevant rules before casting their eyes on other norms.

There might be two further dimensions to discuss when it comes to the relevance of EU platform regulations. The first is naturally the already mentioned "Brussels-effect". Whether the copyright-relevant platform rules can have any such effect on other parts of the globe (especially on the USA), is far from certain. Although the US federal government (especially via the Federal Trade Commission), the Congress,[19] and also the Federal Supreme Court[20] has taken steps to review the immunities of platforms under the two early and still valid US acts, namely under Section 230 of the Communications Decency Act and Section 512 of the Digital Millennium Copyright Act. It is, however, almost certain that the USA will follow its own approach to re-regulate platforms' liability in the field of copyright law.

The other fascinating dimension is connected to the layers of regulating end-users' behaviour.[21] As our findings within the frames of the reCreating Europe project have also shown, there are at least three distinct types of "platform regulation". Namely, "regulations *of* platforms", which are the public/state laws on the functioning of platforms; "regulation *by* platforms", which equal with the service providers' own/internal regulatory sources; and, finally, "regulation *on* platforms", which corresponds to the content management practices of platforms. These three options follow each other in a logical order: content moderations under terms and conditions shall comply with statutory rules. The devil lies, however, in the details. Whether regulation by and on platforms is truly in light of the existing public norms, shall be tested empirically. This is in the focus of our paper.

---

[19] See the bill submitted by Lindsey Graham on the repealing of Section 230 of the CDA: S.2972 - A bill to repeal section 230 of the Communications Act of 1934, 117th Congress (2021–2022).

[20] The Supreme Court found Section 230 constitutional in both of the first two such cases. See: Reynaldo Gonzalez, et al. v. Google LLC, 598 U.S. ___ (2023); Twitter, Inc. v. Taamneh et al., 598 U.S. ___ (2023).

[21] Gorwa (2019), pp. 861–865.

3 Legal Geography and Its Place Among Legal Research Methods

It cannot be stressed enough how geography is an important context, a determinant in geopolitical relations, trade, transport and communication networks, or even in agriculture and environmental protection. Geopolitics shows the geographical location of the natural and other resources available on the planet, the nature of the power entities that control them, including the nature of the social, political and legal arrangements of the power.[22]

The characteristics of space also have a fundamental impact on legal systems, determining the territorial scope of legal norms, the boundaries of the sovereign's jurisdiction, the framework of international cooperation. It is essentially state-based, linked to statehood, which may ignore the heterogeneity of social, ethnic and religious groups.[23] Approaching legal systems from a geographical perspective also provides a basis for comparison, as it is well established that the development of the major legal systems has essentially taken place within a geographical framework. The civil law (Roman law) roots of continental Europe date back to the Roman Empire, which ruled a large part of the continent. The Anglo-Saxon common law system firstly developed in a country which, due to its geographical location, was sufficiently distant from Europe. Foreign conquerors could only with great difficulty, if at all, prevent it from developing independently. England, and later Britain, also owed its colonial empire to its geographical location, which enabled it to reach the world's oceans quickly. In this colonial empire, the legal system that had been established centuries earlier in the old country, England, could easily spread. The aim of legal geography, therefore, is to make visible the interconnections between the two disciplines, focusing on geography, space and place as determinants in jurisprudence,[24] in order to answer the question *"does law determine the functioning of the economy"*[25] or, on the contrary, *"does both law and economy flow from and respond to the geographical context?"*[26] Leah S. Horowitz sees the essence of legal geography in the organization of space, whereby political and economic actors shape the rules of economic production and social coexistence and their control frameworks from the micro to the macro level.[27]

When considering the interface between geography and law, one of the most obvious starting points is property and intellectual property law. Both can be understood in very palpable geographical terms.[28] In the case of property rights, land as a real estate space is well-defined, a key building block of the modern market econ-

[22] Bartel et al. (2013), pp. 345–346.

[23] Robinson (2013), p. 376.

[24] Bartel et al. (2013), pp 339–341. Comp.: Robinson and Graham (2018), p. 3.

[25] Bartel et al. (2013), p. 343.

[26] I.m.

[27] Horowitz (2021), pp. 1192–1193. Comp.: Robinson (2013), pp. 375–376. Delaney (2015), p. 99.

[28] Bartel et al. (2013), p. 342.

omy based on private property, but it was also a defining foundation of feudal medieval monarchies. The same can be said of forms of intellectual property, the territorial nature of which expresses the fact that the sovereign granting protection seeks to ensure the highest possible level of protection for a wide variety of intellectual products on its own territory. This territorial, geographical approach leads to market fragmentation, which hinders the free movement of goods in aspirations such as the EU's drive to create a single internal market. In the European Union, the creation of a single internal market is a key ambition, complemented by the seemingly borderless nature of the internet, which has created a digital market across nation-state borders. In the digital space, content is delivered by companies, most of which are based in the US. The geographical intersection is therefore between, on the one hand, the European Union's desire to create a single internal market and, on the other, the contractual practices of US-based technology giants. It is at this intersection that the European Union's essentially continental author's right system, rooted in the Romano-Germanic civil law, meets the contractual practices of platform services, which are largely based on Anglo-Saxon law, and which gives rise to particular contradictions, since the will of the European legislator and the contractual platform governance operating outside this institutional framework are in conflict.[29] Sebastian Felix Schwemer classifies this form of governance as a form of regulation initiated by private actors, a type of corporate self- and co-regulation, but which can only be considered as soft law. However, if it has an impact on behaviour and is respected by those involved, it is in a functional sense equivalent to hard law.[30] Since these rules are not the product of traditional legislation, they raise the question of the lack of democratic legitimacy and how they can coexist with the legal norms established by the legislator.[31]

The contractual practices that have developed in the platform economy (private ordering mechanism) show similar features to the *lex mercatoria* that governs maritime trade, a private global trade framework that contains selfregulatory norms that exist independently of states and through which international economic actors are interconnected. The lex mercatoria, according to Joshua Barkan, fits into a global economic constitutionalism that exists alongside and in parallel with the constitutional systems of nation states following a territorial logic,[32] and is embodied to a significant extent in the contractual practices followed by transnational corporations. This is a kind of autonomous regulatory role[33] which, due to the supranational form of activity, can extend to several jurisdictions.[34]

International production chains therefore not only involve the flow of goods and services, but also general contractual terms and conditions and organisational

---

[29] Bartel et al. (2013), p. 347.

[30] Schwemer (2019), pp. 18–19.

[31] I.m. pp. 20–22.

[32] Barkan (2011), p. 595.

[33] I.m. p. 600.

[34] I.m. p. 601.

governance norms that interact with the legal system of the host state or regional economic cooperation.[35] For self-regulatory platform providers,[36] rule-making serves two important purposes. On the one hand, to maximise profits[37] and, on the other, to minimise liability[38] for possible infringements. And while on the subject of maritime trade, cross-border content consumption is undoubtedly a focal point and a trigger for disputes that typically start in national courts but end up in the Court of Justice of the European Union, where they provide an opportunity for interpretation of the law. Daniel Kelemen and Tommaso Pavone have shown that EU litigation can arise where a subset of EU rules is particularly relevant to the local socio-economic environment.[39] Examples include trade-related cases, including free movement of goods and services, which typically start in port cities on international shipping routes, and mergers and acquisitions disputes, which can arise near a country's financial centres.[40]

4 Signs of Territoriality in the Contractual Practices of the Analysed Internet Platforms

According to Niall Ferguson, the emergence and expansion of the internet and two-sided platforms in online content delivery does not fit into the path of technological innovation of previous eras, which can be described as innovation—creative anarchy—commercialisation—regulation. In case of the internet, innovative invention and creative anarchy was quickly followed by commercialisation, but regulation was significantly delaysed and not very effective in adapting to the new power

[35] I.m.

[36] For more on the wide-ranging topic of platform governance, see Quintais et al. (2022), pp. 29–32. Comp.: Cohen (2017), pp. 168–175.

[37] An excellent example of profit maximisation is the acquisition of exclusive and worldwide free licences for user-generated content through end-user contracts. For details on the contractual practices of the seventeen key services in the platform economy, see: Mezei and Harkai (2022), pp. 1–20.

[38] It is common for all end-user license agreements to exclude primary liability for user infringements and to operate a notice and takdown mechanism whereby infringing content is removed from the platform after notification from rightholders. Article 17 of Directive (EU) 2019/790 of the European Parliament and of the Council of 17 April 2019 on copyright and related rights in the Digital Single Market and amending Directives 96/9/EC and 2001/29/EC (hereafter the CDSM Directive) imposes a double obligation on online content sharing services. On the one hand, operators have to ensure that only authorised content is uploaded to their platform, which implies the implementation of a prior filtering mechanism. On the other hand, while allowing for limitations and exceptions, as well as the fundamental rights of access to information and freedom of expression, operators are also required to respect safeguards that provide end-users with a means of complaint and redress in the event that end-user content that was not otherwise infringing is removed. On the issue of platform liability, see: Mezei and Harkai (2017), pp. 13–28.

[39] Kelemen and Pavone (2018), pp. 365–366.

[40] I.m.

Table 1 Analysed Platforms

Streaming with hosting	Streaming without hosting	Online marketplaces	Social media
YouTube Twitch DailyMotion Pornhub Soundcloud Bandcamp	Netflix Disney+ Spotify	Steam Electronic Arts Origin Amazon Apple Media Service Google Play	Facebook Instagram Twitter Tiktok

relations that emerged. In the digital markets, duopolies (e.g., Microsoft and Apple in the markets for operating systems and personal computers) and oligopolies (including the platforms examined below) have emerged,[41] partly taking over and partly complementing the rules established by national and international legislators for the provision of content on the internet.

In what follows, we examine the territoriality clauses in the contractual practices of 18 platform services, In what follows, we analyse the territoriality clauses in the contractual practices of 18 platform services, looking at (1) the nationality of the service or its subsidiary, (2) the rules on territoriality, (3) choice of law and conflict of laws, (4) references to specific legal institutions of a legal system other than the European copyright system, and (5) whether the terms of use make specific reference to Community law provisions, and (6) what provisions are included for the use of content by end users.[42]

The Table 1 below lists the analysed platforms.

4.1 Streaming with Hosting

Service of YouTube is provided in the European Economic Area and Switzerland by Google Ireland Limited, a company incorporated in Ireland and operating under Irish law.[43] The relationship between an end-user in the European Economic Area or Switzerland and YouTube is governed by the laws of the country of residence of the user, who may bring proceedings in the local courts.[44] As regards the use of works protected by copyright, the conditions refer to the applicability of both the fair use test and the European limitations and exceptions.[45] The terms also state that consumers in the EEA, once they have accepted the Terms and Conditions, can rely on EU consumer protection rules, which also cover digital content and services for which YouTube is liable for defective or non-conforming performance.[46] By

41 Ferguson (2019), pp. 408–409.

42 Last date to view end-user license agreements for all services was 25 June 2023.

43 YouTube, Your Service Provider.

44 YouTube. Governing Law.

45 Submit a copyright removal request. What to know before you submit a removal request.

46 YouTube, Other Legal Terms, Warranty.

uploading content to the service, end-users grant YouTube a worldwide, non-exclusive, royalty-free, transferable, sublicensable license to use the content.[47] Other end-users are granted a worldwide, non-exclusives, royalty-free licence to use the content in a manner permitted by the service.[48]

Twitch, which specialises in sharing recorded gameplay, refers to US copyright law as the primary law in several of its terms of use. Appeals from arbitration of any disputes are subject to the exclusive jurisdiction of the state of federal courts of Santa Clara County, California. Any dispute between the parties will also be governed by the applicable laws of the State of California and the United States, without giving effect to principles of conflict of laws requiring the application of the law of another jurisdiction.[49] The terms of use allow a derogation from the general rule if the user or the rightholder is domiciled in a jurisdiction in which the provision is unenforceable. Any dispute, claim or cause of action shall be governed by the laws of the jurisdiction in which the end-user is domiciled and shall be decided by the competent civil courts of the jurisdiction in which the end-user is domiciled.[50] Twitch's terms of use are based on the DMCA rules regarding protected content and notice and takedown procedures.[51] With regard to the use of musical content, the terms of use specifically address the issue of permitted uses, stating that, on the one hand, not all musical content is protected by copyright and related rights and not all uses are considered unlawful. Especially if the use falls within the framework of fair use or similar rules.[52] By posting, transmitting, displaying, publishing or storing user content, Twitch and its sublicensees might grant to the maximum extent and for the maximum period permitted by law an unrestricted, worldwide, irrevocable, fully sublicensable, non-exclusive, royalty-free right to use the content.[53]

Dailymotion is a French-based video sharing platform that offers its service not only in Europe, but also in North America and Asia. This is also evident from the terms of use, which differentiate in terms of the nationality of users. If the end-user is a national of the European Economic Area, the United Kingdom or Switzerland, the end-user license agreement is concluded between the end-user and Dailymotion SA (Société anonyme, Paris), a company incorporated in France.[54] However, if the end-user is not a citizen of one of these three entities, the agreement will be between the end-user and Dailymotion Inc. (Delaware corporation, New York).[55] The resolution of any disputes arising from the use of the platform will also depend on the

[47] YouTube, Rights you Grant, Licence to YouTube.

[48] YouTube, Rights you Grant, Licence to Other Users.

[49] Twitch, 18. Disputes, d. Applicable law, point (i).

[50] I.m. point (ii).

[51] Twitch, 13. Respecting Copyright. Using Music on Twitch. DMCA Process. Digital Millenium Copyright Act Notification Guidelines.

[52] Music Guidelines, Uses Permitted by Law.

[53] Twitch, 8. User Content, a. License to Twitch.

[54] DailyMotion, Section 2: Acceptance of these terms. 2.2.1.

[55] I.m. 2.2.2.

nationality of the end-user. If the end-user is a national of the EEA, the United Kingdom or Switzerland, French law will apply, in all other cases the law of the State of New York will apply.[56] Interestingly, for user-generated content, the license granted to the service, which otherwise allows worldwide use, allows the end-user to restrict the use of the content on a territorial basis.[57] The platform operators also reserve the right to use geo-blocking if the uploaded content violates a specific law or regulation in a particular country or territory.[58] Dailymotion's terms of use prohibit the uploading of content that infringes copyright, but also indicate that if the use is subject to the limitations and exceptions, the permission of the rightholder is not required. As regards the limitations and exceptions, they provide for the application of French copyright provisions.[59] In addition, Dailymotion Support specifically mentions that for European uses, the scope of limitations and exceptions may differ from country to country, to which the French and European rules apply. In addition, the rules of the US fair use test may be invoked.[60] By placing content on the platform, the end-user grants Dailymotion non-exclusive, transferable, worldwide rights to use the content, which is also transferable to Dailymotion's affiliates.[61]

Pornhub is one of the largest adult content sharing sites in the world,[62] and although it is based in Canada, its terms of use state that it is registered in Cyprus.[63] The Terms of use accordingly provide for the application of the laws of Cyprus to the use of the website. Any disputes arising from the use of this website shall also be subject to the jurisdiction of the courts of Cyprus, specifically the Limassol courts.[64] The agreement provides for the application of the Federal Arbitration Act for the arbitration of disputes with users located in the United States.[65] The DMCA also applies to the notice and takedown process for infringing content.[66] Given the fact that the service is domiciled in Cyprus, it is legitimate to ask at this point why it was considered important to keep the copyright notice and takedown procedures under the DMCA, when the E-Commerce Directive[67] and the CDSM Directive also

[56] DailyMotion, Section 9: Miscellaneous 9.5.

[57] DailyMotion, Section 3: Your Intellectual Property Rights.

[58] DailyMotion, III. Consequences of Non-Compliance with the Prohibited Content Policy. A. Moderation actions applicable to the content, 3. Moderation Action affecting the accessibility of Content: application of a geo-blocking measures.

[59] DailyMotion, I) Prohibited Content Categories, J.Copyright-Infringing Content.

[60] DailyMotion Support, General questions related to copyright, What are the exceptions to copyright and related rights?

[61] DailyMotion, 3. Your Intellectual Property Rights.

[62] Terms of use also refer to this fact when they mention the results of the visitor data measurement, which closed on 31 January 2023 (https://www.pornhub.com/information/eu_dsa).

[63] Pornhub, Your Comments and Concerns.

[64] Miscellaneous.

[65] Arbitration Agreement & Waiver of Certain Rights.

[66] DMCA – Reporting Claims of Copyright Infringement.

[67] Directive 2000/31/EC of the European Parliament and of the Council of 8 June 2000 on certain legal aspects of information society services, in particular electronic commerce, in the Internal

contain advanced liability rules for internet service providers. By posting user content on the website, user grant an unlimited, worldwide, perpetual, non-exclusive, royalty-free, sublicensable and transferable license to the operators to use the content for promotional or commercial purposes, and other users are granted a non-exclusive, royalty-free license to access the content through the website. The license is also perpetual and irrevocable.[68]

SoundCloud is a German-based service specialised in storing audio content.[69] Accordingly, end-users must respect the platform's community guidelines as background legislation, in addition to the terms of use.[70] The applicable law is the law of Germany, unless otherwise provided by the mandatory laws of the United States or any Member State of the European Union, or the agreement is governed by the United Nations Convention on Contracts for the International Sale of Goods (CISG). The contract provides for the exclusive jurisdiction of the Berlin courts to settle disputes.[71] The terms of use specifically refer to EU copyright limitations and exceptions, including quotation, criticism, review, caricature, parody and pastiche.[72] For each and every content uploaded to SoundCould, the end-users grant a limited, worldwide, non-exclusive, royalty-free and fully paid license to use. License is also granted to other users and websites, applications or platforms, as well as to their users.[73]

Bandcamp is also in the business of making audio content available to the public. In its terms of use, for example, it explicitly refers to geographical restrictions on access to content, stating that the company makes no representation that the content is appropriate or available for use in locations outside of California, and access to the service is prohibited from areas where such content is illegal.[74] The terms provide for the application of North Carolina state law for the arbitration of disputes arising out of the use of the platform, with the exception of the conflict of laws rules. In the event that arbitration is not satisfactory, the United States federal courts or the state courts located in the Eastern District of North Carolina shall have exclusive jurisdiction over the dispute.[75] The removal of copyright infringing content is also subject to the DMCA.[76] Users uploading music as authors grant a worldwide, non-exclusive, royalty-free license to Bandcamp, its sublicensees and distributors.[77] Fans who use the service as users may also upload user content to the platform, for

Market (Directive on electronic commerce).

[68] Pornhub, Rules Applicable to All Content and Uploaders on the Website.

[69] SoundCloud, Disclosure.

[70] Your Use of the Platform.

[71] Applicable Law and Jurisdiction.

[72] Your Content.

[73] SoundCloud, Grant of license.

[74] Bandcamp, International/Non-California Use.

[75] Bandcamp, Dispute Resolution.

[76] Bandcamp, Fees and Payments – Terms for Fans, Intellectual Property Rights – Fans.

[77] Bandcamp, Intellectual Property Rights – Artists.

which the operators of the service acquire a worldwide, non-exclusive, perpetual, irrevocable, royalty-free, fully paid, sublicensable and transferable right to use. Other users of the platform will receive a non-exclusive, personal, non-commercial license to use the content at the time of uploading.[78]

4.2 *Streaming Without Hosting*

A specific feature of the services in this category is that they do not manage end-user creative content at all, nor do they provide hosting services to end-users. Their repertoire consists of pre-licensed audio and audiovisual content for which the operators presented here have themselves concluded strict usage contracts. These contracts often oblige operators to introduce effective technical measures to restrict access to the content, including geographical discrimination.

Netflix's terms of use explicitly mention the practice of geo-blocking content, stating that a subscribing user can access content primarily in the country in which they have established their account and only in the geographic locations where their service is offered and where such content is licensed. The availability of content varies from geographic location to geographic location.[79] Netflix's offline functionality, more specifically the content that can be viewed and accessed offline, may also be subject to geographical restrictions.[80] The terms of use also state that the legal relationship between end-users and the providers is governed by and construed in accordance with Dutch law.[81] In other words, the scope of the EU legal standards covers the conditions of use in question at least indirectly, or directly in the case of for example Portability Regulation.[82]

Disney+ addresses the territorial aspects of content delivery and access in a variety of ways and from many angles. The European market is served by the Dutch subsidiary, which is registered under Dutch law and based in Amsterdam.[83] The terms and conditions are available in different language versions for each country and are limited in scope to that country,[84] as can be seen from for example the English version: "*Only residents of the countries where we offer the Disney+ Service (collectively, the "Territory") are eligible to register for a Disney+ Service account.*"[85] The subscription terms and conditions specifically highlight the role of

[78] Bandcamp, Intellectual Property Rights – Fans.

[79] Netflix, Netflix Service, 4.3.

[80] I.m. 4.5.

[81] Netflix, 6. Miscellaneous, 6.1. Governing Law.

[82] Regulation (EU) 2017/1128 of the European Parliament and of the Council of 14 June 2017 on cross-border portability of online content services in the internal market.

[83] Disney+, Subscriber Agreement.

[84] Disney+, 7. Additional Provisions, q. Prevailing Language.

[85] Disney+, 1. User Eligibility and Registration. a. Eligibility and Age Limitations.

the Portability Regulation in relation to portability, stressing out that Disney+ maintains the geographic limitation of content while respecting the rules of the Regulation. The geolocation of the subscriber may be controlled by different technologies and methods.[86] Disputes between the service and the subscriber shall be settled before the court of the latter's place of residence or domicile,[87] and Hungarian law shall prevail as the applicable law.[88] The subscription contract also states that in some EU jurisdictions there is no possibility to exclude warranty, therefore the Disney+ disclaimer of warranty provisions do not apply to nationals of those jurisdictions.[89]

Spotify is one of the few globally significant platform services that is European, Swedish to be precise, and based in Sweden.[90] Although the conditions of use contain far fewer references to EU and non-EU legal institutions than before, they contain quite detailed rules on choice of law and jurisdiction. In the absence of mandatory rules in the country of residence, the general rule is to apply Swedish law or to submit to the jurisdiction of Swedish courts. For Bulgaria, Cyprus, Estonia, France, the Philippines, Hong Kong, Latvia, Lithuania, Luxemburg, Malta, Monaco, Norway, Portugal, Slovakia, Spain, Turkey, Swedish law is also applicable, but Swedish courts have non-exclusive jurisdiction.

In case of Brazil, Brazilian law is applicable and the courts in the state of Sao Paulo have exclusive jurisdiction. In case of Canada, Canadian law applies except in Quebec, where the law of Quebec is applicable, and the courts of Quebec have jurisdiction. In the rest of Canada, the Canadian law is applicable, and the courts of Ontario have jurisdiction. As regards Argentina, Bolivia, Chile, Colombia, Costa Rica, the Dominican Republic, Ecuador, El Salvador, Guatemala, Honduras, Nicaragua, Panama, Paraguay, Peru and Uruguay, the law of the State of California will be applicable to the end-user license agreements and the competent courts will be exclusively either the state and federal courts of California or the State of New York. In the United Kingdom, the contractual relationship between Spotify and users will be governed by the laws of England and Wales.[91] The terms of use also state that certain products may be subject to U.S. export and re-export control laws and regulations or similar rules in other jurisdictions. The end-user must warrant that it is not located in a country that is subject to an embargo or other economic sanctions imposed by the United States or is not listed as a prohibited or restricted party under any applicable export and re-export laws on any other United States government list.[92] At the time of uploading user content, Spotify acquires an

[86] Disney+, 4. Usage Terms, f. Disney+ Content Availability.

[87] Disney+, 7. Additional Provisions, j. Forum.

[88] Disney+, 7. Additional Provisions, l. Choice of Law.

[89] Disney+, 7. Additional Provisions, i. Disclaimers of Warranty; Liability Limitation.

[90] Spotify, Service Provider.

[91] Spotify, Governing Law, Mandatory Arbitration and Venue, 6.1 Governing Law/Jurisdiction.

[92] Spotify, Export Control and Sanctions.

exclusive, transferable, sublicensable, royalty-free, fully paid, irrevocable, worldwide license to the uploaded content.[93]

4.3 *Online Marketplaces*

Steam, one of the largest digital game stores in the online space, and more specifically its operating company, Valve, is incorporated in Washington State under Washington state law.[94] A clear indication that the content is geographically licensed is that the terms of use prohibit the use of IP proxies or other methods that would allow end-users to hide their place of residence or circumvent geographic restrictions on game content, including ordering or purchasing at prices that do not apply to the geographic area.[95] EU and UK consumers can rely on their legal right of withdrawal.[96] The applicable law differs as regards the place of residence of the subscribers. For end-users outside the EU and the UK, Washington state law applies, excluding conflict of laws principles and the Convention on Contracts for the International Sale of Goods. The state or federal courts in King County, Washington State has jurisdiction to resolve disputes.[97] For EU and UK nationals, the law of the country of habitual residence applies.[98] Steam's terms of use also address the geographic difference between the European Union and the United Kingdom, where service charges including VAT or other value-added taxes.[99] By uploading user content, the end-user grants Valve and its affiliates a worldwide, non-exclusive intellectual property right for the full term to use the content.[100]

The Electronic Arts (EA) video game service (Origin) is operated by Electronic Arts Inc. in the United States and EA Swiss Sarl in Europe.[101] The consumers using the service must be entitled to use the EA service and they must be a resident of a country where the use of the EA service is permitted.[102] The end-user license agreement explicitly declares that content is not guaranteed to be available in all places at all times, nor that the service is available on all devices in all geographical

[93] Spotify, Licenses that you grant us, User Content.

[94] Steam Subscriber Agreement.

[95] Steam, 3. Billing, payment and other subscriptions, A. Payment Authorization.

[96] Steam, I. Refunds and Right of Withdrawal.

[97] Steam, 10. Applicable Law/Mediation/Jurisdiction/Attorneys' Fees, For All Subscribers Outside the European Union and United Kingdom.

[98] I.m.

[99] Steam, 3. Billing, payment and other subscriptions, A. Payment Authorization.

[100] Steam, 6. User generated content, A. General Provisions.

[101] EA, 13. General Terms, B. Applicable Law.

[102] EA, 1. EA Account.

locations.[103] Users may not use the service in a country where EA is not permitted to offer its services under applicable export control laws.[104]

The end-user's place of residence is also a key determinant of the applicable law. Residents of the EEA, the United Kingdom, Switzerland, Brazil, Hong Kong, Mexico or Russia who enter into a contractual relationship with EA Swiss Sarl will be governed by the law of the country of residence of the end-user and will be subject to the jurisdiction of the courts of that country. In case of South Korea, the Swiss-based subsidiary will also be the contracting partner, but Korean law will be the applicable law, and the Korean courts will have jurisdiction over disputes. The legal relationship between EA and consumers residing in the United States, Canada and Japan is governed by the laws of the State of California, and jurisdiction is in the state or federal courts of San Mateo County. If the end user resides in a country other than the above, the contract is between the end-user and the Swiss subsidiary, but the applicable law will be the laws of the State of California and jurisdiction will be the state or federal courts of San Mateo County. The terms of use expressly exclude the applicability of the Vienna Convention on Contracts for the International Sale of Goods.[105] Arbitration of disputes is governed by the US Federal Arbitration Act if the end-user is not resident in Quebec, Russia, Switzerland, Brazil, Mexico, EEA member states, the United Kingdom or the Republic of Korea.[106] By posting user-generated content, EA and its licensors obtain a non-exclusive, perpetual, transferable, worldwide, sublicensable license to use the content, which also extends to all other users who may access or use the content through EA's services.[107]

Compared to the other services, Amazon is rather tight-lipped about the criteria it examines. The end-user license agreement for content on the services that may be protected by copyright and related rights states that such content is the property of Amazon or its content providers and is protected by United States and international copyright laws.[108] The terms of use provides for the exclusive jurisdiction of the state or federal courts in King County,[109] Washington, and the applicable law to be federal law and Washington state law, without regard to conflict of laws principles.[110] For reviews, comments, notices and other content generated by end-users, Amazon grants at time of posting a non-exclusive, royalty-free, perpetual, irrevocable, and fully sublicensable right to use the content throughout the world in any medium.[111]

[103] EA, 4. Availability of EA Services and Updates.

[104] EA, 6. Rules of Conduct.

[105] EA, 13. General Terms, B. Applicable Law.

[106] EA, 15. Dispute Resolutions by Binding Arbitration.

[107] EA, 5. Your UGC.

[108] Amazon, Copyright.

[109] Amazon, Disputes.

[110] Amazon, Applicable Law.

[111] Amazon, Reviews, Comments, Communications, and Other Content.

Apple Media Service's wide range of services are available to end-users in their country or territory of residence.[112] Downloadable content will also be made available to end-users on a differentiated territorial basis, for which the terms also state that the content can be removed from Apple services at any time.[113] The terms also warn that services and content available in the country of residence may not be available when the end-user travels abroad.[114] Apps made available on the Apple Media Service App Store may be used, imported or exported only in accordance with the laws of the United States and the laws of the jurisdiction in which the user obtained the app, which is prohibited conduct if it is directed to countries embargoed by the United States or targets sanctioned persons or entities.[115] For U.S. end-users or for services provided in the United States, the legal relationship between end-users and Apple is governed by the laws of the State of California, excluding its conflict of law provisions. The courts located in Santa Clara County, California shall have personal and exclusive jurisdiction to resolve any disputes arising. In the case of a citizen of a country of the European Union, the United Kingdom, Switzerland, Norway or Iceland, the law of the country of habitual residence shall govern and the courts of that country shall have exclusive jurisdiction. The terms exclude the applicability of the Vienna Convention on the Law of Sales.[116] Apple allows the creation and sharing of UGC (*user-generated content*), over which the service obtains a worldwide, royalty-free, perpetual, non-exclusive license.[117]

Google Play is rather tight-lipped about the geographical aspects of using the service. There is a reference to Ireland being the home country of the service's European subsidiary, and that the availability of content and features varies from country to country, and some content and features may not be available in the end-user's country.[118]

4.4 Social Media

The main service in the Meta product family, Facebook, provides services to European end-users through its Irish subsidiary, Meta Platforms Ireland Limited.[119] End-users must ensure that they comply with applicable laws when using the service, and that they appropriately restrict access to content, including filtering by

[112] Apple Media Service, A. Introduction to our Services.

[113] Apple Media Service, B. Using our Services.

[114] Apple Media Service, Content and Service Availability.

[115] Apple Media Service, F. Additional App Store Terms (Excluding Apple Arcade Apps) License of App Store Content.

[116] Apple, Governing Law.

[117] Apple Media Service, Your Submission to our Services.

[118] Google Play, 2. Your Use of Google Play.

[119] Facebook, 5. Other terms and policies that may apply to you.

geographic location or age.[120] A person who is in a country subject to a trade prohibition under U.S. law or who is on the U.S. Treasury Department's list of specially designated nationals may not engage in commercial activities in connection with Meta products.[121] Disputes arising out of or in connection with use by the consumer shall be settled before any court of competent jurisdiction in the country of residence of the end-user, to which the law of that country shall apply, without prejudice to conflict of laws rules. If the dispute arises in any other capacity, including access or use for business or commercial purposes, the matter will be heard by the competent court in Ireland, to which Irish law will apply, again without regard to conflicting of rules.[122] By uploading end-user content, Facebook acquires a non-exclusive, transferable, sublicensable, royalty-free license without geographical limitations.[123]

As part of the Meta family of products, Instagram follows the same rules as Facebook with respect to the affiliate's Irish domicile,[124] applicable law and courts of jurisdiction.[125] By sharing content, the end-user grants Meta a non-exclusive, royalty-free, transferable, sublicensable and worldwide license to use the content.[126]

Twitter differentiates between users who live in the European Union, EFTA Member States, the United Kingdom[127] or outside the European Union, the United States or other countries.[128] Of the two options, this paper examines the one that applies to end-users in EU or EFTA Member States and the UK. As with many of the services mentioned above, Twitter has a subsidiary registered in Ireland that provides services to non-US end-users.[129] End-users are granted a worldwide, royalty-free, non-transferable and non-exclusive license to use Twitter's software.[130] The protection of services relies on copyright rules in both the United States and other countries.[131] The notice and takedown procedures for copyright infringement are governed by the DMCA,[132] and the terms specifically state that if user conduct

---

[120] Facebook, 4. Additional provisions.

[121] Facebook, 3. Your commitments to Facebook and our community. 2. What you can share and do on Meta Products.

[122] Facebook, 4. Additional Provisions. 4. Disputes.

[123] Facebook, 3. Your commitments to Facebook and our community. 3. The permissions you give us.

[124] Instagram Terms of Use.

[125] Instagram, How we will handle disputes?

[126] Instagram, Your commitments. Permissions you give to us.

[127] Twitter Terms of Service. If you live in the European Union, EFTA States, or the United Kingdom.

[128] Twitter Terms of Service. If you live outside the European Union, EFTA States, or the United Kingdom, including if you live in the United States.

[129] Twitter, 6. General.

[130] Twitter, Your License to Use the Services.

[131] I.m.

[132] Twitter, Copyright policy.

falls within the fair use test, it is not considered unlawful.[133] By posting content on the platform, the end-user grants Twitter a worldwide, non-exclusive, royalty-free, sublicensable license to make the content available to the rest of the world. This license also extends to other end-users.[134]

TikTok's terms of use also differ according to the end-users' place of residence. I will consider the one that applies to end-users resident in the European Economic Area, the United Kingdom and Switzerland. The subsidiaries providing services in Europe are located in Ireland (EEA and Switzerland) and the United Kingdom.[135] The applicable law is the law of the country of residence of the end-user and the courts of the country of residence have jurisdiction to settle disputes. In addition, the parties may have recourse to the courts of the Republic of Ireland or the United Kingdom, which, however, do not have exclusive jurisdiction, depending on whether the dispute arises in relation to the Irish or the British subsidiary. End-users resident in the EEA may also use the European Commission's online dispute resolution platform.[136] TikTok's terms of use provide detailed rules for copyright infringement, specifically stating that not all unauthorised use is infringing. In this respect, there is a reference to the fair use test[137] and a detailed reference to the limitations and exceptions contained in the CDSM Directive.[138] The procedure for removing infringing content is also based on the DMCA[139] or similar laws in other countries. The end-user agreement also contains provisions on consumer protection, stating that EEA consumers are legally guaranteed by European consumer laws.[140] With respect to the right to use the end-user content, TikTok is seeking a non-exclusive, royalty-free, transferable, sublicensable, worldwide license for itself and its partners. Other end-users will also be granted a non-exclusive, royalty-free, worldwide license.[141]

5 Moving Towards "internet lex mercatoria"?

Six variables of the analysed EULAs shed light on a pattern.[142] Every agreement contain references to the domicile of the platforms providing the international service, choice of law and conflict of laws rules, which coincide with either the

[133] I.m.

[134] Twitter, Your Rights and Grant of Rights in the Content.

[135] TikTok, 1. Who you are contracting with.

[136] TikTok, 8. Resolving disputes.

[137] TikTok, Intellectual Property Policy.

[138] TikTok, Intellectual Property Policy. Copyright. Information for Rightsholders.

[139] TikTok, Information for Users: Copyright Infringement Counter-Notification.

[140] TikTok, 5. What we promise to you. 6. Suspending or ending our relationship. Your Rights.

[141] TikTok, Ownership of content and grant of licenses.

[142] These variables and patterns can be clearly seen in the overview tables in the annex.

domicile of the parent company or its subsidiary or the law of the country of establishment. For services that also host content, users grant a worldwide license to the platform operators by posting content. This statement is particularly interesting for two reasons. On the one hand, service providers, who also act as gatekeepers,[143] acquire a transnational, often global, license to use the UGC without paying the fair amount of remuneration. Meanwhile, the use of musical works and phonograms, as well as audiovisual works follows an established practice of licensing on a territorial basis. The gatekeeper role of platforms in the use of user-generated content should be the subject of further research in the future, if only because the relevant standard contractual clauses raise competition issues, in particular with regard to abuse of dominant position.

A further striking similarity in the patterns examined was the reference to the institutions of the Anglo-Saxon copyright system, which has different roots from the European author's rights system based on civil law. This was also particularly evident in the notice and takedown procedures for user-generated content, where end-users could file a counterclaim. Such counterclaims were historically designed by the DMCA to reflect the fair use doctrine of the US Copyright Act.[144] While this does not contradict the principle of freedom of contract, it is striking that instead of the otherwise well-developed EU e-commerce platform liability rules, operators providing services in Europe are being required to apply the rules of a foreign jurisdiction. This is also true in relation to the fair use test, which is the primary reference point for end-users seeking to prove the legitimacy of their use of content. Instead of the typical Anglo-Saxon test developed by case-law, there should be more space for applying the European limitations and exceptions. The CDSM Directive has now introduced several mandatory exceptions for online uses. However, these have been invoked in only four cases.

The players in the internet platform economy operate in a well-defined, interacting physical and digital space. The physical space is fundamentally defined by nation states and economic and political cooperation at regional and possibly international level. In this paper, we attempted to examine the private law-based contractual practices of platform giants operating in digital space. End-user license agreements can be understood as the *lex mercatoria* of the online platform economy, a body of law that operates at least partially independently of states, self-regulating through which the actors of the platform economy—content industry rights holders, service providers, secondary commercial users, end-users—are interconnected. The contractual practice of transnational platform services can also be placed within the framework of the *global constitutionalism* mentioned above, which is an

[143] For detailed characteristics of the gatekeeper role, see: Regulation 2022/1925 of the European Parliament and of the Council on contestable and fair markets in the digital sector and amending Directives 2019/1937 and 2020/1828 (Digital Markets Act) Article 2–3.

[144] 17 U.S.C. §107.

autonomous regulatory role whose norms coexist with the constitutional systems of nation states following a territorial logic, and even cross-jurisdictional.

Thus, the reference to the copyright acquis of the Anglo-Saxon legal system, due to the gatekeeping role and dominant market position of platform providers, provides evidence that, just as geographical exploration and colonialism in previous centuries, the global digital economy today creates the possibility for the exchange of legal institutions between legal cultures, a kind of *"legal colonialism"*, where the norms of different legal systems are mixed in the online spaces of the platform economy.

Links to the Analysed End-User License Agreements

https://www.youtube.com/t/terms?gl=GB
https://support.google.com/youtube/answer/2807622
https://www.twitch.tv/p/hu-hu/legal/terms-of-service/#7-license
https://legal.dailymotion.com/en/terms-of-use/
https://faq.dailymotion.com/hc/en-us/articles/360020018900-Exceptions-to-copyright
https://www.pornhub.com/information/terms
https://www.pornhub.com/information/dmca
https://soundcloud.com/terms-of-use
https://bandcamp.com/terms_of_use
https://bandcamp.com/copyright
https://help.netflix.com/legal/termsofuse
https://www.disneyplus.com/hu-hu/legal/el%C5%91fizet%C5%91i-meg%C3%A1llapod%C3%A1s
https://www.spotify.com/hu/legal/end-user-agreement/
https://store.steampowered.com/subscriber_agreement/?snr=1_4_4__global-responsive-menu#2
https://www.ea.com/legal/user-agreement
https://www.amazon.com/gp/help/customer/display.html?nodeId=GLSBYFE9MGKKQXXM
https://www.apple.com/legal/internet-services/itunes/us/terms.html
https://play.google.com/intl/en_uk/about/play-terms/
https://www.facebook.com/terms.php
https://help.instagram.com/478745558852511/?helpref=hc_fnav
https://twitter.com/en/tos#intlTerms
https://help.twitter.com/en/rules-and-policies/copyright-policy
https://www.tiktok.com/legal/page/eea/terms-of-service/en
https://www.tiktok.com/legal/page/global/copyright-policy/en

Appendix

Streaming with hosting						
	YouTube	Twitch	DailyMotion	Pornhub	Soundcloud	Bandcamp
1. Nationality of service or its subsidiary	EEA and Switzerland→Google Limited, incorporated in Ireland under Irish law	USA	France	Cyprus	Germany	–
2. Rules on territoriality	–	–	Maintaining geo-blocking in case of infringement	–	–	"The Company makes no representation that the Content is appropriate or available for use in locations outside of California, and access to the Service from territories where such Content is illegal is prohibited."
3. Choice of law and conflict of law rules	EEA and Switzerland→the laws of the user's country of residence, the local courts having jurisdiction.	State of California, United States lawJurisdiction of the state or federal courts of California, Santa Clara CountyUnless unenforceable in the State of the user's domicile	EEA, UK, Switzerland: French lawOther countries: New York Sate law	Cyprus law, Courts of LimassolArbitration proceedings under the United States Federal Arbitration Act	The law of Germany, unless otherwise provided by mandatory law of the USA or another EU country or if the agreement is governed by the CISG the courts of Berlin have jurisdiction	North Carolina state law, except conflict of laws rulesUnited States federal courts, state courts located in the Eastern District of North Carolina

Streaming with hosting

	YouTube	Twitch	DailyMotion	Pornhub	Soundcloud	Bandcamp
4. Instruments of legal systems other than the European Union	Fair use test	DMCA Fair use test	Fair use test	DMCA	–	DMCA
5. EU law provisions	European restrictions and exceptions, EU consumer protection rules (for EEA consumers)	–	European limitations and exceptions, French copyright provisions	–	European limitations and exceptions, references to quotation, criticism, review, caricature, parody and pastiche.	–
6. UGC License	License for worldwide use.	Worldwide license for use.	Worldwide, but the user can restrict use on a territorial basis.	Worldwide license for use.	Worldwide license for use.	Worldwide license for use.

Streaming without hosting

	Netflix	Disney+	Spotify
1. Nationality of service or its subsidiary	–	In Europe, the Netherlands, under Dutch law, with its seat in Amsterdam	Sweden
2. Rules on territoriality	Users can access content primarily in the country in which they have created their account and only in the geographic locations where they offer their services and where such content is licensed. The content availability varies by geographical locations.	Only residents of the countries where the Disney+ service is offered (collectively, the Territory) may create an account on the Disney+ service. Verification of subscribers' geolocation using various technologies and methods.	End users must guaranty that they are not located in a country that is subject to an embargo or other economic sanctions imposed by the United States.

Streaming without hosting			
	Netflix	Disney+	Spotify
3. Choice of law and conflict of law rules	Law of the Netherlands.	The law and competent courts of the country of residence of the subscriber.	Main rule: Swedish law, jurisdiction of Swedish courts. Bulgaria, Cyprus, Estonnia, France, Hong Kong, Lativa, Lithuania, Luxemburg, Malta, Monaco, Norway, Portugal, Slovakia, Spain, Turkey, Philippines: Swedish law, Swedish courts with non-exclusive jurisdiction. Brazil: Brazilian law, Sao Paulo state and federal courts. Canada, except Quebec: Canadian law, Quebec law in Quebec, Quebec courts. Argentina, Bolivia, Chile, Colombia, Costa Rica, Dominican Republic, Ecuador, El Salvador, Guatemala, Honduras, Nicaragua, Panama, Paraguay, Peru, Uruguay: California state law, competent courts of California or New York. United Kingdom: laws and courts of England and Wales.
4. Instruments of legal systems other than the European Union	–	–	–
5. EU law provisions	–	Even beside the rules of the Portability Regulation, the service maintains territorial content restrictions. EU consumer protection and warranty rules if the subscriber is an EU national.	–
6. UGC License	–	–	Global license to use.

Online marketplaces

	Steam	EA Origin	Amazon	Apple Media Service	Google Play
1. Nationality of service or its subsidiary	United States, Washington State.	United States: Electronic Arts Inc.Europe: EA Swiss Sarl.	–	–	Ireland (European affiliate).
2. Rules on territoriality	The use of IP proxies or other methods that allow end-users to hide their place of residence or circumvent geographical restrictions on game content is prohibited. In the EU and the UK, VAT is included in the service fees.	Residents of a country where EA provides its service are eligible to use the service. Content availability in all geographical locations and at all times is not guaranteed by the service providers.The Service is not available in any country in which EA is not permitted to provide the Service under applicable export control laws.	–	The service is available in the country or territory where the end-user resides. Services and content available in the country of residence may not be available when the end-user travels abroad.	The availability of content and features varies from country to country, and some content and features may not be available in the country of residence of the user.
3. Choice of law and conflict of law rules	EU and UK: law and courts of the country of habitual residence. Outside the EU and UK: state or federal courts in King County, Washington, Washington state law.	EEA, UK, Switzerland, Brazil, Hong Kong, Mexico, Russia: law and courts of the country of residence of the end-user.South Korea: Korean courts.United States, Canada, Japan: California state law, San Mateo County state or federal courts.	Washington state law and federal law. Washington State King County state or federal courts, without regard to conflict of laws principles.	US users: the laws of the State of California, excluding its conflict of laws provisions. The courts of Santa Clara County shall have jurisdiction. EU, UK, Switzerland, Norway, Iceland: laws and courts of country of habitual residence.	–
4. Instruments of legal systems other than the European Union	–	–	The content is the property of Amazon or its content providers and is protected by United States and international copyright laws.	–	–

Online marketplaces

	Steam	EA Origin	Amazon	Apple Media Service	Google Play
5. EU law provisions	EU and UK residents can invoke their legal right of withdrawal.	–	–	–	–
6. UGC License	–	A license for worldwide use.	A license for worldwide use.	Worldwide license for use.	–

Social media

	Facebook	Instagram	Twitter	Tiktok
1. Nationality of service or its subsidiary	European users: Ireland, Meta Platforms Ireland Limited.	See: Facebook.	EU, EFTA, UK: subsidiary in Ireland.	EEA, UK, Switzerland: subsidiaries in Ireland and the UK.
2. Rules on territoriality	End-users warrant that they will comply with the rules for filtering by geographic location or age.	See: Facebook.	End-users are granted a worldwide license to use Twitter software.	–
3. Choice of law and conflict of law rules	Any court of competent jurisdiction in the country of the user's domicile, according to the law of that country, without prejudice to conflict of law rules. Court with jurisdiction in Ireland under Irish law: any other dispute, including access or use for business or commercial purposes.	See: Facebook.	–	The law and courts of the country of residence of the end-user.
4. Instruments of legal systems other than the European Union	–	–	DMCA, Fair use test.	Fair use test, DMCA.
5. EU law provisions	–	–	–	CDSM Directive limitations and exceptions, European consumer protection rules.
6. UGC License	Permit without geographical restrictions.	See: Facebook.	Worldwide license for use.	Worldwide license for use.

References

Literature

Barkan J (2011) Law and the geographic analysis of economic globalization. Progr Human Geogr 35(5):589–607
Bartel R, Graham N, Jackson S, Prior J-H, Robinson D-F, Sherval M, Williams S (2013) Legal geography: an australian perspective. Geograph Res 51(4):339–353
Bradford A (2020) The Brussels effect: how the European Union rules the world. Oxford University Press
Cohen J-E (2017) Law for the platform economy. University of California, Davis 51:133–204
Delaney D (2015) Legal geography I: constituvities, complexities, and contingencies. Progr Human Geogr 39(1):96–102
Ferguson N (2019) A tér és a torony – Hálózatok, hierarchiák és harc a globális hatalomért (The Square and the Tower. Networks and Power, From the Freemasons to Facebook). Scolar Kiadó, Budapest
Gorwa R (2019) What is platform governance? Inf Commun Soc 22(3):854–871
Horowitz L (2021) Indigenous rights and the persistence of industrial capitalism: capturing the law-ideology-power triple-helix. Progr Human Geogr 45(5):1192–1217
Kelemen R-D, Pavone T (2018) The political geography of legal integration – visualizing institutional change in the European Union. World Polit 70(3):358–397
Mezei P, Harkai I (2017) Enforcement of copyrights over the Internet. A review of the recent ECJ case law. J Internet Law Rev 21(4):13–28
Mezei P, Harkai I (2022) End-user flexibilities in digital copyright law – an empirical analysis of end-user license agreements. Interact Entertain Law Rev 1:1–20
Quintais J-P, Mezei P, Harkai I, Magalhães J-C, Katzenbach C, Schwemer S-F, Riis T (2022) Copyright content moderation in the EU: an interdisciplinary mapping analysis, reCreating Europe Report (https://papers.ssrn.com/sol3/papers.cfm?abstract_id=4210278)
Robinson D-F (2013) Legal geographies of intellectual property, 'Traditional' knowledge and biodiversity: experiencing conventions, laws, customary law, and Karma in Thailand. Geograph Res 51(4):375–386
Robinson D-F, Graham N (2018) Legal pluralisms, justice and spatial conflicts: New directions in legal geography. Geograph J 184:3–7
Schwemer S-F (2019) Licensing and access to content in the European Union. Cambridge intellectual property and information law. Cambridge University Press, Cambridge

The Digital Platforms' Sisyphean Task: Reconciling Content Moderation and Freedom of Expression

Dušan V. Popović

Abstract Given the increasing importance of online platforms as a source of information and opinion formation, content moderation unsurprisingly came into the focus of the recent European Union's legislative efforts. From the freedom of expression perspective, the content moderation activities may lead to excessive filtering of users' content, in contradiction with the formal absence of general monitoring and filtering duty in EU law. Another concern stems from the use of recommender systems. Such algorithm-driven content delivery on social media, search engines and other platforms limit the content to which people are exposed, leads to 'information bubbles' and may negatively affect democratic discourse as a result. Further concern from the freedom of expression perspective is reflected in the use of content demotion mechanisms by online platforms in addressing 'borderline content', i.e. content which is not illegal nor in violation of platforms terms of service but rather undesirable. The use of such techniques clearly generates risk of censorship. The paper addresses these concerns while providing an analysis of relevant provisions of the Copyright in the Digital Single Market Directive and the Digital Services Act.

1 Introduction

Online platforms are the main points for access to, and exchange of, information on the Internet. The central role of online platforms in the flow of information raises the question of their responsibility for allowing the spread of illegal or harmful

This paper represents a contribution to the project of the University of Belgrade Faculty of Law "Contemporary problems of the Serbian legal system".

D. V. Popović (✉)
University of Belgrade, Faculty of Law, Belgrade, Serbia
e-mail: dusan.popovic@ius.bg.ac.rs

D. V. Popović, R. Kulms (eds.), *Repositioning Platforms in Digital Market Law*, European Union and its Neighbours in a Globalized World 15,
https://doi.org/10.1007/978-3-031-69678-7_4

content. Online platforms have consistently been presenting themselves as mere content hosts, emphasizing the distinction between them and the traditional media which exercise editorial control. Such distinction was generally accepted and built-in the legal framework in the form of digital platforms' liability exemption for the content they carried. After initial legislation was adopted in the United States in the nineties,[1] the European Union followed and introduced obligations on Member States to protect online service providers from liability,[2] as well as the possibility of seeking injunctions against an online service provider to prevent infringements.[3] In recent years, these legislative approaches, based on a 'notice-and-action' mechanism,[4] have started being perceived as insufficient to address the outsized effect digital platforms have on our information ecosystem.

The European Commission announced its intention to additionally regulate content-sharing platforms in the Communication "Towards a modern, more European copyright framework" in December 2015.[5] Following a heavily lobbied legislative process from all sides, the Copyright in the Digital Single Market Directive (CDSM Directive)[6] was adopted in May 2019. Many EU Member States struggled to implement the CDSM Directive within the two-year transposition period.[7] One of the main reasons for these difficulties was Article 17, which changes the liability rules for online-content sharing service providers. Departing from the case-law of the Court of Justice of the European Union (CJEU) on the right of communication to the public under Article 3(1) of the InfoSoc Directive, Article 17(1) of the CDSM Directive makes online-content sharing service providers (OCSSPs) directly liable for content uploaded by their users. This means that OCSSPs must themselves obtain the necessary authorization for such uploads. The complexity of the digital platforms' legal and business environment in Europe has further been

[1] See Communications Decency Act of 1996, 47 U.S.C. § 230; The Digital Millennium Copyright Act (DMCA) of 1998, 17 U.S.C. § 512.

[2] See Directive 2000/31/EC of the European Parliament and of the Council of 8 June 2000 on certain legal aspects of information society services, in particular electronic commerce, in the Internal Market (E-commerce Directive), 2000 O.J. (L 178) 1-16, Arts. 12–15.

[3] See Directive 2001/29/EC of the European Parliament and of the Council of 22 May 2001 on the Harmonisation of Certain Aspects of Copyright and Related Rights in the Information Society (InfoSoc Directive), 2001 O.J. (L 167) 10-19, art 8(3); Directive 2004/48/EC of the European Parliament and of the Council of 29 April 2000 on the Enforcement of Intellectual Property Rights (Enforcement Directive), 2004 O.J. (L 195) 16, Art 11.

[4] These mechanisms are commonly referred to as 'notice-and-takedown'. However, a more appropriate term is 'notice and action', which comprises a number of mechanisms intended to eliminate illegal or infringing content from the Internet upon request of the right owner. See Kuczerawy (2020), p. 526.

[5] European Commission, "Towards a modern, more European copyright framework", COM(2015) 626 final (9.12.2015), p. 10.

[6] Directive (EU) 2019/790 of the European Parliament and of the Council of 17 April 2019 on copyright and related rights in the Digital Single Market and amending Directives 96/9/EC and 2001/29/EC, 2019 OJ (L 130) 92.

[7] Only three Member States (Germany, Hungary and The Netherlands) had fully implemented the provisions of the CDSM Directive within the transposition deadline which was set at 7 June 2021.

increased with the adoption of the Digital Services Act (DSA)[8] in October 2022. The DSA separated the online platforms' due diligence obligations from the liability for underlying content. The providers violating the due diligence obligations prescribed under the DSA will be held to account. These violations, however, have no bearing on the provider's preservation of the liability exemptions. Even the providers who are no longer responsible for users are nonetheless responsible for their own failings to be diligent.

A significant part of online platforms' duties relate to content moderation, an activity which is not unequivocally defined. A rare example of a definition of content moderation in EU law is found in the DSA, which specifies that the said activities, automated or not, may be undertaken by providers of intermediary services and are aimed, in particular, at detecting, identifying and addressing illegal content or information incompatible with the terms and conditions, provided by recipients of the service.[9] From the freedom of expression perspective, the content moderation activities may lead to excessive filtering of users' content, in contradiction with the formal absence of general monitoring and filtering duty in EU law (Sect. 2). Another concern stems from the use of recommender algorithms. Such algorithm-driven content delivery on social media, search engines and other platforms limit the content to which people are exposed, leads to 'information bubbles'[10] and may negatively affect democratic discourse as a result (Sect. 3). These activities are generally undertaken automatically, without direct involvement of humans, which adds to the existing controversy. The use of recommender systems may be seen as a specific type of content moderation which does not lead to content removal, but rather to content manipulation, in line with the user's prior interactions with the content and/or user's (alleged) expectations. Further concern from the freedom of expression perspective is reflected in the use of content demotion mechanisms by online platforms in addressing 'borderline content', i.e. content which is not illegal nor in violation of platforms terms of service but rather undesirable. The use of such techniques clearly generates risk of censorship (Sect. 4).

[8] Regulation (EU) 2022/2065 of the European Parliament and of the Council of 19 October 2022 on a Single Market For Digital Services and amending Directive 2000/31/EC (Digital Services Act), 2022 OJ (L 277) 1.

[9] DSA, Art. 2 (p).

[10] Further to 'information bubbles', other terms such as 'echo chambers' and 'filter bubbles' are equally used in literature. An echo chamber is typically defined as an enclosed media environment with the capacity to both amplify the messages delivered within it and isolate them from any counter-argument. Although the two terms are often used interchangeably, a filter bubble is to be understood as a type of echo chamber, which is primarily produced by ranking algorithms engaged in passive personalization without any active choice on the part of the user.

2 Risk of Content Moderation Leading to General Monitoring

The initial European approach to content moderation relied on liability exemptions for both access and hosting providers for unlawful acts of third parties on their networks. Such limited liability regime established by the E-Commerce Directive was based on two principles: (i) the principle of 'notice-and-action'; and (ii) the principle of no-monitoring obligation. The CJEU has further clarified that general proactive monitoring and filtering mechanisms are contrary to EU law. In *Scarlet*[11] and *Netlog*[12] as well as in *L'Oréal*,[13] the CJEU made a clear distinction between general and specific monitoring and filtering. In *Netlog,* referring to hosting providers, the CJEU concluded that EU law must be interpreted as precluding to require a hosting provider to install a system for filtering: (i) information which is stored on its servers by its users; (ii) which applies indiscriminately to all of those users; (iii) as a preventative measure; (iv) exclusively at its expense; (v) for an unlimited period; and (vi) which is capable of identifying electronic files containing musical, cinematographic or audio-visual works.[14] In *L'Oréal*, the CJEU clarified that an active monitoring of all the data of each customer in order to prevent any future infringement would be precluded by EU law. Consequently, an Internet service provider can only be ordered to prevent further infringements: (i) of that kind; (ii) by the same seller; and (iii) in respect of the same trademarks.[15] More recently, in *Glawischnig-Piesczek*, the CJEU has extended the scope of 'monitoring in a specific case' to include the content identified as illegal by national courts. The CJEU concluded that a digital platform (Facebook in the present case) may be requested to block and remove identical content and content with equivalent meaning. However, the equivalent elements should be specifically identified in the injunction and the service provider should not have to carry out any independent assessment of the content.[16]

Some of the criteria set by the courts seem rather complex to comply with, particularly given the current state of technology and the need to avoid general monitoring of users' activities. Moreover, the complexity of the business and legal environment for digital platforms continued to grow with the adoption of the CDSM Directive and the DSA.

---

[11] CJEU, *Scarlet Extended SA v Société belge des auteurs, compositeurs et éditeurs SCRL (SABAM)*, Case C-70/10, 24 November 2011.

[12] CJEU, *Belgische Vereniging van Auteurs, Componisten en Uitgevers CVBA (SABAM) v Netlog NV*, Case C-360/10, 16 February 2012.

[13] CJEU, *L'Oréal SA and Others v eBay International AG and Others*, Case C-324/09, 12 July 2011.

[14] See *Netlog,* § 26 and 52.

[15] See *L'Oréal,* § 141. See also: Guzel (2021), pp. 12–13.

[16] CJEU, *Eva Glawischnig-Piesczek v Facebook Ireland Ltd*, Case C-18/18, 3 October 2019, § 35–37.

2.1 Copyright Content Moderation Under the CDSM Directive

The CDSM Directive introduces new elements into the liability regime of online business players. It also introduces new terminology and a new legal concept—that of 'online content-sharing service providers' (OCSSP). The latter are defined as providers of an information society service whose main purposes is to store and give the public access to a large amount of protected content by its users, provided they organise and promote that content for profit-making purposes.[17] Certain services which are either not aimed primarily at giving access to copyright-protected content and/or are primarily not for-profit are excluded.[18] Consequently, the OCSSPs may be seen as sub-category of 'hosting providers' within the meaning of Art. 14 of the E-Commerce Directive. Articles 2(6) and 17 CDSM Directive introduce a new mechanism of attribution of liability to online service providers. Under the 'old' regime which is based on the provisions of the E-Commerce Directive, the InfoSoc Directive and the Enforcement Directive, the analysis would first focus on whether the activity in question could be qualified as an act of communication to the public; if it could qualify as such, the provider would be directly liable. Under the regime introduced by the CDSM Directive, the liability is attached to a legally specified category of providers: if a provider qualifies as an OCSSP, then direct liability follows.[19] Furthermore, if an act of an OCSSP is covered by Art. 17(1) and (2) of the CDSM Directive, then the hosting liability exemption in Art. 14(1) of the E-Commerce Directive (now: Art. 6 of the DSA)[20] does not apply to that act.[21]

Since the OCSSPs are directly liable for content uploaded by their users, they must themselves obtain the necessary authorization for such uploads. If OCSSPS do not succeed in obtaining the relevant authorizations, for example by concluding licenses with collecting societies, or when the rightholders refuse to grant such licenses, OCSSPs can still escape liability by demonstrating: (i) that they have made best efforts in obtaining the necessary authorisations; (ii) that they ensured that works uploaded without prior authorization and for which the rightholders have provided for the relevant and necessary information are made unavailable on their services; and (iii) that they removed works upon notification by the rightholder in an expeditious manner and prevented their future uploads.[22] The CDSM Directive and the European Commission Guidance on Article 17[23] do not mandate the use of a

[17] See CDSM Directive, Art. 2(6) and Recitals 62–63.

[18] The non-exhaustive list of exclusions contained in Art. 2(6) of the CDSM Directive includes not-for profit online encyclopaedias, providers of electronic communications services, providers of business-to-business cloud services and cloud services, online marketplaces etc.

[19] See also Quintais et al. (2022), p. 92.

[20] The DSA repealed Arts. 12-15 of the E-Commerce Directive. See DSA, Art. 89.

[21] See CDSM Directive, Art. 17(3).

[22] See CDSM Directive, Art. 17(4).

[23] Communication from the Commission to the European Parliament and the Council - Guidance on Article 17 of Directive 2019/790 on Copyright in the Digital Single Market (Guidance on Article 17), COM/2021/288 final.

technological solution nor impose any specific technological solutions on service providers in order to comply with the requirements of Art. 17(4)(b) (making best efforts to remove illegal content that is already uploaded) and Art. 17(4)(c) (preventing future uploads) of the CDSM Directive. Online content-sharing service providers have to act in accordance with high industry standards of professional diligence when making their best efforts to implement any relevant solutions aiming to ensure the unavailability of specific unauthorised content.[24] Consequently, in order to determine whether an OCSSP has made its best efforts in line with high industry standards of professional diligence, one should consider the industry practices on the market at a specific moment in time. This includes the use of technology or particular technological solutions. Nevertheless, the OCSSPs continue to have the freedom to select the technology or the solution to comply with the best efforts obligation.[25] In its Guidance on Article 17, the European Commission did not recommend the use of any specific technology or solution. Instead, it noted that the stakeholder dialogue showed that content recognition technology is commonly used to manage the use of copyright protected content, while other applicable technologies include hashing, watermarking, the use of metadata, keyword search or a combination thereof. Smaller service providers are likely to turn to more basic solutions (such metadata or key word search), whereas larger service providers with a larger audience are expected to employ more sophisticated solutions or technology.

The use of content recognition technology may (or should we say—will) lead to *ex ante* blocking of 'legitimate' content. The CDSM Directive requires the Member States to ensure that any action undertaken together by service providers and rightholders does not lead to the unavailability of content which does not infringe copyright or related rights, including to ensure that the users are able to rely on the existing exceptions or limitations for quotation, criticism, review and use for the purpose of caricature, parody or pastiche when uploading and making available content generated by users on online content-sharing services.[26] The European Commission recognizes that, in the present state of the art, no technology can assess to the standard required in law whether content, which a user wishes to upload, is infringing or represents a legitimate use.[27]

Taking into account the existing limitations of technology, the European Commission suggests the recourse to a 'reasonable practical standard', that of 'manifestly infringing content', to determine whether an upload should be blocked or go online. Given that the content recognition technology may identify specific copyright-protected content for which rightholders have provided relevant and necessary information to service providers, when an upload matches a specific file provided by rightholders, such manifestly infringing uploads should be automatically blocked. Other uploads, which are not manifestly infringing, should in principle go

[24] See Guidance on Article 17, Section V(2).

[25] *Ibid.*

[26] See CDSM Directive, Art. 17(7) and 17(9).

[27] See Guidance on Article 17, Section VI (II).

online and may be subject to an *ex post* human review when rightholders oppose by sending a notice.[28] However, even this 'reasonable practical standard', furthered by the European Commission, will be difficult to implement in practice. For example, uploads of an original work which has been modified in order to hinder its identification (like the frequent adding of an outside frame) should normally be considered as 'manifestly infringing'. On the other hand, an upload which matches only partially with the file provided by the rightholders because the user has modified the work in a creative manner, would generally not be manifestly infringing.[29] Furthermore, in cases of high risk of significant economic harm to rightholders, the European Commission suggests the recourse to a rapid *ex ante* human review by OCSSPs of the uploads containing 'particularly time sensitive content' identified by an automated content recognition tool, like in the case of pre-released music. Although the European Commission asserts that this mechanism should not lead to a disproportionate burden on service providers nor to a general monitoring obligation, it seems rather difficult to avoid both consequences of its deployment.

Given the timing of its adoption as well as its legal form (a communication), the Guidance on Article 17 was not of notable assistance to national legislators striving to transpose the CDSM Directive. The Guidance on Article 17 was adopted only three days before the transposition deadline of the CDSM Directive on 7 June 2021. It was adopted as a communication and is therefore not binding.[30] Moreover, as the Guidance on Article 17 itself states,[31] it might have to be reviewed in light of the CJEU judgment in case *Poland v European Parliament and Council*.[32]

The transposition of Art. 17 of the CDSM Directive into the national copyright laws of the Member States did not (and could not) remedy the intrinsic inconsistency of this provision. The German legislator demonstrated more contemplation and creativity when transposing the said provision, by introducing a the concept of 'uses presumably authorised by law', which must not be blocked automatically. For an upload to qualify as "presumably authorised by law", it needs to fulfil the following cumulative criteria: (i) the use must consist of less than 50% of the original protected work; (ii) the use must combine the parts of the work with other content; and (iii) the use must be minor (a non-commercial use of less than 15 seconds of audio or video, 160 characters of text or 125 kB of graphics) or, if it generates significant revenues or exceeds these thresholds, the user must flag it as being covered

[28] Art 17(9) of the CDSM Directive already comprises a set of procedural safeguards, such as an internal complaint mechanism and redress mechanism, as well as rules on out-of-court redress mechanisms. These procedural safeguards will not be discussed in this paper.

[29] *Ibid.*

[30] See Treaty on the Functioning of the European Union (TFEU), Arts. 288 and 290. However, one should not undermine some normative or coercive effects such 'soft law' measures may have.

[31] See Guidance on Article 17, Section I.

[32] CJEU, *Republic of Poland v European Parliament and Council of the European Union*, Case C-401/19.

by an exception.[33] If these conditions are met, the upload cannot be blocked automatically. The rightholders can stil challenge the legality of such uses but the content remains online until the complaints have been reviewed by the OCSSPs. Regretfully, failure to protect legitimate users' interests has only limited legal consequences. The CDSM Directive is silent on this issue, while the German transposing act merely entitles user associations to claim injunctive relief against an OCSSP who repeatedly and wrongfully blocks authorised uses.[34] The legislator did not prescribe any enforcement mechanism in case of failure to implement the concept of 'uses presumably authorised by the law'.[35]

Although the quantitative approach advanced by the German legislator may seem as an adequate solution for avoidance of over-blocking, one should bear in mind that in some cases the upload of an *entire* copyrighted work or other subject-matter may still fall within the scope of application of a copyright exception. For example, a copyright exception covers an act of reproduction by the press, communication to the public or making available of published articles on current economic, political or religious topics or of broadcast works or other subject-matter of the same character, in cases where such use is not expressly reserved, and as long as the source, including the author's name, is indicated.[36] The use of works or other subject-matter in connection with the reporting of current events, to the extent justified by the informatory purpose, is also covered by the same copyright exception.[37] Depending on the context, it may be justified to use the entire work or other subject matter for the purpose of reporting of current events. Moreover, the use of an entire copyrighted work or other subject-matter for the purpose of quotation may sometimes be covered by the copyright exception for quotation, depending on the context.[38] For example, the CJEU confirmed the application, in principle, of certain exceptions to the upload on a complete manuscript.[39] Indeed, in order to determine whether an uploaded content is covered by a copyright exception, one must consider context, message and a variety of other factors. At the current state of technology, such complex analysis cannot be performed by a software.

Finally, the CJEU rulling in case *Poland v European Parliament and Council* aggravates an already complex legal framework for platform liability. The CJEU admitted that Art. 17(4)(b) and (c) imposes on the OCSSPs monitoring obligations that require them to employ automated content recognition and filtering technologies which restrict freedom of expression and information. However, the exercise of

---

[33] Urheberrechts-Diensteanbieter-Gesetz – UrhDaG (Act on the Copyright Liability of Online Content Sharing Service Providers), Section 9. The translation into English is available at: https://www.bmj.de/SharedDocs/Gesetzgebungsverfahren/Dokumente/UrhDaG_ENG.html.

[34] *Ibid,* Section 18(6).

[35] Brieske and Peukert (2022), p. 12.

[36] See InfoSoc Directive, Art. 5(3)(c).

[37] *Ibid.*

[38] See InfoSoc Directive, Art. 5(3)(d).

[39] CJEU, *Spiegel Online GmbH v Volker Beck*, Case C-516/17, 29 July 2019. See also Geiger and Jütte (2021), pp. 9-10.

freedom of expression and information can be restricted under certain conditions and provided that the principle of proportionality is respected. The CJEU found that the limitation on freedom of expression carried out by Art. 17 of the CDSM Directive is provided for by law. It is the CJEU view that even though Art. 17(4)(c) does not specify what measures the providers are to adopt to ensure the unavailability of specific content, this is not in itself contrary to freedom of expression and information. The CJEU made it clear that lawful content should not be blocked, and technological solutions adopted to comply with Art. 17(4) of the CDSM Directive need to appropriately discriminate between lawful and unlawful uploads. What the CJEU did not say is where to find such technological solutions.

2.2 'General' Content Moderation Under the DSA

The Digital Services Act (DSA) takes a form of an EU Regulation, that is directly applicable and does not need to be transposed into national law. It is a 'horizontal' instrument, that applies in all sectors; consequently, it will coexist with sector specific legislation (consumer protection rules, intellectual property rules, etc.). The DSA explicitly states that specific rules and procedures established under the InfoSoc Directive, Enforcement Directive and CDSM Directive will remain unaffected.[40] Only providers of intermediary services that have a substantial connection to the European Union are subject to the DSA. Such substantial connection is considered to exist if a provider has an establishment in the EU or, in the absence of such an establishment, where the number of recipients of the service in one or more Member States is significant in relation to the population thereof, or on the basis of the targeting of activities towards one or more Member States.[41] The providers of relevant digital services that are established in the EU are subject to primary supervision by a national Digital Service Coordinator (DSC) of the state in which they have their main establishment. If they have no establishment in the EU, they are subject to supervision by a DSC of the state of their designated legal representative. Very large online platforms and very large online search engines are subject to European Commission's exclusive competence for special due diligence obligations.[42]

The liability exemptions under the DSA largely resemble the system set forth in the E-Commerce Directive more than twenty years ago. The DSA employs the 'traditional' terminology to define the intermediaries, which are divided into three categories – mere conduit, caching and hosting.[43] However, the DSA also introduces novel concepts, that of a 'very large online platforms (VLOPs)' and 'very large

[40] See DSA, Recital 11.

[41] See DSA, Art. 2 and Recital § 8.

[42] *Ibid*, Arts. 49–50 and 56.

[43] *Ibid*, Arts. 4–6.

search engines (VLOSEs)', which have a number of average monthly active recipients of the service in the EU equal to or higher than 45 million.[44] VLOPs and VLOSEs are subject to additional duties. The DSA sets asymmetric due diligence obligations on different types of intermediaries depending on the nature of their services as well as on their size and impact, to ensure that their services are not misused for illegal activities. Some of the largest digital platforms, such as YouTube for example, may meet the criteria to be considered as both an OCSSP within the meaning of the CDSM Directive, and a VLOP within the meaning of the DSA. In case of such regulatory overlap, the hosting safe harbour prescribed by the DSA will still apply to OCSSPs for purposes falling outside the scope of the CDSM Directive.[45] Consequently, if the relevant content a platform hosts relates to copyright, the CDSM Directive applies. If, however, the content relates to any other illegal activity (e.g. hate speech), the DSA applies.

The DSA introduces certain transparency reporting obligations which are related to content moderation. All intermediaries, unless they qualify as micro or small enterprises,[46] must publish annual reports specifying what orders they have received from authorities (e.g., to remove content), and how they operate their content moderation practices, divided by different categories of actions. The annual reports must include, *inter alia*, information about the content moderation in which the provider engaged at its own initiative, any use of automated means, as well as the measures taken to provide training and assistance to persons in charge of content moderation. In case the provider used the automated means for the purpose of content moderation, the report must include a qualitative description, an indication of the exact purposes, indicators of the accuracy and the possible rate of error of the automated means used in fulfilling those purposes. The provider must also indicate any safeguards applied. The European Commission published (draft) templates to facilitate compliance with this obligation, in line with Art. 15 of the DSA.

In addition, hosting providers (including online platforms) are obliged to comply with some procedural obligations when conducting their content moderation. The DSA lays down detailed rules according to which such 'notice and action'

---

[44] *Ibid,* Art. 33. The threshold represents approximately 10% of the European Union's population. In April 2023, the European Commission designated the following platforms as VLOPs: Alibaba AliExpress, Amazon Store, Apple AppStore, Booking.com, Facebook, Google Play, Google Maps, Google Shopping, Instagram, LinkedIn, Pinterest, Snapchat, TikTok, Twitter, Wikipedia, YouTube, and Zalando. Bing and Google Search were designated as VLOSEs.

[45] See CDSM Directive, Art. Article 17(3)(2). See also Quintais and Schwemer (2022), pp. 195-198.

[46] The DSA refers to definitions of small and micro enterprises in the Commission Recommendation concerning the definition of micro, small and medium-sized enterprises (2003 O.J. (L124) 36–41). Under Art. 2 of the Recommendation, a small enterprise is defined as an enterprise which employs fewer than 50 persons and whose annual turnover and/or annual balance sheet total does not exceed EUR 10 million. A microenterprise is defined as an enterprise which employs fewer than 10 persons and whose annual turnover and/or annual balance sheet total does not exceed EUR 2 million. Transparency reporting obligations specified in Art. 15 of the DSA shall not apply to small and micro enterprises so as long they do not qualify as VLOPs within the meaning of Art. 33 of the DSA.

mechanisms should be implemented.[47] Hosting service providers must set up procedures that would enable any individual or organization to alert them to the existence of any content on their platform that they believe to be illegal. Such notifications must be precise and adequately substantiated, and contain the following elements: (i) explanation of the reasons why the individual or entity alleges the information in question to be illegal content; (ii) indication of the exact electronic location of that information; (iii) name and email address of the individual or entity submitting the notice, except in the case of information regarding sexual abuse and sexual exploitation of children and child pornography; and (iv) a statement confirming the bona fide belief of the individual or entity submitting the notice that the information and allegations contained therein are accurate and complete. In line with CJEU rulling in *Poland v European Parliament and Council,* the DSA requires that such notifications must allow a diligent hosting provider to identify the illegality of the relevant activity or information 'without a detailed legal examination'.[48] The hosting providers must provide to content uploaders an explanation on grounds and reasons for the imposed restrictions. Such explanations should enable the content uploaders to seek redress through, where applicable, internal complaint-handling mechanisms, out-of-court dispute settlement and the courts. The DSA also requires hosting providers to notify the relevant authorities about illegal content that gives rise to a suspicion that a criminal offence involving a threat to the life or safety of a person, if they become aware of it (e.g. when conducting content moderation).

A number of additional duties apply to online platforms, a sub-category of hosting providers. These include duties related to content moderation, fair design of services, advertising, amplification, and transparency. Three set of rules are particularly relevant for content moderation engaged in by the providers of online platforms. First, online platforms are asked to give priority in the assessment process to notifications submitted by 'trusted flaggers'. The status of 'trusted flagger' is awarded, upon application, by the DSC of the Member State in which the applicant is established, to an entity that has demonstrated that it meets the following cumulative conditions: (i) it has particular expertise and competence for the purposes of detecting, identifying and notifying illegal content; (ii) it is independent from any provider of online platforms; and (iii) it carries out its activities for the purposes of submitting notices diligently, accurately and objectively.[49] Such status should only be awarded to entities, and not individuals, that meet the prescribed criteria.[50] Second, providers of online platforms are required to provide recipients of the service, including individuals or entities that have submitted a notice, with access to an effective internal complaint-handling system. Such system should allow users to electronically and without cost file complaints against the online platform provider's decision upon receiving a notice. The recepients of the service must also be able

[47] *Ibid,* Arts. 16–18.

[48] Compare CJEU, *Poland v European Parliament and Council,* § 91 with DSA, Art. 16(3).

[49] See DSA, Art. 22.

[50] *Ibid,* Recital § 61.

to lodge a complaint against the decisions taken by the provider of the online platform on the grounds that the information provided by the recipients constitutes illegal content or is incompatible with its terms and conditions.[51] This includes the decisions whether or not to remove or disable access to or restrict visibility of the information. Providers of online plartforms should also inform the recepients of their service of a possibility to have access to an out-of-court dispute settlement mechanism (usually for a fee). In any event, the recipients of the service have the right to contest the decisions taken by the providers of online platforms before a court.[52] Third, the DSA prescribes additional due diligence obligations on transparency for providers of online platforms. The latter are required to report on the the disputes submitted to the out-of-court dispute settlement bodies, on the suspensions to complainants that frequently submited notices or complaints that were found to be manifestly unfounded, as well as on the number average monthly active recipients of their service in the EU. Moreover, the providers of online platforms are required to submit to the European Commission their decisions about content, along with explanation, which would then be included in a publicly accessible machine-readable database managed by the Commission. In complying with this obligation, the providers must ensure that the submitted information does not contain personal data.[53]

A separate set of due diligence obligations introduced by the DSA is applicable to VLOPs and VLOSEs only. One of such duties is to identify, analyse, and assess, at least once a year, any systemic risks stemming from the design, functioning and use made of their services. Such risk assessment activities have to be focused on, *inter alia*, illegal content on their services (e.g. hate speech, copyright infringements). The actions expected to overcome these challenges typically include redesign of their amplification and moderation tools, or adjustment of their content moderation rules. The risk reports prepared by the VLOPs and VLOSEs are to be submitted to independent auditors who would assess compliance with these due diligence obligations.[54] Moreover, under the additional transparency reporting obligations prescribed for VLOPs and VLOSEs, the latter must specify the human resources that they dedicate to content moderation in respect of the service offered in the European Union.[55]

The DSA reiterates that (all categories of) providers of intermediary services have no general obligation of monitoring the information they transmit or store, nor of actively seeking of facts or circumstances indicating illegal activity.[56] Trying to avoid the introduction of general monitoring duty, the legislator resorted to some 'creative' solutions, such as random cheking of users. For example, providers of

[51] *Ibid,* Arts. 20–21.

[52] *Ibid.*

[53] DSA, Art. 24.

[54] *Ibid,* Arts. 34–35, 37.

[55] *Ibid,* Art. 42.

[56] *Ibid,* Art. 8.

online platforms that allow consumers to conclude distance contracts with traders are required to make reasonable efforts to randomly check in any official online database or online interface whether the products offered were identified as illegal.[57]

In addition to the ban of general monitoring, the DSA introduces 'Good Samaritan' protection that did not previously exist under the E-Commerce Directive. Few years before the adoption of the DSA, the European Commission started encouraging the voluntary removal of content, for example in the 2016 Code of Conduct on hate speech,[58] or the 2017 Communication on Tackling Illegal Content.[59] The introduction of the 'Good Samaritan' protection into the EU intermediary liability regime prescribed by the DSA was inspired by the Section 230(c) of the US Communications Act of 1934 (as amended by the Telecommunications Act of 1996).[60] Section 230 protects intermediaries when they act with good intentions to restrict access to content or to restrict its availability. Moreover, it protects intermediaries when they do not act against such content, regardless of whether they have knowledge of it or not, provided that this is not content that violates federal criminal law. However, the DSA offers only half of the US-type 'Good Samaritan' protection. Intermediaries in the European Union would not lose the immunity if they took voluntary action resulting in the removal of unlawful or infringing content, but they would not be protected if they remained passive.

Under the DSA, if intermediaries, in good faith and in a diligent manner, carry out voluntary own-initiative investigations into, or take other measures aimed at detecting, identifying and removing, or disabling access to, illegal content, or take the necessary measures to comply with the requirements of EU law and national law, they may still benefit from the liability exemptions.[61] Consequently, the DSA 'Good Samaritan' protection is conditional on the intermediary service provider acting in good faith and diligently. Recital 26 of the DSA explains how those principles should be interpreted: "*The condition of acting in good faith and in a diligent manner should include acting in an objective, non-discriminatory and proportionate manner, with due regard to the rights and legitimate interests of all parties involved, and providing the necessary safeguards against unjustified removal of legal content, in accordance with the objective and requirements of this Regulation. To that aim, the providers concerned should, for example, take reasonable measures to ensure that, where automated tools are used to conduct such activities, the technology is sufficiently reliable to limit to the maximum extent possible the rate of errors.*" The components of good faith in Recital 26 are objectivity, non-discrimination, proportionality, due regard of rights and interests of users and neces-

[57] See DSA, Art. 31(3).

[58] In May 2016, the European Commission agreed with Facebook, Microsoft, Twitter and YouTube a "Code of conduct on countering illegal hate speech online".

[59] Communication from the Commission to the European Parliament, the Council, the European Economic and Social Committee and the Committee of the Regions - Tackling Illegal Content Online: Towards an enhanced responsibility of online platforms, COM(2017) 555 final.

[60] 47 U.S. Code § 230 - Protection for private blocking and screening of offensive material.

[61] See DSA, Art. 7.

sary safeguards in place to ensure automated technologies are sufficiently reliable. The principle of non-discrimination may particularly be at risk through automated moderation, since moderating algorithms may have implicit biases. By training algorithms on certain datasets, results of their monitoring might disproportionately affect minority groups, thus causing discrimination. The DSA has addressed this risk by prescribing mandatory risk assessment for fundamental rights by VLOPs and VLOSEs.[62]

3 Risk of Content Moderation Leading to 'Information Bubbles'

Further to the activities aimed at detecting, identifying and addressing illegal content or information incompatible with the platform's terms and conditions, content moderation *in extenso*[63] may comprise the use of recommender systems by online platforms. Recommender systems are fully or partially automated systems used by online platforms to suggest in their online interface specific information to recipients of the service or prioritise that information, including as a result of a search initiated by the recipient of the service or otherwise determining the relative order or prominence of information displayed.[64] The filtering algorithms used by online platforms do not select content for every user according to the same criteria but rather select content tailored to the user's interests. In time, owing to machine learning, these algorithms improve their suggestions based on the user's interactions with the content (likes, comments, page visits etc). As a consequence, the users find themselves in 'information bubbles', having access only to content that corresponds to their views and values. Indeed, in recent years, the business model of online platforms lead to creation of multiple groups of users that share similar (political) views and values. Such business model undoubtedly contributes to the radicalisation and division of society. Moreover, a central component of this business model is the moderation of content in order to encourage users to spend more time on the platform and share more personal data.[65]

Facebook's 'Feed', Twitter's 'Timeline', TikTok's 'For You' page, and YouTube's 'Up Next' list all have a similar recommendation system. Still, the manner in which these algorithms operate is diverse. There are many ways of classifying recommender systems.[66] One possible distinction is between 'open' and 'closed' systems. Open systems are those that allow anyone to contribute to the content inventory. For

---

[62] *Ibid,* Art. 34(1).

[63] The DSA defines content moderation more narrowly, referring only to illegal content or information incompatible with the platform's terms and conditions. See DSA, Art. 3(1)(t).

[64] See DSA, Art. 3(1)(s).

[65] Buiten (2021), p. 361.

[66] Bobadilla et al. (2013), pp. 109–132.

example, Google indexes and ranks content from across the internet. In contrast, closed systems index and rank only 'first-party' content. One could also distinguish between push and pull recommendations. Push recommendations proactively suggest content to audiences. Pull recommendations, on the other hand, suggest content in response to a user's request. For example, users of search engines 'pull' recommendations from a platform by specifying a search query. Social media, like Facebook for example, typically use hybrid system which allows users to receive 'pushed' content by scrolling through their feed, but also to search the platform and 'pull' content from a specific page. Recommender systems can also be categorized based on their degree of personalization. A highly personalized system would typically generate recommendations according to user's location, age or activity. Recommender systems can obtain personal information through mechanisms such as browser cookies. Contemporary recommender systems allow for a certain degree of customization. Platform users can only to some extent adjust how recommender systems select their content. For example, users can 'hide' content they do not wish to be exposed to in their feeds or choose the frequency of receiving notification on specific content.[67]

Prior to the adoption of the DSA, the European legislator was generally focused on a narrow view of content moderation; that is, the question what content gets removed from online locations.[68] The discussion on the consequences of the use of filtering algorithms has been treated as an 'afterthought'. The DSA departs from that approach and prescribes a number of preventive measures aimed at insuring better protection of users and their fundamental rights online. The DSA refers explicitly to the social implications of recommending, by acknowledging that recommender systems can have a significant impact on the ability of recipients to retrieve and interact with information online, including to facilitate the search of relevant information for recipients of the service and contribute to an improved user experience. The DSA also notes that such recommender systems may play an important role in the amplification of certain messages, the viral dissemination of information and the stimulation of online behaviour.[69]

The DSA includes a number of provisions that explicitly address the role of recommender systems. First, VLOPs and VLOSEs are required to identify, analyse and assess any systemic risks in the Union stemming from the design or functioning of their service and its related systems, including algorithmic systems, or from the use made of their services. Such risks include the dissemination of illegal content, negative effects for the exercise of fundamental rights, negative effects on civic discourse and electoral processes, and public security, negative effects in relation to

---

[67] *Ibid.*

[68] Although this chapter is not dedicated to the specific issue of disinformation, it is worth noting that, even prior to the adoption of the DSA, the European Union has taken certain steps to counter the spread of disinformation by adopting, *inter alia*, the Communication on Tackling Online Disinformation in 2018 (COM/2018/236 final) and the Code of Practice on Disinformation in 2018 (revised in 2022). See Cavaliere (2022), pp 486–491.

[69] See DSA, Recital § 70.

gender-based violence, the protection of public health and minors and serious negative consequences to the person's physical and mental well-being. When conducting such risk assessments, VLOPs and VLOSEs should assess how the design of their recommender systems and any other relevant algorithmic system the identified systematic risks.[70] Thus, recommender systems are explicitly listed as risk factors and their adjustment as a risk mitigation measure. Second, providers of online platforms, regardless of their size, are required to use recommender systems in transparent manner. They must set out in their terms and conditions, in simple and comprehensible manner, the main parameters used in their recommender systems, as well as any options for the recipients of the service to modify or influence those main parameters.[71] While this requirement is a positive development in the regulation of recommender systems, it is disputable whether the provider's terms and conditions are the best online location for disclosure of such information. It seems more transparent and user-friendly to publish the key parameters for recommender systems optimization at a dedicated page, in a visual and interactive manner. Third, in addition to the transparency obligations applicable to all online platforms, the DSA requires VLOPs and VLOSEs to offer at least one version of their recommender system that does not rely on profiling.[72] The DSA does not provide for a definition of profiling, but refers to the General Data Protection Regulation (GDPR) instead.[73]

Further to duties related to risk assessment and transparency, the DSA prescribes a number of duties which may directly or indirectly affect the use of recommender systems, like those related to independent auditing, researcher access to data, provisions on platforms' terms and conditions, and statements of reason. Under the DSA, VLOPs and VLOSEs are subject to independent audits to assess compliance with the the obligations set out in Chapter III of the DSA which includes obligation to ensure recommender system transparency.[74] Moreover, at the request of either DSC or of the European Commission, VLOPs and VLOSEs must explain the design, the logic, the functioning and the testing of their algorithmic systems, including their recommender systems. Upon a reasoned request from a DSC, VLOPs and VLOSEs must provide access to data to vetted researchers.[75] Indeed, researchers access is crucial for better understanding of potential risks of recommending, as well as for

[70] *Ibid,* Art. 34.

[71] *Ibid,* Art. 27.

[72] *Ibid,* Art. 38.

[73] The GDPR defines profiling as 'any form of automated processing of personal data consisting of the use of personal data to evaluate certain personal aspects relating to a natural person, in particular to analyse or predict aspects concerning that natural person's performance at work, economic situation, health, personal preferences, interests, reliability, behaviour, location or movements'. See Regulation (EU) 2016/679 of the European Parliament and of the Council on the protection of natural persons with regard to the processing of personal data and on the free movement of such data, and repealing Directive 95/46/EC, 2016 OJ (L 119) 1, Art. 4.

[74] See DSA, Art. 37.

[75] *Ibid,* Art. 40.

proper assessment of the effectiveness of remedies. However, sharing of platform data with external researchers raises significant data protection concerns, given that the data of greatest interest to researchers often represent sensitive information about the beliefs and attitudes of platform users. Therefore, when ensuring platform transparency one must be mindful of protecting the fundamental rights of platform users. Bearing that in mind, the European Digital Media Observatory proposed a code of conduct on researcher access to platform data, which discusses relevant concerns and safeguards in this regard.[76] One of the proposed measures includes the researchers' access to data through 'clean rooms'- secured and monitored research environments from which no data may be taken without prior privacy review. Next, all providers of intermediary services are required to include in their terms and conditions information on any restrictions that they impose in relation to the use of their service in respect of information provided by the recipients of the service.[77] Finally, providers of hosting services are required to provide a clear and specific statement of reasons to any affected recipients of the service for any restrictions of the visibility of specific items of information provided by the recipient of the service, including removal of content, disabling access to content, or demoting content.[78]

4 Risk of Content Demotion Leading to Censorship

While content moderation *stricto sensu* may result in content removal, the mechanism is generally applied in a transparent manner: the poster is informed of any request for removal, may respond to it and, ultimately, request review of the decision about reported content. A certain degree of transparency is also to be expected in relation to the use of recommender algorithms, particularly following the adoption of the DSA. The users will be better informed of the key parameters used for content optimization, and will be allowed to influence upon those parameters, to a certain extent. However, content demotion or content suppression techniques, although widely used, remain largely outside of the legislative focus in many countries. Content demotion is a visibility remedy applied by online platforms that does not cut off access to content entirely, but instead make the content less visible through discovery features such as search and recommendation. Content demotion, also known as shadowbanning, relates to 'borderline' content which does not violate platforms' policies or terms of services, but may come close to violate it. We are presently lacking an understanding of the rate of such interventions from platforms.

Several online platforms acknowledged using these techniques. For example, YouTube stated that content demotion is used to '*(…) reduce the spread of content*

[76] EDMO, Report of the European Digital Media Observatory's Working group on platform-to-researcher data access, 31 May 2022.

[77] See DSA, Art. 14.

[78] *Ibid,* Art. 17.

that comes close to - but doesn't quite cross the line of - violating the Community Guidelines (...)'.[79] An important step towards transparency of content demotion techniques employed by online platforms was made by Facebook in September 2021. Facebook clarified what content it identifies as 'borderline' or likely violating their community standards.[80] The social media acknowledged employing content demotion techniques towards several categories of content, such as: (i) content borderline to the community standards; (ii) content likely violating the community standards; (iii) content posted by repeat violators of our policies; (iv) posts that indicate suspicious virality; (v) unsafe reporting about suicide. Still, examples given for each of content categories remain in rather broad terms. For instance, photo of a person wearing minimal clothing may be demoted although it does not violate the Adult nudity and sexual activity policy. Similarly, content that Facebook considers to be '*sensationalist or provocative and can bring down the overall quality of discourse on the platform*' may be supressed, although it does not violate the community standards.[81]

There seems to be three main characteristics that unite various understandings of content demotion. First, there is a particular form of secrecy surrounding the use of such techniques. Although content demotion mechanisms can exclude the users from public conversations, they leave them unaware or merely suspecting of platforms' intervention.[82] Contrary to more traditional methods of takedown and account suspension, content demotion leaves little or no trace. Second, 'borderline' content will still be hosted, although it will no longer be recommended or, *in extremis*, will no longer be searchable. Content reduction only pertains to where content is offered up or suggested, not where it stays in the archive.[83] Third, demoted content is not illegal nor contrary to platforms' principles, community guidelines or standards, but is nevertheless 'inappropriate' in the platforms' view. Indeed, the lack of clear guidelines on 'borderline' content makes the platforms' content demotion policies questionable from the freedom of expression perspective. While content demotion may make sense when it comes to fake news or clickbait posts, such policies may nevertheless limit visibility of other categories of content which should not be disputed, like sexualized but not explicit content, or jokes that might offend someone despite not being abusive.

The Regulation on promoting fairness and transparency for business users of online intermediation services (P2B Regulation)[84] was the first EU legislation to

---

[79] The YouTube Team, Continuing Our Work to Improve Recommendations on YouTube, 25 January 2019. Available at: https://blog.youtube/news-and-events/continuing-our-work-to-improve.

[80] Facebook, What content we demote, 23 September 2021. Available at: https://transparency.fb.com/features/approach-to-ranking/types-of-content-we-demote/.

[81] *Ibid.*

[82] Gahntz (2022), p. 9.

[83] Gillespie (2022), p. 3.

[84] Regulation (EU) 2019/1150 of the European Parliament and of the Council of 20 June 2019 on promoting fairness and transparency for business users of online intermediation services, 2019 O.J. (L 186) 57.

regulate transparency in content visibility policies. The P2B Regulation requires providers of intermediation services which decide to restrict or suspend the provision of its online intermediation services to a given business user in relation to individual goods or services offered by that business user, to provide the latter with a statement of reasons for that decision. Such business user should be given the opportunity to clarify the relevant facts and circumstances in the framework of the internal complaint-handling process.[85] Although the relevant provisions do not explicitly mention content demotion, the latter is referred to in the Recital in connection with restrictions of individual listings of business users.[86] The P2B Regulation also requires the providers of online intermediation services to ensure that their terms and conditions set out the grounds for decisions to suspend or terminate or impose 'any other kind of restriction' upon the provision of their services to business users.[87] However, the P2B Regulation is rather limited in scope, as it applies only to business users of online intermediation services.

The DSA makes a further step in explicitly regulating content demotion by including visibility restrictions in the definition of content moderation.[88] The DSA Recital clarifies that visibility restrictions may consist in demotion in ranking or in recommender systems, as well as in limiting accessibility by one or more recipients of the service or blocking the user from an online community without the user knowing it.[89] Consequently, content demotion is recognised as content moderation action, and is therefore subject to the DSA's notice-and-action procedures.[90] These procedures reflect the basic principles of due process: every sanction must be governed by clear and precise rules, must be notified to the concerned party, and must be subject to appeals. This leaves limited margin for shadow banning of content contrary to platforms' terms and conditions.[91] In addition, the DSA demands that the rules governing online intermediaries' content moderation actions must be published in their terms and conditions, in 'clear and unambiguous language'.[92] However, some authors fear that excessively detailed terms and conditions may not be desirable due to tradeoffs with flexibility, which could impede content moderators in unforeseen circumstances.[93]

Despite significantly contributing to platforms' transparency, these rules might not resolve all issues pertaining to content demotion. In most cases, content demotion actions are applied to content which is not violating the platform's terms and conditions but is 'close to' violating it. In contrast, the content moderation rules

---

[85] See P2B Regulation, Art. 4.

[86] *Ibid,* Recital § 22 and 24.

[87] *Ibid,* Art. 3(1)(c).

[88] See DSA, Art. 3(t).

[89] *Ibid,* Recital § 55.

[90] See *supra* Sect. 2.2 of this paper.

[91] See DSA, Arts. 17 and 20–21.

[92] *Ibid,* Art. 14.

[93] Leerssen (2023), p. 6.

prescribed by the DSA apply to content which is either illegal or contrary to the platforms' terms and conditions. Still, content demotion actions could, to a certain extent, be scrutinized under the DSA rules on transparency of recommender systems, which require that main parameters used in such systems are made public.[94] This could at least provide some limited insight into demotion actions related to removal from content recommendations.

5 Concluding Remarks

Given the increasing importance of online platforms as a source of information and opinion formation, content moderation unsurprisingly came into the focus of the recent European Union's legislative efforts. The EU's approach towards content moderation is twofold -copyright content moderation is regulated by the CDSM Directive, while 'general' content moderation rules are prescribed by the DSA. From a legal-technical perspective, the CDSM Directive falls short of its stated objectives of harmonization and legal certainty. This is partly due to its design, given the margin of discretion left to the national legislators, but also due to the complexities of the text. It is highly likely that many of the ambiguities in the CDSM Directive text will need to be raised before the CJEU by way of preliminary references. On the other hand, 'general' content moderation rules are prescribed by the DSA which takes the form of an EU Regulation – a certainly more suitable legal instrument to achieve the proclaimed goals of establishing of the European Digital Single Market. The DSA reitirates, with slight modifications, the pre-existing 'safe harbor' regime, outlines a comprehensive 'notice and action' mechanism, and set out duties of care for certain types of intermediaries. What is really innovative about this framework is that it applies not only to content prohibited by law, but also to content prohibited under the platform's terms and conditions. Regretfully, the DSA does not harmonise what type of content or behaviour is considered illegal. Apart from EU rules specifying illegality in certain areas, like intellectual property, this remains under the sovereignty of Member States, and the DSA basically refers to the national legal systems of EU Member States to define what is illegal. Another concern is related to the platforms' significant discretion in articulating its terms and conditions, and establishing the violation thereof. Finally, the enforcement of certain visibility reduction sanctions towards the content which does not violate but gets 'close to' violating the platforms' terms and conditions is particularly controversial, from the freedom of expression perspective.

Despite certain deficiencies of the European Union's legal framework for online platforms, which were identified in this paper, the readiness of the European legislator to address the complex issue of co-existence of freedom of expression and freedom to conduct business is to be welcomed. It is yet to be seen whether the European approach will be followed in other parts of the world sharing the one and same Internet.

[94] See DSA, Art. 27.

References

Bobadilla J, Ortega F, Hernando A, Gutierrez A (2013) Recommender systems survey. Knowl-Based Syst 46(2013):109–132

Brieske J, Peukert A. (2022) Coming into Force, not Coming into Effect? The Impact of the German Implementation of Art. 17 CDSM Directive on Selected Online Platforms. CREATe Working Paper 2022/1. Available at https://zenodo.org/record/5865619#.ZFKOzXZBzrd

Buiten MC (2021) The digital services act from intermediary liability to platform regulation. JIPITEC – J Intell Prop Inf Technol E-Commer Law 12(2022):361–380

Cavaliere P (2022) The truth in fake news: how disinformation laws are reframing the concepts of truth and accuracy. Eur Conv Human Rights Law Rev 3(2022):481–523

Gahntz M (2022) Towards responsible recommending: recommendations for policymakers and large online platforms. Mozilla Foundation Report. Available at: https://assets.mofoprod.net/network/documents/Mozilla_Towards-Responsible-Recommending.pdf

Geiger C, Jütte BJ (2021) The EU Commission's Guidance on Article 17 of the Copyright in the Digital Single Market Directive – A Guide to Virtue in Content Moderation by Digital Platforms? Available at SSRN. https://doi.org/10.2139/ssrn.3876608

Gillespie T (2022) Do not recommend? Reduction as a form of content moderation. Soc Media Soc 8(3):1–13

Guzel S (2021) Article 17 of the CDSM Directive and the fundamental rights: shaping the future of the internet. Eur J Law Technol 1(2021):1–29

Kuczerawy A (2020) From 'Notice and Take Down' to 'Notice and Stay Down': risks and safeguards for freedom of expression. In: Frosio G (ed) Oxford handbook of online intermediary liability. Oxford University Press, Oxford, pp 524–543

Leerssen P (2023) An end to shadow banning? Transparency rights in the digital services act between content moderation and curation. Comput Law Secur Rev 48(2023):1–13

Quintais JP, Schwemer SF (2022) The Interplay between the digital services act and sector regulation: how special is copyright? Eur J Risk Regul 13(2):191–217

Quintais J. P, Mezei P, Harkai I, Magalhães J. C, Katzenbach C, Schwemer SF, Riis T (2022) Copyright Content Moderation in the EU: An Interdisciplinary Mapping Analysis. reCreating Europe Report. Available at https://www.recreating.eu

Moving Towards More Transparent Online Platforms Under the Digital Services Act

Magdalena Knapp and Anna Piszcz

Abstract The DSA introduces a multi-layered framework of obligations tailored to various categories of providers of online intermediary services, many of which aim to increase transparency of online environment. This chapter aims, first, to propose the categorization of transparency obligations and, second, to identify them in the DSA. These objectives are combined with the objective of the assessment of the primary obligations from the perspective of a transparency goal of the DSA, whereas more detailed analysis of meta-obligations related thereto is left aside. The research methods employed in this chapter primarily include a doctrinal legal method as well as systemic and teleological approaches. The authors conclude, first, that though the layered structure of the obligations and self-assessment model puts the burden of enforcement on providers of online platforms, it also invites more actors to the process, therefore, third parties, such as consumers, civil society and SMEs, will play role in enforcing the transparency obligations set out in DSA. Second, one of the most challenging imprecisions in the DSA results from that, in many instances, the DSA is silent on the scope and/or the form of providing the required access to data, for example in Article 40. Third, the DSA applies its own logic (different from that of EU consumer law) resting heavily on ex ante primary fairness obligations, while the consumer law relies upon ex post prohibition of unfair practices. Fourth, the pyramid-like structure of transparency obligations under the DSA can be considered an obstacle to the increase of consumer protection by exempting smaller pro-

Sections 3, 4 and 7 were written by Magdalena Knapp, Sects. 5 and 6 were written by Anna Piszcz whilst Sects. 1, 2 and 8 are common parts.

M. Knapp (✉)
University of Warsaw, Faculty of Management, Warsaw, Poland
e-mail: mknapp@wz.uw.edu.pl

A. Piszcz
University of Bialystok, Faculty of Law, Bialystok, Poland
e-mail: piszcz@uwb.edu.pl

D. V. Popović, R. Kulms (eds.), *Repositioning Platforms in Digital Market Law*, European Union and its Neighbours in a Globalized World 15,
https://doi.org/10.1007/978-3-031-69678-7_5

viders from most of primary obligations. However, in general, the authors consider the DSA as representing a promising development in online platform governance.

1 Introduction

In digital economy online platforms thrive on a large user base that continuously generates data, and thus enhancing the development of more accurate algorithmic models. It is also what extends their market power. Many people rely on information supplied by online platforms, using them as a primary source for obtaining and staying up to date with the latest news. Online platforms influence how they perceive world and surrounding reality. It may be alarming when there is no or very little Internet governance. Our underlying assumption that is not discussed further is that transparency is needed: (1) due to the size of some online platforms and their social impact; (2) in order to regain control over data; (3) in order to reduce information asymmetry. We assume that more transparency on aggregation, moderation and use of data is needed in order to prevent abuses and safeguard democratic values and fundamental rights. For many years states were reluctant to regulate these issues. However, European Union (EU) tried to address them by introducing package of regulations relating to digital markets. Digital Services Act (DSA),[1] adopted in record time,[2] is one of the key instruments in that package. At the time of writing this chapter, the DSA is in the last phases of its implementation. The European Commission is currently in the process of adopting executing and delegating acts that shape the implementation of the DSA.

The DSA, in the form of a directly applicable regulation, is an unprecedented initiative aimed at regulating aspects of Internet activity, including its transparency. The DSA is novel both in the area it is covering and the model of its enforcement. It has ambitious goal of regulation of social media, including regulation of data privacy, access to data, accountability of online service providers, and most of all, the topic that is central to this chapter—transparent and safe online environment by making providers of online platforms operate in a transparent way. To this end, the DSA introduces a multi-layered framework of obligations, tailored to various categories of providers of online intermediary services, leading us to choose transparency obligations provided for in the DSA as our research object. This contribution focuses on primary obligations aimed at transparency, leaving aside more detailed analysis of meta-obligations related thereto. It does not discuss, however, overlaps between these obligations and obligations stemming from other rules, such as—in particular—the general data protection regime or laws regulating AI. Additionally,

[1] Regulation (EU) 2022/2065 of the European Parliament and of the Council of 19 October 2022 on a Single Market for Digital Services and amending Directive 2000/31/EC, OJ L 277, 27.10.2022, pp. 1–102 (Digital Services Act or DSA).

[2] Proposal 15 December 2020, published in the Official Journal in October 2022 and entered into force on 1 November 2022.

content moderation issues, which are directly related to transparency, have been omitted since they are analysed in the preceding chapter.

The objectives of our research are twofold. First, we aim to propose the categorization of transparency obligations and to identify them in the DSA. Second, we intend to assess the introduced primary obligations from the perspective of a transparency goal of the DSA.

This chapter is divided into seven parts and a conclusion. The first part is the introduction. The second part discusses the categorization of transparency obligations and methods of analysis. The third part defines obliged entities and beneficiaries of obligations. Next parts analyse and assess key primary obligations of providers of online platforms relating to transparency, and introduce concisely to the issue of meta-obligations. Last, we present the key findings and conclusions of the assessment. The research methods employed in this contribution include a doctrinal legal method as well as systemic and teleological approaches.

2 Transparency Obligations in the DSA in General

In market-oriented terms, it is said that transparency would increase competition in the market of platforms.[3] Indirectly it may also influence market power problems by reducing information asymmetry. Whereas one of the main objectives of the DSA is ensuring a safe and transparent online environment,[4] the DSA aims to shift the power asymmetry related to gathered data. On one hand, it means giving more rights to recipients of services i.e. consumers, businesses and other users, on the other, it translates to more obligations for providers of online platforms.

The preamble to the DSA explains the means to achieve the objective to ensure a safe and transparent online environment. Pursuant to motive 40 DSA, in order to achieve the objectives of the DSA, and 'in particular to (…) ensure a safe and transparent online environment, it is necessary to establish a clear, effective, predictable and balanced set of harmonised due diligence obligations for providers of intermediary services'.

The excessive length of the DSA (156 motives and 93 articles) hinders its clarity. Navigating through all the articles to identify connections between them and related obligations is challenging. Some articles are explicit in their descriptions, while others require to be interpreted with caution. Considering the sheer volume of obligations scattered throughout the DSA, it appears that additional soft law and guidelines are essential. We can already see the emergence of a regulatory environment aimed at improving the enforcement of the DSA, with a focus on transparency. It consists of:

[3] See Rodríguez de las Heras Ballell (2021), p. 84.

[4] Motive 40 DSA.

- delegated acts;[5]
- new databases (e.g. transparency database[6]);
- non-binding analyses, e.g. internal working documents of the European Commission,[7]
- recommendations,[8]
- documents from supporting institutions, e.g. European Centre for Algorithmic Transparency (ECAT),[9]
- voluntary codes of conduct and protocols.[10]

We have mapped and categorized obligations provided for in the DSA that aim to increase digital transparency. We have examined both transparency-related provisions and associated motives preceding them. We looked for transparency obligations identified through keywords such as, in particular, 'transparent', 'clear' 'comprehensible', 'accessible' or 'publicly available'.[11] Additionally, we have taken into account the content and purpose of the relevant provisions. As was stated above, we have not analysed any overlaps, in particular with the general data protection regime, where transparency is generally considered as related to how one's personal data are processed. We have focused on overall transparency related to the functioning of the online platforms.

A first attempt at the categorization of due diligence obligations for providers of online platforms let us state that two main categories can be found among them: (1) those that are intended to achieve the goal of a transparent online environment, and

[5] I.e. Draft delegated Regulation supplementing Regulation (EU) 2022/2065 of the European Parliament and of the Council, by laying down rules on the performance of audits for very large online platforms and very large online search engines, 20.10.2023, C(2023) 6807 final; Commission Delegated Regulation (EU) 2023/1127 of 2 March 2023 supplementing Regulation (EU) 2022/2065 of the European Parliament and of the Council with the detailed methodologies and procedures regarding the supervisory fees charged by the Commission on providers of very large online platforms and very large online search engines, C/2023/1257.

[6] https://transparency.dsa.ec.europa.eu/ (all Internet references cited in this article were last visited in November 2023).

[7] Commission Staff Working Document, Overview of elements accounted for the estimation of the amount of external assigned revenues stemming from the supervisory fee pursuant to Article 6(1) of Commission Delegated Regulation (EU) 2023/1127, 30.6.2023, SWD(2023) 242 final, https://digital-strategy.ec.europa.eu/en/library/dsa-overview-elements-accounted-estimation-amount-external-assigned-revenues-stemming-supervisory.

[8] Recommendations on coordinating responses to incidents in particular arising from the dissemination of illegal content, https://digital-strategy.ec.europa.eu/en/library/coordinating-responses-incidents-particular-arising-dissemination-illegal-content.

[9] ECAT will support enforcement of DSA by taking over some of the European Commission responsibilities, including tasks like analyzing transparency reports, risk assessments and independent audits reports, https://algorithmic-transparency.ec.europa.eu/index_en.

[10] See Articles 45–48 DSA.

[11] So, we interpret transparency in a broader sense, as an intuitive high-level concept, and not only as the 'disclosure of certain information that may not previously have been visible or publicly available'; see Gorwa and Ash (2020), p. 286.

(2) those that are intended to achieve the goal of a safe online environment. This simple 'bipartition' would not be satisfactory as the two main categories merge with each other creating further third category, i.e.: (3) obligations intended to achieve both goals combined, but typically in such a way that transparency implies safety. The first and third categories are our focus here. The obligations that can be linked only to achieve the goal of a safe online environment (second category) are not discussed in this contribution. Examples of such obligations can be found in Article 30(1)(b)-(c) DSA that obliges providers of online platforms to obtain information ensuring traceability of traders (a copy of the identification document of the trader or other electronic identification; the payment account details of the trader), verify it (para 2), store it (para 5 sentence 1) and share it with public authorities (para 6). Providers of online platforms are not obliged to disclose this information to their users, moreover they are obliged to delete the information after a required period of storage (para 5 sentence 2).

Another way to look at due diligence obligations for providers of online platforms is to examine them from the perspective of the 'level' of obligations. Consequently, first we have identified primary (first tier) obligations. In addition to them, the DSA introduced new meta- (second tier) obligations that are secondary in nature, refer to obligations relating to the execution of another (primary) obligation(s), and revolve around the online platform provider's accountability for meeting other (primary) obligations which includes being both responsible and capable of demonstrating compliance.[12] Combined, the DSA provisions on both these categories intend to set new standards for the accountability of online platforms providers.

The above categorization of transparency obligations is a point of departure for our further analyses. Based on our analyses, Fig. 1 presents the proposal of the division of transparency obligations into these two categories.

Our analysis points towards differences between transparency obligations listed in the DSA accounted for by their addressees or beneficiaries (see part 3 below). Under the DSA transparency obligations are structured as a pyramid ('or layer-cake'), whereas moving up the pyramid reveals increasingly stringent obligations that apply to fewer and fewer categories of providers.[13]

[12] Distinguishing these categories of transparency obligations in the case of obligations provided for in the DSA partly corresponds to the categorization of transparency initiatives for platforms that distinguishes, besides voluntary transparency around freedom of expression and for content takedowns, and self-transparency around advertising and content moderation, legally mandated transparency regimes (here, primary obligations); and third-party tools, investigations, and audits (here, meta-obligations). Cf. Gorwa and Ash (2020), pp. 294–295.

[13] G'Sell (2023), p. 89. Van Cleynenbreugel refers to different 'layers' of regulatory obligations on specific categories of information society services providers; see Van Cleynenbreugel (2021), p. 669. Mocanu and Sibony emphasize the DSA's new perspective introducing a new focus on who can use what data, and conclude that this takes the form of asymmetric obligations that bear on very large platforms and reduce their access to certain sources of data; see Mocanu and Sibony (2023), p. 240.

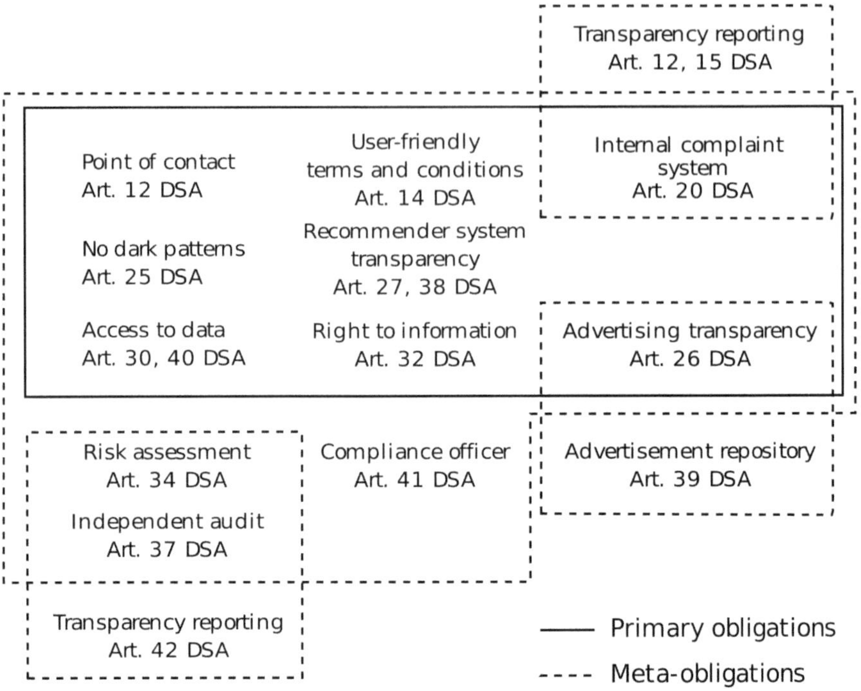

Fig. 1 Proposal of categorization of transparency obligations. Source: authors' own elaboration based on the DSA

Transparency obligations listed in the DSA are also significantly differentiated when it comes to their form and duration. They take form of written reports, setting up databases, restrictions, providing access to information/data (general or restricted), introducing new mechanisms for users or requiring specific action. They are general in nature which may cause problems with their enforcement. It should be emphasised here that their enforcement relies mostly on a self-assessment model.[14] This approach results from failure to achieve anticipated outcomes of self-regulation despite European Commission's past efforts to promote self-regulation among online platforms. Therefore, in the DSA, monitoring the compliance with obligations is largely left to providers of online platforms. There is an oversight mechanism allowing authorities to intervene in case of non-compliance. This design is economically efficient as it reduces the costs of supervision and enforcement on regulators' side. The only unknown is whether this model proves to be effective.

[14] We distinguish self-assessment model from self-regulation which indicates lack of external intervention. While self-assessment refers to periodic or continuous process of evaluating one's actions and compliance with established set of regulations.

3 Obliged Entities and Beneficiaries of Obligations

The DSA distinguishes several categories of addressees of the obligations. The broadest category consists of providers of intermediary services. The DSA applies to all providers of intermediary services, regardless of where they are established as long as they provide services to recipients that are located in the EU. The provisions of the DSA take a horizontal, cross-sector approach, applying to providers irrespective of the specific type of services they offer or the sector they operate in.

However, some of the obligations are addressed to other parties such as regulators or trusted flaggers, both of which have transparency reporting obligations to comply with.

The analysis of transparency obligations focuses on one category of providers of intermediary services—providers of online platforms (hereafter also as OPs). Definition of online platform laid down in Article 3(i) DSA is rather broad and encompasses all social media and e-commerce platforms, but also any platform that hosts and shares content, e.g. gaming platforms, education or entertainment platforms. The recipient of the service and the operating model of the platform (C2C, B2C, B2B) are not relevant. What defines an online platform are two key conditions: (1) the storage of information provided by users upon request, and (2) the subsequent sharing of that information with the public.

Providers of a particular category of OPs, so-called very large online platforms (VLOPs), are subject to additional due diligence obligations because of the size and status of VLOPs. The threshold for online platform to be considered a VLOP is an average monthly number of active recipients equal to or higher than 45 million in the EU.[15] Based on information provided by OPs, European Commission adopted the decision designating 17 VLOPs on 25 April 2023.[16] It has already been contested by two OPs, namely Zalando[17] and Amazon,[18] that brought action before the CJEU aiming to drop the status of VLOP. In case of the latter, General Court partially suspended the Commission's decision and resulting obligation of publishing advertisement repository (Article 39 DSA).[19]

Micro and small enterprises have special status under the DSA. They are exempt from most of the primary obligations imposed on providers of OPs, unless they qualify as VLOPs. In such case, they have to comply with Article 24(3) DSA which

---

[15] Art. 33(1) and 33(4–6) DSA.

[16] Very large online platforms and very large search engines designated pursuant to Article 33(4) of Regulation (EU) 2022/2065 of the European Parliament and of the Council of 19 October 2022 on a Single Market For Digital Services and amending Directive 2000/31/EC, 2023/C 249/02, OJ C 249, 14.7.2023, pp. 2–2.

[17] Action brought on 27 June 2023 — Zalando v Commission (Case T-348/23), OJ C 314, 4.9.2023, pp. 9–11.

[18] Action brought on 5 July 2023 — Amazon Services Europe v Commission (Case T-367/23, OJ C 296, 21.8.2023, pp. 41–42.

[19] Judgement of General Court, 27.09.2023, Case T-367/23 R, *Amazon Services Europe v Commission*.

obliges them to provide information on the average monthly active recipients of the service in the EU, upon request of the regulator. The aim of exemption expressed in Motives 49 and 57 is avoiding imposition of disproportionate burden on smallest enterprises. Though, this category of providers of OPs still has to comply with certain primary obligations, i.e. designate points of contact for recipients of services and ensure that their terms and conditions are user-friendly, meaning transparent, simple and easy to understand. They are also relieved from transparency reporting obligations stated in Article 15 DSA.

Providers of OPs had to publish information on their average monthly active recipients by 17 February 2023. VLOPs have to comply with their obligations to ensure transparency, accountability and responsibility for their actions from 26 August 2023.[20] By 17 February 2024 all DSA provisions will apply regardless of the status of the online intermediary.

It is also possible to look at transparency obligations from the perspective of their beneficiaries, i.e. mainly those who receive access to information/data etc. From this point of view, transparency can be enjoyed by:

1. anyone (due to obligations to make information/data publicly available)—Articles 12, 14, 25, 27 and 38, 32 (also Articles 15, 24, 42 and 39);
2. recipients of the service—Articles 20, 26, 30;
3. others (researchers, research associations, NGOs, regulators)—Article 40.

It may be important to emphasize here that the OP's accountability for meeting these obligations implies the obligation (meta-obligation) to make information/data available to specific 'beneficiaries' such as regulators (Articles 15, 24, 42, 34, 41) and organisation carrying out the audit (Article 37).

4 Primary Obligations Regarding OP's Functioning

The DSA mandates that providers of OPs' enhance the accessibility and user-friendliness of their platforms. This involves operating in a way that enables users to understand the legal and operational framework, the content moderation process, and the mechanism for resolving any dispute or issue that may arise from interacting with the platform.

One way of addressing user needs and ensuring OPs transparency is establishment of easily accessible points of contact. Providers of OPs are obliged to designate single electronic points of contact guaranteeing effective communications with recipients of the service relating to matters covered by the DSA (Article 12). The same requirement is imposed by Article 11 in relation to communication with authorities for compliance and accountability reasons. Points of contact should be

[20] Articles 33(6) and 92 DSA stipulate that obligations apply within 4 months of the European Commission's designation decision.

easy to find and reach out to for any user, including vulnerable users. Accessibility is a key in that context and might be understood as follows:

- finding information about the point of contact should be effortless, interface cannot hinder access to that information;
- allowing users to reach platform should be possible via different means of communication, such as telephone numbers, email addresses, electronic contact forms, chatbots or instant messaging[21];
- the process of communication should be straightforward and devoid of complex procedures; OPs interface should facilitate the process;
- users should be explicitly informed when they are interacting with chatbots and allowed to switch the means of communication;
- point of contact should be available for users during reasonable hours and ensure timely response;
- language of communication should not constitute a barrier.

The DSA directly stipulates that points of contact cannot be fully automated which is crucial for the weakest group of users—consumers. Chatbots are usually designed to provide only limited number of answers and options to proceed with the matter at hand. This may lead to the dead-end as some users will not know how to find alternative way to reach provider or simply will give up. Also, the interaction with chatbot and quality of its design directly affects the effectiveness of this mean of communication. Conversational agents, such as chatbots still lack trustworthiness among users.[22]

The DSA encourages providers of OPs to take extra measures also with regard to their terms and conditions. Article 14 DSA stipulates general rules on the content and how terms should be presented to recipients of the service. The main requirements refer to:

- the official language in which terms and conditions are published (obligation imposed on VLOPs),
- the content of terms and conditions e.g. providers of OPs should include information related to processing users' data, restrictions imposed on users or rules of procedure of their internal complaint-handling system,
- accessible format of terms and conditions; providers of OPs are obliged to provide summary of the terms and conditions in plain language; use of graphics or interactive features is recommended (obligation imposed on providers of VLOPs).

While most of providers of VLOPs have already implemented those rules, smaller providers of OPs will have to significantly adjust their terms and conditions.

Beside setting the organizational design, terms and conditions distribute the rights and obligations between users and platform provider. Consequently, it is a

[21] Motive 43 of the DSA.

[22] More on chatbot acceptance and trustworthiness among users e.g. Janson (2023); Cabrero-Daniel and Sangustin Cabrero (2023).

mean of allocating the risks. The way it is done is increasingly becoming the subject of governments' scrutiny.[23] Readability of the terms and conditions is crucial to giving informed consent. However, it was confirmed on numerous occasions that users do not read terms and conditions,[24] unless they are forced to do it.[25] Therefore, even different form of presenting them (such as to ensure that complexity and excessive length are not overwhelming) might not achieve expected result.

Article 20 DSA sets the framework for OPs' internal complaint-handling system. All major platforms already have that kind of systems in place and their importance is only increasing with the number of content moderation decisions. Practice shows it is the first redress mechanism that users seek, and frequently the last, despite the availability of out-of-court dispute settlement mechanism.[26]

The dispute settlement system established by providers of OPs and further developed by DSA contributes to and accelerates shift from judicial scrutiny of such cases to private entities which, as commentators point out, might be detrimental in the long run.[27] Design of internal complaint system, along with terms and conditions, further empowers and increases societal role of OPs. The providers of biggest OPs are deciding on the scope of rights and obligations of the users, their enforcement and adjudicate any dispute arising from the interaction with the platform, creating self-sufficient governance system.[28]

5 Primary Obligations to Provide (Access to) Information/Data

As mentioned above in part 2, the obligations to obtain, verify, store and share trader information with public authorities referred to in Article 30(1)(b)-(c) DSA (ID, the payment account details) are not transparency obligations but obligations aimed at safety of online environment. Similarly, these obligations apply to information referred to in Article 30(1)(a), (d)-(e) DSA, i.e.: the name, address, telephone number and email address of the trader; where the trader is registered in a trade register or similar public register, the trade register in which the trader is registered and its registration number or equivalent means of identification in that register; a self-certification by the trader committing to only offer products or services that comply with the applicable rules of EU law. Additionally, however, the provider of the online platform is obliged to make information referred to in Article 30(1)(a),

[23] Helberger et al. (2018), p. 4.

[24] See Karanicolas (2021), pp. 3–4.

[25] See Steinfeld (2016).

[26] Ortolani (2022).

[27] Ibid; Wimmers (2021), pp. 398–401.

[28] Petersen et al. (2018), pp. 39–41.

(d)-(e) available on its online platform to the recipients of the service 'in a clear, easily accessible and comprehensible manner' (para 7 sentence 1). That information shall be available at least on the online platform's online interface where the information on the product or service is presented (para 7 sentence 2). This is mostly due to transparency (implying safety) reasons, therefore the above-mentioned 'know-your-trader' obligations regarding such information are considered a set of transparency obligations by us. One additional obligation can change the qualification of the entire set of obligations. The attribution of a goal of transparency to these obligations has also been reflected in literature.[29]

A transparency (implying safety) obligation is also provided for in Article 32 DSA (titled 'Right to information'). Pursuant to its paragraph 1, if a provider of an OP allowing consumers to conclude distance contracts with traders becomes aware, irrespective of the means used, that an illegal product or service has been offered by a trader to consumers located in the EU through its services, that provider shall inform, insofar as it has their contact details, consumers who purchased the illegal product or service through its services of the following:

(a) the fact that the product or service is illegal;
(b) the identity of the trader; and
(c) any relevant means of redress.

However, the obligation laid down in the first subparagraph of Article 32(1) DSA is limited to purchases made within 6 months preceding the moment that the provider became aware of the illegality.

Where the provider of the OP allowing consumers to conclude distance contracts with traders does not have the contact details of all consumers concerned, that provider shall make publicly available and easily accessible on its online interface the information concerning the illegal product or service, the identity of the trader and any relevant means of redress.

It is as if providers of OPs have to do everything possible to prevent the consumer from being harmed by the distance sale of illegal products or services.[30] However, critics claim that the DSA is a missed opportunity to more effectively tackle the ever-increasing amount of illegal products and services sold online, among others, by extending these obligations to all online intermediaries, even the smallest ones.[31]

The other issue that arises as part of providing access to information/data is a set of obligations provided for in Article 40. It obliges providers of VLOPs (or of very large online search engines, hereafter VLOSEs, but we do not focus on them here)

[29] See Cauffman and Goanta (2021), pp. 761–763.

[30] Tommasi (2023), p. 26.

[31] AIM, the European Brands Association, News & Positions - April 2022. The Digital Services Act should help crack down on illegal goods but is not future-proof. https://www.aim.be/news/the-digital-services-act-should-help-crack-down-on-illegal-goods-but-is-not-future-proof/.

to provide access to data not only to the Digital Services Coordinator of establishment or the European Commission monitoring and assessing compliance with the DSA, but also to vetted researchers referred to in Article 40(8) DSA, for the sole purpose of conducting research that meets requirements of Article 40(4) DSA. The most challenging and significant problem under Article 40 DSA regime is in determining the scope of data covered by these obligations. Similarly, Article 40 DSA is silent on the form of providing access to data, whereas in practice it can take many forms.

The obligation towards researchers is an important measure enabling them VLOP-related research focusing on systemic risks in the EU referred to in Article 34 DSA. The literature indicates that only the active participation of researchers can assure full accountability of providers (and regulators) to the latest scientific advances, and, without Article 40 the DSA's risk mitigation system will be very weak and resemble a formalistic exercise.[32] However, it should be noted that pursuant to Article 40(5)(b) DSA, providers of VLOPs can reject data access requests due to that giving access to the data will lead to significant vulnerabilities in the security of their service or the protection of confidential information, in particular trade secrets. This provision is 'almost paradoxically broad',[33] but it needs to be interpreted with caution. An important caveat is that according to motive 97 the mere consideration of the commercial interests of providers should not lead to a refusal to provide access to data necessary for the specific research objective. As a rule, the conclusion of non-disclosure agreements between providers of VLOPs and researchers should be sufficient to solve the risk of public disclosure of data. However, the devil will be in the detail of such agreements. Therefore, non-disclosure agreements should be standardised by regulators in order to prevent that providers of VLOPs use their bargaining position to impose undue conditions. Finally, regulators should follow the lessons learned from practices existing in the area of court-appointed experts (for instance, in competition law court cases).

6 Primary Obligations Regarding Online Interfaces

There are many different forms that the dark patterns can have, e.g. the ones that: (1) lead user towards one option rather than the other, (2) try to make it as difficult as possible to find something the user is looking for, (3) use the easiest path for the user to take, even though the choice would benefit the service provider more than the user, etc. Article 25(1) DSA obliges providers of OPs not to design, organise or operate their online interfaces in a way that deceives or manipulates the recipients of their service or in a way that otherwise materially distorts or impairs the ability of the recipients of their service to make free and informed decisions.

[32] See Husovec (2023), p. 3.

[33] Leerssen (2021), p. 59.

This provision might seem to have the potential to increase protection of consumers. However, first, Article 25(2) DSA provides for an exception to paragraph 1. The prohibition in Article 25(1) DSA is not applicable to practices covered by Directive 2005/29/EC ('Unfair Commercial Practices Directive')[34] or Regulation (EU) 2016/679 (GDPR).[35] During the legislative process, this exemption was criticized, but was nevertheless integrated in the final version of the DSA.[36]

In addition, Article 25 DSA refers to 'recipients' of the services, a broad category of beneficiaries with business users among them. In Article 25 there are no references to the average consumer standard, whereas the EU legislature chose the reception of this standard in Article 6 and Recital 24 DSA. As a result, there does not seem to be a clear pattern regarding misleading information in the DSA. It would seem coherent to employ the average consumer standard with regard to misleading practices in both Article 6 and Article 25 DSA.[37] Otherwise, it is unclear what type of approach courts will take to appraising deception and manipulation when consumers are concerned.

Importantly, the DSA contains in Article 26 a set of transparency obligations for advertisements. Advertising systems on online platforms used to be considered as functioning with no more than a clear definition of the desired results (e.g., installs, page views, impressions, etc.).[38] According to Article 26 DSA, providers of OPs shall be obliged:

1. to ensure that for each specific advertisement presented on the online interfaces to each individual recipient, the recipients of the service are able to identify, in a clear, concise and unambiguous manner and in real time (para 1):
   – that the information is an advertisement;
   – on whose behalf the advertisement is presented and who paid for the advertisement;
   – meaningful information directly and easily accessible from the advertisement about the main parameters used to determine the recipient to whom the advertisement is presented and, where applicable, about how to change those parameters;
2. to ensure that (para 2):

[34] Directive 2005/29/EC of the European Parliament and of the Council of 11 May 2005 concerning unfair business-to-consumer commercial practices in the internal market and amending Council Directive 84/450/EEC, Directives 97/7/EC, 98/27/EC and 2002/65/EC of the European Parliament and of the Council and Regulation (EC) No 2006/2004 of the European Parliament and of the Council, OJ L 149, 11.6.2005, pp. 22–39.

[35] Regulation (EU) 2016/679 of the European Parliament and of the Council of 27 April 2016 on the protection of natural persons with regard to the processing of personal data and on the free movement of such data, and repealing Directive 95/46/EC, OJ L 19, 04.05.2016, pp. 1–88.

[36] See Micklitz (2023), p. 86.

[37] See e.g. Mocanu and Sibony (2023), p. 247.

[38] Ranganathan (2023), p. 206.

- recipients of the service are provided with a functionality to declare whether the content they provide is or contains commercial communications;
- in the case of such a declaration, other recipients of the service can identify in a clear and unambiguous manner and in real time that the content provided by the recipient of the service is or contains commercial communications, as described in that declaration;

3. not to present advertisements to recipients of the service based on profiling using special categories of personal data in the meaning of GDPR provisions[39] (para 3).

Among these different obligations, the latter is considered in the literature as hardly effective against recommendations exploiting emotions or addressing fears. The wording od Article 26(3) DSA can potentially mean that targeting information based on sensitive data that was inferred from other non-sensitive data is not prohibited.[40]

Furthermore, by leaving 'meaningful information' open for interpretation and allowing platforms the power to determine the degree of abstraction by which they make their advertising operations legible to the public (breakdown by age brackets, gender, etc.), Article 26(1)(d) DSA will allow companies to disclose only as much non-threatening information as their business models permit.[41] The same provision creates a consumer right to control parameters of personalised advertisement, but the reach of this right is 'very limited because the choice of whether to offer several personalisation options remains that of the platform'.[42] This means that if platforms decide to give a choice between ad personalisation based on previous purchases or ad personalisation based on previous purchases, search history, and social media activity, they are obliged to make this choice clear and salient.[43] In other words, for advertisement, consumer empowerment through information is mediated by law but in the hands of platforms.[44]

Another set of obligations under scrutiny is encompassed by Article 27 DSA imposing obligations on providers of OPs using recommender systems in the meaning of Article 3(s) DSA. The imposition of transparency obligations regarding recommender systems seems to be particularly important. Recommender systems are perceived as opaque. Concerns over their transparency often refer to the obscure complex (and confidential) algorithms used to produce recommendations, as well as the organisations surrounding recommender systems, 'which also tend to be poorly documented'.[45] Article 27 DSA provides for obligations to:

---

[39] Regulation (EU) 2016/679 of the European Parliament and of the Council of 27 April 2016 on the protection of natural persons with regard to the processing of personal data and on the free movement of such data, and repealing Directive 95/46/EC, OJ L 19, 04.05.2016, pp. 1–88.

[40] Grisse (2023), pp. 123–124.

[41] Ranganathan (2023), p. 207.

[42] Mocanu and Sibony (2023), p. 243.

[43] Ibid, p. 244.

[44] Ibid.

[45] Leerssen (2023), pp. 53–58.

- set out in their terms and conditions, in plain and intelligible language, the main parameters used in their recommender systems,[46] as well as any options for the recipients of the service to modify or influence those main parameters (paras 1–2),
- make available a functionality (directly and easily accessible from the specific section of the online platform's online interface where the information is being prioritised) that allows the recipient of the service to select and to modify at any time their preferred option, where several options are available (para 3).

Its provisions should be seen alongside VLOP- (and VLOSE-) related Article 38 DSA. The latter provision obliges them to provide at least one option for each of their recommender systems which is not based on profiling.

Article 38 DSA still allows a solution where users actively must choose the free-of-profiling option (reject the default option). However, most users do not read the information but only continue to click on the default options to progress with the process they visited a certain platform for.[47] An open question is the sufficiency of the general requirement of fair interface design contained in Article 25 DSA. In literature, it is argued that there should be precise requirements for the design of a personalisation opt-out.[48] Otherwise, Article 38 DSA does not necessarily imply an increasing level of protection.

Additionally, in the literature it has been noted that the scope of Article 38 limited to VLOPs is too narrow; it can be that recommender systems based on profiling are used also in certain niche areas by other OPs and the obligation in question applied to them could be of importance for their users.[49]

7 Meta-Obligations of Providers of Online Platforms

Meta-obligations correspond directly with primary obligations as it was presented in Fig. 1. They are complementary in their nature. Obligations related to transparency that we have identified within this category include:

1. risk assessment (Article 34 DSA),
2. publishing online advertisement database (Article 39),
3. conducting independent audit (Article 37),
4. establishing compliance officer (Article 41),
5. transparency reporting obligations (Article 15, 24, 42).

Most of the meta-obligations relate to providers of VLOPs, except for the transparency reporting obligation stipulated in Article 15 that is imposed on all providers of

[46] E.g., characteristics, preferences, and networks of the user; respectability or popularity of a source; trends, etc. von Ungern-Stenberg (2023), p. 49.

[47] For more see Bergram et al. (2020).

[48] Mocanu and Sibony (2023), p. 253.

[49] Gössl (2023), p. 23. Also Grisse (2023), pp. 123–124.

OPs. It is a reasonable strategy because VLOPs are larger, have a bigger impact on both users and the society, and, as a result providers of VLOPs should have more responsibilities. The latter have resources at their disposal like data, models, infrastructure, network of users or global reach, to develop most sophisticated algorithms for content recommendations. They have the means to decide what is shown to single users, influencing their choice. Whether it is a targeted advertisement inciting to purchase goods or services, or hiding some content from particular users.

For instance, targeted advertisements are more effective, and therefore, more valuable. However, advertisements tailored to potential consumers exploit their vulnerability. While it has been pointed out in part 6 that primary obligation for advertisement transparency might not produce the desired outcome and be less effective mean of providing safety, disclosing information about whole advertisement campaigns might be helpful in discovering the patterns by providing the big picture. It is one of the meta-obligations imposed on providers of VLOPs in Article 39 DSA and one that was already contested. There are limits to transparency and it should not be absolute. However, the EU legislature already did the balancing while drafting Article 39 DSA and decided to grant public access to that information. What, perhaps, needs further discussion is not the obligation itself but its implementation. Article 39 DSA is not very detailed but it allows the Commission to issue additional guidelines relating to this obligation.

In fact, meta-obligations are designed in a way that gives wiggle room for providers of OPs. It makes sense because the model of enforcement is based on self-assessment. On the other hand it necessitates establishment of many guidelines to address specific details, such as templates or instructions for reports (transparency reports, systemic risk assessment, independent audit). The least problematic meta-obligation from the point of view of providers of OPs seems to be establishment of internal unit responsible for compliance function (Article 41). While complete uniformity is not necessary, mapping out some technical requirements is essential to prevent potential conflicts, such as, how to mitigate risks of non-compliance of providers of OPs' and satisfy the requests at the same time, or how to avoid overburdening the providers of OPs while ensuring that the objective of obligation is not compromised.

It is not within the scope of this chapter to analyse individual meta-obligations in details, however, we consider them an area requiring further research.

8 Conclusions

The DSA introduces a set of due diligence obligations aimed at fostering a transparent online environment. However, the mechanism itself may lack the desired level of transparency. The excessive length of the act and numerous interconnected provisions add to the complexity of the legal framework. It requires navigating through many sections to understand the full scope and implications of the DSA. Therefore, delegating acts will play critical role in specifying many open-ended articles, providing recommendations and guidelines for compliance with the DSA to providers of OPs and authorities oversighting its implementation. The layered structure of the obligations and self-assessment model shifts the burden of enforcement to providers of OPs. It also invites more actors to the process, therefore, third parties, such as consumers, civil society and SMEs, will play role in enforcing the transparency obligations set out in DSA.

The EU's interest in regulating functioning of online intermediaries is a powerful factor in shaping policies and practices of providers of OPs that operate globally. This influence begins with obligation to establish clear and understandable terms and conditions, enabling recipients of the services to make informed decisions. Considering the fact that most of the recipients are overwhelmed by the complexity of terms and conditions, leading to blind acceptance, functionalities that are more beneficial to users should be set by default. Given the societal impact that providers of the OPs have, it is essential for their communication and internal dispute resolution systems to be accessible and user-friendly. This is particularly important for users, especially consumers, as it may be the only redress mechanism they opt to use. Consequently, those decisions of providers of OPs will not be subjected to judicial review.

One of the most challenging uncertainties and imprecisions in the DSA results from that, in many instances, the DSA is silent on the scope (and/or the form) of providing the required access to data, e.g. in Article 40. Certainly, transparency as a goal is set against providers of OPs' rights and interests. Examining the obligations highlights that there may be many conflicts of interests to settle, when it comes to the scope/form of providing the access to data or other requirements. The first test run of balancing the need for transparency with commercial confidentiality will be the *Amazon* case mentioned in part 3 above.

Even though our analysis has not included overlaps between the DSA and the EU law on consumer protection, it can be seen that they both apply a different logic. The consumer law relies upon *ex post* prohibition of unfair practices, while the DSA rests heavily on *ex ante* primary fairness obligations. In terms of fairness, Article 25 DSA regarding fair interface design is a fundamental provision and a lot will depend on its enforcement. In this chapter, certain DSA's features disadvantaging consumers are reported, e.g. the DSA's inconsistent approach to the application of the average consumer standard or the very limited reach of a consumer right to control parameters of personalised advertisement. However, as our analysis shows, consumers can benefit from that the DSA gives tighter control over data for consumers. On the other hand, the risk exists that they will neither notice the change nor use new possibilities to make better and informed decisions regarding the use of their data. Therefore, we recommend that fairness by design requirements (Article 25 DSA) and meta-obligations such as reporting obligations need to coexist with education raising consumer awareness.

The very pyramid-like structure of transparency obligations under the DSA can be considered an obstacle to the increase of consumer protection. Whereas micro and small enterprises are exempt from most of the primary obligations imposed on providers of OPs, it would be advisable to extend obligations provided for in Article

32 (regarding illegal products and services sold online) to all online intermediaries, regardless of their status (even the smallest ones). Furthermore, in some cases also the scope of Article 38 regarding recommender systems based on profiling (limited to VLOPs) could be extended, as obligations resulting therefrom will not be applicable to some small providers of OPs present in certain niche areas and using recommender systems.

In conclusion of our research, however, we consider the DSA as representing a promising development in online platform governance.

References

Bergram K, Bezençon V, Maingot P, Gjerlufsen T, Holzer A (2020) Digital nudges for privacy awareness: from consent to informed consent?. In: Proceedings of the 28th European Conference on Information Systems (ECIS), An Online AIS Conference, June 15–17, 2020. https://aisel.aisnet.org/ecis2020_rp/64

Cabrero-Daniel B, Sangustin Cabrero A (2023) Perceived trustworthiness of natural language generators. In: 1st International Symposium on Trustworthy Autonomous Systems, July 11–12, 2023, https://doi.org/10.1145/3597512.3599715

Cauffman C, Goanta C (2021) A new order: the digital services act and consumer protection. Eur J Risk Regul 21:758–774

G'Sell F (2023) The digital services act: a general assessment. In: von Ungern-Sternberg A (ed) Content regulation in the European Union: the digital services act. Volume 1. Verein für Recht und Digitalisierung e.V. Institute for Digital Law, Trier

Gorwa R, Ash TG (2020) Democratic transparency in the platform society. In: Persily N, Tucker J (eds) Social media and democracy: the state of the field and prospects for reform. Cambridge University Press

Gössl SL (2023) Recommender systems and discrimination. In: Genovesi S, Kaesling K, Robbins S (eds) Recommender systems: legal and ethical issues. Springer, Cham

Grisse K (2023) Recommender systems, manipulation and private autonomy: how European civil law regulates and should regulate recommender systems for the benefit of private autonomy. In: Genovesi S, Kaesling K, Robbins S (eds) Recommender systems: legal and ethical issues. Springer, Cham

Helberger N, Pierson J, Poell T (2018) Governing online platforms: from contested to cooperative responsibility. Inf Soc 34(1):1–14

Husovec M (2023) How to facilitate data access under the digital services act. https://papers.ssrn.com/sol3/papers.cfm?abstract_id=4452940

Janson A (2023) How to leverage anthropomorphism for chatbot service interfaces: the interplay of communication style and personification. Comput Hum Behav 149:1–17

Karanicolas M (2021) Too long; didn't read: finding meaning in platforms' terms of service agreements. https://papers.ssrn.com/sol3/papers.cfm?abstract_id=3887753

Leerssen P (2021) Platform research access in article 31 of the digital services act. In: Richter H, Straub M, Tuchtfeld E (eds) To break up or regulate big tech? Avenues to constrain private power in the DSA/DMA package. Max Planck Institute for Innovation and Competition, Munich

Leerssen P (2023) Seeing what others are seeing: studies in the regulation of transparency for social media recommender systems [thesis, fully internal]. University of Amsterdam, Amsterdam

Micklitz HW (2023) The role of standards in future EU digital policy legislation: a consumer perspective. BEUC, Brussels

Mocanu D, Sibony AL (2023) EU consumer law meets digital twins. Revue européenne de droit de la consommation 1:229–257

Ortolani P (2022) If you build it, they will come: the DSA's "Procedure Before Substance" approach, VerfBlog, 7.11.2022. https://verfassungsblog.de/dsa-build-it/, https://doi.org/10.17176/20221107-095646-0

Petersen CS, Ulfbeck VG, Hansen O (2018) Platforms as private governance systems—the example of Airbnb. Nordic J Commer Law 1:39–60

Ranganathan N (2023) Regulating influence, timidly. In: van Hoboken J, Quintais JP, Appelman N, Fahy R, Buri I, Straub M (eds) Putting the digital services act into practice: enforcement, access to justice, and global implications. Verfassungsblog gGmbH, Berlin

Rodríguez de las Heras Ballell T (2021) The background of the digital services act: looking towards a platform economy. ERA Forum 22:75–86

Steinfeld N (2016) "I agree to the terms and conditions": (how) do users read privacy policies online? An eye-tracking experiment. Comput Hum Behav 55:992–1000

Tommasi (2023) The risk of discrimination in the digital market: from the digital services act to the future. Springer, Cham

Van Cleynenbreugel P (2021) The Commission's digital services and markets act proposals: first step towards tougher and more directly enforced EU rules? Maastricht J Eur Comp Law 28(5):667–686

von Ungern-Sternberg A (2023) Freedom of speech goes Europe—EU laws for online communication. In: von Ungern-Sternberg A (ed) Content regulation in the European Union: the digital services act, vol 1. Verein für Recht und Digitalisierung e.V. Institute for Digital Law, Trier

Wimmers J (2021) The out-of-court dispute settlement mechanism in the digital services act—a disservice to its own goals. J Intell Prop Inf Technol E-Commer Law 12:381–401

Stakeholder Engagement in EU Digital Platform Regulations: Ways Forward and Persisting Gaps

Giulia Schneider

Abstract The chapter questions whether the issued European digital platform regulations can be inscribed in the newly emerging sustainable business paradigm and be considered an example of corporate digital responsibility norms regarding digital platforms in the European legal system. More precisely, the analysis tests two different hypotheses: (i) to which extent EU digital platform regulations address corporate digital sustainability interests; and (ii) whether the considered regulations employ, as a regulatory technique, co-regulation mechanisms leveraging on stakeholder engagement capacities for the attainment of the relevant interests. To these ends, the study first identifies the "digital sustainability" interests underlying the considered regulations, detecting the stakeholders that would have a legitimate claim for engagement in view of the declared regulatory objectives. Then it illustrates the codified tools for stakeholder-driven co-regulation within digital platforms' public and private ordering spheres. Conclusions will highlight persistent downsides and gaps of the assessed stakeholders' participatory spaces in the digital platform ecosystem.

G. Schneider (✉)
Università Cattolica del Sacro Cuore, Milan, Italy
e-mail: giulia.schneider@unicatt.it

D. V. Popović, R. Kulms (eds.), *Repositioning Platforms in Digital Market Law*, European Union and its Neighbours in a Globalized World 15,
https://doi.org/10.1007/978-3-031-69678-7_6

1 Digital Platforms and Third Parties' Interests: DMA and DSA as Corporate Digital Responsibility Norms

Digital platforms' regulation in the European Union is appears to have moved a qualitative step further—compared also to other competing legal systems[1]—with the entering into force of the Digital Markets[2] and the Digital Services Act.[3] Taking the more severe form of a regulation, both legislative acts intend to control and curb the market power of digital giants operating in multisided markets, introducing behavioral and structural responsibilities designed in accordance with a proportionality approach.[4]

The ambition of these interventions is thus to capture under the European legal order—and its foundational values—the elusive countenance of the transnational private digital ecosystems,[5] which base their business models on the factual control and exploitation of data and information of the participants to self-reinforcing networks.[6]

While the Digital Markets Act addresses the conducts of gatekeepers mainly from a horizontal market perspective encompassing the relationship with business users,[7] the Digital Services Act intervenes on the vertical side of the effects that the digital platform organization has onto its end-users.[8] Both regulations thus appear to deal with the external impact that the distinctive business model of digital platforms have onto the interests of the recalled third parties.[9] In this respect, it can be said that the issued provisions pursue digital sustainability objectives, in the sense that they promote digital platforms' responsibility in considering external stakeholders' individual and collective interests affected by their (varied) business activities.

However, as a wide strand of the literature has now been observing,[10] the concrete identification and protection of third parties' interests proves to be extremely difficult in digital markets.

---

[1] Bradford (2023), pp. 33–149.

[2] Regulation (EU) 2022/1925 of the European Parliament and of the Council of 14 September 2022 on contestable and fair markets in the digital sector and amending Directives (EU) 2019/1937 and (EU) 2020/1828 (Digital Markets Act), OJ L 265/1.

[3] Regulation (EU) 2022/2065 of the European Parliament and of the Council of 19 October 2022 on a Single Market For Digital Services and amending Directive 2000/31/EC (Digital Services Act), OJ L 277/1.

[4] For comments about the new regulatory framework see Akman (2022), p. 85; Ibanez Colomo (2021), p. 561; Monti (2021), p. 90; Larouche and De Streel (2021), p. 542; Richter et al. (2021); Belloso and Petit (2023), p. 391; Leistner (2021), p. 778; De Streel et al. (2021); Busch and Mak (2021), p. 109; Di Porto et al. (2021), p. 84; Falce (2021), p. 10; Colangelo (2022), p. 597.

[5] Bassan (2021), p. 84 ff.

[6] Graef (2015), p. 473; Robertson (2022), p. 161; Colangelo and Maggiolino (2018), p. 224.

[7] Art. 1 DMA.

[8] Art. 1 DSA.

[9] De Gregorio and Dunn (2022), p. 473; Husovec (2023).

[10] One out of many, Zuboff (2019); and more recently Matsumi and Solove (2023).

The digital environment shares indeed structural features that appear to be hardly governed through a traditional top down or through "command and control" regulatory techniques[11] for the purposes of protecting public or collective interests. As the DMA impact assessment outlines, ex ante regulations face the challenge of mediating between legal certainty objectives and the urge for context-sensitive responses, which is particularly pressing in the fast-changing technological setting of digital platforms. Traditional regulatory techniques may be relevant for ensuring legal certainty in a stable market environment but reveal all their shortcomings in structurally volatile and dynamic environments.[12]

Digital markets appear to fit in this latter category: they are characterized by highly complex business relations not only between the digital platform and its end users, but also between the business users the digital platforms itself connects as an intermediary.[13] The complexity of the open ended and networked setting blended with the fast pace of technological progress gives rise to genetically incomplete contractual agreements among involved economic actors and thus to an overall unpredictable economic context.[14]

The uncertainty of market conditions makes it hard to identify the interests that are exactly linked to (one of the many) business activities originating from the digital (multisided) platform, and in the eventual pathological phase of a damage causation, the type, the chronological moment as well as the quantification of the occurred damages are much more difficult to assess than what occurs in a stable scenario. As a result, pre-existing templates for collaborations between undertaking and relevant Authorities (be it regulatory or judicial ones) appear largely unsuited.[15]

Digital markets' distinctive traits contribute to what can be defined the "regulatory sovereignty" of digital platforms,[16] resulting into parallel transnational jurisdictional systems that have proven to be largely elusive of States' legislative dictates, and with public regulators encountering difficulties in verifying ex post compliance with set regulatory obligations.[17] Among the main reasons for digital platforms' legal "impenetrability", information asymmetries in technological matters, advanced by a stratified use of legal and technical control measures, as well as the long procedural stages of public investigations by regulatory or judicial authorities are to be considered.[18]

Moreover, shifting from the public supervisory dimension to internal corporate supervisory mechanisms, it must be recalled that digital platforms often have a

[11] Black (2001), p. 103.

[12] Svetiev (2020), p. 51.

[13] Ranchordás (2017), p. 1.

[14] Hart and Moore (1988), p. 755; Ayres and Gertner (1989), p. 87.

[15] Svetiev (2020), p. 58.

[16] Cohen (2016), p. 369; Bamberger and Lobel (2017), p. 1051.

[17] De Gregorio and Radu (2022), p. 68.

[18] Bassan (2023), p. 1103.

pyramidal corporate governance structure,[19] in which only a very few investors have voting powers in the shareholder assembly and are thus capable of excercising an effective control over executives' strategic choices. Decision-making rights are thus hierarchically allocated in the hands of very few subjects (namely executives as supervised by "controlling" shareholders with voting rights), thus restricting the scope of internal active scrutiny by shareholders, well before other stakeholders.[20]

In light of the traced scenario, the question arises how the issued European digital platform regulations effectively pursue digital sustainability objectives, and whether, as a result, these can be inscribed in the broader sustainable business paradigm emerging at European normative level. After having described the major features of the European sustainable business paradigm (para 2), the chapter will explore the "digital sustainability" interests underlying the considered regulations, detecting the stakeholders that would have a legitimate claim for engagement in view of the declared regulatory objectives (para 3). Then it illustrates the codified tools for stakeholder-driven co-regulation within digital platforms' public and private ordering spheres (para 4 and 5). Conclusions will highlight ways forward and persistent gaps of the assessed stakeholders' participatory spaces in the digital platform ecosystem (para 6).

2 The Emerging European Sustainable Business Paradigm and the Rise of Sustainability-Oriented Co-regulation

As generally known, the twist towards sustainable business practices and structures is currently promoted at European level by reforms that have been primarily concentrated onto the sectoral domain of (sustainable) financial markets[21] and (sustainable) due diligence law.[22] Further interventions have occurred in the national venues: Germany and France have issued laws such as the *Sorgfaltspflichtengesetz*[23] and the

[19] Jones and Samples (2023), p. 172.

[20] Shill (2023), p. 221.

[21] The latest relevant normative text in the field of sustainable finance and business law is the corporate social reporting directive. Directive (EU) 2022/2464 of the European Parliament and of the Council of 14 December 2022 amending Regulation (EU) No 537/2014, Directive 2004/109/EC, Directive 2006/43/EC and Directive 2013/34/EU, as regards corporate sustainability reporting, 23 February 2022, OJ L 322/15.

[22] Directive (EU) 2024/1760 of the European Parliament and of the Council of 13 June 2024 on corporate sustainability due diligence and amending Directive (EU) 2019/1937 and Regulation (EU) 2023/2859, 5 July 2024.

[23] Gesetz über die unternehmerischen Sorgfaltspflichten in Lieferketten, 16 luglio 2021, in Bundesgesetzblatt, 2021, 46, 2959.

Loi Pacte,[24] which pose binding provisions differently reconsidering the notion of business purpose in accordance with environmental and human rights interests.[25]

Ultimately, the broad goal of binding private economic initiatives to the consideration of public and collective interests has been newly stressed in some Constitutional Charters, as the Italian one, where art. 41 Cost. now requires the freedom of business to be excercized while respecting—thus without producing any harm to—social interests, as human dignity and liberty but also health and the environment.[26] Outside the realm of hard law, many soft law documents as national corporate governance codes,[27] and at international level the revised version of the OECD principles of corporate governance[28] further 'institutionalize' the consideration of stakeholder interests within businesses' organization and governance structures.[29]

If at substantial level this implies the need for businesses acting in the EU internal market to find solutions to complement profit maximization objectives with non-financial interests,[30] at procedural level, the emerging framework requires businesses to open up to the dialogue with relevant third parties so as to identify the social interests that are relevant to the specific business activities and to find ways to address the spotted negative externalities.[31]

From the standpoint of the employed regulatory techniques, the consolidating sustainable business law framework appears to resort to forms of "co-regulation"[32]

---

[24] LOI n° 2019-486 du 22 mai 2019 relative à la croissance et la transformation des entreprises, https://www.legifrance.gouv.fr/jorf/id/JORFTEXT000038496102/.

[25] For the literature see Sjafjell and Mähönen (2022), p. 69; Möslein and Sorensen (2021), p. 7.

[26] Finmanò (2023), p. 777.

[27] Siri and Zhu (2021), p. 175.

[28] G20/OECD Principles of Corporate Governance 2023, 11 September 2023, https://www.oecd-ilibrary.org/governance/g20-oecd-principles-of-corporate-governance-2023_ed750b30-en.

[29] In some strand of the business scholarship, the attempt to incorporate within corporations' functioning social interests has been appointed as 'institutionalist approach', which suggest that corporations should take on also some 'institutional' tasks of protecting social interests, as opposed to a purely 'contractualist' vision of the corporation as a mere profit-oriented contract between the corporation itself and its shareholders. For the literature see Cottino (2005), p. 693. Ricolfi (2022), p. 46.

[30] This operation of complementation between financial and social-oriented interests can be graded differently. Indeed, next to stakeholder capitalist conceptions, also milder enlightened shareholder theories have been affirmed. Among these see Hart and Zingales (2022), p. 196.

[31] Apart from provisions relating to the need of the board to enact a "dialogue" with stakeholders, as demanded by some corporate governance codes, as the Italian corporate governance code under art. 1, Principle IV, the European Commission's proposal of a corporate sustainability due diligence directive requires businesses to "carry out consultations with potentially affected groups including workers and other relevant stakeholders to gather information on actual or potential adverse impacts" (so art. 6(4) of the proposed directive).

[32] The European Union provides the following definition of co-regulation: 'the mechanism whereby a Community legislative act entrusts the attainment of the objectives defined by the legislative authority to parties which are recognized in the field (such as economic operators, the social partners, non-governmental organizations, or associations)'. See art. 18 of the Interinstitutional

for the pursuing of sustainability objectives, and thus for the protection of stakeholders' interests within the course of business initiatives.

Co-regulatory instruments and templates originate from market regulation and competition law, as well expressed by commitments decisions.[33] These had been elaborated to pursue static and dynamic market efficiency. The method adopted by the European legislator to the attainment of these objectives was indeed characterized by i) the delegation of public regulatory competences upon private actors; ii) a cooperative effort between businesses and relevant stakeholders; iii) the use of co-designed open-ended and less prescriptive guidelines. On the enforcement side, compliance in co-regulatory settings largely relies onto iv) the firms' commitment and v) the oversight and monitoring activities by competent public supervisory authorities.[34]

The new legislative interventions in the sustainable business realm seek to graft onto such templates a rights protection mandate: they thus appear to rely on a mixture between public and private ordering solutions for the purposes of the achievement of public policy objectives, as social or environmental ones.

Also outside the recalled regulatory calls in the sustainable business law framework, multi-stakeholder initiatives (MSIs) are increasingly considered in the business practice as a means of addressing adverse impacts in areas such as human rights and climate change, and verify businesses' social performance.[35]

The initiatives in this area differ in the mechanisms with which third parties come to interact with the concerned businesses:[36] some of these only define broad principles of engagement without any monitoring or certification commitments, as has occurred in the UNGC;[37] some use certification criteria so as to evaluate supply chains, as occurs with the social accountability 8000 initiative;[38] and others are centered on reporting frameworks for the circulation of knowledge regarding non-financial parameters, as well reflected in the Global Reporting Initiative.[39] Despite the differences in the employed means and goals, these initiatives all resort to collaborative patterns in the definition of the standards needed for the pursuing of sustainability objectives, crossing the state/non-state and profit/non-profit-boundaries.[40]

Agreement between the European Parliament, the Council of the European Union and the European Commission on Better Law-Making, 13 April 2016, OJ L 123/1. For the literature see Bassan (2023), p. 1103, observing how in respect to self-regulation a co-regulatory technique is characterized by a higher degree of government involvement in rulemaking and enforcement and combines elements of self-regulation with command and control legislation.

[33] Svetiev (2020), pp. 61–71.

[34] Bassan (2023), p. 1103.

[35] Rasche et al. (2022), p. 309.

[36] Gilbert et al. (2011), p. 23.

[37] Jastram and Klingenberg (2018), p. 775.

[38] See Möslein (2019), p. 669.

[39] Bosetti (2022), p. 1706.

[40] Rasche et al. (2022), p. 309.

A regulatory model centered on channels of stakeholder engagement has been considered by the European Commission also in the context of digital markets,[41] where the need of the creation of new "industry tools for ensuring application of legal requirements and appropriate monitoring mechanisms" has been felt, in particular at the design and preparation phase, and at the implementation phase of the policy cycle.[42]

In particular, co-regulatory solutions involving stakeholders as external monitoring peers of digital platforms' private ordering processes appear to be particularly relevant for the protection of interests that are exogenous to the ordinary business activity of digital platforms. A few factual drivers point in this direction. First, in line with the rising regulatory pressure in the matters of technology safety, large digital businesses are increasingly exposed to reputational risks which could incentivize these businesses to turn to relevant stakeholders to safeguard their image. On the opposite site, the strengthening of public authorities' engagement in digital markets[43] is consolidating stakeholders', as business users' and end users', awareness in respect to their rights and contractual powers they have vis à vis digital platforms.[44]

Against this backdrop, the questions arise: i) to which extent EU digital platform regulations address corporate digital sustainability interests; and ii) whether the considered regulations employ, as a regulatory technique, co-regulation mechanisms leveraging on stakeholder engagement capacities for the attainment of the relevant interests.

[41] European Commission, Communication from the Commission to the European Parliament, the Council, the European Economic and Social Committee and the Committee of Regions, Online Platforms and the Digital Single Market Opportunities and Challenges for Europe, 25 May 2016, COM(2016) 288 final.

[42] European Commission, Communication from the Commission to the European Parliament, the Council, the European Economic and Social Committee and the Committee of Regions, Better Regulation for Better Results- An EU Agenda, 19 May 2015, COM(2015) 215 final; and more recently European Commission, Communication from the Commission to the European Parliament, the Council, the European and Social Committee and the Committee of the Regions Better Regulation: Joining forces to make better laws, 2021, https://commission.europa.eu/system/files/2021-04/better_regulation_joining_forces_to_make_better_laws_en_0.pdf. Among the tools mentioned for a better law making, the European Commission includes impact assessments, public and stakeholder consultation and feedback, and ex-post evaluation of the existing legislation. For the literature on co-regulatory solutions in digital markets, see Finck (2018), p. 33.

[43] See Monti and De Streel (2022).

[44] See Beuc (2023).

3 The Objectives of Digital Platform Regulations: From Market Power to Platforms' CSR

In order to verify the first hypothesis regarding the nature of corporate digital responsibility norms of the provisions laid down under the DMA and DSA, reference must be first made to the definition of "digital sustainability" or "digital responsibility" that has been shaped by the literature.

As opposed to a technology neutral approach that has characterized the first phase of the European effort in regulating the digital sphere,[45] the digital sustainability approach assumes that technology and data management practices as "freely" determined by businesses in the interstices of regulatory dictates encounter the limit of balancing the material (efficiency) with fundamental rights and dignity; a balance that arguably lies at the core of the idea of "sustainable markets" and "sustainable business governance" as emerging in the above recalled framework.[46]

Building on the direct efficacy (*drittwirkung*) of constitutional precepts, as the ones enshrined in the European Charter of Fundamental Rights, corporate digital responsibility demands a responsible risk culture attitude for the integration of fundamental legal and ethical values in the design and supervision of digital technologies and data.[47] Originating in the realm of businesses' self-regulation,[48] corporate digital responsibility principles appear to have creeped into the latest legislative "texture" in digital matters.

The final version of the European AI Act[49], for instance, intends to address systemic risks of general purpose artificial intelligence models; these are defined as risks that are "specific to the high-impact capabilities of general-purpose AI models, having a significant impact on the Union market due to their reach, or due to actual or reasonably foreseeable negative effects on public health, safety, public security, fundamental rights, or the society as a whole, that can be propagated at scale across the value chain".

The cited definition, in its general scope expresses a dynamic and flexible conception of AI governance, which warrants to materialize third parties' fundamental rights in digital capitalism vis à vis the unpredictability of technological progress, through a polycentric, inclusive and self-correcting attitude sensitive to long-term effects of digital infrastructures.

---

[45] Maxwell and Bourreau (2015), p. 1; Greenberg (2016), p. 1495. For more recent reflections on the principles of technological neutrality from the perspective of the upcoming AI Act, see Grady (2023).

[46] Yokoi et al. (28 April 2023).

[47] Lobschat et al. (2021), p. 875; Dörr (2022); Balboni and Francis (2022).

[48] Möslein (2020), p. 805.

[49] Regulation (EU) 2024/1689 of the European Parliament and of the Council of 13 June 2024 laying down harmonised rules on artificial intelligence and amending Regulations (EC) No 300/2008, (EU) No 167/2013, (EU) No 168/2013, (EU) 2018/858, (EU) 2018/1139 and (EU) 2019/2144 and Directives 2014/90/EU, (EU) 2016/797 and (EU) 2020/1828, 12 July 2024 (hereafter AI Act), see especially arts. 3(65); and 51 ff.

Interestingly, the declared objectives of the DMA and DSA, regulating the specific perspective of digital platforms' responsibilities, appear in line with such approach.

As generally known, the DMA intends to regulate digital platforms' activities in accordance with the principles of contestability and fairness.[50] Contestability exactly relates to the "ability of undertakings (…) to challenge the gatekeepers on the merits of their products and services" overcoming the barriers to entry given by the features of platform services in the digital sector, as given by "network effects, strong economies of scale, and benefits from data".[51] As defined in these terms, contestability of third business parties vis à vis digital platforms has not only a competitive market significance, meaning their ability to engage in competition with digital platforms to attain a competitive market position, but also the qualitatively different bearing of the ability of third business parties to oppose an action or a strategy stemming from a digital platform as mistaken or wrong, on the basis of the eventual violation of the same third party's interests.[52]

This last understanding of contestability well matches with the "relational" dimension of digital market's fairness, which provides a criterion to detect an eventual "imbalance between the rights and obligations of business users where the gatekeeper obtains a disproportionate advantage".[53] Hence, the balancing exercise required by the fairness principles, demands digital platforms to structure the relations with business partners alongside commercial practices that are perceptive of the negative societal and economic externalities of their business organizational and governance options onto their business users.

Although very broadly defined, the contestability and fairness principles under the DMA appear to majorly regard business users' economic (contractual) rights vis à vis digital platforms. Broadening the perspective beyond business users, the DSA takes a substantially different stance, and primarily considers societal interests touched by digital platforms' business activities. From this standpoint, the DSA identifies different types of so-called "systemic risks".[54]

A first category of systemic risk regards the "extreme" hypothesis of illegal activities conducted by or by means of digital platforms, which impact on personal fundamental rights, as children's rights or personhood rights protected by criminal provisions and by product liability regulations.[55] The rights that are related to this hypothesis of systemic risk are evidently linked with public interests pursued by the branches of law that come to protect the said rights, by means of a prohibition or of a severe restriction of practices considered to be risky in the mentioned domains.

---

[50] On these notions see Schweitzer (2021), p. 509.

[51] Recital 32 DMA.

[52] Crémer et al. (2023), p. 973.

[53] Recital 33 DMA.

[54] Frosio and Geiger (2023), p. 31.

[55] Recital 80 DSA.

To the contrary, the other categories of systemic risks are related to the "actual or foreseeable" negative externalities of digital platforms' ordinary commercial services: these can either adversely impact individual or collective personal fundamental rights, generally relating to human dignity, as the right to private life and the right to data protection, consumer protection rights and non-discrimination rights, media freedom and pluralism;[56] or on public interests, relating to the political sphere, as the well-functioning of democratic and electoral processes,[57] or the public health realm, including physical and mental well-being or gender-based violence interests.[58]

As a result, the systemic risks targeted by the DSA make a turnaround from the pure economic and market efficiency perspective and capture the interference of digital platforms' activities with public and group-based interests that are traditionally generously guarded by State-derived regulations, starting from constitutional charters. Along these lines, the DSA oversteps the consideration of the structural market imbalances arising from the platform ecosystem and considers the substantially different "eco-systemic" effects linked to platform-based business model between the market and the private sphere of users and even the public sphere.

3.1 *The Sustainable "Well-Functioning" of Digital Markets*

The varied notion of systemic risks provided by the DSA intend to "secure" a highly blended virtual market dimension in which platforms have enabled—upstream—commodification trends of the person and of the public interest through the means of data (of both personal and public nature) collection[59] and analysis and—downstream—the exercise of activities in which commercial aspects merge with public interest-related outcomes.[60] These have been well perceived, for example, in the case of the censorship functions conducted by digital platforms in the course of online content moderation processes.[61] In some cases, digital information flows skewed by the platforms have been capable of sensitively orienting the "material" pattern of public debates or even of democratic votes.[62]

Traditional legal paradigms, strictly attached to the generally accepted public/private divide, have turned out to be largely unsuited for the detection of the mentioned platforms' economic and societal externalities.[63] Also the attempts on both sides of the regulatory sphere (the private and the public law ones) to seize the

[56] Recital 81 DSA.

[57] Recital 82 DSA.

[58] Recital 83 DSA.

[59] Seidl (2023), p. 1; Cohen (2024).

[60] Simoncini and Longo (2021), p. 27.

[61] Eder (2023).

[62] See European Parliament (October 2023).

[63] De Gregorio and Radu (2022), p. 68. See also Bietti (2023).

recalled spillover effects of digital services offered by the platforms have provided questionable, or at least to date uncertain, solutions. Just to mention a few, as far as public regulation is concerned, no agreement has been found to date to effectively use corporate tax law to control the returns associated with the massive use of users' data and thus with the commercial exploitation of their personal rights.[64]

Conversely, in the field of market regulation (broadly intended), there is an ongoing effort in both the scholarly debate and the enforcement sites to curb the general competition framework to the attainment also of non-economic goals.[65] This interpretative path, which is currently being advanced under the green competition law discourse, has historically originated from the need felt in the platform economy to overcome a sole economic-based notion of market efficiency and consumer welfare.[66] Along these lines, for example, the prohibition of abuse of dominant position has been tentatively applied also to conducts harming consumers' personal fundamental rights, as the right to data protection.[67]

The ineffectiveness of public enforcement interventions, together with the tailored and ex post nature of evolving competition enforcement methodologies, have paved the way for new regulatory solutions, which are sensitive to the direct reflexes of the platforms' activities over the protection not only of individual but also of collective fundamental rights. In this last respect, the DSA appears to overtake the grandfather of European digital regulations, the GDPR, which had only considered the impact of digital technological progress onto the strictly individual and private sphere.

However, the systemic risks targeted by the DSA reveal an even greater step forward in the regulation of the digital sphere at European level: the consideration of the "systemic" relevance of digital platforms' business activities is indeed the prerequisite for an equally blended notion of the "well-functioning" of the internal market: as suggested by art. 1(1) DSA, the regulation is aimed at contributing to the proper functioning of the internal market for intermediary services by setting out "harmonized rules for a safe, predictable and trusted online environment that facilitates innovation and in which fundamental rights enshrined in the Charter, including the principle of consumer protection, are effectively protected". Hence, under the new regulatory paradigm, the internal market's well-functioning cannot be assessed without internalizing in the measurement of the markets' efficiency the evaluation of (the degree of) fundamental rights' protection.

This regulatory conception of a "sustainable" well-functioning of digital markets mirrors the long-term methodology to profit maximization objectives that sustainable business law provisions intend to inflect in the corporate governance realm.

Moreover, in order to substantiate this "systemic" bearing of the notion of internal markets' well-functioning, the DSA relies on a proportionality method that is

[64] Beretta (2021), p. 31.

[65] Andriychuk (2023), p. 1.

[66] Ezrachi (2017), p. 49; Lianos (2018), p. 161; Miazad (2022), p. 1637.

[67] Persch (2021), p. 542.

directly based on the size of the considered digital corporations: it indeed links the economic power of "very large online platforms" and of "very large online search engines" with greater social responsibilities arising from the systemic risks resulting from the design, functioning and use of their services, as well as from the potential misuses by the recipients of the service.[68]

Hence, the systemic responsibilities of these "very large" platforms should account not only for the negative impacts *directly* stemming from their commercial activities, but also for the ones *indirectly* activated and propagated by end-users *through* the platform ecosystem. In this respect, the size of platforms (very large) also grounds a form of vicarious or "rebound" social liability for the protection of both individual and collective interests on behalf of third parties that have a qualified user relation with the offered service.

Hence, the bigger the market size governed by a platform is, the wider the monitoring duty of systemic risks which materially originate from the digital infrastructure becomes: this general monitoring duty encompasses the duty to identify potentially affected parties, to evaluate the potential irreversibility of the damage, or the difficulty to remedy and restore the situation prevailing prior to the potential impact.[69] This evaluation phase should be functional to design the "appropriate mitigating measures in observance of fundamental rights".[70]

The traced analysis shows how both the DMA and DSA structure a legally mandated obligation for digital platforms to actively balance economic interests with third-party interests, along the lines of a relational and integrated notion of the well-functioning of the digital internal market.

The flipside of the defined regulatory objectives, and of platforms' social monitoring as well as intervention duties, should be that of the ability of relevant third parties to effectively intervene and orient the protection of their fundamental rights as given by the "integration" options chosen by the digital platforms. In other terms, the defined regulatory superstructure should have as its "systemic" effect that of enabling third interested parties' "sovereignity" over the digital economy,[71] by shifting onto these the bargaining power in establishing and challenging the platforms' social obligations.

But how much has this procedural flipside of the declared regulatory objectives effectively been mingled in the DMA and DSA' normative architecture?

The next paragraphs will enquire the codified channels of stakeholder engagement in digital platform regulations, considering the two different cases of i) regulators' engagement as stakeholders in a platform-driven regulatory process and of ii) third parties impacted by platforms' organizational and governance choices regarding employed digital infrastructures.

---

[68] Recital 79 DSA.

[69] Recital 79 DSA.

[70] Recital 79 DSA.

[71] On the notion of digital sovreignity, see Andriychuk (2021), p. 261.

4 Regulators' Engagement in the DSA and DMA

The first active "stakeholders" to be considered in the realm of digital platform regulations are the regulatory market authorities, which have the public mandate of supervising the protection of individual, collective and public interests that may be affected by the described systemic reach of digital platforms' business activities.

In the considered regulatory framework, regulators do not only have an ex-post enforcement role but are attributed wide margins of technical discretion in designing and substantiating a deliberately open-ended normative super-structure, relying on a dialogical regulatory format.[72]

On the side of traditional enforcement activities of the "standard" regulatory layer of the digital platform regulations, the European Commission is given in both the DMA and DSA a rich regulatory toolkit for securing effective enforcement options.[73] The European Commission's enforcement tasks are further complemented by the role of national authorities, which are expected to submit national compliance reports to the European Commission[74] and are granted the residual competence to investigate breaches occurring at the national level and to send their findings to trigger the European Commission's enforcement.[75]

In addition to the traditional enforcement role, the new regulations envisage an even more active involvement of the European Commission, and, as a reflex, within the limits of their competences also for national authorities, not only for the establishment of the adequate sanctions in the event of normative violations (ex post perspective), but also for the (ex ante) definition of the regulatory burden to be specifically tailored upon the features of monitored market players.

From this second standpoint, both the DMA and DSA turn to the iterative and peer-reviewed methodologies that have been well embodied by commitment decisions in competition law cases,[76] coalescing the dialogical flexibilities of such regulatory techniques in the general ex ante regulatory template. In particular, the regulatory choice proposed by the new framework is that of a "semi-flexible" approach, involving a qualitatively progressive regulatory burden that relies on a constant involvement of regulators for the purposes of:

(i) ***a "movable" application of stricter legal regimes***. This is well reflected in the dynamic definition of gatekeepers captured by the DMA. Art. 4(1) DMA provides that the Commission may, also on its own initiative "reconsider, amend or repeal at any moment a designation decision", in accordance with the change of the factual circumstances on which the designation decision was originally based or on the reconsideration of the information upon which the initial decision was grounded.

[72] Andriychuk (2021), p. 261.

[73] See Chapter V DMA and Chapter IV DSA.

[74] Art. 11 DMA. see also art. 29 DMA that establishes the Commission's discretion in triggering a non-compliance procedure based on reasons for the efficient allocation of resources.

[75] Art. 20 DMA.

[76] Svetiev (2020), pp. 61–71.

Moreover, the Commission has outright reviewing duties of the list of gatekeepers, with the power to amplify or otherwise amend it.

Similarly, also the DSA lays down a gradually more burdensome normative regime, structured on both quantitative and qualitative parameters. On the first side, as already mentioned, it establishes stricter obligations for very large online platforms and very large online search engines to manage systemic risks. To these ends, under art. 33 DSA, the definition of the quantitative thresholds for the qualification of these very large online platforms can be changed by the European Commission's delegated acts, which may adjust the number of average monthly active recipients of the service in the Union,[77] in accordance with a population increase or with "market and technological development". Interestingly, in accordance with art. 33(4) DSA, the adoption of a decision of a very large online platform or very large search engine must be preceded by a period of ten working days in which the concerned platform shall be given the opportunity to submit its views on the Commission's preliminary findings and on its intention to designate the online platform or the online search engine as a very large online platform or as a very large online search engine, respectively. The Commission shall take due account of the views submitted by the provider concerned.

As occurs under the DMA, thus, also in the DSA, the European Commission is entrusted with the power of flexibly setting the ultimate standard determining the applicability of a more severe regulatory burden. This movable regime in turn intersects with the further progressive obligations for online platforms directly envisaged by the law: in this respect, based on the nature of the provided service, the DSA codifies additional obligations applicable to providers of hosting services;[78] providers of online platforms;[79] providers of online platforms allowing consumers to conclude distance contracts with traders.[80]

In both of the considered regulations, a higher compliance burden equals to a sort of indirect behavioral sanction for the riskier business activity detected.[81]

(ii) ***a "case-by-case" development of compliance strategies.*** The DMA not only enables the Commission to further specify the obligations under art. 6, but also entrusts the regulator with the possibility to open a proceeding pursuant art. 20 DMA, through which the Commission may adopt, *on its own initiative or at the request of a gatekeeper*, an implementing act as defined art. 8(2) DMA "specifying the measures that the gatekeeper concerned is to implement in order to effectively comply with the obligations laid down in Articles 6 and 7". Moreover, under art. 8(3) DMA a gatekeeper itself can reach out to the regulator in order to know whether

---

[77] Art. 33(1) DSA sets the threshold for very large online platforms and very large search engines in a number of average monthly active recipients of the service in the Union equal to or higher than 45 million.

[78] Art. 16–18 DSA.

[79] Art. 19–28 DSA.

[80] Art. 29–32 DSA.

[81] Andriychuk (2021), p. 261. In this sense the framework could be subsumed in the scheme of default penalty rules. See Maskin (2006), p. 557.

"the measures that that gatekeeper intends to implement or has implemented to ensure compliance with Articles 6 and 7 are effective in achieving the objective of the relevant obligation in the specific circumstances of the gatekeeper". In these cases, the interactive availability of the regulator has to be calibrated upon the principles of equal treatment, proportionality and good administration.[82]

Compliance strategies may however be tailored also at procedural level in respect to timing aspects. In relation to gatekeepers' interoperability obligations, for example, the Commission may, exceptionally and upon a reasoned request by the gatekeeper, extend, in accordance with art. 7(6) DMA, the time limits for compliance where the gatekeepers demonstrates that this is necessary to ensure effective interoperability and to maintain the necessary level of security, including end-to-end encryption.

Also the DSA considers some form of active involvement of the European Commission in the design of tailored regulatory solutions, to be however more traditionally found, differently than what occurs in the DMA, at soft law level integrating the codified regulatory principles.

Under art. 35(3) DSA, the Commission, in cooperation with the Digital Services Coordinators, may issue guidelines on the fulfilment of the monitoring duties over systemic risks by very large online platforms to present best practices and recommend possible measures, having due regard to the possible consequences of the measures on the fundamental rights of all parties involved. Moreover, the Commission is demanded to support the development of voluntary standards in some specific matters, as the templates for communicating with the recipients of the service in a user-friendly manner on restrictions resulting from terms and conditions and changes thereto; the implementation of interoperability obligations; or the definition of auditing strategies of very large online platforms.[83] Ultimately, the Commission shall promote the drawing up of codes of conduct, "taking into account in particular the specific challenges of tackling different types of illegal content and systemic risks, in accordance with Union law in particular on competition and the protection of personal data".[84]

As can be derived from the traced framework, the manners of compliance may vary in accordance with an operator- and service-dependent assessment along the lines of a functional and "forward looking" compliance methodology.[85]

(iii) ***"Reflexive" or "dialogic" techniques at enforcement level.*** The identified modes for regulators' engagement at the initial stages of the regulatory design chain open up further venues of dialogue also at the final enforcement phase. The initial moments of the regulatory dynamic already suggest the blurring of the commonly accepted distinction between ex ante compliance dictates and ex post enforcement interventions. Indeed, the extension of tailored compliance requirements already

[82] Art. 8(3) DMA.

[83] See art. 44 DSA.

[84] Art. 45 DSA.

[85] Armour et al. (2020), p. 1.

equals to an indirect form of enforcement of the standard requirements that form the general regulatory baseline and that the European Commission is called to dialectically substantiate. Despite this structural blend between conventionally different junctures of the regulatory cycle, also at the final level of enforcement some type of dialogic techniques can be identified in the assessed regulatory framework. In the DMA, for example, in case of non-compliance with the different regulatory layers identified above, the Commission can adopt an implementing act of non-compliance under art. 29 DMA, where the Authority is asked to illustrate the findings relating to non-compliance. Before formally adopting the non-compliance decision, the Commission has a duty to communicate its preliminary finding to the interested gatekeeper, foreshadowing to the concerned undertaking the measures it considers taking or that the gatekeeper should "take in order to effectively address the preliminary findings".[86] The initiative of this regulatory dialogue preceding the issue of a sanction for non-compliance, evidently enables the gatekeeper to anticipatedly remedy its non-compliant behavior, in case it is possible, so as to avert the issuing of a sanction, or to anyhow influence the choice and amount of the potential penalty,[87] either in a favorable manner through a collaborative attitude, or in a negative way in case the gatekeeper is not sufficiently responsive to the regulator's solicitations.[88]

Also the DSA establishes some form of dialogical enforcement practices, first of all enabled by digital platforms' organizational requirements regarding the prompt "communication" with relevant authorities. Digital platforms are indeed required to appoint a single point of contact to enable them to communicate directly, by electronic means, with Member States' authorities, the Commission and the Board referred to in Article 61 for the application of the DMA.[89] The platforms which do not have an establishment in the Union, but which offer services in the Union shall designate, in writing, a legal or natural person to act as their legal representative in one of the Member States where the provider offers its services. The legal representative shall act as a direct communication point for the Member States' competent authorities, the Commission and the Board, on all issues necessary for the receipt of, compliance with and enforcement of decisions issued in relation to the DSA.[90] Moreover, all very large online platforms are required under art. 41 DSA to appoint a compliance officer which is meant to collaborate with the Digital Services Coordinator of establishment and the Commission for enforcement purposes. In this respect, the head of the compliance function shall report directly to the management body the information eventually transmitted by the regulator, raising concerns and

---

[86] Art. 29(3) DSA.

[87] The DMA envisages various penalty measures: periodic penalty payments under art. 31; fines up to the 1% of the total worldwide turnover in the precedent financial year under art. 30(2) DMA; and fines up to the 20% of the total worldwide turnover in the precedent financial year for the violation of the provisions under art. 5;6; 7 DMA under 30(1) DMA.

[88] Andriychuk (2021), p. 261.

[89] Art. 11 DSA.

[90] Art. 13 DSA.

warning, when needed, the same management body about detected risks, also of enforcement interventions.

On the same enforcement side, the Digital Services Coordinator has the power to accept commitments offered by the providers of intermediary services to strengthen compliance with normative dictates. Following art. 51(2) lett. a) DSA, the Digital Services Coordinator can make those commitments binding. Moreover, the Digital Services Coordinator has the power to take further measures in case all other powers to effectively bring about an infringement have been exhausted and the infringement has not been remedied and is causing serious harm. These further measures listed under art. 51(3) DSA enable the Digital Services Coordinator to require the management body of the relevant provider to adopt and submit an action plan for the termination of the infringement, or even to order the temporary restriction of access of recipients to the service concerned by the infringement or, only where that is not technically feasible, to the online interface of the provider of intermediary services on which the infringement takes place.

Finally, where extraordinary circumstances lead to a serious threat to public security or public health in the Union or in significant parts of it, and a "crisis" in the sense of art. 36 DSA occurs, the Commission may adopt a decision, requiring one or more providers of very large online platforms or of very large online search engines to take some specific measures. These may regard the conduction of an assessment regarding how the provided service contributes to the crisis; the implementation of remedies mitigating the threat; the activation of a regular communication channel with the Commission so as to inform the Authority about the progress and effectiveness of the measures taken.

The traced provisions confirm the persistence of an interactive and dynamic process also in the pathological moment of enforcement, aligning this last fragment of the regulatory loop to the other initial moments of the setting of the regulatory burden (sub. i) and its needed adjustment and tailoring (sub. ii).

Overall, each of the described moments of interaction appear to structure a type of regulatory contract,[91] which contingently identifies the specific obligations that the considered digital undertaking should fulfil so as to more effectively attain the set social interests targeted by the considered regulations.

However, the fruitful activation of the said cooperative regulatory technique faces the obstacle of the structural information asymmetries between supervisors and the market affecting, with even more severe traits, the digital platforms ecosystem.

The fueling of relevant information flows towards the regulator is an aspect to which the DSA gives specific consideration as an outright pre-condition for the Commission's or the Digital Services Coordinator's engagement for the safeguard of collectively and publicly relevant rights. In this respect, for example, art. 24(5) DSA requires providers of intermediary services to submit to a publicly accessible machine-readable database managed by the Commission, the decisions and the

[91] Svetiev (2020), p. 64.

statements of reasons issued by the same providers to any affected recipients of the service for any restriction of the visibility of specific items of information provided by the recipient of the service; suspension of termination of monetary payments; or even suspension or termination of the recipient of the service's account in accordance with art. 17(1) DSA. The recalled provision well matches the obligation under art. 13 DSA similarly binding providers of intermediary services to "make publicly available, in a machine-readable format and in an easily accessible manner, at least once a year, clear, easily comprehensible reports on any content moderation that they engaged in during the relevant period".

The requirement to disclose relevant information in a machine-readable format may suggest the intention of the European legislator to facilitate the adoption by competent Authorities of risk-sensitive technological solutions (so called reg-tech solution) for a more rapid and customized governance of supervisory processes.[92] These solutions appear to be particularly suited for an anatomically technology-intensive market as that of digital platforms.

Although the creation of a solid information basis proves essential for molding regulators' bargaining effort with digital platforms at the variously detected regulatory levels, it may also underpin the risk of "regulatory capture" of the same supervisory authorities by digital platforms.[93] This risk proves to be greater in case the regulatory process faces substantial timing pressures. Moreover, regulators' engagement may give rise to solutions, which over time result to be increasingly standardized,[94] this undermining concrete protection needs.

This is why, despite its undoubted innovative character, the sustainable governance of digital markets needs a further layer of engagement within the described regulatory circle: that of directly interested parties for the unmediated protection of their fundamental rights and the development of truly socially responsible business models by digital platforms.

[92] Although the reflection on regtech tools has mainly originated in the financial compliance sector, innovative regulatory and supervisory solutions relying on digital tools may be extremely relevant also for digital markets' compliance. See Arner et al. (2016), p. 79. On the limits of automated regulatory tools, see Pasquale (2019), p. 2.

[93] Already observing the risk of regulatory capture in economic regulation Stigler (1971), p. 3. In relation to digital markets, see the considerations by Carugati (27 February 2023); Ranchordas and Vinci (2023).

[94] The risk of standardization of regulatory solutions appears to equally arise in other co-regulatory settings as that of regulatory sandboxes. For an assessment of the risks arising from experimentation policies, see Philipsen et al. (2021), p. 1128.

5 Third Interested Parties' Engagement: Contestability as Group-Based Digital Sovereignty

In line with the declared objectives of promoting digital markets' contestability and systemic risk management, the considered regulations also take the more ambitious step of setting means for the involvement of interested third parties in the orientation of digital platforms' business activities. Stakeholder involvement is meant to support the above-described regulators' engagement, also in view of public authorities' limited budgetary and human resources. Moreover, if correctly internalized within the platforms' functioning, it could prevent public authorities' more severe adjustment of the compliance burden.

In the DMA and DSA, third parties' engagement appears to take the three major forms of technological; political and businesses' informal dialogue with stakeholders.

On the technological side, the DMA envisages specific technology-related rights of business users, alternative providers of services and end users enabled by interoperability rights regarding the provided operating system, hardware and software;[95] the right to uninstall any software application on the operating system of the provider;[96] and the right to the portability of data provided by the end users or generated through the activity of the end user in the context of the use of the relevant core platform service.[97] To advance the right to data portability, the platform is required to provide means to facilitate the provision of continuous and real-time access to relevant data.[98] In the same vein, the more specific category of advertisers and publishers, and of third parties authorized by advertisers and publishers, is entitled to have access to the performance measuring tools of the gatekeepers and to the data necessary for advertisers and publishers to carry out their own independent verification of the advertisements inventory.[99] Access to these technological facilities enables advertisers and publishers to run their own verification and measurement tools to assess the performance of the core platform services provided for by the gatekeepers.[100]

Similarly, the DSA formulates some form of technology-driven interaction between third interested parties and online platforms. In particular, the regulation requires under art. 16 DSA providers of hosting services to enact easy to access and user-friendly mechanisms to allow any individual or entity to notify, also exclusively by electronic means, to the provider of the presence on their service of specific items of information that the individual or entity considers to be illegal content. Moreover, particular attention is given under art. 40 DSA to the issue of data access in respect to providers of very large online platforms and of very large online search

[95] Art. 6(7) DMA.

[96] Art. 6(3) DMA.

[97] Art. 6(9) DMA.

[98] Art. 6(9) DMA.

[99] Art. 6(8) DMA.

[100] Art. 6(8) DMA.

engines, which shall give without undue delay access also to real-time data to researchers, including those affiliated to not for profit bodies, organizations and associations who perform research that contributes to the detection, identification and understanding of platforms' systemic risks.[101]

Although mainly providing the obligation on the side of gatekeepers and online providers to open up their technological assets and data to the "communication" with the technological equipment of users, the cited framework also indirectly enables these same users to verify the openness of gatekeepers' digital infrastructures, empowering them to engage in a technological "dialogue" between their own technologies and the ones of the relevant platforms. The structural flexibilities required by interoperability and portability obligations avert users' lock-in situations and thus prevent the gatekeepers' and online platforms' technological code from limiting users' actions.[102]

Thanks to the described technological "mobility", users can more freely use their technologies in connection with digital platforms and this is supposed to incentivize providers of online services to safeguard the interests and rights of their users so as to keep them attached to their services (from which they may easily turn away thanks to interoperability capabilities). In this light, the mentioned requirements imply a technology-driven engagement of users purportedly monitoring and thus evaluating digital platforms' technical structural choices.

In addition to technology-channeled interactions, third interested parties are expected to have an active role also for the purposes of the supervision of digital platforms' compliance in accordance with the above-described regulatory cycle.

When it comes to compliance decision under art. 8(2) DMA, the Commission shall publish a non-confidential summary of the case and of the measures it is considering to enact so as to enable third interested parties to provide comments.[103] Moreover, third parties may be consulted by the Commission in case of the issuing of a non-compliance decision under art. 29(4) DMA.

On a different note, it is interesting to recall that the gatekeepers' compliance function, which is in direct contact with the regulatory authority, shall inform and advise not only the management but also the employees of the gatekeeper on compliance matters.[104] Employees' interest over the compliance degrees of the digital platforms they work for is becoming an increasingly important driver of employees' collective action, as fuelled by specific ideological conceptions regarding a business' research and development activities.

---

[101] Art. 40(8) DSA: "Upon a duly substantiated application from researchers, the Digital Services Coordinator of establishment shall grant such researchers the status of 'vetted researchers' for the specific research referred to in the application and issue a reasoned request for data access to a provider of very large online platform or of very large online search engine a pursuant to paragraph 4 (…)".

[102] On the importance of interoperability see Hovenkamp (2021), p. 1952.

[103] Art. 8(6) DMA.

[104] Art. 28(5) lett. b) DMA. See also art. 41(3) lett. d) DSA.

Amazon's workers, for example, have lately threatened a massive walkout from the company on grounds of the company's climate failure, forcing the CEO to commit to a so-called "Climate Pledge".[105] As the case well illustrates, businesses' compliance choices as advocated by employees strictly intersect with corporate strategies. This is further confirmed by the recent involvement of Microft-owned Open AI's workers in the discussion regarding AI safety, which has led to the temporary firing of the CEO Sam Altman. Also on this occasion, employees' activism and threat of massive resignation has had a decisive impact on the board's decision to hire the CEO back.[106]

At financial level, employees' engagement in digital platforms is to be traced back to the large use of stock options or profit participation units (PPUs)[107] enacted for incentivizing employees' willingness to actively contribute to the business' activities. As apparent, the greater the financial interests of employees in the corporation are, the more they are likely to engage in an investor-styled behavior towards their employer.

Especially in this last case, the creation of dialogical channels fueling employment relationships' transparency and trust proves essential. If ordinary corporate governance systems do not pay much attention to the board-employees' interaction,[108] also the regulatory framework specifically regarding digital platforms has not further delved into this particular aspect. A more direct engagement of employees in respect to businesses' compliance strategies may be relevant for advancing the same business and regulators' interface on compliance matters.

While the DMA majorly focuses on stimulating the dialogue between gatekeepers' third interested parties and regulators, the DSA promotes a more informal dialogue between online platforms and relevant stakeholders for the purposes of platforms' private and self-regulatory options.

This holds true in particular for providers of very large online platforms and very online search engines. These have the twofold obligation of (i) mapping systemic risks stemming from the design or functioning of their services and (algorithmic) systems—or from the use made of their services—[109] and (ii) to put in place reasonable, proportionate and effective mitigation measures tailored to the specific identified systemic risks, with particular consideration to the impacts of such measures on fundamental rights.[110] To these specific ends, the DSA encourages online platforms' cooperation with different categories of stakeholders.

A first category relates to "trusted flaggers" in accordance with art. 22 DSA, which is an entity that has demonstrated a particular expertise and competence for the purposes of detecting, identifying and notifying illegal content; is independent

[105] See Amazon Employees for Climate Justice (26 May 2023).

[106] Cooper (3 January 2024).

[107] Aran (2024).

[108] The German model is an exception.

[109] Art. 34 DSA.

[110] Art. 35 DSA.

from any provider of online platforms; and carries out its activities for the purposes of submitting notices diligently, accurately and objectively. Trusted flaggers have the task of submitting notices of illegal content to the platform and are thus expected to have a specific knowledge about digital platforms' systemic risks. Therefore, these entities' opinions may be relevant in aiding digital businesses in the development of strategies for the detection and mitigation of systemic risks.[111]

In second stance, large digital platforms may coordinate with other providers of online platforms or of online search engines, establishing means of information regarding systemic risks, also through the setting of shared standards codified in codes of conduct.[112]

An important role in the advancement of the management of systemic risks by providers of digital services is further given by organizations carrying out independent audits under art. 37 DSA. These entities shall provide the cooperation and assistance necessary for digital platforms to conduct the audit regarding the compliance features of their businesses. By doing so, the organizations conducting independent audits have the task of providing the digital platforms with strategic advice for filling eventual knowledge gaps or for highlighting the specific risks related to the different "sides" of multisided platforms' business activities.

Interestingly, needed insights should be drawn by large digital providers also at vertical level, from recipients of the services, as business users or consumers. To these ends, digital platforms are asked to take awareness-raising measures, providing the recipients of the needed information to understand the reality of systemic risks. These actions are evidently a precondition for grasping from the recipients of the digital services feedbacks and reactions that may be useful for designing more effective responsive measures, which should take into particular account the interests of those stakeholders who bear the consequences of the platforms' strategic choices firsthand,[113] including children.[114]

To these specific ends, the DSA appears to further amplify—although through a non-binding provision—the participative governance techniques of digital platforms. In recital 90 DSA, providers of very large online platforms and very large search engines are recommended to ensure that their risk assessment and mitigation procedures are rooted "in the best available information and scientific insights". In order to do so, the groups which are "most impacted by the risks and the measures they take" shall be consulted by the concerned undertakings. In particular the recital suggests the involvement within risk assessments of "representatives of the recipients of the service, representatives of groups potentially impacted by their services, independent experts and civil society organisations". Consultations with these groups should be integrated into platforms' methodologies for assessing the risks and designing mitigation measures, including, as appropriate, through the

[111] Art. 35(1) lett. g) DSA.
[112] Art. 35(1) lett. h) DSA.
[113] Art. 35(1) lett. i) DSA.
[114] Art. 35(1) lett. j) DSA.

employment "of surveys, focus groups, round tables, and other consultation and design methods".

Although only in the recitals, the DSA thus ultimately appears to consider more specific dialogical methods with relevant stakeholders. The proposed methodologies interestingly suggest the opportunity—not yet the obligation—for digital platforms to ground the identification of systemic risks and the development of adequate remedial strategies in empirical and even scientific investigations with interested parties. The recommended engagement tools should thus ensure an ongoing and updated monitoring of the constantly new emerging threats to social values arising from a fast-changing digital setting thanks to the confrontation with other members of society, which may be passive addressees of the enacted activities. For digital platforms, it should be an exercise of mutual learning, whereas for the interested third parties a precious occasion of activism.

As far as the categories of stakeholders are concerned, recital 90 DSA testifies the importance of assessing systemic risks arising from developed technological solutions in accordance with a cohort-based approach sensitive to the adverse impacts onto specific groups of stakeholders. This reflects the acknowledgment that a regulatory perspective solely focused on the business-individual subject relationship, as the one adopted by most data protection laws as the GDPR, is incapable of guaranteeing effectiveness of protection of involved legal interests.[115]

Only a group-based interface with "tech giants" may be relevant for the construction of the counterpowers needed for the tangible attainment of collective digital sovereignty; an intuition the DSA has however only marginally substantiated.

6 Conclusions

The chapter has questioned i) the extent to which the European regulatory framework regarding digital platforms under the DMA and DSA addresses platforms' social responsibilities arising from their technology-driven businesses and ii) whether co-regulatory techniques based on the involvement with relevant stakeholders have been envisaged in order to identify and reduce the adverse impacts to digitally provoked systemic risks. Ultimate objective of the study has been that of evaluating, in accordance with the said substantial and procedural parameters, the consideration, within the said regulations, of digital markets' sustainability aspects.

Against this backdrop, the evaluation of the legal interests targeted by the assessed framework confirms the European legislator's intent to depart from a purely efficiency- and competition-driven conception of the well-functioning of digital platforms' markets. Along these lines, the regulatory technique deployed for the attainment of these objectives appears to align with the methodologies currently

[115] Along these lines, some strand of the literature has called for a group-based approach to privacy: see Floridi (2014), p. 1; Floridi (2016), p. 83; Van der Sloot (2016), p. 159.

adopted by general European sustainable business laws, which increasingly require the involvement of interested external stakeholders within businesses' organizational and strategic decision-making processes.

Similarly, as the conducted analysis demonstrates, the DMA and DSA integrate within the frame of digital platforms' regulation both methods of public and private co-regulation, variously relying on the three main tools of i) negotiation; ii) monitoring; and iii) peer review by relevant third interested parties in respect to digital platforms' institutional choices. From this standpoint, it appears that the analysed regulations have internalised some regulatory mechanisms that can be ascribed to the realm of so-called experimentalist governance,[116] which genetically aims at coordinating undertaking's decisions with the interests of different stakeholders at both vertical (top down, public authorities and bottom up, consumers) and horizontal (e.g. other competing or non-competing businesses) level with the function of filling empirically grounded protection needs.

Indeed, the DMA and DSA load digital platforms with result-based governance structures for the pursuing of systemic interests that public regulation or traditional supervisory arrangements fail to adequately address. This failure drives the urgency of incentivising socially responsible practices by powerful digital market operators.

To these ends, the digital platforms' reflexive stances over the iterative monitoring excercised by regulators (mainly the European Commission) appears to be effectively promoted along the lines of an innovative pyramidal architecture variously blending ex ante compliance and ex post enforcement measures. However, in order to avert some natural risks arising from regulators' dialogue with digital platforms, as the recalled risk of regulatory capture or of standardised decision-making, the confrontation of digital platforms with third interested stakeholders, as the (business) users of service, proves essential for the enactment of digital businesses socially responsible governance choices.[117]

Although equally structured around dialogical methods, this second operational line seems, to date, to be structurally closer to a more traditional paradigm of self-regulation, lacking direct enforcement channels by affected parties[118] and eventually depending on the eventual ambitions of digital businesses to secure reputational gains.[119]

As noted, the DMA and DSA establish relevant technology-related enforceable rights as the rights over data portability and infrastructure interoperability and foresee the possibility of interested parties to express their viewpoint to the regulator. However, the margins of direct contestability of digital platforms by non-institutional stakeholders, outside established technological or regulatory channels, still prove to

[116] Ranchordas (2015), p. 871; Sabel and Zeitlin (2008), p. 271; Svetiev (2010), p. 79; Monti and Rangoni (2022), p. 851.

[117] Assessing digital platforms' responsibilities from the perspective of their global value chain, Micklitz and Villanueva (2021), p. 263.

[118] Observing the difficulties in distinguishing co-regulatory tools from self-regulation at the implementation stage, Bassan (2023), p. 1103.

[119] Rasche et al. (2022), pp. 312–313.

be weak, as the case of employees' engagement shows, in view of the absence of more specific procedures of verification of expressed positions or even of complaints procedures in case employed mitigation strategies do not prove to be effective.[120]

This path has not yet been sufficiently concretised by the European legislator, which considers the relevance of group-based engagement only within the recalled recital 90 DSA, without tracing clearer procedures for it. An opportunity the currently introduced digital platform regulations appear to have missed, overlooking the risk that a large number of subjects will be harmed by the same harmful practice and with that further weakening, at its foundations, an already fragile collective enforcement system in European digital markets.[121]

References

Akman P (2022) Regulating competition in digital platform markets: a critical assessment of the framework and approach of the EU Digital Markets Act. ELR 47:85–114

Amazon Employees for Climate Justice (2023) Amazon is failing its own climate pledge. Medium. https://amazonemployees4climatejustice.medium.com/amazon-is-failing-its-own-climate-pledge-c6ff60fceccd

Andriychuk O (2021) Shaping the new modality of the digital markets: the impact of the DSA/DMA proposals on inter-platform competition. World Compet 44:261–286. https://kluwerlawonline.com/journalarticle/World+Competition/44.3/WOCO2021017

Andriychuk O (2023) EU digital competition law: the socio-legal foundations. Camb Yearb Eur Stud, pp 1–23

Aran Y (2024) RSU time bomb: regulating startup equity compensation in the unicorn era. In: Broughman B, De Fontenay ED (eds) Research handbook on the structure of private equity and venture capital. Elgar Publishing, Cheltenham, forthcoming

Armour J, Gordon JN, Min G (2020) Taking compliance seriously. Yale J. on Reg. 37:1–66

Arner DW, Barberis JN, Buckley RP (2016) The emergence of Regtech 2.0: from know your customer to know your data. J Fin Transform 44:79–86

Ayres I, Gertner R (1989) Filling gaps in incomplete contracts: an economic theory of default rules. Yale Law J 99:87–130

Balboni P, Francis KE (2022) Data protection as corporate social responsibility. Edward Elgar, Cheltenham

Bamberger KA, Lobel O (2017) Platform market power. BTLJ 32:1051–1091

Bassan F (2021) Digital platforms and global law. Edward Elgar, Cheltenham

Bassan F (2023) Digital platforms and blockchains: the age of participated regulation. EBLR 34:1103–1133

Belloso NM, Petit N (2023) The EU Digital Markets Act (DMA): a competition hand in a regulatory glove. ELR 48:391–409

[120] Stakeholders' complaints procedures have been foreseen in the first proposal of the proposed directive on corporate sustainability due diligence (art. 9).

[121] Articles 42 and 52 DMA open the door for "representative actions brought against infringements by gatekeepers of provisions of [the DMA] that harm or may harm the collective interests of consumers" under the RAD. However, as known, the RAD majourly regards consumers, and thus leave out, business users, including SMEs. See Hornkohl and Ribera Martínez (20 November 2023).

Beretta G (2021) The new rules for reporting by sharing and gig economy platforms under the OECD and EU initiatives. EC Tax Rev 30:31–38
Beuc (2023) Connected but unfairly treated. Consumer Survey Results on the Fairness of Digital Markets. https://www.beuc.eu/sites/default/files/publications/BEUC-X-2023-113_Fairness_of_the_digital_environment_survey_results.pdf
Bietti E (2023) A genealogy of digital platform regulation. Geo Law Tech Rev 7:3–68
Black J (2001) Decentring regulation: understanding the role of regulation and self-regulation in a "post-regulatory" world. Curr Leg Problems 64:103–146
Bosetti L (2022) Global reporting initiative standards. In: Idowu S, Schmidpeter R, Capaldi N, Zu L, Del Baldo M, Abreu R (eds) Encyclopedia of sustainable management. Springer, Cham, pp 1706–1719
Bradford A (2023) Digital empires: the global battle to regulate technology. OUP, Oxford
Busch C, Mak V (2021) Putting the Digital Services Act into context: bridging the gap between EU consumer law and platform regulation. EuCML 10:109–114
Carugati C (2023) A model for a participative approach to digital competition regulation. Policy Brief. https://www.bruegel.org/policy-brief/model-participative-approach-digital-competition-regulation#:~:text=The%20participative%20approach%20involves%20three,demonstrate%20compliance%20to%20the%20regulator
Cohen JE (2016) The regulatory state in the information age. Theor Inq Law 17:369–414
Cohen JE (2024) Informational capitalism as phase shift: challenges for digital constitutionalism. In: Giovanni De Gregorio G, Pollicino O, Valcke P (eds) Oxford handbook of digital constitutionalism. Oxford University Press, forthcoming 2024. https://ssrn.com/abstract=4667197
Colangelo G (2022) The European Digital Markets Act and Antitrust Enforcement: a Liaison Dangereuse. ELR 5:597–621
Colangelo G, Maggiolino M (2018) Data accumulation and the privacy–antitrust interface: insights from the Facebook Case. IDPL 8:224–239
Cooper P (2024) What OpenAI teaches us about employee power. HR. https://www.hrmagazine.co.uk/content/comment/what-openai-teaches-us-about-employee-power
Cottino G (2005) Contrattualismo e istituzionalismo (Variazioni sul tema da uno spunto di Giorgio Oppo). Riv soc 4:693–709
Crémer J et al (2023) Fairness and contestability in the Digital Markets Act. Yale J Regul 40:973–1012
De Gregorio G, Dunn P (2022) The European risk-based approaches: connecting constitutional dots in the digital age. CMLR 59:473–500
De Gregorio G, Radu R (2022) Digital constitutionalism in the new era of Internet governance. Int J Law Inf Technol 30:68–87
De Streel A, Feasey R, Krämer J, Monti G (2021) Making the Digital Markets Act more resilient an effective. Cerre Centre on Regulation in Europe
Di Porto F, Grote T, Volpi G, Invernizzi R (2021) "I See Something you Don't See". A computational analysis of the Digital Services Act and Digital Markets Act. Stanford Comput Antitrust 1:85–116
Dörr S (2022) Corporate digital responsibility. Managing corporate responsibility and sustainability in the digital age. Springer, Berlin
Eder N (2023) Making systemic risk assessments work: how the DSA creates a virtuous loop to address the societal harms of content moderation. https://papers.ssrn.com/sol3/papers.cfm?abstract_id=4491365
European Parliament (2023) Artificial intelligence, democracy and elections. https://www.europarl.europa.eu/thinktank/en/document/EPRS_BRI(2023)751478
Ezrachi A (2017) Sponge. J Antitrust Enforce 5:49–75
Falce V (2021) Digital markets between regulation and competition policy. Converging agendas. Eur J Priv Technol 1:10–18
Finck M (2018) Digital co-regulation: designing a supranational legal framework for the platform economy. ELR 41:33–67

Finmanò F (2023) Art. 41 della Costituzione e valori ESG: Esiste davvero una responsabilità sociale dell'impresa? Giur Comm 5:777–806
Floridi L (2014) Open data, data protection and group privacy. Philos Technol 27:1–3
Floridi L (2016) Group privacy: a defence and an interpretation. In: Taylor L, Floridi L, Van der Sloot B (eds) Group privacy: new challenges of data technologies. Springer, Cham, pp 83–100
Frosio G, Geiger C (2023) Taking fundamental rights seriously in the Digital Service Act's Platform Liability Regime. ELJ 29:31–77
Gilbert DU, Rasche A, Waddock S (2011) Accountability in a global economy: The emergence of international accountability standards. Business Ethics Quarterly, 21:23–44
Grady P (2023) The AI act should be technology-neutral. Centre for Data Innovation. https://www2.datainnovation.org/2023-ai-act-technology-neutral.pdf
Graef I (2015) Market definition and market power in data: the case of online platforms. World Compet 38:473–506
Greenberg BA (2016) Rethinking technological neutrality. Minn Law Rev 100:1495–1562
Hart O, Moore J (1988) Incomplete contracts and renegotiation. Econometrica 56:755–785
Hart O, Zingales N (2022) New corporate governance. Univ Chic Bus Law Rev 1:196–216
Hornkohl L, Ribera Martínez A (2023) Collective actions and the Digital Markets Act: a bird without wings. Kluwer Competition Law Blog. https://competitionlawblog.kluwercompetitionlaw.com/2023/11/20/collective-actions-and-the-dma-a-bird-without-wings/
Hovenkamp H (2021) Antitrust and platform monopoly. Yale Law J 130:1952–2273
Husovec M (2023) Rising above liability: the Digital Services Act as a blueprint for the second generation of global internet rules. BTLJ 38. https://papers.ssrn.com/sol3/papers.cfm?abstract_id=4598426
Ibanez Colomo P (2021) The Draft Digital Markets Act: a legal and institutional analysis. JECLAP 12:561–575
Jastram S, Klingenberg J (2018) Assessing the outcome effectiveness of multi-stakeholder initiatives in the field of corporate social responsibility – the example of the United Nations Global Compact. J Clean Prod 189:775–784
Jones LS, Samples TR (2023) On the systemic importance of digital platforms. Univ Pa J Bus Law 25:141–207
Larouche P, De Streel A (2021) The European Digital Markets Act: a revolution grounded on traditions. JECLAP 12:542–560
Leistner M (2021) The Commission's Vision for Europe's Digital Future: Proposals for the Data Governance Act, the Digital Markets Act and the Digital Services Act—a critical primer. JECLAP 16:778–784
Lianos I (2018) Polycentric competition law. Curr Leg Problems 71:161–213
Lobschat L et al (2021) Corporate digital responsibility. J Bus Res 122:875–888
Maskin E (2006) On the rational for penalty default rules. Fla St Univ Law Rev 33:557–562
Matsumi H, Solove D (2023) The prediction society: algorithms and the problem of forecasting the future. GWU Legal Studies Research Paper No. 2023-58. https://papers.ssrn.com/sol3/papers.cfm?abstract_id=4453869
Maxwell WJ, Bourreau M (2015) Technology neutrality in internet, telecoms and data protection regulation. CTLR 1:1–4
Miazad A (2022) Prosocial antitrust. Hastings Law J 73:1637–1696
Micklitz H, Villanueva AA (2021) Responsibilities of companies in the algorithmic society. In: Micklitz HW, Pollicino O, Reichman A, Simoncini A, Sartor G, De Gregorio G (eds) Constitutional challenges in the algorithmic society. CUP, Cambridge, pp 263–280
Monti G (2021) The digital markets act: improving its institutional design. Eur Compet Reg Law Rev 5:90–101
Monti G, De Streel A (2022) Improving institutional design to better supervise digital platforms. Cerre Centre on Regulation in Europe
Monti G, Rangoni B (2022) Competition policy in action: regulating tech markets with hierarchy and experimentalism. JCMS 60:1106–1123

Möslein F (2019) Certifying 'good' companies. A comparative study of regulatory design. In: Sjafjell B, Bruner CM (eds) Corporate law, corporate governance and sustainability. CUP, Cambridge, pp 669–681
Möslein F (2020) Corporate digital responsibility: Eine aktienrechtliche Skizze. In: Grundmann S, Merkt H, Mülbert PO (eds) Festschrift für Klaus J. Hopt zum 80. Geburtstag am 24. August 2020, De Gruyter, Berlin, Boston, pp 805–824
Möslein F, Sorensen KE (2021) Sustainable corporate governance: a way forward. Eur Company Law 18:7–14
Pasquale F (2019) A rule of persons, not machines: the limits of legal automation. George Wash Law Rev 87:2–55
Persch J (2021) The role of fundamental rights in antitrust law – a special responsibility for undertakings with regulatory power under Art. 102 TFEU? Eur Compet J 17:542–566
Philipsen F, Stamhuis EF, De Jong M (2021) Legal enclaves as a test environment for innovative products: toward legally resilient experimentation policies. Regul Gov 15:1128–1143
Ranchordas S (2015) Innovation experimentalism in the age of the sharing economy. Lewis Clark Law Rev 19:871–924
Ranchordás S (2017) Peers or professionals? The P2P-Economy and competition law. CoRe 1:1–14
Ranchordas S, Vinci V (2023) Regulatory sandboxes and innovation-friendly regulation: between collaboration and capture. Ital J Public Law 1. https://papers.ssrn.com/sol3/papers.cfm?abstract_id=4696442
Rasche A, Gwozdz W, Lund Larsen M, Moon J (2022) Which firms leave multi-stakeholder initiatives? An analysis of delistings from the United Nations Global Compact. Regul Gov 16:309–326
Richter H et al (2021) To break up or regulate big tech? Avenues to constrain private power in the DSA/DMA Package. Max Planck Institute for Innovation & Competition Research Paper No. 21-25
Ricolfi M (2022) Istituzionalismo, contrattualismo, storia. In: Callegari M, Cerrato SA, Desana ER (eds) Studi in Onore di Paolo Montalenti. Giappichelli, Torino, pp 46–63
Robertson VHSE (2022) Excessive data collection: privacy considerations and abuse of dominance in the era of big data. CMLR 57:161–189
Sabel CF, Zeitlin J (2008) Learning from difference: the new architecture of experimentalist governance in the EU experimentalist governance in the EU. ELJ 14:271–327
Schweitzer H (2021) The art to make gatekeeper positions contestable and the challenge to know what is fair: a discussion of the Digital Market Act Proposal'. ZEuP 3:503–544
Seidl T (2023) Commodification and disruption theorizing digital capitalism. Weizenbaum J Digit Soc 3:1–35
Shill G (2023) The social costs (and benefits) of Dual Class Stock. Ala Law Rev 75:221–274
Simoncini A, Longo E (2021) Fundamental rights and the rule of law in the algorithmic society. In: Micklitz HW, Pollicino O, Reichman A, Simoncini A, Sartor G, De Gregorio G (eds) Constitutional challenges in the algorithmic society. CUP, Cambridge, pp 27–41
Siri M, Zhu S (2021) Integrating sustainability in EU Corporate Governance Codes. In: Busch D, Ferrarini G, Grünewald S (eds) Sustainable finance in Europe. Corporate governance, financial stability and financial markets. ESBMCL Palgrave MacMillan, London, pp 175–224
Sjafjell B, Mähönen J (2022) Corporate purpose and the misleading shareholder vs stakeholder dichotomy. Bond Law Rev 34:69–112
Stigler GJ (1971) The theory of economic regulation. Bell J Econ Manag Sci 2:3–21
Svetiev Y (2010) Networked competition governance in the EU: delegation, decentralization or experimentalist architecture ? In: Sabel CF, Zeitlin J (eds) Experimentalist governance in the European Union: towards a new architecture. OUP, Oxford, pp 79–120
Svetiev Y (2020) Experimentalist competition law and the regulation of markets. Hart, Oxford
Van der Sloot B (2016) Do groups have a right to protect their group interest in privacy and should they? Peeling the Onion of Rights and Interests Protected under Article 8 ECHR. In: Taylor L,

Floridi L, Van der Sloot B (eds) Group privacy: new challenges of data technologies. Springer, Cham, pp 159–173
Yokoi T et al (28 April 2023) Infusing digital responsibility into your organization. Harvard Business Review. https://hbr.org/2023/04/infusing-digital-responsibility-into-your-organization
Zuboff S (2019) The age of surveillance capitalism: the fight for a human future at the new frontier of power. Public Affairs, New York

Below the DMA-Threshold: Access Between Data Protection and Unfair Competition

Rainer Kulms

Abstract The Digital Markets Act is silent on data access to platforms or *de facto* owners of data that do not qualify as gatekeepers. This calls for an evaluation of regulatory strategies for data access below the DMA's gatekeeper threshold. The paper will explore the data access scenarios under the P2B-Regulation, the EU's new Data Act, the GDPR and German competition law. As fairness has become a crucial element of digital market policy, the potential of unfair trading law for developing access standards will be examined. After surveying current sectoral approaches to data access, a recent legislative proposal for access to data in the US automobile industry will be assessed. As unfair trading laws as such are ill-equipped to bring forth workable access criteria, the paper argues for a fine-tuned sectoral access approach to balance the business interests of dataholders against those who depend on access for competing on aftermarkets.

1 Introduction

1.1 Platform Scenarios

The platform economy has ushered in new forms of digital coordination and property configurations. Transaction platforms operate as online marketplaces facilitating the sale of merchandise or services or enabling users to share information and content.[1] Innovation platforms establish a technological foundation where members on one side develop innovations for the other side.[2] Network effects emerge which

[1] Gawer (2021). See the surveys in: Podszun (2020), p. F 19 et seq.; Krause et al. (2017), p. 50 et seq.
[2] Gawer (2021); Schreieck et al. (2022).

R. Kulms (✉)
Affiliate Max Planck Institute for Comparative and International Private Law, Hamburg, Germany
e-mail: kulms@mpipriv.de

D. V. Popović, R. Kulms (eds.), *Repositioning Platforms in Digital Market Law*, European Union and its Neighbours in a Globalized World 15,
https://doi.org/10.1007/978-3-031-69678-7_7

build on relational power, self-governing norms and governance structures that challenge traditional business models.[3] Once platforms have attained market power, gatekeepers are able to exploit users for their own benefit.[4] Unfair trading conditions imposed on platform users stand for stipulations, conferring a disproportionate advantage on a gatekeeper.[5]

Market failure analysis builds on the assumption that platform users should not be required to unduly provide personal data in exchange for access to products or services of a business company.[6] The DMA[7] and the new Data Act[8] usher in a regulatory strategy which concentrates on shaping markets.[9] In its Explanatory Memorandum to the DMA,[10] the EU Commission associates core platform services with problematic access to digital markets, dependencies for business users and unfair practices.[11] Under the presumptions of art. 3 (2) DMA, size and turnover are crucial. Platforms below the DMA-statutory threshold and other digital ecosystems do not qualify as gatekeepers and, hence, are under no obligation to grant business users access to data or their communication facilities, unless art. 20 GDPR applies. For intermediation services below the DMA-threshold, business users and consumers, the P2B-Regulation,[12] unfair trading laws[13] and national contracts laws retain their relevance.[14] The P2B-Regulation associates information asymmetries with a market failure,[15] to be remedied by transparency, fairness and effective redress possibilities for the users of online intermediation services and corporate websites (art.

[3] See the analysis in: Monopolkommission (2021), p. 8 et seq.; Paal and Kieß (2022), p. 5 et seq.

[4] Eifert et al. (2021), p. 988 et seq.

[5] See Recital 33 to the DMA; Schweitzer (2021), p. 516 et seq.; Monopolkommission (2021), p. 17 et seq.

[6] See Economides and Lianos (2021); Botta and Wiedemann (2019), p. 474 et seq.

[7] Regulation (EU) 2022/1925 of 14 September 2022 on contestable and fair markets in the digital sector and amending Directives (EU) 2019/1937 and (EU) 2020/1828 (Digital Markets Act), O.J. L. 265/1 of 12 October 2022.

[8] Regulation (EU) 2023/2854 of 13 December 2023 on harmonised rules on fair access to and use of data and amending Regulation (EU) 2017/2394 and Directive (EU) 2020/1828 (Data Act), O.J. L series of 22 December 2023.

[9] Cf. ibid.; Metzger and Schweitzer (2023), p. 42 et seq.

[10] European Commission, Proposal for a Regulation on contestable and fair markets in the digital sector (Digital Markets Act) – Explanatory Memorndum (Brussels 15 December 2020 (COM (2020) 842 final) (available at https://eur-lex.europa.eu/legal-content/EN/TXT/PDF/?uri=CELEX:52020PC0842).

[11] Ibid.

[12] Regulation (EU) 2019/1150 on promoting fairness and transparency for business users of online intermediation services of 20 June 2019, O.J. L 186/57 of 11 July 2019.

[13] See Drexl, J., in German Federal Ministry of Justice and Consumer Protection, Max Planck Institute for Innovation and Competition (2021), p. 477 et seq. (at 519 et seq.)

[14] Cf. Bania (2022); Wais (2023), p. 589.

[15] See Busch (2022) (-Podszun), art. 7 n. 73.

1 (1), (2)). But art. 9 of the P2B-Regulation stops short of conferring a statutory access right on businesses.[16] Moreover, the Regulation remains silent on the transition from purely contractual structures via hybrids to quasi-firm structures where elements of one-sided power may come into play.[17]

Art. 20 (1) GDPR enshrines the right to portability of personal data, irrespective of whether the data controller is a gatekeeper, a platform below the DMA-threshold or a small business.[18] But 'portability' as understood under the GDPR is too narrow: It overlooks that portability has become a function of the data subjects' and data users' economic interests to qualify data as a commodity.[19] This applies to both, personal and non-personal data,[20] although privacy concerns impose a much stricter regime with respect to the data subject's consent for using personal data. Although the great variety of applications with personal and non-personal data presents a challenge to regulators,[21] it is a general feature of portability rules that they combine enabling with restrictive effects. Access to data protects the economic freedom of the data subject and the viability of aftermarkets.[22] But access also imposes constraints on the dataholders' businesses[23] and their legitimate interests to protect their own business secrets.[24]

Access to data plays a prominent role in the car industry for automated, connected cars and with respect to the internet of things.[25] To facilitate data exchange, the automobile industry operates with platforms organised by manufacturers, open telematic platforms or shared server concepts.[26] In the U.S. House of Representatives, a bill has been introduced for a "Right to Equitable and Professional Auto Industry Repair Act".[27] The regulatory technique envisaged by this bill aspires to create a market for repair services and related data by construing data exchange mechanisms without invoking traditional concepts of antitrust policy.[28]

---

[16] See Tribess (2020), p. 442 et seq.

[17] See e.g. Lande (2008).

[18] Kieß (2023), p. 330.

[19] Cf. Kieß (2023), p. 330 et seq., and Schweitzer and Metzger (2023), p. 342 et seq.

[20] See Schweitzer and Metzger (2023), p. 344 et seq.

[21] See Schweitzer (2019), p. 571 et seq.

[22] See Schweitzer et al. (2018), p. 173 et seq.

[23] Kieß (2023), p. 136.

[24] Schweitzer (2019), p. 571.

[25] Kerber and Gill (2019), p. 246. From an antitrust law perspective: Kühne, A, in: Kühne and Nack (2022), p. 132 et seq.

[26] Wiebe et al. (2023), p. 36 et seq.

[27] 118th Congress (2023-2024), H.R. 906 (Repair Act) (available at https://www.congress.gov/118/bills/hr906/BILLS-118hr906ih.pdf).

[28] See infra, sub III.2.f.

When the EU Commission assessed the availability of advanced technologies for the industry,[29] it highlighted data access and sharing problems of small and medium-sized enterprises (SME's).[30] SME access to data is to strengthen their participation in the internet of things;[31] it will also result in greater consumer choice.[32] The industry emphasizes data protection problems in the context of mixed data sets of personal and non-personal data.[33] An SME position paper favours a voluntary code of conduct under the auspices of a data sharing support centre.[34] Regulatory intervention is recommended when real-time access cannot be guaranteed and market failure becomes evident.[35] The EU's Code of Conduct on Agricultural Data Sharing with its focus on non-personal data reiterates the concept of allowing data access through voluntary acceptance of contractual standards in the context of data portability rules,[36] but remains silence on regulatory sanctions if cooperative behaviour breaks down.

Shaping markets as a policy choice may build on reducing market dominance, but it may also usher in equitable fairness thinking. In this context, portability and access to data are committed to shaping the market for digital information as an institution, where public and private enforcement overlap. Successful digital regulation by litigation[37] is predicated on meaningful behavioural standards for private actors on the market for data. The development of an efficient digital platform law hinges on a meaningful interface between competition law, the law on unfair competition law and consumer protection law.[38]

---

[29] See generally: Martens et al. (2020).

[30] See European Commission, Advanced Technologies for Industry – Technology Focus on Data Sharing (April 2021) (available at https://ati.ec.europa.eu/reports/technology-watch/technology-focus-data-sharing); cf. OECD, SME's in the data economy:_ from cloud computing to digital security (4 October 2022) (available at https://www.oecd.org/cfe/smes/D4SME%20Webinar%20SMEs%20in%20the%20Data%20Economy%20-%20Key%20Highlights%20-%20October%202022.pdf).

[31] Cf. Suciu et al. (2021), p. 6357 et seq.

[32] See European Commission Staff Working Document, Final Report – Sector Inquiry into Consumer Internet of Things (Brussels 20 January 2022 (SWD2022/ 10 final) (available at https://competition-policy.ec.europa.eu/system/files/2022-01/internet-of-things_final_report_2022_staff_working_document_0.pdf).

[33] Position Paper SME United, SME United's position paper on Access to Data (8 July 2020) (available at https://www.smeunited.eu/publications/position-paper-on-access-to-data).

[34] Ibid.

[35] Ibid.

[36] EU Code of Agricultural Product Sharing by Contractual Agreement (2020) (available at https://www.effab.info/wp-content/uploads/2022/10/eu_code_of_conduct_on_agricultural_data_sharing-1.pdf).

[37] See the title of the book by Viscusi (2002).

[38] Schweitzer and Gutmann (2021), p. 6.

1.2 Outline of the Paper

The DMA is under-inclusive as it regulates access to data from gatekeepers, but does not address access rights for businesses dealing with smaller platforms or de facto owners of data under the internet of things.[39] This paper will therefore focus on data access scenarios below the DMA-threshold. It will first explore the regulatory strategies behind the DMA, the P2B-Regulation, the Data Act, before moving to data protection law aspects and the German law against restraints on competition. In accordance with the current policy focus on fairness on digital markets the analysis will then assess the potential of (German) unfair trading law for facilitating access to data. Currently, regulators take a pragmatic approach towards access vy fairness as they appear to favour sectoral regulation. The EU's sectoral access policies will be scrutinized, before access to information in the U.S. automobile under a legislative proposal in the House of Representatives sets the framework for a concluding statement on whether unfair trading law is capable of supplying workable criteria for shaping access rights in the market for digital information.

2 Regulatory Access Strategies

2.1 Digital Markets Act

2.1.1 Policy Approach

Art. 1 (VI) DMA elevates the EU's new platform law to the status of a specific regulatory instrument, separate from antitrust law: The DMA can be invoked without prejudice to the anti-cartel and and anti-monopoly prohibitions of artt. 101 and 102 TFEU. In the face of multiple data access scenarios and underlying business strategies[40] the DMA chooses an addressee-informed policy approach by singling out gatekeepers for complying with data-specific obligations.[41] Although art. 1 (1) DMA focuses on 'contestable and fair markets in the digital sector', the DMA does not allow for a calibration between the free flow of data-related information and the need to limit the exchange of information in the interest of efficient competition.[42] Instead, the DMA builds on the Commission's decision-making practice in policing anti-competitive by imposing a per-se catalogue of behavioural duties on the

[39] See recommendations by the Monopolkommission (2021), sub □169, and Bruegel (2021).

[40] See Schweitzer (2019), p. 571 et seq.

[41] See art. 5 et seq. of the DMA.

[42] See on this policy dilemma: Schweitzer (2019), p. 571.

gatekeeper.[43] A right to argue an efficiency defense on the part of the gatekeeper is not granted.[44]

The classification as a gatekeeper by the Commission can be challenged before the Court of Justice of the European Union (CJEU).[45] Gatekeepers are entitled to rebut the presumption that their core platform services have a significant impact on the market, thereby building on an endurable position in their operations.[46] If unsuccessful, the behavioural duties under artt. 5 and 6 DMA are automatically triggered. Once gatekeepers within the meaning of art. 3 DMA have been unable to rebut the presumption that their core platform services have a significant impact on the market, Art. 5 (1) imposes ex ante specific duties with respect to the use of personal data obtained from endusers or other platform services.[47] Artt. 5 and 6 DMA prescribe factual situations under which gatekeeprs have to grant access to data they hold. This includes scenarios where business users or authorised third parties seek access as a condition for offering services on aftermarkets.[48] Due to its regulatory focus on gatekeepers' duties the DMA does not explore at what stage a refusal to supply data for facilitating aftermarket services would constitute abusive behaviour under TFEU competition rules.[49]

Although art. 8 (1) DMA is mindful of the protection of personal data under the GDPR and its portability rules, it does not clarify whether machine-generated data would also be covered by the per-se access duties imposed on gatekeepers.[50] In the face of two-sided markets, the DMA places fairness in the framework of a bilateral relationship, surprisingly insulated from market-oriented thinking.[51] Regrettably, the DMA falls short of clarifying the relationship between public and private enforcement,[52] although art. 42 DMA opens the door for collective enforcement mechanisms in the interest of consumers if a DMA norm designed to protect consumer interest has been breached or is likely to be breached.[53] Conversely, art. 1 (5) DMA might be read as placing an implicit limitation on private litigation under Member State unfair trading laws: Art. 1 (5) DMA bars Member States from

[43] See Monopolkommission (2021), pp. 10, 62; Paal and Kieß (2022), p. 20.

[44] See Westermann (2022), p. 332; Monopolkommission (2021).

[45] Podszun (2023a) (-Podszun/Schwab), art. 5 (1) n. 7.

[46] See also Zalando v. Commission, Action brought on 27 June 2023 (Case no. T-348/13, O.J. C 314/9 of 4 September 2023), challenging the classification as 'very large online platform' under the Digital Services Act.

[47] Paal and Kieß (2022), p. 19.

[48] See art. 5 (10) DMA.

[49] See regulatory policy proposals for access to non-personal data with respect to aftermarkets: Crémer (2019), p. 87 et seq.

[50] Access to machine-generated data is covered by the new Data Act: Paal and Fenik (2023), p. 255 et seq.; Schweitzer and Metzger (2023), p. 346.

[51] Monopolkommission (2021), p. 15.

[52] See the plea by Podszun (2021b), p. 254 et seq., for broad private enforcement facilities against digital gatekeepers.

[53] Podszun (2023a) (-Gappa/Käseberg), art. 42 □3.

imposing additional obligations on gatekeepers to ensure contestable and fair markets. Although this does not extend to national policy matters not conditioned on the status as gatekeepers, this appears to privilege gatekeepers over enterprises below the DMA-threshold once national unfair trading laws kick in.[54] Arguably, reading discrimination into art. 1 (5) DMA might also open up a policy discussion whether the strict application of national unfair trading laws will jeopardise the innovative potential of gatekeepers and other dataholders.[55]

2.1.2 A Platform Jurisprudence Prior to the DMA

The Commission's digital policy calls for an assessment of potential litigation risks for gatekeepers, although art. 42 DMA is confined to facilitating collective actions against gatekeepers.[56] This raises the question whether the pre-DMA jurisprudence of the CJEU or national unfair trading laws[57] have the potential of boosting private access litigation. In the Towercast case, the CJEU[58] held that merger projects below the threshold criteria of the Merger Regulation 139/2004 ex-ante, may nonetheless be scrutinised ex post, if anti-competitive behaviour within the meaning of art. 102 TFEU is found. This holding will push DMA-gatekeepers into a precautionary strategy. They are likely to notify the Commission of envisaged merger projects with other platforms even if the threshold of the Merger Regulation is not met.[59]

At the outset, both, antitrust and digital law enforcement under the DMA are intended to stave off negative welfare effects.[60] Public enforcement operates as a shield against macroeconomic harms,[61] whereas private actions operate as a 'sword' against the infringer.[62] In analysing antitrust sanctions against unilateral practices on digital markets, Schweitzer/Gutmann have emphasised the predominant role of public enforcement: With respect to access scenarios, they point to the fear of retaliation, but also to the diffulty of devising a successful litigation strategy in uncharted

[54] Hoffmann et al. (2023), p. 17 et seq., Gatekeeper's potential privilege—the need to limit DMA decentralisation.

[55] See passim Schweitzer (2019), p. 571, with respect to data access rights.

[56] See the criticism by Podszun (2021), p. 254 et seq.

[57] See infra sub III.

[58] CJEU, judgment of 16 March 2023, Case no. C-449/21, Towercast SASU v. Autorité de la Concurrence et al., ECLI :EU:C:2023:207.

[59] Dentons, Blog of 24 March 2023, CJEU Decision in the Towercast case – Ex-post review of deals by the back door? (available at https://www.dentons.com/en/insights/articles/2023/march/24/cjeu-decision-in-the-towercast-case-ex-post-review-of-deals-by-the-back-door).

[60] From an antitrust law perspective: Hüschelrath, K., in: Hüschelrath and Schweitzer (2014), p. 9 et seq. (in the context of anti-cartel enforcement).

[61] Cf. Ohlhausen and Okuliar (2015), p. 152 et seq.

[62] See Komninos (2008), p. 2et seq.; Wurmnest and Gömann (2022), p. 154 et seq.

legal territories.[63] These difficulties are magnified if it is unclear whether disclosure of data and strict portability rules frustrate or trigger competition on digital markets.[64] Moreover, private parties are faced with national burden of proof rules for establishing harm.[65] It is therefore no coincidence that the CJEU's data privacy cases against Google were brought by or with the help of national data protetction agencies.[66]

The Towercast judgment is an important reminder that the CJEU's pre-DMA typology of platform cases will continue to impact business strategies and tactics with respect to potential competitors and litigation for data access. In the following, the focus is not on a detailed assessment of the CJEU's jurisprudence. Rather from a public and private enforcement perspective, a typology of pre-DMA platform cases is offered at the intersection between platform law, the law of contracts, data protection law, antitrust and unfair trading law.

The 2007 Microsoft judgment acknowledged a right to data access in the case of an abuse of a dominant decision.[67] It had reached the European judges as a public enforcement case, based on a fine the European Commission had imposed. It seems that potential victims of abusive market practices under art. 102 TFEU have a preference for lodging a complaint with the European Commission which may then commence a formal antitrust investigation.[68] When the first Airbnb case came up to the CJEU,[69] the European judges were asked to determine whether the accommodation platform could be classified as a provider of an information society services, benefiting from the freedoms under the TFEU. Paris hotel owners had complained to local authorities that Airbnb was in breach of a French law on letting property, thus triggering the commencement of criminal law proceedings. In its judgment on the request for a prelimnary ruling from a Paris criminal law court, the CJEU made an analysis of Airbnb's business model and governance structures, and found that the platform's activities did not amount to those of a real estate broker subject to specific registration duties.[70]

---

[63] Schweitzer and Gutmann (2021), p. 10.

[64] See Körber (2016), p. 350 et seq.

[65] Heinemann, A., in: Hüschelrath and Schweitzer (2014), p. 170 et seq.

[66] See judgments of 13 May 2014, case no. C-131/12, Google Spain SL et al. v. Agencia Española de Protecciǿn de Datos (AEPD), Mario Costeja González, ECLI:EU:C:2014:317, and of 24 September 2019, case no, C-507/17, Google LLC v. Commission nationale de l'informatique et des libertés (CNIL), ECLI:EU:C:2019:772.

[67] European Court of First Instance, judgement of 17 September 2007, Case no. T-201/04, Microsoft Corp. v. Commission of the European Communities, ECLI:EU:T:2007:289.

[68] Cf. the November 2022 complaint by the Cloud Infrastructure Service Providers in Europe, attacking Microsoft's licensing practices. Microsoft had attempted to alleviate criticism by changing the terms of its licensing conracts: Euroactiv (2022); ZDNet/Cloud (2022).

[69] European Court of Justice, judgment of 19 December 2019, Criminal Proceedings against Unknown Person, case no. C-390/18, ECLI:EU:C:2019:1112.

[70] Ibid.

In 2017, Italy introduced a law subjecting the income form short-term rental contracts to a specific form of taxation. Airbnb took the Italian tax authorities to court, arguing that its right to provide information services had been infringed. The CJEU refused to locate this case in platform law.[71] Instead, both the Advocate-General[72] and the Court acknowledged a Member state's right to determine the tax regime applicable to platforms.

Nonetheless, Airbnb got caught when the European Commission examined whether Airbnb's standard terms were compatible with consumer protection law. In a coordinated action with the consumer protection authorities of some Member States, the European Commission found that Airbnb was practising discriminatory practices towards consumers, exacerbated by a lack of transparency with respect to the total amount of costs involved for using the platform services.[73] Ultimately, Airbnb succumbed to pressure from Member States' consumer protection authorities, pledging to amend its standard terms and to supply more detailed information on the total cost of Airbnb-based transactions and on venues to pursue a claim for damages.[74] Although this case is informed by consumer protection concerns, it foreshadows the control of standard terms as an element of an emerging platform law.[75] In a pre-Brexit public enforcement case initiated by the UK competition authority, a 2020 judgment of the English Court of Appeal relied on EU competition law to facilitate access to online shopping platforms.[76] A manufacturer of clothes had inserted its 'internet sales policy' terms into the contracts with dealer, banning online sales. The Court of Appeal found a breach of art. 101 TFEU, but pointed out that the manufacturer was entitled to impose certain selling conditions.[77]

The first Spanish Uber case before the CJEU goes back to a private enforcement action, based on unfair trading law. The local Barcelona taxi association had sued Uber for breach of Spanish unfair trading law, since Uber with its on-demand booking system had not complied with local taxi regulations.[78] The CJEU rejected Uber's argument that the 2019 Airbnb judgment on information society services was

[71] European Court of Justice, judgment of 22 December 2022, case no. C-83/31, Airbnb Ireland et al. v. Agenzia delle Entrate, ECLI:EU:C:2022:1018.

[72] See Opinion of Advocate-General Szpunar, of 7 July 2022, Case C-83/21.

[73] European Commission Press Release, 20 September 2018, EU Consumer Rules: Airbnb commits to complying with EU Commission and EU consumer authorities' demands (available at EU consumer rules: Airbnb commits to complying with European Commission and EU consumer authorities' demands (europa.eu)).

[74] Europäisches Verbraucherzentrum Österreich (2018). For an assessment of Airbnb's business model in the aftermath of the COVID pandemic: Polisetty and Jikku Susan Kurian (2021).

[75] See infra sub III.1.a.,b.

[76] Ping Europe Ltd. v. CMA, [2020] EWCA Civ 13.

[77] Ibid.

[78] CJEU, judgment of 20 December 2017, case no. C-434/15, Asociación Profesional Élite Taxi v. Uber Systems Spain SL, ECLI:EU:C:2017:981.

applicable to the services offered by the Uber platform.[79] Compared to Airbnb, Uber's business model connecting of non-professional drivers relies on a much greater amount of de-facto integration. The CJEU emphasized that the nature of the services proffered via the Uber platform goes much beyond the sheer provision of online intermediation services. The CJEU agreed with the Spanish Court, which had asked for a preliminary ruling, pointing to the governance structure of the Uber platform and the nature of the transport services. As a consequence of this line of reasoning, Uber became subject to the EU's and the relevant transport laws.[80] Moreover, potential disregard of national transport law lowers the threshold of applying unfair trading law to Uber's platform.

According to the CJEU's July 2023 holding in the Facebook/Meta case, a breach of the GDPR does not automatically establish an abuse of an dominant position under art. 102 TFEU.[81] However, it would seem that a breach of European Union law can indicate a breach of natonal unfair trading law: French and Italian courts treat a breach of obligations under the GDPR as an incidence of 'concurrence déloyale' (unfair competition).[82] The courts appear to be guided by the notion that—by breaching mandatory EU law—business people are likely to obtain an unjustified advantage over their law-abiding competitors. From a broader regulatory policy perspective, this invites an analysis to what degree unfair trading law can be instrumentalized to ensure platform behaviour that does not unduly exploit information asymmetries or breach data rights of the parties dealing with online platforms. It is noteworthy that the CJEU has opined that data privacy rights are not absolute, but need to be calibrated with under fundamental freedoms, subject to a proportionality anaylsis.[83]

In imposing a fine on Facebook, the Italian Autorità per la Concorrenza ed il Mercato (AGCM) had accused the platform of misleading consumers and aggressive commercial practices which dissuaded consumers from transferring their data to third-party websites.[84] It is interesting that the Italian AGCM relies on consumer protection law in order to police Facebook's anticompetitive behaviour. This is partly due to the fact, that contrary to the German Bundeskartellamt, the AGCM is also empowered to enforce consumer protection law. What is noteworthy, though, is that the policy thrust of the Italian decision differs from its Bundeskartellamt counterpart. The AGCM's focus is not directed at market power, but at certain business practices detrimental to consumers.

---

[79] Ibid.

[80] Ibid.

[81] CJEU, judgment of 4 July 2023, Case no. C-252/21, Meta Platforms Inc. (formerly Facebook Inc.) et al., v. Bundeskartellamt, ECLI:EU:C:2023:537.

[82] See Tribunal de grande instance de Paris, judgment of 15 April 2022 (no. RG 19/12628) (available at https://juricaf.org/arret/FRANCE-TRIBUNALDEGRANDEINSTANCEDEPARIS-20220415-1912628); for an Italian perspective see Colomba (2021).

[83] See the analysis on art. 15 GDPR in: CJEU, judgment of 12 January 2023, case no. C-154/21 , RW v. Österreichische Post, E CLI:EU:C:2023:3.

[84] Botta and Wiedemann (2019), p. 442 et seq.; Colomba (2021).

A Barcelona taxi licensing case from 2023 suggests that EU law imposes limits on policing digital platforms. The CJEU emphasised that established case law required a proportionality analysis under art. 49 TFEU.[85] Morever, policy objectives of purely economic nature would not amount to an overriding public interest, justifying an encroachment of a fundamental freedom.[86] This seems to impose limits on an unfair trading law analysis, informed by general policy considerations.

2.2 *P2B-Regulation*

2.2.1 Legislative Policy

The P2B-Regulation[87] focuses on unilateral business practices which grossly deviate from good commercial conduct or are contrary to good faith and fair dealing.[88] It is intended to supplement Member State laws on unilateral conduct or unfair commercial practices (art. 1 (4)). Art. 3 of the Regulation calls for the scrutiny of the standard terms of the provider of online intermediary services. Moreover, as is typical in long-term business relationships, envisaged changes of the standard terms or the scope of online intermediary services have to be announced beforehand.[89] This is a traditional law of contracts approach[90] which focuses on the imbalance of terms or potential lock-in effects of long-term contracts without directly assessing the competitive structure of the relevant market or the economic potential of competitors.[91] Nonetheless, art. 5 of the Regulation acknowledges the potential market effects of ranking as it calls for transparency of the parameters applied by the platform. Similarly, transparency is mandated if the provider of online intermediation services applies discriminating criteria with respect to platform access or related remuneration schemes (art. 7). Under the P2B-Regulation, this is confined to express contractual stipulations and related transparency obligations. The emphasis on contractual stipulations has provoked a query whether third party rights might be

[85] CJEU, judgment of 8 June 2023, case no. C-50/21, Prestige and Limousine SL v. Área Metropolitana de Barcelona et al., ECLI:EU:C:2023:448.

[86] Ibid., see also European Court of Justice, judgment of 22 December 2010, case no. 338/09, Yellow Cab Verkehrsbetriebe GmbH v. Landeshauptmann von Wien, ECLI:EU:C:2010:814 ECLI:EU:C:2010:814, at □51: Mere profitability concerns in favour of a competing bus service are of a purely economic nature, but of an overriding public interest which might justify a restriction on fundamental freedoms.

[87] Regulation (EU) 2019/1150 of 20 June 2019 on promoting fairness and transparency for business users of online intermediation services, O.J. L 186/57 of 11 July 2019.

[88] See Recital 2 to the Regulation.

[89] See art. 4 of the Regulation.

[90] See Tribess (2020), p. 443, on contractual enforcement mechanisms in case of breach of obligations imposed by the P2B-Regulation.

[91] See also the criticism by Iamiceli (2019), p. 404, that the P2B-Regulation does not contain a list target terms and clauses detrimental business and consumer interests,

read into access stipulations under art. 8 of the Regulation.[92] Business partners of commercial platform users would then attain the status of third-party beneficiaries if technological necessities dictate continued access to information stored on the platform. But such an approach would unduly stretch the limits of contractual interpretation. Moreover, reading third-party effects into the agreement between the online service provider and commercial platform users is likely to jeopardise consumers' personal data protection rights, protected by art. 9 of the Regulation and the GDPR.[93] Art. 9 of the Regulation offers transparency instead of regulated access.[94] Nonetheless, transparency enables commercial platform users to specify with greater certainty to which data they would like to have access.[95] As a corollary, regulatory attempts to open up access to data beyond the DMA will have to supply a clear specification which data are to be covered by a statutory access stipulation.[96]

2.2.2 Enforcement

The P2B-Regulation does not confer individual rights of litigation on business users of platform services.[97] Instead, artt. 13, 14 P2B-Regulation favour collective redress mechanisms. Under art. 13 P2B-Regulation, the Commission invites Member States to encourage the establishment of alternative dispute settlement mechanisms (mediation) through business organisations established by online service providers. Art. 14 (9) of the P2B-Regulation approves of Member State mechanisms to police breaches of obligations of through collective or individual redress litigation under national laws.[98] It should be noted that standing and the individual or collective rights to police non-compliance with the P2B-Regulation will have to be conferred by national laws: a breach of P2B-obligations triggers litigation if national law so provides.[99]

---

[92] See Busch (2022) (-Graf von Westphalen), art. 8 n. 51 et seq., and Vischer (2021).

[93] Ibid., art. 8 n. 54.

[94] Tribess (2020), p. 441 et seq.

[95] Busch (2022) (-Podszun), art. 9 n. 128.

[96] Ibid., art, 9 n. 52 et seq., 128.

[97] See, however, the judgment of 12 May of 2021 of the Landgericht München I (local district court), MMR 2021, 995 (sub □75), which invokes art. 4 of the Regulation to specify the fairness requirements to be observed by Amazon prior to blocking a vendor account.

[98] This includes proceedings brought by platform-competitors policing breaches of obligations under the P2B-Regulation with the help of national unfair trading laws: Tribess (2020), p. 444.

[99] See Tribess (2020), p. 444.

2.3 The EU's New Data Act

The EU's Data Act is motivated by the conviction that "barriers to data sharing ... [frustrate] ... the optimal allocation of data".[100] The Data Act recognises that the freedom of contract is of fundamental importance in B2B-relationships and intends to subject only those contract terms to an unfairness test which are unilaterally imposed.[101] This policy approach is not inspired by a strict market failure analysis, but rather about concerns about remedying imbalances in negotiating power. Artt. 3 et seq. of the Data Act favour shaping markets over redressing shortcomings in the market for data from an antitrust perspective.[102] It should be noted that third-party access is predicated on the user's consent and agreement between the dataholder and the user (art 5 (1) of the Data Act). The third party cannot act upon its own initiative.

In analysing potential legislative interventions for access to data two major scenarios have to be distinguished:[103] Market participants contributed to generating data and now request to individual-level generated data by their use (including authorization of third parties to use such data). Conversely, third parties absent from the original generation of data need access to bundled individual-level or aggregate sets of data to offer services within a network for creating value. Art. 4 (1) of the Data Act requires data holders to make available to the user the data, generated by using a product. The user may request the data holder to make such data available to a third party (art. 5 (1) of the Data Act). But trade secrets shall only be disclosed for executing the contract between the data user and the third party. Details of the disclosure shall be agreed upon in an agreement between the data holder and the third party (art. 5 (9) of the Data Act). According art. 6 (2) (e) of the Data Act, data obtained under a request for access may not be used for developing a product that may compete with the connected product from which the data originate. Art. 5 (8) of the Data Act is mindful of the portability rights under the GDPR. Moreover, the Data Act does not purport to assign an independent role to third parties or independent businesses, seeking to establish themselves on aftermarkets or new markets in the context of the internet of things. Schweitzer/Metzger correctly question the legislative motive for non-compete clauses as an instrument for entrenching the data holder's position on the primary market.[104]

---

[100] Recital 2 of the Data Act (Regulation (EU) 2023/2854 of 13 December 2023, O.J. L of 22 December 2023).

[101] Recital 59 of the Data Act.

[102] See Schweitzer and Metzger (2023), p. 338 et seq.

[103] See on this and the following: Schweitzer and Metzger (2023), p. 338.

[104] Schweitzer and Metzger (2023), p. 346.

2.4 *Data Protection Law Aspects*

In its July 2023 judgment on Meta/Facebook, the CJEU noted that the efficient administration of competition law required Member State authorities to assess whether the non-observance of obligations under the GDPR facilitates the built-up of a dominant position and its abuse within the meaning of art. 102 TFEU.[105] The CJEU cautions, however, that the infringement of the GDPR does not automatically trigger a finding that art. 102 TFEU has also been breached.[106] While this line of reasoning has been greeted as an acknowledgment of the close interface between competition and data protection law,[107] the contours of a portability right remain unclear, once a request for releasing data goes beyond the scope of art. 20 GDPR.[108]

Art. 20 GDPR codifies the privacy rights of the data subject, but also operates to stimulate competition between platforms, as data can be freely moved from one dataholder to another.[109] It refers to personal data voluntarily transmitted by the data subject, but does not refer to inferred data, whereas the legal treatment of observed data is uncertain.[110] Although portability is intended to facilitate switching and multi-homing in the interest of competitive data markets, it comes at a specific for endusers desirous to change. The current version of the GDPR requires the endusers' consent, but does not provide for (independent) third party providers to realise portability on behalf of the data subjects.[111] Under the Data Act, it would seem that this becomes standard practice, as third-party service providers seek access to data from the data-holder upon presenation of the data subject's consent[112]

The DMA purports to supplement portability rights under the GDPR by placing the gatekeeper under the obligation to grant access to data.[113] It will be difficult to separate personal from non-personal elements if raw data received from an enduser have been refined, or the gatekeeper has developed new data which are a derivative of the enduser's raw data.[114] Ultimately, this turns into a debate on what a gatekeeper may do for legitimate internal purposes (including the installation of cybersecurity mechanisms) and how to ensure real-time portability of data.[115] Moreover, it still has

---

[105] CJEU, judgment of 4 July 2023, Case no. C-252/21, Meta Platforms Inc. (formerly Facebook Inc.) et al., v. Bundeskartellamt, at □□ 46 et seq., 51.

[106] Ibid., at □ 47.

[107] Bundeskartellamt (2023b).

[108] See e.g. for data access with respect to aftermarkets: Kieß (2023), p. 160 et seq.

[109] See Botta and Wiedemann (2019), p. 476.

[110] Krämer (2022).

[111] See Monopolkommission (2021).

[112] Metzger and Schweitzer (2023), p. 58.

[113] Gérardin et al. (2022).

[114] See the comments by European Data Protection Supervisor (2021), p. 11 and p. 11 fn. 27.

[115] See CEP Blog, Pavlova (1 February 2022), Data Dilemma: Will Europe Favor Privacy or a Crackdown on Gatekeepers?, and Steinrötter (2023) (-Mendelsohn/Richter), at □20, 44, on the fundamental policy conflict between mandatory data protection law and a free market for data.

be ascertained whether a gatekeeper may refuse to disclose if third-party personal or business interests would be jeopardised. Platform owners or dataholders might be tempted to argue that a duty to disclose or transfer data would constitute an infringement of their own fundamental freedoms under the TFEU.[116]

Under the jurisprudence of the CJEU, dominance criteria and the prohibition of abuse of market power operate as a deterrent for powerful market players, desirous to avoid an antitrust investigation by the EU Commission.[117] The threat of an investigation under art. 102 TFEU is likely to incentivise gatekeepers into sharing data.[118] It is unclear whether platform owners and data holders below the DMA-threshold would be motivated to adopt a similar strategy if faced a claim under national unfair trading laws for sharing or disclosing data.

2.5 *National Access Rules: The German Law Against Restraints of Competition*

In amending the German Act against Restraints of Competition (Gesetz gegen Wettbewerbsbeschränkungen (GWB)), the Federal Government pledged to adapt antitrust law to the challenges of the digital economy. § 19 (1) of the amended Act proscribes the abuse of a dominant position through one or several enterprises. § 19 (4) of the Act clarifies that a dominant enterprise evidences abuse of its position if,—against payment of a reasonable fee—access to data is denied that is necessary to compete on after-markets, thereby jeopardising the existence of competition on such markets. The amended version of § 19 GWB is protect the competitive potential of the platform while acknowledging that network effects, control over data and self-enforcing effects of the foregoing may generate concentration at an early stage.[119] On the other hand, sanctioning the denial of access to data as a consequence of abusing dominant position is not intended to extend the law against anticompetitive restraints to policing breaches of non-market related norms.[120]

§ 19a (1) GWB adopts a regular technique similar to the DMA's classification mechanisms for gatekeepers:[121] The Federal Cartel Office (Bundeskartellamt) is authorised to classify enterprises which are—to a substantial degree active on markets as enterprises of outstanding importance for competition. Such a classification triggers specific behavioural duties, which are sanctioned by the Bundeskartellamt

[116] See Kieß (2023), pp. 162, 165; Gérardin et al. (2022).

[117] See the judgment in Towercast, supra fn. 58.

[118] See e.g. Chee (2022), Blog 13 June 2022, UE; Amazon va proposer un partage de données pour éviter une amende des autorités antitrust, selon des sources (available at https://www.reuters.com/article/ue-amazon-com-antitrust-idFRKBN2NU0Z0).

[119] See official reasoning Deutscher Bundestag (2020), p. 73, for amending the GWB.

[120] Ibid., at p. 71; see also: Paal and Kieß (2022), p. 11 et seq.

[121] See the commentary on § 19a GWB in: 10. GWB-Novelle (2021) (-Käseberg), p. 58 et seq.; for an analysis of § 19a GWB and its relationship with the DMA: Kieß (2023), p. 454 et seq.

if a breach occurs. The Bundeskartellamt has already classified Alphabet/Google, Meta/Facebook and Amazon as companies of outstanding market relevance.[122] In April 2023, Apple was made to join this club of companies: The Bundeskartellamt noted that Apple had a cross-market position of economic power which allowed Apple to explore patterns of behaviour, not normally available under market conditions.[123] Moreover, the German cartel authority diagnosed that Apple with its proprietary products and its AppStore occupies key positions for competition and access to the digital ecosystem.[124]

For the benefit of businesses in aftermarkets with no alternative choice, § 20 (1) GWB extends the prohibition of an abuse of a dominant position to enterprises with relative market power and to intermediaries for multi-sided markets. Under § 20 (1a) GWB, dependence on an enterprise with relative market power may be engendered if the business activities of another enterprise are predicated on access to data under control of the enterprise with relative market power. Refusal of access to such data against payment of a reasonable fee constitutes an undue obstruction (Behinderung) of business activities. The data access right under § 20 (1a) GWB[125] is not conditioned on pre-existing business transactions with data. According to the reasoning advanced by the German Federal Government dependence and, hence the need for a statutory data access right is found to exist in two distinct factual situations.

Dependence may be found in complex multi-stakeholder settings in after-market and IoT scenarios, typically based on a network of contracts where the creation of additional value is in the interest of both sides.[126] In this context, legality control will normally be relegated to the law of contracts and judicial control of standard term contracts.[127] A different legal treatment is warranted if the negotiating power of the parties to a contract is imbalanced and access to data is not granted under the stipulations of a contract.[128] The second alternative of dependence under § 20 (1a) GWB refers to data access problems of third parties who want to offer services without having had a prior business or contractual relationship with the data holder. The official reasoning submitted by the Federal Government recommends a cautious approach so that a data access should only be envisaged if competition on aftermarkets risks being thwarted due to already existing power structures.[129] The denial of access could also be unreasonable if the dependent enterprise cannot realise a substantial increase in business value. Conversely, denial of access is justified if the claimant could gain access via third-party users or the original ‘owner’ of the data.[130]

[122] Bundeskartellamt (2023a).

[123] Ibid.

[124] Ibid.

[125] See the commentary by 10. GWB-Novelle (2021) (-Brenner), p. 56 et seq.

[126] Deutscher Bundestag (2020), p. 80.

[127] Ibid.

[128] Ibid., at p. 81.

[129] Ibid.

[130] Ibid., at p. 82.

3 Access to Data from a Fairness Perspective

According to the then Commissioner Vestager, competition operates to ensure both, efficiency and fairness.[131] This includes ensuring efficient price competition on the markets, but also protecting consumers so that they enjoy the benefits of competition.[132] Under the DMA, unfairness relates to an "imbalance between the rights and obligations of business users where the gatekeeper obtains a disproportionate advantage".[133] 'Fairness' appears to govern bilateral relationships with no reference to traditional competition law standards for digital market analysis,[134] but does not expressly refer to private users.[135] The new Data Act is committed to harmonising rules on fair access to and the use of data.[136] The P2B-Regulation refrains from interfering directly with the competitive process.[137] Under the P2B-Regulation, 'fairness' is confined to offering interpretive guidance.[138]

When the EU Commission announced its strategy for data, it pledged to impose mandatory and fair access to data only if market failure can be established and competition law does not provide an appropriate remedy.[139] Under national law, it is a truism that unfair trading law remedies should not be available where competition law remains silent for the benefit of free market competition.[140] Thus, more far-reaching notions of fairness should not automatically override competiton law goals.[141] Nonetheless (sector-inspired) fairness norms are attractive to regulators, because 'fairness' properly understood dispenses with the need to prove abuse of market power or market failure.[142] Currently, mandatory rules on fair data access appear to be welcome by small and medium-sized enterprises in the context offering services in the internet of things and for smart homes.[143]

[131] Vestager Key note speech at the European competition day in Prague 10 October 2022, "Fairness and Competition Policy" (available at https://ec.europa.eu/commission/presscorner/detail/en/SPEECH_22_6067).

[132] Ibid.

[133] See recital 33 and art. 12 (5) (b) DMA, and Steinrötter (2023) (-König), at □11, 23.

[134] Monopolkommission (2021), p. 22.

[135] Podszun et al. (2021), p. 62.

[136] See also: European Commission, Proposal for a Regulation on harmonised rules on fair access to and the use of data (Data Act), Brussels 23 February 2022 (2022/0547 (COD)).

[137] Zimmer and Nittenwilm (2022), p. 835.

[138] Steinrötter (2023) (-Louven), at □16.2.

[139] European Commission, Communication of 19 February 2020, A European strategy for data (COM (2020) 66 final), p. 13 and fn. 39 (available at https://eur-lex.europa.eu/legal-content/EN/TXT/PDF/?uri=CELEX:52020DC0066), see Busch, P2B-VO – Kommentar (-Podszun) (München 2022), art. 9 n. 131.

[140] Stuyck (2011), p. 475, citing the judgment of the Belgian Cour de Cassation of 7 January 2000, R.C.J.B. 2001, 256–269. See also the fairness analysis by Göhsl, at p. 413 et seq., 420.

[141] See Schweitzer (2021), p. 517 et seq.; Monopolkommission (2021), p. 22.

[142] Morton et al. (2019), p. 90.

[143] See the study by Podszun (2021a).

In the following, unfair trading law and sector-specific data access instruments will be explored in order to assess their potential for facilitating access to data,[144] ensuring distributive justice between dataholders and users[145] and implementing competition-related policy aims.[146]

3.1 EU Unfair Trading Law

Under EU law, B2B commercial practices of gatekeepers and platforms below the DMA threshold are covered by the Directive 2005/29(EC) on Unfair Commercial Practices.[147] Under this Directive, businesses which play by the codified rules of the marketplace, guarantee fair competition.[148] Businesses which disregard the standards of fair competition harm consumers and potential competitors.[149] Arguably, the Directive might therefore be understood as an instrument to supplement the P2B-Regulation where consumer protection is indirect, as consumers derive benefits from platforms observing standards of market fairness.

3.1.1 German Unfair Trading Law I: Statutory Concepts

In transposing the Unfair Commercial Practices Directive into national law, Germany has extended the scope of application of unfair trading law to online platforms. With respect to ensuring access to data below the DMA-threshold, two norms of the German Act against Unfair Competition[150] (UWG) are particularly apposite. § 3a UWG sanctions business activities which build on a breach of law, capable of infringing consumer interests and those of competitors. 'Law' in the sense of § 3 UWG are norms which prescribe specific duties for rendering professional services, product- and distributed-related statutory duties, including norms on data protection, access to industrial data and platform regulation.[151] This includes the EU sector-specific rules on access to automobile data,[152] but also artt. 35 and 44 of the

[144] See Drexl, J in: German Federal Ministry of Justice and Consumer Protection, Max Planck Institute for Innovation and Competition (2021), p. 519 et seq.; and Kerber (2019), who highlights data-access solutions below the threshold of competition law which build on new theories of harm.

[145] Cf. Zimmer and Nittenwilm (2022), p. 824; Schweitzer (2021), p. 513.

[146] See Steinrötter (2023) (-König), at □11, 22, 24, on fairness-conditioned policy regulation as an instrument to protect competition on secondary markets.

[147] O.J. L 149/22 of 11 June 2005.

[148] See recital 8 to the Directive.

[149] Ibid.

[150] Gesetz gegen den unlauteren Wettbewerb (UWG) in der Fassung der Bekanntmachung vom 3. März 2010, BGBl. I 254,

[151] Ohly and Sosnitza (2023) (-Ohly), § 3a UWG □ 31 et seq.

[152] See infra, sub III.2.a.

amended Payment Services Directive,[153] which grant a statutory right to payment service providers and payment service users to access payment systems. Similarly, § 48 of the German law on the supervision of payment services provides for a statutory right of access if the payor has agreed to a disclosure of his data to a payment service provider.[154] However, industry practice or trading standards will only be covered by § 3a UWG, if they have attained the force of customary law.[155] Thus, standards developed by business associations such as the code of access to agricultural data would need to be elevated to the quality of norms with statutory force to be covered by § 3a UWG. It remains to be seen whether competition authorities need to be authorised by the legislator to shape specific markets for data, by conferring normative character on such industry codes. § 4 (4) UWG proscribes business activities which deliberately obstruct competitors. Under current German unfair trading law, litigation against competitors will only be successful if an existing competitive relationship ('Wettbewerbsverhältnis') can be established.[156] Unless the German or the EU legislator intervene, third-party service providers are precluded from seeking access to data for commencing business activities in the internet of things.

3.1.2 German Unfair Trading Law II: Case Law

There is a line of cases which recognise a breach of fair competition standards, once personality rights or ownership rights of businesses or potential platform users have been infringed.[157] But this does not usher in a focus on potential business ownership rights of a third-party newcomers who want to offer data-based services in the internet of things. In handling litigation about access to data, German courts take a cautious approach by relying on a combination of unfair trading law rules and a user-friendly interpretation of contract law.

Unfair trading law applied when Amazon blocked its online marketplace for traders. The courts caution, however, that unfair trading law will only ensure continued access to amazon's market place, if both, Amazon and the trader are competitors.[158] Blocking access to a platform is only justified for anti-virus protection measures.[159] Tort law bars Facebook from automatically generating a company

---

[153] Directive (EU) 2015/2366 of 25 November 2015 on payment services in the internal market, amending Directives 2002/65/EC, 2009/110/EC and 2013/36/EU and Regulation (EU) 1093/2010 and repealing Directive 2007/64/EC, O.J. 337/35 of 23 December 2015.

[154] § 48 Gesetz über die Beaufsichtigung von Zahlungsdiensten(Zahlungsdiensteaufsichtsges etz - ZAG).

[155] Metzger, A and Eichelberger, J in: Peifer (2020), § 3a UWG □ 49.

[156] See ibid., § 3a UWG □□35, 58.

[157] Köhler et al. (2020) (-Köhler), Einl. UWG □7.3 et seq.

[158] See Landgericht Stuttgart, Decision of 22 April 2021, MMR 2021, 1000 (Motion for Injunction).

[159] Cf. Landgericht (local district court) Lüneburg, 27 September 2007. MMR 2008, 61.

profile without having obtained prior consent of the company.[160] In taking a law of contracts approach, the Hamburg appellate court enjoined Facebook from shutting down an account without giving the user a reasoned notice and a chance to comment.[161] The Berlin appellate court forced Apple to change its internal data protection rules as they were in breach of the German law on standard terms in contracts.[162] This amounts to a control of platform business services from the perspective of consumer protection law. Interestingly, the reasons given by the Berlin appellate court make a reference to the GDPR, thereby pointing to the potential impact of data protection law on controlling platforms, including those under the DMA threshold.

At this stage, German courts emphasize that the GDPR does not supersede national unfair trading law. In fact, unfair trading law operates to enforce obligations under the GDPR: Breach of information duties under the GDPR triggers cease and desist orders under unfair trading law,[163] or leads courts to impose specific duties to disclose the identity of those using a platform.[164] Conversely, a telecommunications service provider may not automatically disclose customer data to a third party for advertisement purposes.[165] A judgment of the Berlin administrative court of June 2021 highlights the interface between the EU's e-commerce law and data protection rules for platforms: Local authorities required Airbnb to disclose the data of property owners who were allegedly in breach of local laws on renting out private apartments.[166] The Berlin Court invokes the e-commerce Directive, as its art. 15 (2)[167] authorizes Member States to compel information society service providers to disclose user data for the purposes of investigating alleged illegal behaviour.

In exploring the nature of legal protection available to the owner of an internet website under unfair trading law, the Frankfurt appellate court has emphasised that the owner's rights do not amount to an absolute right enjoyed by the owner of a house.[168] A case of unfair obstruction of business activities does not exist when an energy producing company refuses to transmit customer data to an energy broker engaged by a customer of the energy producing company.[169] In assessing an obstruc-

---

[160] Landgericht Hamburg, judgment of 13 February 2020, ZD 2020, 477. See also Landgericht Hamburg, judgment of 11 December 2020, GRUR-RS 2020, 59.

[161] Oberlandesgericht Hamburg, judgment of 29 June 2022, GRUR-RS 2022, 24844.

[162] Kammergericht, judgment of 27 December 2018, ZD 2019, 27. See also Amtsgericht Hamburg-Blankenese, judgment of 31 August 2016, BeckRS 2016, 137.

[163] Oberlandesgericht München, judgment of 7 February 2019, BB 2019, 1108; Oberlandesgericht Stuttgart, judgment of 27 February 2020, ZD 2020, 472.

[164] Oberlandesgericht München, judgment of 27 January 2022, GRUR-RR 2022, 398.

[165] Oberlandesgericht (Appellate Court) Stuttgart, 22 February 2007, FD-GewRS 2007, 220.

[166] Verwaltungsgericht (Administrative Court) Berlin, judgment of 23 June 2021, NVwZ-RR 2021, 934.

[167] Directive 2000/31/EC of 8 June 2000 on certain legal aspects of information society services, in particular electronic commerce, in the Internal Market ('Directive on electronic commerce'), O.J. L 178/1 of 17 July 2000.

[168] Oberlandesgericht Frankfurt/Main, 5 March 2009, MMR 2009, 400.

[169] Landgericht Karlsruhe, 30 March 2017, BeckRS 2017, 105706.

tion scenario, courts are willing to grant the owners of a concert hall a substantial amount of discretion, allowing them to preserve their own business strategy.[170] The allegation of obstructing a business has been rejected where a product was not granted access to a chain of stores.[171] Offering a software device to customers for blocking third-party offers does not in itself constitute unfair obstruction.[172] In a law of contracts litigation, a Bavarian district court has determined that denying access to software for further use on the customer's server does not justify the charge of having supplied a defective product, if the underlying contract does not contain a corresponding stipulation for the transfer of such data.[173]

3.2 Sector Regulation and Fair Access

3.2.1 Access to Automobile Manufacturing Data

The EU's rules on access to vehicle repair and information are motivated by the belief that market conditions for the exchange of machine data and repair-related information need to be maintained:[174] Recital 8 to Regulation (EC) No. 715/2007.[175] and recital 12 to Regulation (EU) No. 566/2011[176] emphasise the legislative focus on effective competition in the market for information, including information to be supplied to independent operators other than retailers. Art. 6 (1) of Regulation (EC) No. 715/2007, as amended, is inspired by fairness by requiring manufacturers to provide unrestricted and standardised access to independent operators via websites in a standardised format in a non-discriminatory manner, compared to authorised dealers and repairers. Art. 6 (2) of the Regulation specifies the list of items to be included in the requested information. Art. 7 of the Regulation is reminiscent of a licensing regime, as it entitles the manufacturer to charging a reasonable and proportionate fee for granting access. Art. 7 (1) disapproves of fees which discourage access if they disregard the extent to which the independent operator uses it. From the perspective of legislative technique, Regulation (EU) No. 715/2007 assumes that there is a risk of market failure potentially affecting the market for

[170] Landgericht Hamburg, 2 September 2022, GRUR-RR 2023, 39.

[171] Landgericht Frankfurt/Main, 31 July 2019, GRUR-RS 2019, 33432.

[172] Oberlandesgericht Hamburg, 15 March 2018, BeckRS 2018, 6040.

[173] Landgericht Passau, 30 July 2014, BeckRS 2021, 37532.

[174] See generally on legislative instruments to stimulate the market for trading machine-related data: Fries and Scheufen (2019), p. 725 et seq.

[175] Regulation (EC) No. 715/2007 of 20 June 2007 on type approval of motor vehicles with respect to emissions and commercial vehicles (Euro 5 and Euro 6) and on access to vehicle repair and maintenance information, O.J. L 171/1 of 29 June 2007.

[176] Commission Regulation (EU) No. 566 of 8 June 2011 amending Regulation (EC) No. 715/2007 as regards access to vehicle repair and maintenance information, O.J. L 158/1 of 16 June 2011.

machine-related information, which requires legislative intervention.[177] Thus, legislative intervention dispenses with the need to establish market failure in each individual case. Breaches of the duty to facilitate access to manufacturing can be policed under Member State law.[178] A judgment of the Frankfurt appellate court combines German unfair trading law sanctions for breaching statutory law with an interpretation of Regulation (EC) 715/2007 on access to machine-vehicle related data:[179] The car manufacturer complies with the statutory duty to grant access to data if independent service providers can access the manufacturer's website. But the manufacturer is under no obligation to facilitate access to a data connecting point, so that third party service providers could connect data with a specific motor vehicle number and process them automatically.[180]

As car maintenance data become portable, the judgment of the Frankfurt appellate court demonstrates the limitations of the EU's current statutory approach. It also highlights the difficult to predict its welfare effects.[181] With the help of telematics, car data can be transmitted in real time from the car to a server under the exclusive control of the manufacturer. As a corollary, the manufacturer in turn can send messages to the car. Portability and data access rules will then determine whether the manufacturer can engage in price discrimination strategies between official dealers with a franchising contract and independent service providers.[182] If drivers were entitled to export data obtained from manufacturers to independent third-party intermediaries, they would be able to compare prices of independent service providers on aftermarkets, not confined to repair work.[183] Multi-sided, independent consumer media platforms with strong network effects would then severely restrict the domineering role of manufacturers with respect to car data.[184] Before such a competitive scenario exists, SME's may have to join franchise networks organised by manufacturers or independent contractors in order to reduce cost and to ensure reliable access to technical support for complex technical vehicles.[185]

---

[177] See on the role of statutory instruments in remedying market failure situations: Fries and Scheufen (2019), p. 725.

[178] Art. 13 (2) (e) of Regulation (EC) 715/2007.

[179] Oberlandesgericht Frankfurt, judgment of 23 February 2017, GRUR-RR 2017, 231 (232).

[180] Oberlandesgericht Frankfurt, judgment of 23 February 2017, GRUR-RR 2017, 231 (232).

[181] Cf. Crémer et al. (2019), p. 71, on the difficulty to predict specific consumer welfare effects of platform regulation.

[182] See the analysis by Martens and Mueller-Langer (2020), p. 118 et seq.

[183] Ibid., p. 125 et seq.; see also Kerber and Gill (2019), p. 247 et seq. on the impact on aftermarkets.

[184] Martens and Mueller-Langer (2020), p. 136. On the technical aspects see Falkhofen (2018), p. 166 et seq. See also Podszun (2023b), p. 32 et seq. on the advantages of data pools for facilitating access to secondary markets.

[185] EU Commission, Study on the operation of the system of access to vehicle repair and maintenance information - Final Report (2014), sub □5.6.1 (available at https://op.europa.eu/en/publication-detail/-/publication/c2c172a5-3f49-4644-b5bb-c508d7532e4a).

3.2.2 E-call Rules

Regulation (EU) no. 2015/738 prescribes the installation of 112-based eCall in-vehicle systems in newly manufactured cars.[186] In case of an emergency, the in-vehicle sensors will automatically trigger an alarm, transmitting data on the location of the vehicle to emergency services.[187] The Regulation envisages eCall in-vehicle systems, based on interoperable and standardised open-access platforms so that the technology could be extended to future in-vehicle application for services.[188] Recital 16 classifies these requirements as an instrument to "ensure open choice for customers and fair competition".[189] Art. 5 (7) of the Regulation acknowledges the right of stakeholders, including independent operators to offer additional emergency or added value services:[190] After payment of a reasonable fee the eCall in-vehicle shall be accessible to independent contractors without discrimination for repair and maintenance services in accordance with the provisions of the Regulation on access to automobile manufacturing data. The fee shall not exceed a nominal amount. It requires little imagination to anticipate in-vehicle systems which allow for tracing cars and construing exact traveling profiles. Thus, art. 6 of Regulation (EU) 2015/758 reiterates data protection rules and proscribes constant tracking systems.[191] Once eCall systems transcend emergency systems for vehicles in distress, they have the potential of signalling machine failures to manufacturers via the internet of things,[192] thus raising the question to what extent independent contractors for repair services should be entitled to access to technical data.

[186] Regulation (EU) 2015/758 concerning type-approval requirements for the deployment of the eCall in-vehicle system based on the 112 service of 29 April 2015, O.J. L 123/77 of 19 May 2015.

[187] See Falkhofen (2018), p. 167; and the description of an eCall system by CreaLog (2023). Software-Entwicklung und Beratung GmbH, Notrufweiterleitung und Call Steering (August 2023) (available at https://www.crealog.com/de/produkte-loesungen/notrufweiterleitung/).

[188] Recital 16 to Regulation (EU) 2015/758.

[189] Ibid.

[190] See also Recital 15 to Regulation (EU) 2015/758.

[191] Art. 6 (4) of the Regulation. See also the information supplied by the Austrian Bundesministerium der Finanzen/A-SIT Zentrum für sichere Informationstechnologie, Kfz-Notrufdienst eCall: Funktion und Datenschutz (11 September 2023) (available at https://www.onlinesicherheit.gv.at/Services/News/eCall-Notrufsystem-KfZ-Ueberblick.html).

[192] See e.g. Heidelberger Druckmaschinen AG, eCall Notfallsupport für Druckmaschinen (available at https://www.heidelberg.com/global/de/services_and_consumables/digital_services/ecall_1/ecall.jsp); Monstarlab, Cases/IoT Entwicklung: ein Ecosystem für die Verwaltung von Aufzügen (available at https://monstar-lab.com/de/cases/otis-iot-entwicklung/).

3.2.3 IVS: Systems

The Delegated Regulation (EU) 2022/670[193] purports to provide a framework for the market for the provision of real-time traffic information while facilitating future innovation.[194] Holders of in-vehicle generated data and service providers collecting data on the state of the network may be required by traffic authorities and (private) road operators to make such data accessible under fair, reasonable and non-discriminatory (FRAND) conditions.[195] This includes payment of a fee and, if applicable, the conclusion of a licence agreement.[196]

3.2.4 Energy

Directive (EU) 2019/44 on common rules for the international market for electricity is intended to establish "common rules for the generation, transmission, distribution, energy storage and supply of electricity, together with consumer protection provisions, with a view to creating truly integrated competitive, consumer centred, flexible, fair and transparent electricity markets in the Union".[197] This includes free choice of the supplier at market-based supply prices,[198] smart metering systems,[199] customer access to their data[200] and interoperability to facilitate such access[201] (including third-party access)[202]

3.2.5 Agriculture

'Smart farming' builds on agriculture-related data sets to develop solutions tailored to the needs of specific farms.[203] In oligopolistic markets, upstream input producers offer digital agricultural services to downstream markets, relying on data they have

[193] Commission Delegated Regulation (EU) 2022/670 supplementing Directive 2010/40/EU with regard to the provision of EU-wide real-time traffic information services of 2 February 2022, O.J. L 122/1 of 25 April 2022.

[194] Recital 6 to the Delegated Regulation (EU) 2022/670.

[195] Artt. 6 (5), 7 (3) of the Delegated Regulation.

[196] See Recital 6 and art. 6 (5,7), 7 (3,5) of the Delegated Regulation.

[197] Art. 1 of the Directive (EU) 2019/44 on common rules for the international market for electricity and amending Directive 2012/27/EU of 5 June 2019, O.J. L 158/125 entitling consumers for better energy management.

[198] Artt. 4, 5 of the Directive.

[199] Art. 19 of the Directive.

[200] Art. 23 (3), (5) of the Directive. See also Schweitzer and Metzger (2023), p. 343 et seq.

[201] Art. 24 (3) of the Directive.

[202] Art. 6 of the Directive.

[203] Atik (2023), p. 382 et seq., addressing data access problems in the emerging agriculture sector, potential of the refusal to deal case law to complement *ex-ante* regulation.

collected from farmers.[204] Producers of agricultural machines frequently cooperate with the downstream subsidiaries of the upstream input producers.[205] With respect to collecting data, the downstream subsidiaries of input producers play a crucial role as they channel digital information obtained from the farmer to their parent company. This creates lock-in situations once farmers seek access to 'their' data sets as soon as they want to switch suppliers of agricultural services.[206] Moreover, newcomers to the market of agricultural services will only be successful if they can operate with data sets stored by upstream input producers. This has led a coalition of associations from the EU's agri-food business to negotiate—with the blessing of the EU Commission—an 'EU Code of Conduct on Agricultural Data Sharing by Contractual Agreement'[207] with a predominant focus on non-personal data.[208] As in the context of digital service intermediaries, the Code recognises the right the (data-storing) operator of the agri-chain to grant access to data and permit their use.[209] However, data originating from a farm or farming operations 'belong' do not 'belong' to the operator of the agri-chain and their use should be conditioned on payment of a compensation to the farmer.[210] Therefore, the Code recommends to conclude a data-sharing agreement which clarifies the purpose of collecting, sharing and processing the data, details on the software to be used and provides for verification mechanisms for the data originator.[211] The Code reiterates the legislative policies on personal data under the GDPR and its protection of personal data, emphasising the need for pseudonymisation and portability.[212] With respect to policing the contractual stipulations of the data sharing agreement, the Code builds on transparency for the benefit of the data originator and credible threats to be realised by the data originator:[213] Data originators should be able to exercise a contractual right to reject unilateral changes of the stipulations and to opt out.[214] The Code's recommendations on liability are confined to data originators' guarantees as to the accuracy and completeness of the data transferred and to intellectual property rights.[215]

[204] Ibid., at p. 383.

[205] Ibid., at p. 384.

[206] Ibid., at p. 384 et seq., see Top et al. (2022).

[207] EU Code of Conduct on Agricultural Data Sharing by Contractual Agreement (2018) (available at https://www.effab.info/wp-content/uploads/2022/10/eu_code_of_conduct_on_agricultural_data_sharing-1.pdf).

[208] See van der Burg et al. (2021), p. 186 et seq.

[209] EU Code of Conduct on Agricultural Data Sharing, sub 'Attribution of the underlying rights to derive data (Also referenced as data ownership)'.

[210] Ibid.

[211] Ibid.

[212] Ibid., sub 'Data access, control and portability'.

[213] Ibid., sub 'Data protection and transparency'.

[214] Ibid.

[215] Ibid., sub 'Liability and intellectual property rights'.

The Code's approach to shaping a market for agricultural data is contractual. Adherence to it is voluntary.[216] It is intended to settle data-related conflicts of interest by supplying principles for a fair contractual arrangement.[217] The Code is likely to operate in a scenario of a network of existing contracts, but also opens up the market for agricultural data for newcomers. Regrettably, the Code remains silent on the consequences of a breach of contractual obligations by the operator of the agri-chain or a cybersecurity incident in his operations. The Code shies away from classifying newcomers as third-party beneficiaries from the contractual pledge to adhere to its stipulations. If the Code were elevated to the rank of a statement on data practices in the agricultural industry, it could be envisaged that individual companies or business associations could enforce them under national unfair trading laws[218] or statutory rules on standing, similar to those of art. 14 (9) of the P2B-Regulation.

3.2.6 Access to Information in the US Automobile Industry: H.R. 906

The bill for a 'Right to Equitable and Professional Auto Industry Repair Act', introduced in the U.S. House of Representatives in February 2023,[219] aims at improving markets in the automobile repair industry. At the outset, it builds on an implicit finding of market failure to the detriment of consumers and providers of repair services. Under the congressional findings of sec. 2 (5) of the bill, the emphasis is on competition in the motor vehicle industry to be fostered by communication and innovation.[220] Motor vehicle manufacturers shall grant, inter alia, consumers, their designees and motor vehicle repair facilities access to critical repair information at fair, reasonable and non-discriminatory cost.[221] The Federal Trade Commission will be charged with the implementation of the statutory obligations envisaged by this bill, including manufacturers' specific duties in the context of granting access to vehicle-generated data.[222]

Connecting cars opens up new markets for offering services such as individual insurance tariffs or optimisation of the use of gas.[223] The draft Repair Act attempts to pave the way for rules on access to data on 'vehicle-generated' data (sec. 5 (a) of the bill. Access to such data will be obtained via a 'standardized access platform'. Under sec. 7 (a) (17) of the bill, a standardized access platform "means a cybersecure authentication and authorization system developed by a mobile vehicle manu-

---

216 Ibid., sub 'Introduction'.

217 See preamble to the Code and van der Burg et al. (2021), p. 193.

218 See from the perspective of platform liability under German Unfair Trading Law: Hofmann (2022), p. 780 et seq.

219 See supra fn. 27.

220 Ibid.

221 Sec. 3 (2) of the bill.

222 See sec. 6 of the bill.

223 Kühne and Nack (2022), p. 56.

facturer. … [This system shall have] … the ability to securely access and communicate vehicle generated data emanating directly from a motor vehicle via direct local and remote wireless data connections bidirectionally and in real time".[224] This platform does not assume the role of a data trustee,[225] although the bill is mindful of the interface between sharing data and trust: Thus, the U.S. National Highway Safety Administration shall assign to an independent entity the task of establishing and administering access to vehicle-generated data transmitted by standardised access platforms.[226] This independent entity shall not be controlled by one or more vehicle manufacturers.[227] Instead, the entity shall consist of representatives from industry stakeholders, aftermarket part manufacturers, telematics service providers and motor vehicle manufacturers.[228] It would seem that this independent entity could also define threshold criteria for eliminating frivolous claims for access to vehicle-generated data, thus side-stepping the issue to what extent standards of antitrust law would kick in. In order to facilitate requests for access to vehicle-generated data, access criteria could be translated into smart contracts.[229] Vehicle manufacturers would then employ blockchain technology to safely store data and share them with parties with a legitimate access interest via the standardized platforms.[230]

4 Conclusion

For the EU Commission, the DMA is to address problematic access to digital markets. Dependencies by business users from core platform services and platform sevices stand for problematic access to digital markets, depencies for business users and unfair practices.[231] In conditioning access to data on threshold criteria for gatekeepers, the DMA is under-inclusive. Access to data controlled by smaller platforms and businesses is relegated to the P2B-Regulation, the Data Act, sectoral regulation and national unfair trading laws. Currently, the Data Act will only apply to access scenarios where data subjects have given their consent.

The interface between the GDPR and the rules for shaping digital markets is overshadowed by the distinction between personal and non-personal data rights. Art. 20 GDPR with its portability right and access to one's own data embodies the data's subject entitlement to privacy. But the exclusive focus in privacy in art. 20

[224] Sec. 7 (a) (17) of the bill.

[225] Cf. on data trustee solutions: Specht-Riemenschneider, L in; German Federal Ministry of Justice and Consumer Protection, Max Planck Institute for Innovation and Competition (2021), p. 407 et seq.

[226] Sec. 5 (b) (1) of the bill. See Podszun (2023b), p. 33, on data pools.

[227] Sec. 5 (b) (1) of the bill.

[228] Sec. Sec. 5 (b) (2) of the bill.

[229] See Duveen et al. (2021).

[230] Cf. In the context of sharing health-related data: Sun et al. (2022).

[231] European Commission, Explanatory Memorandum for the Proposal for a Digital Markets Act.

GDPR ignores that portability is essentially a function of the data subject's decision to handle personal data as a commodity. Once personal and non-personal data attain the status of a commodity, it is unclear how rules for the digital market as an institution should be set. In this context, neither the DMA' gatekeeper criteria nor the traditional antitrust criteria are of great help, as data for access to aftermarkets and the internet of things become crucial.

The EU Commission appears to be committed to ensuring access to platforms below the DMA-threshold and to data held by other businesses, even if competition law does not apply. In such a case, the EU Commission conditions access regulation on a finding of market failure. But as digital markets are fast developing, it is a considerable challenge to determine at what stage access regulation should step in. Portability and access rights are designed to protect the interests of consumers and those businesses seeking access to data for offering services on aftermarkets and in the internet of things. Conversely, portability and access rights restrain dataholders from developing their businesses. In this context, national unfair trading laws are capable of enforcing EU sectoral standards,[232] but unfair trading law as such is currently ill-equipped to develop access standards below the DMA-threshold: As portability and access rights are a function of the data subject's decision to use data as a commodity, unfair trading law is too unspecific to accommodate scenarios where actual proof of market failure has been dispensed with.

While it has been observed that sectoral rules might diversify the concept of portability and access into a state of disharmony,[233] sectoral regulation is currently the only mechanism for substituting market failure analysis and the proof of 'competitive harm'.[234] Current sectoral access rules allow for a fine-tuned approach.[235] By necessity, they are highly technical in order to limit the application of an overly broad concept of access to digital markets (including aftermarkets).[236] The current project in the U.S. House of Representatives takes a similar approach. Morever, it introduces a governance scheme whereby access to data is jointly administered by dataholders, interested business on aftermarkets and consumers. While this does not come close to data-sharing, it de facto establishes a system for administering joint criteria for access, open for sophistication by smart contracts ad artificial intelligence.

It should be noted, however, that centralised data sharing agencies are only a policy option[237] where data are sufficiently standardised and the risk of being

[232] For a broader approach under unfair trading law see: Drexl, J in: German Federal Ministry of Justice and Consumer Protection, Max Planck Institute for Innovation and Competition (2021), p. 523.

[233] Cf. Schweitzer and Metzger (2023), p. 340.

[234] Cf. Kerber (2019).

[235] Cf. the advice by Metzger and Schweitzer (2023), p. 58, to avoid a broad mandatory access approach.

[236] See Kieß (2023), p. 136, for a warning of fishing expeditions based on overly broad data access rights, and Göhsl (2022), p. 420.

[237] See the proposals by Graef and Prüfer (2021) and Krämer and Schnurr (2021).

excluded from aftermarkets is sufficiently high.[238] Where centralised data sharing agencies are not feasible,[239] especially SME's would still be relegated to a combination of sectoral access rules and private law instruments. Thus, sectoral regulatory attempts to get hold of data access problems on an EU level are predicated on workable private law rules for sharing data in an access scenario. This would also require to introduce meaningful rules for calculating a reasonable access fee. The EU's code on access to agricultural data highlights a specific regulatory challenge if markets are under development so that regulation might be considered as coming too early, thereby stifling competition. In this case, codes on digital access might offer an acceptable solution, controlling the interpreatation of contracts. For non-contractual scenarios, national unfair trading laws should be amended to classify breaches of such codes as seeking a benefit by disregarding industry standards.

The Data Act and current portability rules condition third-party access to data on the consent of the data subject. If data access in an industry is controlled by adherence to a code through a bilateral contract between data subject and data holder, third-party beneficiary rights should be read into the contract to facilitate services for aftermarkets and in the internet of things. As sectoral rules develop, national laws of civil procedure need to bring forth specific burden of proof rules where access to data is likely to be jeopardised by information asymmetries at the intersection between antitrust, data protection, unfair trading law and sectoral access rule.

References

10. GWB-Novelle (2021) Bien F et al (eds) Die 10. GWB-Novelle – Das neue Kartellrecht. Beck, München

Atik C (2023) Addressing data access problems in the emerging agriculture sector, potential of the refusal to deal case law to complement *ex-ante* regulation. Eur Compet Law J 19:380–409

Bania K (2022) Fitting the Digital Markets Act in the existing framework; the myth of the "without prejudice". Eur Comp Law J:116–149

Botta M, Wiedemann K (2019) The interaction of EU competition, consumer, and data protection law in the digital economy: the regulatory dilemma in the Facebook Odyssey. Antitrust Bull 64(3):428–446

Bruegel (2021) Blog Post of 14 December 2021, Which platforms will be caught by the Digital Markets Act? The 'gatekeeper' dilemma (available at https://www.bruegel.org/blog-post/which-platforms-will-be-caught-digital-markets-act-gatekeeper-dilemma)

Bundeskartellamt (2023a) Press Release, Digitalwirtschaft: Apple unterliegt den Digitalvorschriften nach § 19a GWB (5 April 2023) (available at https://www.bundeskartellamt.de/SharedDocs/Meldung/DE/Pressemitteilungen/2023/05_04_2023_Apple_Abschluss.html)

Bundeskartellamt (2023b) Press Release of 4 July 2023, CJEU decision in Facebook proceding: Bundeskartellamt may take data protection rules into consideration (available at https://www.

[238] Metzger and Schweitzer (2023), p. 57.

[239] In view of multitude of factual scenarios below the DMA-threshold it is unrealistic to insist on introducing limitations on private enforcement. See Komninos' plea for a precedence of public enforcement, in: Liber Amicorum Elinor Fox (2021), p. 425 et seq.

bundeskartellamt.de/SharedDocs/Meldung/EN/Pressemitteilungen/2023/04_07_2023_EuGH.html;jsessionid=48FD6AE3EF0BB664A439991CD10447D5.1_cid508?nn=3591568)
Busch C (ed) (2022) P2B-VO – Verordnung (EU) 2019/1150 zur Förderung von Fairness und Transparenz für gewerbliche Nutzer von Online-Vermittlungsdiensten. Beck, München
CEP Blog (2022) Pavlova, Y (1 February 2022), Data Dilemma: Will Europe Favor Privacy or a Crackdown on Gatekeepers? (available at https://cepa.org/article/data-dilemma-will-europe-favor-privacy-or-a-crackdown-on-gatekeepers/)
Chee FY (2022) Blog 13 June 2022, UE; Amazon va proposer un partage de données pour éviter une amende des autorités antitrust, selon des sources (available at https://www.reuters.com/article/ue-amazon-com-antitrust-idFRKBN2NU0Z0)
Colomba V (2021) Blog 24 February 2021, Facebook vs Apple: quando il diritto alla privacy diventa strumento di concorrenza sleale (available at https://www.agendadigitale.eu/mercati-digitali/facebook-vs-apple-quando-il-diritto-alla-privacy-diventa-strumento-di-concorrenza-sleale/)
CreaLog (2023) CreaLog Software-Entwicklung und Beratung GmbH, Notrufweiterleitung und Call Steering (August 2023) (available at https://www.crealog.com/de/produkte-loesungen/notrufweiterleitung/)
Crémer J et al (2019) Competition policy for the digital era – Final Report, European Commission
Dentons, Blog of 24 March 2023, CJEU Decision in the Towercast case – Ex-post review of deals by the back door? (available at https://www.dentons.com/en/insights/articles/2023/march/24/cjeu-decision-in-the-towercast-case-ex-post-review-of-deals-by-the-back-door)
Deutscher Bundestag (2020) 19. Wahlperiode (10 October 2020), Drucksache 19/23492, Gesetzentwurf der Bundesregierung, Entwurf eines Gesetzes zur Änderung des Gesetzes gegen Wettbewerbsbeschränkungen für ein fokussiertes, proaktives and digitales Wettbewerbsrecht 4.0 und anderer wettbewerbsrechtlicher Regelungen (GWB-Digitalisierungsgesetz) (available at https://dserver.bundestag.de/btd/19/234/1923492.pdf)
Duveen S et al (2021) Fine-grained access control for a blockchain-based healthcare system, Delft University of Technology Paper (available at https://repository..nl/islandora/object/uuid%3A3fe6b070-5961-4463-b84f-53074bd7e324)
Economides N, Lianos I (2021) Restrictions on privacy and exploitation in the digital economy: a market failure analysis. J Compet Law Econ 17(4):765–845
Eifert M et al (2021) Taming the giant: the DMA/DAS Package. CMLR 58:987–1028
Euroactiv (2022) Microsoft confronté à une plainte pour pratiques déloyales auprès de l'UE (November) (available at https://www.euractiv.fr/section/competition/news/microsoft-confronte-a-une-plainte-pour-pratiques-deloyales-aupres-de-lue/)
Europäisches Verbraucherzentrum Österreich (2018) Press Release of 21 September 2018, Neue AGB bei Airbnb (available at https://europakonsument.at/de/news/neue-agb-bei-airbnb)
European Data Protection Supervisor (2021) Opinion 2/2021 on the Proposal for a Digital Markets Act (available at https://edps.europa.eu/system/files/2021-02/21-02-10-opinion_on_digital_markets_act_en.pdf https://edps.europa.eu/system/files/2021-02/21-02-10-opinion_on_digital_markets_act_en.pdf)
Falkhofen B (2018) Car data platforms and the EU Acquis. Comput Law Rev Int 19(6):165–174
Fries and Scheufen, Märkte für Maschinendaten – Eine rechtliche und rechtsökonomische Standortbestimmung, MMR 2019, 721 (725 et seq.)
Gawer A (2021) Digital platforms' boundaries – the interplay of firm scope, platform sides, and digital interfaces. Long Range Planning 54(5)
Gérardin D et al (2022) The interplay between the Digital Markets Act and the General Data Protection Regulation (https://papers.ssrn.com/sol3/papers.cfm?abstract_id=4203907)
German Federal Ministry of Justice and Consumer Protection, Max Planck Institute for Innovation and Competition (eds) (2021) Data access, consumer interests and public welfare. Nomos, Baden-Baden
Göhsl J-F (2022) Marktübergreifendes Wachstum in der Digitalwirtschaft. Nomos, Baden-Baden
Graef I, Prüfer J (2021) Governance of data sharing: a law & economics proposal. Res Policy 50:104440

Hoffmann J et al (2023) Gatekeeper's potential privilege – the need to limit DMA decentralisation. J Antitrust Enforce:1–23
Hofmann F (2022) Lauterkeitsrechtliche Haftung von Online-Plattformen – Die neuen Transparenzvorgaben im UWG 2022 im Kontext lauterkeitsrechtlicher Plattformregulierung. GRUR:780–786
Hüschelrath K, Schweitzer H (eds) (2014) Public and private enforcement of competition law in Europe, ZEW Economic Studies, vol 48. Springer-Verlag, Heidelberg
Iamiceli P (2019) Online platforms and the digital turn in EU contract law: unfair practices, transparency and the (pierced) veil of digital immunity. ERCL 15(4):392–420
Kerber W (2019) Data-sharing in IoT ecosystems from a competition law perspective – the example of connected cars. J Compet Law Econ 15(4):381–426
Kerber W, Gill D (2019) Access to data in connected cars and the recent reform of the motor vehicles type approval regulation. Jipitec 10:244–256
Kieß F (2023) Regulierung von digitalen Ökosystemen – Implikationen durch § 19a GWB and Digital Markets Act. Nomos, Baden-Baden
Köhler et al (eds) (2020) Gesetz gegen den unlauteren Wettbewerb, 8th edn. Beck, München
Komninos A (2008) EC private antitrust enforcement - decentralised application of EC competition law in national courts. Hart Publishing, Oxford/Portland
Körber T (2016) "Ist Wissen Marktmacht?"- Überlegungen zum Verhältnis von Datenschutz, "Datemmacht" und Kartellrecht - Teil 2. NZKartR 348–356
Krämer J (2022) Data access provisions in the DMA - Issue Paper November, Centre on Regulation in Europe (available at https://cerre.eu/wp-content/uploads/2022/11/DMA_DataAccessProvisions-2.pdf)
Krämer J, Schnurr D (2021) Big data and digital markets contestability: theory of harm and data access remedies. J Compet Law Econ 18(2):255–322
Krause T et al (2017) IT-Plattformen für das Internet der Dinge (IoT) – Basis intelligenter Produkte und Services. Fraunhofer Verlag, Stuttgart
Kühne A, Nack R (eds) (2022) Rechtshandbuch Connected Cars. Beck, München
Lande RH (2008) Market power without a large market share: the role of information and other "consumer protection" market failures. The American Antitrust Institute Working Paper No. 07-06 (available at https://papers.ssrn.com/sol3/papers.cfm?abstract_id=1103613)
Liber Amicorum Elinor Fox (2021) Charbit N, Gachot S (eds). Institute of Competition Law, New York
Martens B, Mueller-Langer F (2020) Access to digital car data, and competition in aftermarket maintenance services. J Compet Law Econ 16(1):116–141
Martens B et al (2020) B2B – data sharing: an economic and legal analysis. European Commission, JRC Technical Report – JRC Digital Economy Working Paper 2020-05 (2020-5) (available at https://joint-research-centre.ec.europa.eu/system/files/2020-07/jrc121336.pdf)
Metzger A, Schweitzer H (2023) Shaping markets: a critical evolution of the draft data act. ZEuP:42–82
Monopolkommission (2021) Sondergutachten 82, Empfehlungen für einen effektiven und effizienten Digital Markets Act (available at https://www.monopolkommission.de/images/PDF/SG/sg_dma_volltext.pdf)
Morton FS et al (2019) Market Structure and Antitrust Committee, in: Chicago Booth – The Stigler Center for the Study of the Economy and the State, Stigler Committee on Digital Platforms, Final Report (16 September 2019) 23- 138 (available at https://www.chicagobooth.edu/research/stigler/news-and-media/committee-on-digital-platforms-final-report)
Ohlhausen M, Okuliar AP (2015) Competition, consumer protection, and the right (approach) to privacy. Antitrust Law J 80:121–156
Ohly A, Sosnitza O (eds) (2023) UWG – Gesetz gegen den unlauteren Wettbewerb (Kommentar), 8th edn. Beck, München
Paal B, Fenik M (2023) Access to data in the data act proposal. ZfDR:249–262
Paal B, Kieß F (2022) Digitale Plattformen im DSA-E, DMA-E und § 19a GWB. ZfDR:1–33

Peifer K-N (ed) (2020) UWG – Gesetz gegen den unlauteren Wettbewerb – Großkommentar, 3rd edn. De Gruyter, Berlin
Podszun R (2020) Empfiehlt sich eine stärkere Regulierung on online-Plattformen und anderen Digitalunternehmen? – Gutachten F zum 73. Deutschen Juristentag Hamburg 2020/Bonn 2022. Beck, München
Podszun R (2021a) Handwerk in der digitalen Ökonomie – Rechtlicher Rahmen für den Zugang zu Daten, Software and Datenplattformen. Nomos, Baden-Baden
Podszun R (2021b) Private enforcement and gatekeeper regulation: strengthening the rights of private parties in the Digital Markets Act. J Eur Compet Law Pract 13(4):254–267
Podszun R (ed) (2023a) Digital Markets Act – Gesetz über digitale Märkte. Nomos, Baden-Baden
Podszun R (2023b) Der EU Data Act und der Zugang zu Sekundärmärkten am Beispiel des Handwerks. Nomos, Baden-Baden
Podszun R et al (2021) The Digital Markets Act: moving from competition law to regulation for large gatekeepers. EuCML:60–67
Polisetty A, Jikku Susan Kurian JS (2021) The future of shared economy: a case study on Airbnb, 2021 FIIB Business Review 1
Schreieck M et al (2022) From product platform ecosystem to innovation platform ecosystem: an institutional perspective on the governance of ecosystem transformations. J Assoc Inf Syst 23(6):1354–1385
Schweitzer H (2019) Datenzugang in der Datenökonomie: Eckpfeiler einer neuen Informationsordnung. GRUR:569–580
Schweitzer H (2021) The art to make gatekeeper positions contestable and the challenge to know what is fair: a discussion of the Digital Markets Act Proposal. ZEuP:503–544
Schweitzer H, Gutmann F (2021) Unilateral practices in the digital market: an overview in EU and National Case Law, e-Competitions Special Issue Unilateral practices in the digital market (available at https://awards.concurrences.com/IMG/pdf/article-101045.pdf?72864/61e38c0d8650bcb359bdf12a1a30dd0f69de153a0f0d338671b31f9c9e3b68bc)
Schweitzer H, Metzger A (2023) Data access under the Draft Data Act, competition law and the DMA: opening the data treasures for competition and innovation? GRUR Int 74(2):337–356
Schweitzer H et al (2018) Modernisierung der Missbrauchsaufsicht für marktmächtige Unternehmen. Nomos, Baden-Baden
Steinrötter B (ed) (2023) Europäische Plattformregulierung – Rechtshandbuch. Nomos, Baden-Baden
Stuyck J (2011) Réflexions sur une meilleure intégration du droit de la concurrence et du droit des pratiques commerciales déloyales. XXV Rev Int Dr Écon:455–479
Suciu A-D et al (2021) IoT technologies as instruments for SMEs' innovation and sustainable growth. Sustainability 13:6357
Sun Z et al (2022) A blockchain-based secure storage scheme for medical information. J Wireless Com Network 2022:40 (available at https://jwcn-eurasipjournals.springeropen.com/articles/10.1186/s13638-022-02122-6)
Top J et al (2022) Cultivating FAIR principles for agri-food data. Comput Electron Agric 196:106909
Tribess A (2020) Datenzugangsrechte in der Plattformökonomie - Auswirkungen der P2B-Verordnung im Bereich datenschutzrechtlicher Transparenzpflichten. ZD:440–444
van der Burg, Wiseman, Krkeljas (2021) Trust in farm data sharing: reflections on the EU code of conduct for agricultural data sharing. Ethics Inf Technol Sharing 23:185–198
Vischer (2021) Blog 9 September 2021, Schweizer Banken in die Cloud – so geht es (und so nicht) on contractual third-party access rights in the context of outsourcing data to clouds (available at https://www.vischer.com/know-how/blog/schweizer-banken-in-die-cloud-so-geht-es-und-so-nicht-39214/)
Viscusi WK (ed) (2002) Regulation through litigation. Brookings, Washington, D.C.
Wais H (2023) Datenzugang des gewerblichen Plattformnutzers und Grundlagen der Privatautonomie. ZEuP:582–606

Westermann K (2022) Die geplante Digital Markets Act: Europäische Regulierung zentraler Plattformdienste außerhalb des Kartellrechts? ZHR 186:325–338

Wiebe A et al (2023) Studie zur Notwendigkeit und Ausrichtung von spezifischen Datenzugangsregelungen im Bereich des vernetzten Fahrzeugs in der Automobilwirtschaft, Bundesnetzagentur

Wurmnest W, Gömann M (2022) Comparing private enforcement of EU competition and data protection law. JETL 13(2):154–182

ZDNet/Cloud (2022) Blog 1 September 2022, Microsofts Lizenzänderungen lassen Wettbewerber kalt (available at ZDNet/Cloud (2022), Blog 1 September 2022, Microsofts Lizenzänderungen lassen Wettbewerber kalt)

Zimmer D, Nittenwilm N (2022) For whose sake, and by which means? Fairness concepts in European law – a reflection on the occasion of recent European legislation , especially the passage of the Digital Markets Act. ZEuP:820–828

Self-Preferencing Practices and Their Future After the DMA

Giacomo Tagiuri

Abstract The chapter describes the self-preferencing prohibition of Art. 6.5 DMA and the main interpretive problems that are likely to emerge in its enforcement. Certain features of the prohibition and its functionality are relatively clear: for example, the fact that it applies exclusively to rankings, and that it demands disclosures by gatekeepers of their ranking parameters. As the discussion in the chapter shows, however, identifying the types of ranking that will precisely substantiate the prohibited self-preferencing conduct presents several difficulties. The difficulties are linked mainly to the need of distinguishing between user-serving features of a ranking algorithm (e.g. the intention to privilege the quality of the results shown) and platform bias that works to the detriment of consumers, as it reduces choice and quality, and business users, as it deprives them of the benefits of their economic contribution to the platform. Based on these observations, as well as design choices of the DMA with regard to its enforcement (e.g. the importance of compliance reports), the chapter argues that Art. 6.5 is unlikely to really work as a per-se rule for the ex-ante identification of prohibited conduct, which is how the DMA prohibitions are mostly described in the scholarship. Most likely, article 6.5 will work as a form of quality standard for the design and presentation of rankings by vertically integrated platforms, to be enforced collaboratively with the undertakings. This functionality does not undermine the overall impulse of the DMA to facilitate scrutiny over digital platforms through a shift away from effects analysis, which had proven difficult in more traditional antitrust. As the chapter begins to show, the form of quality control over rankings that Art. 6.5 prefigures is different from an economic analysis of competitive effects. It focuses not so much on welfare effects and efficiencies, or the analysis of counterfactuals, but rather on explainability of the ranking parameters, and the design of the consumer interface design, to minimize platform bias and, where it had to emerge, its harmful effects. This interpretation points at a vision of the DMA as offering consumers constant monitoring of the

G. Tagiuri (✉)
University of Amsterdam, Amsterdam, Netherlands
e-mail: g.tagiuri@uva.nl

D. V. Popović, R. Kulms (eds.), *Repositioning Platforms in Digital Market Law*, European Union and its Neighbours in a Globalized World 15,
https://doi.org/10.1007/978-3-031-69678-7_8

quality of the platform, and specifically its rankings, which in turn ensures opportunities for business users to thrive on the platform and potentially, on the long run, contest its role.

1 Introduction

This contribution deals with one of the substantive prohibitions of the Digital Markets Act (DMA) that is receiving most scholarly attention—the so called self-preferencing prohibition of art 6.5. The phrases *self-preferencing, favoring,* or *treating more favorably*, which I here use interchangeably, describe a constellation of business practices whereby the provider of a vertically integrated platform favors its own products or offers on the platform (first party products) to the detriment of products and offers by third parties. This happens mostly, but not only, through awarding some form of visual prominence to the platform provider's own offers when the said offers are shown to consumers after a query.

These practices have recently come under the scrutiny of antitrust authorities in Europe and beyond.[1] The best known investigation into this type of conduct resulted in the record fine imposed by the EU Commission on Google for the favoring of its own shopping comparison service on the search results.[2] The Court of Justice of the EU, in upholding the decision, also implicitly confirmed that self-preferencing can describe a self-standing type of abuse under the law of art. 102 TFEU without the need to reconduct the conduct within more established types of exclusionary abuse such as the essential facility doctrine or tying.[3]

The EU Commission also scrutinized the conduct of Amazon, and in particular the criteria that Amazon uses to select the winner of its buy box, a visually

---

[1] See among others: Commission Decision of 27.06.2017, Case AT.39740 – *Google Search (Shopping)*; Commission Decision of 20.12.2022, Cases AT.40462 – *Amazon Marketplace* and AT.40703 – *Amazon Buy Box*; Autoritá Garante della Concorrenza e del Mercato (Italian Competition Authority), Decision of 30 November 2021, Case A 528 – *FBA Amazon*. See also the pending Commission investigation, Case AT.40684 – *Facebook Marketplace*. In the United States, the Federal Trade Commission sued Amazon for practices including self-preferencing. See Federal Trade Commission, *FTC Sues Amazon for Illegally Maintaining Monopoly Power*, September 26, 2023, available at: https://www.ftc.gov/news-events/news/press-releases/2023/09/ftc-sues-amazon-illegally-maintaining-monopoly-power.

[2] Commission Decision of 27.06.2017, Case AT.39740 – *Google Search (Shopping)*.

[3] Case T-612/17, *Google and Alphabet v Commission (Google Shopping)*, ECLI:EU:T:2021:763. While a decision on appeal by the ECJ is pending, the advocate general opinion confirmed the approach of the general court: Case C-48/22 P, *Google LLC, Alphabet, Inc. v European Commission*, Opinion of Advocate General Kokott, ECLI:EU:C:2024:14 ('the self-preferencing of which Google is accused constitutes an independent form of abuse through the application of unreasonable conditions of access to competing comparison shopping services, provided that it has at least potentially anticompetitive effects', para 90).

prominent area of its interface which allows consumers to complete a purchase faster.[4] Furthermore, scrutiny was brought onto the criteria used by Amazon to select the sellers that are allowed to offer products to Prime users, meaning those consumers that purchase the Prime loyalty program.[5] The concern of the Commission was that Amazon was favoring its own retail business, or, its own logistics and delivery services, in a way that harmed competition and 'marketplace sellers, their independent carriers, other marketplaces, as well as consumers that may not get to view the best deals'.[6] These investigations were concluded with the acceptance by the Commission of commitments by Amazon to, among others, treating all sellers equally when ranking for the selection of the Buy Box winner; and to showing a second offer from a different seller when this is sufficiently differentiated on price and/or delivery—basically doubling the Buy Box.[7] The Commitments were further strengthened after market-testing and are being monitored by an independent trustee.[8]

National competition authorities have also adopted infringement decisions for similar conduct. Most notably, the Italian NCA has imposed a record fine on Amazon for favoring its logistics and delivery services.[9] Amazon allegedly did so indirectly by giving preferential access to its Prime program to those third party-sellers that also purchased delivery services provided by Amazon (Fulfillment by Amazon - FBA). The Italian NCA decision has received ample attention, because it confirms the Google Shopping approach of treating self-preferencing as an independent category of abuse in the law of article 102. Because of its avoidance of questions concerning whether the foreclosed logistics providers were as efficient as Amazon, the decision has been dubbed by some as the first Neo-Brandeisian decision in Europe.[10] Furthermore, the Commission deploys the language of favoring or

[4] European Commission, Press Release, 17 July 2019, *Antitrust: Commission opens investigation into possible anti-competitive conduct of Amazon*, https://ec.europa.eu/commission/presscorner/detail/en/IP_19_4291.

[5] European Commission, Press Release, 10 November 2020, *Antitrust: Commission sends Statement of Objections to Amazon for the use of non-public independent seller data and opens second investigation into its e-commerce business practices*, https://ec.europa.eu/commission/presscorner/detail/en/ip_20_2077.

[6] European Commission, Press Release, 14 July 2022, *Antitrust: Commission seeks feedback on commitments offered by Amazon concerning marketplace seller data and access to Buy Box and Prime*, https://ec.europa.eu/commission/presscorner/detail/en/ip_22_4522. See also European Commission, Market Test Notice in Case AT.40703 *Amazon – Buy Box* and AT.40462 - *Amazon Marketplace*, O.J. C 278/8 (2022).

[7] Commission Decision of 20.12.2022, Cases AT.40462 – *Amazon Marketplace* and AT.40703 – *Amazon Buy Box*. See also Press Release, 20 December 2022, *Antitrust: Commission accepts commitments by Amazon barring it from using marketplace seller data, and ensuring equal access to Buy Box and Prime* https://ec.europa.eu/commission/presscorner/detail/en/ip_22_7777.

[8] *Ibid.*

[9] Autoritá Garante della Concorrenza e del Mercato, Decision of 30 November 2021, Case A 528 – *FBA Amazon.*

[10] For an account of the debate see Vezzoso (2022).

self-preferencing in pending 102 investigations against Google's treatment of its own 'online display advertising technology services to the detriment of competing providers of advertising technology services, advertisers and online publishers'[11] as well as the conduct of Facebook in relation to its marketplace.[12] And some of the practices by Apple vis a vis third party developers on the App store, as the object of investigations and litigation worldwide, may also be described, albeit the language is less explicit in the relevant cases, as favoring some of Apple services or products.[13]

The wealth of cases that has emerged in recent years is remarkable. These cases target all major digital companies that attract regulatory attention, and place self-preferencing practices at the center of discussions about reigning in the digital giants. To be sure, the phrase self-preferencing is a new qualifier for practices that have always existed in situations of vertical integration.[14] Think of the vertically integrated supermarket which may favor its own brands through prominent placement in the aisles. The new qualifier seeks to draw attention to the novel concerns that these practices generate in the digital economy. Indeed, there is ample agreement among economists and competition policy experts that the types of conduct mentioned above contribute significantly to the entrenchment of the gatekeeper's power with potential negative consequences for consumers, business users and competing platforms.[15] Despite disagreement on the specific theory of harm,[16] most scholarship would agree that at least some forms of self-preferencing are concerning.

Decisions such as Google Shopping, however, illustrate the difficulties of effectively tackling self-preferencing conduct through traditional ex post antitrust enforcement as based on article 102. First, as often remarked in the scholarship, the decision in Google shopping arrived too late, after Google competitors have suffered the negative consequences of Google's conduct for too long,[17] and a final

---

[11] Case AT.40670 *Google - Adtech and Data-related practices*. See European Commission, Press Release, 14 June 2023, *Antitrust: Commission sends Statement of Objections to Google over abusive practices in online advertising technology*, https://ec.europa.eu/commission/presscorner/detail/en/ip_23_3207.

[12] Case AT.40684 – *Facebook Marketplace*.

[13] Epic Games, the publisher of popular videogames such as Fortnite, sued Apple in US Courts for certain practices related to its pricing policy in the Apple store. See Nicas and Griffith (2021). See also the Dutch competition authority decision concerning Apple's conditions on the Apple store vis a vis dating app providers: Netherlands Authority for Consumers and Markets, Case ACM/19/035630, 24 August 2021, https://www.acm.nl/sites/default/files/documents/summary-of-decision-on-abuse-of-dominant-position-by-apple.pdf. The Commission has opened at least two cases against Apple: Case AT.40716 *Apple App Store Practices (music streaming)*; Case AT40452 *Apple – Mobile Payments*. For the latter, Apple proposed commitments to the commission: Proposal of Commitments to the European Commission, https://ec.europa.eu/competition/antitrust/cases1/202403/AT_40452_9866037_9192_4.pdf.

[14] See on this point Caminade et al. (2022).

[15] Cabral et al. (2021) (calling for placing self-preferencing among the black-listed practices to be prohibited ex ante, including because of the difficulty of ex post monitoring). See also Hagiu et al. (2022); Caminade et al. (2022); Motta (2023); Peitz (2023).

[16] See Motta (2023); Iacobucci and Ducci (2018).

[17] Crémer et al. (2019); Wytt (2023), p. 630.

decision by the ECJ is yet to come. Secondly, by seeking to ground self-preferencing in the law of article 102 as in independent form of abuse, the decision generated uncertainty and even controversy, because of the Commission's departure from better established forms of abuse, with alleged negative consequences for legal certainty, among others.[18]

It is in this context that the EU legislator has formalized a self-preferencing prohibition in the DMA. As per the functioning of the DMA, the provision is set up as a *per-se, ex ante,* prohibition, meaning that no proof of the prohibited conduct's harmful effects—not only on competition, but also on the DMA's declared objectives of contestability and fairness—is needed.[19] Furthermore, the prohibitions in the DMA are often described as *form-based,* namely they prohibit conduct based on some formal characteristics of the said conduct.[20] These features of the DMA's substantive rules are there to facilitate the modification of conduct that experience gathered through traditional antitrust enforcement has shown to be harmful.[21] While I preliminarily accept the above characterization of the DMA substantive provisions as per-se, form-based, rules, some of the findings in this chapter question the said characterization, at least in relation to self-preferencing. Far from closing the debate on the future of self-preferencing, the substantive rule of art 6.5 leaves us with significant uncertainty concerning which practices are allowed and which prohibited.

To reduce this uncertainty, the chapter offers a description of the prohibition, discusses the main interpretive questions that it presents, and offers some preliminary answers to the said questions. The answers presented in this chapter rely on a reading of the DMA in the broader context of EU regulatory efforts to govern the digital economy, with particular attention to EU competition law cases that have foreshadowed the formalization of the art. 6.5 prohibition. Through its focus on the self-preferencing prohibition, the chapter also aims to illuminate some of the key features of the DMA in its relationship with the EU competition rules and contributes to the conceptualization of the DMA, its goals, and functionalities. As the chapter shows, the self-preferencing prohibition occupies a special role in the architecture of the DMA as it is paradigmatic of the broader concerns that animate the Act and well illustrates some of the key features of its enforcement. A reading of the

[18] Ibanez Colomo (2020); Iacobucci and Ducci (2018); Eben (2018); Deutscher (2021); Cf. Bouzoraa (2022).

[19] This feature of the DMA is amply emphasized in the scholarship. See among others Petit (2021); Wytt (2023). For a distinction between a rule-based and standard base approach in relation to the DMA see Kerber (2021).

[20] Most explicitly, de la Mano et al. (2021).

[21] This characterizes many of the substantive prohibitions of article 5, 6 and 7 of the DMA. For example the prohibition of Art. 5.2 on combination and cross-use of end-user data collected on a core platform for the provision of other services by the gatekeeper mirrors the German Bundeskartellamt Facebook decision: Bundeskartellamt, B-22/16, Decision of 15.02.2019, Facebook, *Exploitative business terms pursuant to Section 19(1) GWB for inadequate data processing*. These features bring scholars to describe competition law as 'embedded in the DMA'. See Kuenzler (2023), p. 139.

prohibition in the light of the DMA's broader goals and functionalities helps to reduce some of the interpretive uncertainty that the self-preferencing prohibition presents us with.

The contribution is structured as follows. The next Sect. 2 describes the prohibition as it appears under the DMA, and surveys its goals and key features. The following Sect. 3 highlights the main interpretative questions that are likely to emerge in the application of the provision and offers some preliminary answers. Section 4 introduces some practical constraints that partially problematize the answers offered in Sect. 3. This section allows to further substantiate my point about the paradigmatic nature of the prohibition and as an entry point into a deeper understanding of the DMA. The fifth section concludes.

2 The Self-Preferencing Prohibition in the DMA

Article 6.5 of the DMA states that designated gatekeepers 'shall not treat more favorably, in ranking and related indexing and crawling, services and products offered by the gatekeeper itself than similar services or products of a third party'. This is the self-preferencing prohibition narrowly understood. Furthermore, a second sentence in the article prescribes that gatekeepers 'shall apply transparent, fair and non-discriminatory conditions to such ranking'. Given the combination of these two substantive rules, Art 6.5 can be seen as a provision aimed at regulating ranking by gatekeepers. When producing rankings, the gatekeeper should not only refrain from favoring its own products and offers, but also ensure that transparent, fair, and non-discriminatory conditions apply to the said rankings. While this contribution focuses mostly on the prohibition in the first sentence, the general duty inserted in the second sentence offers guidance on how to interpret the prohibition itself.

An immediate question that the provision generates is what ranking is. The DMA defines ranking in Art. 2.22.[22] The provision of 2.22 does three things. First, it offers a basic definition of ranking as the process of giving 'relative prominence' to goods or services (or 'relevance' to search results on a search engine). Second, it defines the types of core platform services which can engage in ranking. These are online intermediation services (including online marketplaces and application stores),[23] online social networking services, video-sharing social platform services, virtual assistants, and search engines. Third, Art. 2.22 clarifiers that ranking has to do with the ways in which products and offers are presented, organized or communicated

[22] The definition mirrors the one in Art. 2.8 of Regulation (EU) 2019/1150 of the European Parliament and of the Council of 20 June 2019 on promoting fairness and transparency for business users of online intermediation services O.J. L 186/57 (2019) (hereinafter Platform to Business regulation or P2B Regulation).

[23] Art 2.5 DMA refers to Art 2.2 P2B Regulation for the definition of online intermediation services. Pursuant to recital 11 of that regulation, these include e-commerce marketplaces (including for example Amazon) and Apple stores.

'…irrespective of the technological means used for such presentation, organization or communication and irrespective of whether only one result is presented or communicated'. Despite the presence of a definition, the scope of ranking presents uncertainty, to which I return in Sect. 3.2.

More clarity exists regarding the subjective scope of application of the provision. Like all substantive rules of the DMA, art 6.5 applies to conduct engaged by a *gatekeeper* insofar as it provides a *core platform service*.[24] In September 2023, the Commission designated a first batch of 6 gatekeepers in relation to 22 core platform services.[25] Since art 6.5 only applies in the context of ranking, and the definition of ranking specifically refers to only a subset of the possible core platform services to which the DMA applies, we take art. 2.22 to limit the scope of application of the self-preferencing prohibition.[26] Based on the designation, and the helpful narrowing down of the types of core platform services that can engage in ranking, the provision will apply for example to Google Search, the Apple Store and Amazon Marketplace. On all these platforms (unlike in other types of core platform services such as operating systems and web browsers), the presentation of offers, products or search results to consumers typically involves ranking: prominence is awarded to some offers over others when the said offers are communicated or presented to consumers.

Another element of relative clarity concerns the types of markets for which the self-preferencing prohibition is devised, namely two-sided (at least) markets dominated by a vertically integrated platform. As made clear by Recital 51 DMA, Art. 6.5 aims to regulate problems which derive from the fact that 'gatekeepers are often vertically integrated'. This means that the gatekeeper offers products or services (first party products[27]) that are additional to, or *separate* from, the core platform services through which they are offered. First-party products are offered in competition with third-party products on the platform. Whether vertical integration is a sufficient or necessary descriptor for what enables self-preferencing may be questioned: some of the platforms that the prohibition covers are better described as ecosystems[28] and/or conglomerate settings[29] than as vertically integrated. But to

---

[24] Wytt (2023), p. 636.

[25] European Commission, Press Release, 6 September 2023, *Digital Markets Act: Commission designates six gatekeepers, https://ec.europa.eu/commission/presscorner/detail/en/ip_23_4328.* The designated gatekeepers *are* Alphabet (the provider among others of the core platform services Google Search, Google Shopping, and Google Maps); Amazon (Amazon Marketplace); Apple (as the provider of the App Store and Safari); Bytedance (TikTok); Meta (Facebook, Instagram and Meta Marketplace); and Microsoft (as the provider of Linkedin and the Microsoft OS).

[26] In other words, a gatekeeper can violate the self-preferencing prohibition only insofar as it provides one of the five core platform services listed above: only on these types of platforms *ranking* happens. It is unclear whether the list is conclusive.

[27] Economics literature routinely speaks of first party offers to indicate the offers offered directly by the vertically integrated platform, while of third party offers to indicate offers by business users on the platform. See e.g. Peitz (2023); Hagiu et al. (2022). This language is not used by the DMA itself.

[28] Hornung (2023).

[29] Bourreau and de Streel (2019).

think about the vertically integrated platform is helpful because it allows to visualize the types of situations in which the provision applies. Furthermore, the emphasis on vertical integration facilitates the bringing into focus that two separate services or products must be present for self-preferencing to exist, a point I further explore in Sect. 3.1.

Recital 51 of the DMA provides illustrative examples of the forms of integration that may lead to self-preferencing. The first mention goes to situations in which a gatekeeper provides its own online intermediation service through an online search engine—similar to the situation of Alphabet providing its own shopping comparison service, Google Shopping, through Google search. Another scenario is the one of software applications developed by the gatekeeper distributed through online application stores which are designated as a core platform service—think Apple distributing its own apps through the Apple store. Furthermore the recital mentions 'videos distributed through a video-sharing platform'; 'products or services that are given prominence and display in the newsfeed of an online social networking services' (think here the pending antitrust investigation concerning Meta favoring Facebook Marketplace on the Facebook social network[30]); and finally 'products or services ranked in search results or displayed on an online marketplace' or offered through a virtual assistant (think Amazon, which on top of operating a marketplace also retails its own products and offers on the marketplace, including its Amazon basics).

The emphasis placed on vertical integration is also helpful because it allows some preliminary observations on the goals of the self-preferencing prohibition. The DMA explicitly links the ability of the gatekeeper to favor its own products and offers to the *dual role* performed by the gatekeeper as both 'intermediary for third-party undertakings and as undertaking directly providing product or services.'[31] The language of the *dual role* has been widely deployed in debates on the regulation of the digital economy. For example, in the years preceding the adoption of the DMA, concerns have emerged in both the popular press[32] and scholarly debates[33] around Amazon's dual role. As mentioned, formal antitrust scrutiny has followed suit, where the language of the dual role, and the characterization of Amazon as a dual platform, were also frequent.[34]

[30] European Commission, Press Release, 19 December 2022, *Antitrust: Commission sends Statement of Objections to Meta over abusive practices benefiting Facebook Marketplace* https://ec.europa.eu/commission/presscorner/detail/en/ip_22_7728.

[31] The language is also employed by economists which describe platforms as operating in a dual mode. See Hagiu et al. (2022); Etro (2022).

[32] US Senator Elizabeth Warren has notoriously evoked this dual role by reference to a sport metaphor: 'You don't get to be umpire and have a team.' The statement was part of Warren public campaigning for legislation that would break up digital corporations. Warren's words evoke the conflict of interest of the platform. See Kaufman (2019).

[33] See among others Khan (2017, 2019).

[34] In Europe, Commission Decision of 20.12.2022, Cases AT.40462 – *Amazon Marketplace* and AT.40703 – *Amazon Buy Box*; Autoritá Garante della Concorrenza e del Mercato (Italian Competition Authority), Decision of 30 November 2021, Case A 528 – *FBA Amazon,* para 746.

While the precise concerns entailed by the emphasis on a platform's dual role may be hard to pin down,[35] the DMA explicitly links the dual role to the *conflict of interest* it generates. Because of the said conflict of interest, the gatekeeper has an incentive to design and run the platform, not in the best interest of its business users and consumers (which would entail for example showing consumers, at the top of the ranking, the lowest priced offer, or the offer that best matches their search parameters), but to favor its own products. When the platform acts upon the said conflict of interest, it is said to engage in what economists call platform bias.[36] The gatekeepers of the digital economy can do so more or less unconstrained, because of their sizeable power on the market for the platform service, where intense positive network effects, consumer loyalty induced through various ancillary or integrated products, as well as other economies of scale, make it hard for a rival platform to challenge the incumbent by competing on the quality of the matching and ranking alone.[37]

To delve a bit deeper into the goals of the prohibition, it is first helpful to discuss in which way the obligation of art. 6.5 relates to the two stated objectives of the DMA, namely contestability and fairness. Contestability as defined in recital 32 of the DMA is the ability of a competitor to challenge the gatekeeper on the merit of their products or services. As mentioned, this would require overcoming the barriers to entry or expansion as linked to network effects, economies of scale, and benefits from data, that characterize the digital economy.[38] Insofar as it emphasizes the ability of competitors to challenge the gatekeeper, contestability may be seen as having an ordo-liberal pedigree[39] as linked to the normative value assigned to access to markets, economic participation, and in turn consumer choice.[40] But the DMA also points at how weak contestability is a problem for consumer welfare. As explicit in recital 32, weak contestability 'reduces the incentives to innovate and improve products and services for the gatekeeper, its business users, its challengers and

[35] The role of images like the dual role, or the umpire/player, in driving public scrutiny into the conduct of platform providers and its regulation has been questioned by economists who advocate more clarity and theory in the study of competition on the platforms and its functioning. See Caffarra et al. (2020) warning against the role of "*subjective priors*" in driving regulatory intervention.

[36] Many studies seek to define and measure platform bias—see e.g. Reimers and Waldfogel (2023).

[37] These features of the digital economy are amply described in various reports that have preceded the formal adoption of legislation on competition in the digital economy, including the DMA. See Crémer et al. (2019) commissioned by the EU Commission. The DMA summarizes the findings of the reports in its initial recitals 1–7. Analogous reports have been adopted in several countries including in the UK - the Digital Competition Expert Panel (2019) s.c. Furman Report – and the US - Nadler and Cicilline (2020).

[38] This is largely in line with the description of digital markets in Crémer et al. (2019).

[39] Peitz (2023), p. 311 (with specific reference to recital 32). Emphasizing the ordo-liberal roots of the DMA see de De Streel (2020); De Streel and Larouche (2021); Caffarra and Scott Morton (2021). But cf. Woersdoerfer (2023).

[40] For an overview of ordoliberal values and approaches in relation to the digital economy see Woersdoerfer (2023).

customers and thus negatively affects the innovation potential of the wider online platform economy'.[41]

As it is clear from the recitals, contestability aims to dislodge both the entrenched power of the gatekeeper on the market for the platform (inter-platform competition) and the power that the gatekeepers often grow downstream (intra-platform competition). This is explicit in the last sentence of recital 31, which reads that the obligations in the Regulation should not only ensure contestability and fairness with respect to core platform services, but also with respect 'to other digital products and services into which gatekeepers leverage their gateway position, which are often provided together with, or in support of, the core platform services'.

Self-preferencing certainly reduces intra-platform competition, which the DMA sees as part of, and conducive to, contestability. This is explicit in recital 51, as self-preferencing is described as undermining 'directly the contestability' for those products or services that compete with the favored products, 'to the detriment of business users which are not controlled by the gatekeeper'. This is in line with the economics literature which identifies in different forms of foreclosure the main risks from self-preferencing.[42]

Furthermore, as observed by economists, self-preferencing reduces the quality of the offer on the platform as self-preferencing may result in an unwillingness of competitors downstream to innovate and compete on the merit: even if they offer a better product, the gatekeeper will still favor its own offers when communicating with consumers, either through rankings or by asking higher commissions from third parties.[43] Less incentives to innovate lead to less product variety on the platform, and product variety on the platform is strictly linked to the product quality of the platform. Indeed, self-preferencing leads to presenting consumers with a poor representation of the existing offer, which can be construed as a degradation of product quality. In a competitive market this type of quality degradation would be constrained by entrants or existing competitors upstream (in the market for platform services), but lack of inter-platform competition, coupled with the well documented barriers to entry which exist in the digital economy preclude this from happening.[44]

The relationship between inter-platform and intra-platform competition deserves a few more observations. As recital 32 acknowledges, while the goal of the DMA is that competitors will have the ability to contest the role of the gatekeeper in the provision of the core platform service (inter-platform competition), 'the role of the gatekeeper may be entrenched to such an extent that inter-platform competition is not effective in the short term, meaning that intra-platform competition must be created or increased'. The importance of this statement is hard to overstate for understanding the overall nature of the DMA. The ambition to preserve together

---

[41] A rich discussion of the meaning of contestability and fairness can be found in Crémer et al. (2023b). N.B. The use of contestability in the DMA has nothing to do with the economic theory of Contestable Markets as developed by Baumol (1982).

[42] Motta (2023); Iacobucci and Ducci (2018).

[43] Peitz (2023), p. 311.

[44] Crémer et al. (2019).

competition for the platform (inter-platform) and competition on the platform (intra-platform) is characteristic of the DMA, unlike other similar proposals, which may instead accept the incontestability of the gatekeeping role and aspire to regulate in the interest of platform neutrality.[45]

From this perspective, the DMA, rejects the binary between decentralization through break-up and mere regulation for access and portability, which has characterised much of the existing debates in competition law.[46] The EU legislator insists on preserving a horizon where the contestability of the platform, which is inter-platform competition is preserved. In turn, the approach is pragmatic, and it acknowledges that inter-platform competition might be practically reduced to such an extent that it needs to be built from scratch. As research has shown contestation of the platform's entrenched position may be more likely to come from within the ecosystem, where other competing platforms are also often active downstream with their products or services:[47] hence, another reason for the emphasis on intra-platform competition. As we further explore later in the chapter, meaningful intra-platform competition requires design choices that work to the benefit of consumers and business users.

The self-preferencing prohibition also serves the specific notion of fairness pursued by the DMA. Indeed, when the DMA speaks of unfairness, it has something precise in mind: it aims to remedy an imbalance between the rights and duties of the business users and the gatekeeper, which is unfairness in the vertical chain. This notion of unfairness is animated by a concern that market participants should be able to 'adequately capture the benefits resulting from their innovative or other efforts', which may be precluded by the said imbalance, an imbalance that as recital 33 specifies 'may ... consist in excluding or discriminating against business users, in particular if the latter compete with the services provided by the gatekeeper'. This is not the unfairness of excessive (unfair) prices as proscribed by art. 102 TFEU, a type of abuse which exploits consumers. It is unfairness on the business side, more akin to the concerns that guide national unfair competition laws or more recently interventions aimed at remedying the imbalance of power in business-to-business

---

[45] Platform neutrality is a concept which creates a parallel between the regulation of digital platforms and the model of essential facility or natural monopoly regulation as found in the networked industries or public utilities. As such this approach is less focused on competition and more on regulation. See CNNum (2014).

[46] I take this binary to be one of the features of what Kuenzler (2023) calls second-generation competition law.

[47] Jacobides and Lianos (2021). The importance of competition in adjacent or complementary markets for the contestability of the target market is also recognized in pre-digital settings: consider for example the Commission guidance on tying and bundling, which recognizes that tying may lead to foreclosure not only in the tied but also in the tying market. European Commission, Communication from the Commission – Guidance on the Commission's enforcement priorities in applying Article 82 of the EC Treaty to abusive exclusionary conduct by dominant undertakings O.J. C 45/7 (2009), para. 50; para. 52.

relations in specific sectors.[48] From this perspective, the DMA is responsive to growing concerns for the dependence of business users from the platform,[49] concerns that are more deeply engrained in the competition laws of at least some member states.[50] Think of Amazon's third-party sellers, which are often small if not micro businesses, and as such are very vulnerable to exclusion from, or penalization on, the platform. The insistence, visible elsewhere in the DMA, that business users must have the ability to multi-home, is also indication of this type of concern.[51] Finally, it is worth mentioning that this notion of fairness is also often evoked through the metaphor of creating a *level playing field*, which while mostly absent in the law itself,[52] abounds in commentary and institutional communication around the introduction of the DMA.[53]

Contestability and fairness concerns are not mutually exclusive. To the contrary, they are closely intertwined.[54] As noted in recital 34, 'the lack of, or weak, contestability for a certain service can enable a gatekeeper to engage in unfair practices. Similarly, unfair practices by a gatekeeper can reduce the possibility of business users or others to contest the gatekeeper's position. A particular obligation in this Regulation may, therefore, address both elements'. This appears to be the status of the self-preferencing prohibition as self-preferencing can undermine both contestability and fairness.

To be sure, the concerns with self-preferencing may also map onto further goals. At stake with the power of gatekeepers are issues that while still largely beyond the concerns that competition law and policy are comfortable to pursue explicitly, have become unavoidable considerations in the regulation of the digital economy.[55] Think for example of media pluralism and cultural production.[56] A gatekeeper who

---

[48] In the digital sector see the P2B Regulation; See more generally Directive (EU) 2019/633 of the European Parliament and of the council of 17 April 2019 on unfair trading practices in business-to-business relationships in the agricultural and food supply chain, O.J. *L 111/59 (2019).*

[49] DMA recital 2; recital 40.

[50] Germany and France among other countries prohibit unilateral conduct not only by dominant companies, but also by companies that have superior bargaining power vis a vis third parties. Germany notably does so through its competition law: see section 20 of the German Competition Act (Gesetz gegen Wettbewerbsbeschränkungen – GWB). See also Art. L442-1, para. 2 of the French Code of Commercial Law, and the recently introduced Article I.6. Belgian Code of Economic Law. For an overview of national interventions concerned with reducing economic dependance and imbalance of power in retail supply chains see Cafaggi and Iamiceli (2018).

[51] DMA Recital 40.

[52] One reference can be found in DMA Recital 54.

[53] See the European Council dedicated page: https://www.consilium.europa.eu/en/policies/digital-markets-act/#:~:text=The%20Digital%20Markets%20Act%20focuses,biggest%20share%20of%20the%20market. See Neves (2023). See the P2B regulation, where this is much more explicit a concern.

[54] Crémer et al. (2023b).

[55] Ezrachi (2017); Svetiev (2020).

[56] These concerns are quite explicit also in the governmental reports, especially Nadler and Cicilline (2020). See also Kuenzler (2022, 2023).

provides a news feed and that favors its own news insensitively to consumer preferences may harm the viability of independent media outlets to the detriment of media pluralism and the quality of independent reporting.[57] Furthermore, as social media platforms are major avenues for self-expression through content creation, gatekeeping platforms are in a position to deprive pro-sumers of the benefits of their creativity. Such concerns have a collective dimension as expressed in anxieties for the detrimental effects of concentration in digital markets on an open society and democracy.[58]

While a complete mapping of the goals of the DMA is beyond the scope of this paper it is worth noting that the DMA signals a departure from the need to justify the harm of the practices it prohibits in narrow competition terms, which is in the language of efficiency and/or consumer welfare. In contrast, the frame offered by the goals of contestability and fairness is broad enough to allow for the inclusion of all the considerations mentioned above. In the interpretation of each specific conduct rule of the DMA, it is thus possible and desirable to be inclusive of the broader set of goals that animate the DMA.

We have so far roughly visualized which types of situations art 6.5 aims to regulate and for which aims. But what conduct exactly can be prohibited by the first sentence of art. 6.5 still requires clarification. To get closer to answering this question three sets of interpretative issues should be addressed. These involve, in order, the issue of what constitutes separate products; more precision on the notion of ranking; and finally, which types of practices amount to favoring.

When discussing the self-preferencing rule in the DMA and the interpretive uncertainty it generates, we must keep in mind that the provision, as included in Art. 6 DMA, is one of the substantive rules that may be subject to further specification by the European Commission (hereinafter the Commission). The Commission may clarify the conduct rules listed in Art. 6 and 7 DMA in two ways; through implementing acts aimed at clarifying the measures that a gatekeeper needs to adopt to comply with them (Art. 8.2); and by engaging in regulatory dialogue upon request by the gatekeeper, to determine whether the compliance measures adopted by the gatekeeper are effective in achieving the objectives of the relevant obligation (Art. 8.3). Furthermore, it is worth mentioning that the enforcement of the substantive obligations in the DMA relies on collaboration between the Commission and the gatekeepers. For example, enforcement starts with an analysis of the compliance measures proposed by the gatekeeper pursuant to art. 11 DMA within 6 months from designation. This suggests that in DMA enforcement there may be a much less clear-cut distinction between the finding of a violation and the remedies imposed to

---

[57] The Digital Services Act, Regulation (EU) 2022/2065 of the European Parliament and of the Council of 19 October 2022 *on a Single Market For Digital Services and amending Directive 2000/31/EC*, O.J. L 277/1 (2022) is more narrowly tailored towards issues of quality of and access to information. But provisions of the DMA, including art. 6(5) could be deployed to advance these goals. See Kuenzler (2023).

[58] Among many contributions see Cohen (2019).

ensure compliance than under more traditional competition law.[59] This has implications for our substantive analysis and the level of uncertainty that the conduct rules can tolerate. While the next Sect. 3 provides answers to the interpretive issues emerging in relation to Art. 6.5 that largely ignore constraints coming from the enforcement structure of DMA, these constraints are reintroduced in Sect. 4.

3 The Main Interpretative Issues

This section builds on the above to delve into the three main interpretative questions that have been discussed in the scholarship and are likely to emerge in the application of Art. 6.5. These are: what constitutes separate products; what constitutes ranking; what constitutes favoring.

3.1 Separate Products

As it emerges from the prohibition and the recitals, two distinct products or services must exist for the self-preferencing prohibition and Art 6.5 more broadly to kick in: one is the core platform service; the second is the additional service or product that is being favored. The issue of separateness of the products has been identified in the scholarship as one of the points of uncertainty in the future enforcement of Art. 6.5.[60] The core platform service must be one of those which relies on *ranking* for the provision of the service, namely, as mentioned above: online intermediation services (including online marketplaces and application stores), online search engines, online social networking services, video-sharing social platform services and virtual assistants. The additional service or product that is being favored may be another designated core platform service (think, for example, of Google Search and Google Shopping, which are both designated as core platform services), but also a digital service that does not meet the standards to be designated as core platform (think the various Apple apps which are sold on the Apple store) and even a non-digital product or service (e.g. the Amazon Basics sold on the marketplace, or also the Amazon fulfillment services).

While separateness may seem a trivial category to assess, it is not always easy to determine whether the core platform service and the object of the favoring are

---

[59] Although that distinction is blurring also in competition enforcement also due to the growing use of commitments. See Svetiev (2020).

[60] Peitz (2022); See also Graef I, *Disentangling Article 6.5 of the Digital Markets Act*, Presentation at the Technical Workshop on the Effective Implementation of the Digital Markets Act, *DMA workshop - Applying the DMA's ban on self-preferencing: how to do it in practice?*, 5 December 2022 https://digital-markets-act.ec.europa.eu/events/dma-workshop-applying-dmas-ban-self-preferencing-how-do-it-practice-2022-12-05_en.

separate. Separateness may thus become a point of contention in the application of the provision. It is plausible that gatekeepers will seek to question the existence of separate products or services, for example through the notion of ecosystems, which indeed aspires to overcome over-narrow definitions of product markets in the description of vertically integrated online marketplaces.[61] From this perspective, it is not surprising that the DMA, in Recital 51, describes instead the problem of self-preferencing as one of the vertically integrated gatekeepers. As mentioned, while vertical integration may be an insufficient descriptor for some of the situations that the provision wants to capture,[62] it makes clear that separate products are at stake and that one product is necessary for the provision of the other.

To illustrate the ways in which separateness may become an issue, the Google Shopping case is helpful. As Google argued in challenging the decision, the services that the Commission qualified as comparison shopping services were just part of the general search: '…the Commission's definition of a comparison-shopping service implies a "separate stand-alone service [that] in response to queries […] returns product offers from merchants" website [and offers] search tools that are specific' to product search. The function of Product Universals[63] [...] was, however, to provide relevant responses to user queries, like all results on Google's general search results pages…'.[64] Similarly Google claimed that the Shopping Unit was not a comparison shopping service but rather an improved form of showing Google's own advertised results (AdWords).[65] These arguments were dismissed by the Commission by reference to the fact that both the Product Universal and, later on, the Shopping Unit were not comparison shopping services as such, but some of the avenues through which Google favored its comparison shopping service, which despite changing name and business model showed continuity as a separate service.[66] As these arguments illustrate, the uncertainty may surround not so much the existence of a separate service in the abstract (Google seemed to implicitly acknowledge that Search and Shopping Comparison are two separate services) but whether certain functionalities and/or features of the consumer interface (e.g. Google's Product Universal and the Shopping Unit) amount to providing the said separate service.

Further indications that separateness may become contentious are found, for example, in debates around the Commission 102 investigation into META,

[61] Hornung (2023).

[62] In digital ecosystems, it is hard to describe what is upstream and what is downstream, for example.

[63] Product Universal was how Google named the integration of its Google Product Search (the name of Google's shopping comparison from 2007 until it was renamed Google Shopping in 2012) into the general Google search. With the renaming Google also changed the business model of its shopping comparison services as it started to charge merchants every time their offer was clicked on via Google Shopping. Product Universal is the equivalent of the Google shopping unit. Commission Decision of 27.6.2017, (AT.39740 - Google Search (Shopping)), paras 28–32.

[64] *Ibid.*, para 403.

[65] *Ibid.*, para 404.

[66] *Ibid.*, paras 408–423.

concerning a potential leveraging of Facebook dominance from its core service—the Facebook Social Network—into a related service, the Facebook marketplace,[67] based on a theory of harm that, after the CJEU Google Shopping decision may well be amounting to mere self-preferencing.[68] As suggested by Eliana Graces, former Director of Economic Policy at META, investigations such as the one into the Facebook Marketplace seem grounded on a rather static idea of the separate markets that may exist in the digital economy.[69] Indeed, while integrated solutions and products may be pervasive in the digital economy, they are not always supply-driven—the product of a strategy by the provider of the core platform to enter a separate market. As Graces observed, more often 'the service that appears on the side is … generative, almost like an evolution of your product that ends up creating another product…'[70] This is the case of Facebook where what is now labelled as Facebook Marketplace started as a user-generated innovation (buy-sell groups created by consumers), which were later regulated by Meta and integrated into a separate set of functionalities on the platform.

Facebook and the Meta marketplace have been separately designated as core platform services, although Meta has appealed the designation of its marketplace including on the grounds that a consumer-to-consumer service cannot fall under the label of an online intermediation service.[71] A separate designation would seem to completely preclude arguments that rely on the lack of separateness to resist application of the self-preferencing prohibition and Facebook's appeal is likely motivated also by a willingness to keep this line of argument open.

While designation of both services may reduce uncertainty by certifying the separate nature of the products, self-preferencing can benefit endless products and services, including non-digital ones, thus we expect to see deliberation and, potentially, even litigation on what constitutes separate products. This possibility is made even more plausible by the explicit mention in the DMA that even services which are perfectly integrated within the core platform service may be subject to scrutiny.[72] This foreshadows a type of uncertainty similar to the one emerged in the

---

[67] Case AT.40684, *Facebook Marketplace*, Statement of Objection, https://ec.europa.eu/commission/presscorner/detail/en/ip_22_7728.

[68] T-612/17, *Google and Alphabet v Commission*, ECLI:EU:T:2021:763. See also the opinion of AG Kokott on appeal, Case C-48/22 P, ECLI:EU:C:2024:14.

[69] Eliana Garces, Director of Economic Policy at Meta (at the time of the event), observations at the roundtable *Platform Neutrality and Self-Preferencing: a Competition and Innovation Policy Perspective*, May 31 2022, SDA Bocconi School of Management, https://www.sdabocconi.it/en/school-events/platform-neutrality-and-self-preferencing-a-competition-and-innovation-policy-perspective-online-20220531. Recording available at: https://www.youtube.com/watch?v−TWk73UwZp2w.

[70] *Ibid.*

[71] Mukherjee and Yun Chee (2023).

[72] Para 52 DMA insofar as it specifies that ranking also covers situations in which the core platform service presents or communicates only one result to the user. See the interpretation of Peitz (2023), for which this would describe scenarios such as the Amazon buy box or voice assistants, p. 315.

Google shopping case, whereby doubt is cast on whether certain functionalities offered in the consumer interface amount to providing a specific service.

To be sure, the likely challenges to the notion of separate products that may come from business are not to be dismissed as mere circumvention strategies. The question of when a new set of functionalities or uses, which are home-grown to a platform, become a separate product for which a competitive market should be aspired to, is certainly a difficult one, which in turn points at some difficult questions about the definition of separate markets and products in digital ecosystems and even about how competition can look like in the digital economy.[73] It is precisely due to the intractable nature of these questions that scholars have called for a more limited role of market definition in the development of competition policy for the digital economy.[74] The DMA can also be seen as addressing the need to overcome questions about market definition: for example, it sets up the process of designation as a gatekeeper as narrowly rule-based and contains an explicit warning that market definition should not provide a justification to escape designation as a gatekeeper.[75] As here illustrated, however, the very idea of self-preferencing relies on a notion of separate products, which is an unavoidable step to identify whether the characteristics of the outlawed conduct are present. This identification can create interpretive problems, short of cases where also the favored products are also designated as core platform services. As it repeatedly will emerge in our story, the aspiration to set-up DMA prohibitions as narrowly rule-based is hardly tenable and differentiation emerges at several points.[76]

When faced with questions concerning the separate nature of the products, some guidance may be found in CJEU decisions that had to answer a similar question in relation to forms of abuse of dominance that also rely on the existence of distinct products, such as tying or bundling.[77] As both the case law and the Commission enforcement guidance that builds on it make clear, whether the products are distinct depends fundamentally on customer demand.[78] While some of the indications may be trivial or provide little help in the context of multi-sided platforms,[79] others appear intuitively more helpful, for example the indication by the Court to look at

[73] Crémer et al. (2019). For a theorization of different types of uncertainty especially in the digital economy see Svetiev (2020).

[74] Crémer et al. (2019), p. 46. Cf. Franck and Peitz (2021).

[75] DMA, recital 23.

[76] See on this point Kerber (2021).

[77] See European Commission, Guidance on the Commission's enforcement priorities in applying article 82 of the EC Treaty to abusive exclusionary conduct by dominant undertakings, O.J. C 45/02, 2009, para 50, by reference to case T 201/04, *Microsoft v Commission,* ECLI:EU:T:2007:289, paras 842; 859.

[78] Guidance on the Commission's enforcement priorities, para 51.

[79] Evidence to determine whether products are different may include evidence showing whether customers, when given a choice, purchase the product separately by different suppliers. See Guidance on the Commission Enforcement priorities, para 51, by reference to Hilti v. Commission, Case T 30/89, ECLI:EU:T:1991:70, para 67. This type of reasoning may be harder to apply to platforms where often the main product is some form of intermediation service, which enables the

whether there is a presence on the market of undertakings specialized on the sale of one product and not the other.[80] In Microsoft, to carry some weight were also the fact that Microsoft offered a version of the Media player not integrated with Windows for use on Apple and others; the fact that Microsoft released upgrades for the media player which were independent of upgrades to the Windows PC operating system; and that promotions existed specifically targeting Media Player users.[81] Furthermore the Court has reiterated in several decisions that complementary products can be separate products.[82]

All in all, the weight to be given to the notion of separateness will depend on what we think the concerns behind the self-preferencing prohibition are. In the enforcement under article 102, self-preferencing practices have been sanctioned as instances of leveraging, with an emphasis on preventing the use of the market power which an undertaking holds in one market to reduce competition and grow market power in a downstream or adjacent market. Insofar as the self-preferencing prohibition is mainly aimed at preventing leveraging, then two markets must exist and in the interest of legal certainty and of the companies' right of defense, arguments on the separateness of the two products must be carefully assessed in the application of Art. 6.5, with a standard to be developed by building on previous 102 decisional practice and case law, for example Microsoft. However, as discussed, leveraging is only one, and possibly not the main concern, that animates the ex-ante self-preferencing prohibition of the DMA. For example, in the DMA there is much more emphasis on the fact that business users on the platform be rewarded for their economic contribution,[83] or, as some have argued, on the integrity/quality of the consumer representation of the existing offer.[84] A prevalence of this latter type of concerns may point at a relative marginalization of the issue of separateness with more limited space and time devoted to proving and questioning the separate nature of the products.

In any event, as the Google shopping case aptly illustrates, the existence of separate product may not be the most contentious issue in the enforcement of a self-preferencing prohibition: more complex is the assessment of what constitutes the promotion and presentation of those separate products in a complex user interface, and what amounts to favoring in that context - issues which are more thoroughly explored in the next two sub-sections.[85]

---

search or distribution of the ancillary or complementary product which are home-grown to the platform—see the discussion on Facebook above.

[80] *Ibid.* See also *Microsoft v Commission,* para 927.

[81] *Microsoft v. Commission,* paras 928–930.

[82] *Ibid.,* para 921. See also most recently European Commission, Notice on the definition of the relevant market for the purposes of Union Competition Law, O.J. C-1645/01 (2024), paras. 99-104

[83] DMA, recital 33.

[84] Kuenzler (2020). See also Guidelines on *ranking transparency pursuant to Regulation (EU) 2019/1150 of the European Parliament and of the Council*, O.J. C-424/01 (2020) (hereinafter the Ranking Transparency Guidelines), para 12.

[85] In Google shopping the Commission, in response to Google's arguments, went at great length to show how the Product Universals and the Shopping Unit as specific features of the consumer interface amounted to means of favoring Google Shopping Comparison service, rather than constituting the

3.2 The Notion of Ranking

Art 6.5 is the key provision in the DMA aimed at regulating ranking by gatekeepers on core platform services. A focus on ranking was also present in previous EU interventions in the regulation of the digital economy[86] and is justified by an awareness that the quality of ranking as essential to preserve consumer choice is one of the main parameters on which online platforms compete, and a key source of value for both consumers and business users. The focus of the DMA on the regulation of ranking is also rooted in an awareness that only non-discriminatory ranking can adequately reward the contribution of business users, mostly smaller firms, to the digital economy, as vital to entrepreneurship and the maintenance of competition on the platform. As observed in the Guidelines on Ranking Transparency adopted pursuant to the Platform to Business Regulation, whose relevance in the application of art 6.5 DMA is made explicit by Recital 52 DMA, 'as the economy continues to move online, ranking in search and on online intermediation services becomes increasingly central to entrepreneurship and EU businesses' commercial success will increasingly depend on their visibility and discoverability online'.[87]

The DMA only creates an ex-ante prohibition for self-preferencing in relation to rankings. As I argue in this sub-section, this is of fundamental importance to identify what art. 6.5 outlaws. While many types of self-preferencing may exist, only those that manifest through rankings are prohibited *ex ante* by the DMA; the rest being left to a case-by-case evaluation under article 102 TFEU, or potentially other substantive provisions of the DMA. Hence the self-preferencing which Art. 6.5 DMA prohibits ex ante is merely a subset of a broad constellation of practices with similar consequences.

The notion of ranking specifies the context in which the prohibited conduct of 'treating more favorably' one's own products can happen, and is the main practice that Art. 6.5 aims to regulate. But article 6.5 also mentions the related practices of indexing and crawling. This addition is aimed at avoiding circumvention by clarifying that self-preferencing can happen also 'before ranking following a query'. Crawling is defined as the 'discovery process by which new and updated content is

comparison-shopping service itself. Commission Decision of 27.06.2017, Case AT.39740 – *Google Search (Shopping)*, paras 402–443, in particular 408.

[86] Regulation (EU) 2019/1150, P2B Regulation, in particular recitals 25–27. See also Art. 7(4a) Unfair Commercial Practices Directive, Directive 2005/29/EC of the European Parliament and of the Council of 11 May 2005 concerning *unfair business-to-consumer commercial practices in the internal market* O.J. L 149/22 (2005) as amended by Directive (EU) 2019/2161 of 27 November 2019 on *better enforcement and modernisation of Union consumer protection rules*, O.J. L 328/7 (2019). The new provision specifies that parameters of product rankings are considered material information, to be provided 'in a specific section of the online interface that is directly and easily accessible from the page where the query results are presented': failure to do so can constitute a misleading omission in the meaning of the UCPD. For a broader discussion see Jablonowska and Tagiuri (2023).

[87] Ranking Transparency Guidelines, para 12.

being found', while indexing is the process of 'storing and organizing of the content found during the crawling process'. The addition of indexing and crawling was necessary because the favoring of one's own products or offers may not only materialize when showing results to users, but also during activities which precede the showing and have to do with the search and organization of the information that leads to the results shown to users.[88]

As mentioned, the DMA provides a definition of ranking in Art. 2.22 as the practice of giving 'relative prominence' to goods or services (or 'relevance' to search results on a search engine). Thus-defined ranking is pervasive: every time there is intermediation between a consumer and traders through some form of digital interface that communicates, presents, or organizes offers, products, services, or more generally information, in the interest of users, there will be ranking. This is clearly the case in situations in which several results are presented to consumers as it routinely happens on search engines, online shopping, and social media, as the said presentation would always give prominence to some results over others. But ranking also materializes in situations where just one result is communicated to consumers as it may be the case for virtual assistants based on generative and conversational AI.[89] And there is also a debate concerning whether ranking includes presentation of results after queries by business users (in interfaces that are internal to the platform on the business users' side), for example as linked to the search of ancillary services.[90]

The standard mode of presenting results to users on a platform is through a list.[91] A list would always involve ranking as, by placing some results at the top, it assigns relative prominence. In theory it is possible to imagine ways of listing results that assign prominence in a random way or present results in alphabetical or chronological order. While a literal understanding of ranking would also capture these types of organizing results, a purposive interpretation of the concept would probably exclude the said type of listing, because in these situations favoring could not possibly emerge. In any event, this is just a theoretical possibility as the order of presentation through which digital platforms communicate results to users is routinely based on complex algorithms. Our understanding of these algorithms is constrained, but we

[88] Mentions to indexing and crawling were later addition to the Commission proposal. See Tan et al. (2022).

[89] DMA Art. 2.22; Recital. 52. The clarification concerning the fact the prohibition also covers the communication of a single result to end users appeared in the final version of the act, not being present in the original commission proposal. This is instrumental to make sure that virtual assistants (e.g. Amazon's Alexa) are covered by the rule and may potentially also target fitness wearables. See on these points Tan et al. (2022). Speculations that this clarification may go as far as covering the pre-installation of a specific browser on an operating system seem unfounded as these practices fall outside of ranking and operating systems are not mentioned as the types of core platform services which can engage in ranking pursuant to Art 2.22.

[90] See Peitz (2022, 2023). I do not address this question explicitly in the paper. But given that there is no indication that Art. 6.5 only regulates rankings vis a vis consumers, these practices seem to me must be included in the scope of the prohibition.

[91] Ranking Transparency Guidelines, para 37.

know that the said algorithms typically rank results based on various parameters, for example, the match with the search, the quality of the website, price (where at stake), and personalization based on consumer characteristics or previous search habits, among others.[92]

It is also possible to imagine forms of data visualization different from a list that may avoid ranking, as they are non-hierarchical and do not assign relative prominence, for example through bubbles of equal size, or other forms of non-linear presentation. But, again, this would seem a mere theoretical possibility, as consumers plausibly accrue value exactly from a hierarchical presentation of results.[93] What is more, most platforms assign prominence in ways that are more conspicuous than a mere list, namely through design features of the interface that give special prominence to the very best results or offers. Think of the Amazon Buy Box or the Google shopping unit. Hence, as observed by many, the application of art. 6.5 brings scrutiny also onto the design choices of a gatekeeper consumer interface.[94] These observations are in line with scholarship that emphasizes how product design, as an element of product quality, is one of the key elements of competition in the digital economy, which the DMA also contributes to regulate.[95]

Given the nature of two-sided platforms, ranking will often, if not always, be implicated in the activity of platform providers. In this context, the limitation of the favoring prohibition to rankings may appear to be rather inconsequential. But on closer look, the limitation of the prohibition to the context of ranking serves a precise function: namely to exclude from the scope of the prohibition forms of favoring through practices different than the presentation, organization, or communication of different results to users, which is rankings. This interpretation would exclude from the scope of the prohibition forms of self-preferencing that do not rely on presentation, organization, or communication. Think of the pricing practices through which the gatekeeper favors its first party offers in comparison to third party offers.

There has been scholarly discussion concerning whether the self-preferencing prohibition may also outlaw practices like the charging of high commissions to third party sellers to get access to the platform, as customary in online application stores.[96] One of the concerns emergent in the litigation is for example that Apple charges high commission fees to app developers while it does not charge similar

[92] Despite difficulties in accessing the algorithms and lack of disclosure by platform, a rich body of scholarship now exists describing the phenomenon. See among many Pasquale (2015).

[93] Some of these non-linear forms of presentation to consumer were discussed as the first executive workshop for DMA compliance, 5 December 2022, https://webcast.ec.europa.eu/dma-first-workshop-05-12-22.

[94] See Vanessa Turner, Senior Advisor for Competition at BEUC (The European Consumer Organization), observations at the online roundtable *DMA and Self-Preferencing*. Digital Markets Research Hub, https://www.youtube.com/watch?v=nUwjSvqly2I at minute 15 (emphasizing how self-preferencing depends as much on the design of the algorithm as on features of the user interface design or online choice architecture).

[95] Kuenzler (2022, 2023).

[96] Peitz (2022, 2023). In general economics literature offers these pricing practices as examples of self-preferencing. See Padilla et al. (2022).

commissions to its own applications.[97] As it has been argued, even where these fees had to be symmetrical, meaning charged to all developers in the same amount including Apple's own apps, for Apple they would be a transfer within the same firm, and hence they may constitute a form of favoring.[98] But insofar as they are mere conditions for access to the platform, such type of pricing schemes, while they may trigger antitrust scrutiny, including as forms of self-preferencing, do not influence the ranking of the offers in any meaningful way. Given the formulation of art. 6.5 and its insistence on ranking I thus maintain that these types of pricing practices are not outlawed by DMA Art. 6.5.

To be sure, there are other pricing practices that may affect ranking, such as situations in which the fees paid by sellers or the developers on the platform are one, or the main, parameter in the ranking—what in the context of the platform to business regulation is referred to as paid-ranking.[99] Paid ranking would seem to adequately describe the auction system that Google devised in response to the remedy imposed by the Commission in Google shopping: under such a system Google competes with other comparison shopping services to show results in its shopping unit.[100] The fact that paid ranking is part of ranking and thus would be scrutinized in the context of the self-preferencing prohibition of Art. 6.5 seems out of question. Again this seems confirmed by the Guidelines on Ranking Transparency to which Recital 52 of the DMA makes explicit reference. Some have suggested that paid ranking may run into the self-preferencing prohibition even if it were to apply also to first party offers, again because for the platform it would be easier to pay the highest fee as it would amount to a transfer within the same economic unit.[101] Such a conclusion would have far-reaching consequences as it may mean that the vertically integrated gatekeeper should abandon the use of paid rankings.[102]

As argued above, the notion of ranking significantly constraints the scope of the self-preferencing practices outlawed by article 6.5. It is however possible that some self-preferencing practices that do not include ranking are outlawed by virtue of the anti-circumvention prohibition contained in art 13 of the DMA, in particular paras 3 and 4 thereof.[103] Any such move, however, would need to be careful about

[97] See Netherlands Authority for Consumers and Markets, Case ACM/19/035630, 24 August 2021; European Commission, Case AT.40716 *Apple App Store Practices (music streaming)*; European Commission, Case AT40452 *Apple – Mobile Payments*. This is on top of broader concerns raised about Apple preferencing its own apps on the apple store: Nicas and Collins (2019).

[98] Peitz (2023), p. 314.

[99] See Art. 5(2) P2B Regulation and paras 32–34 Guidelines on Ranking Transparency.

[100] See Gerardin (2020). Some competition authorities have in turn looked again into the solution devised after the remedy. See Balki and Bugrahan (2020).

[101] Peitz (2023).

[102] There is however significant disagreement on the issue. For an opposite view See Auer (2021).

[103] Art. 13.3 DMA provides that 'the gatekeeper shall ensure that the obligations of Articles 5, 6 and 7 are fully and effectively complied with'. Art 13.4 reads 'The gatekeeper shall not engage in any behaviour that undermines effective compliance with the obligations of Articles 5, 6 and 7 regardless of whether that behaviour is of a contractual, commercial or technical nature, or of any other nature, or consists in the use of behavioural techniques or interface design.'

preserving the functionality of the DMA as aimed at facilitating scrutiny over practices whose harmfulness is amply recognized. Again, to push the scope of the prohibition beyond ranking through article 13 would have far-reaching consequences as it may altogether outlaw the types of pricing schemes employed by App Store providers as based on high commission charged to third party developers. Similarly, such a broad interpretation of self-preferencing may catch other practices that while they may favor the vertically integrated company's products do not concern ranking—think tying or bundling. This inclusion would be in sharp contrast with ample judicial precedence that tells us to only consider such practices unlawful after a careful analysis of their effects, and proof that as efficient competitors are foreclosed. For the reasons above, a reading of the anti-circumvention provision that would push the scope of art. 6.5 far beyond rankings seems an unlikely scenario.

A further indication that closely links the self-preferencing prohibition to rankings is the second sentence of Article 6.5. As mentioned, beyond the prohibition to self-preference, Art. 6.5 contains a general rule that regulates ranking in the form of a duty to design rankings, and the algorithms that govern them ('the conditions that apply' to rankings)[104] in a way that is generally fair, transparent, and non-discriminatory. The provision reiterates for gatekeepers a series of obligations about transparency and explainability of rankings, which already applied to all digital platforms pursuant to the Platform to Business Regulation, at least in their relationship with business users.[105] The duty of the second sentence exists irrespective of whether self-preferencing is involved, but it is explicitly aimed at ensuring the effectiveness of the self-preferencing prohibition.[106] In order to interpret this duty, the DMA makes explicit reference to the Guidelines on Ranking Transparency adopted to facilitate compliance with art. 5 of the Platform to Business regulation (P2B).

Article 5.1 of the P2B regulation requires that the providers of a platform service must specify the main parameters based on which rankings happen, and the 'reasons for the relative importance of those main parameters as opposed to other parameters.' Furthermore, Art 5.5 P2B requires the description of the parameters to explain how the said parameters take into account the characteristics of the goods and services offered on the platform and the relevance of those characteristics to consumers. As clarified in the Guidelines, the description should be aimed at ensuring that business users can also optimize their products and offers so as to thrive on a specific platform.[107] The P2B also clarify that Article 5 is not to be interpreted as requir-

[104] DMA, Recital 52.

[105] P2B Regulation, in particular Art. 6 and 7.

[106] DMA, Recital 52.

[107] As para 94 of the Ranking Transparency guidelines read: 'As a general remark, it is important to note thatby obtaining an adequate understanding of how ranking functions, users will be able to compete on a more level playing field when deciding their sales strategies. These strategies potentially encompass both good and service optimisation as well as investment in online visibility, including search engine optimisation and paid ranking. Users should reasonably be able to decide whether or not to invest more in particular elements of their goods and services and to make a better determination of whether and if so, how to invest in 'ranking strategies'.

ing disclosure of the detailed functioning of the ranking mechanisms, which is disclosure of the algorithm itself. This is in the interest of preserving the ability of the platform providers 'to act against bad faith manipulation of rankings' which would harm consumers.[108] But a general description of the main ranking parameters can never be considered too intrusive and will always be due.[109]

The guidelines further require that the platform providers must present users with 'meaningful explanations' of their ranking mechanisms, and the main parameters used, where what is meaningful depends on who the average user of a given service is.[110] This information should be provided in plain and intelligible language and, for online intermediation services, must form part of the terms and conditions. In the ranking transparency guidelines, emphasis is given to the explanation of the reasons why a parameter is employed, which may require, for example, the description of 'the company internal thought process that was used for identifying the main parameters, as a way to also derive the reasons for their relative importance'[111]

To delve further into the details of these guidelines is beyond the scope of the contribution, but their relevance in the interpretation of art. 6.5 DMA is hard to overstate. First, the guidelines support the above proposed reading of ranking as a serious constraint to an overbroad interpretation of the prohibition. As the guidelines and the second sentence of art 6.5 make clear, the prohibition regulates rankings and the design choices of the algorithms that govern them; it is not designed to catch pure pricing practices or other practices that have little to do with ranking. Secondly, and relatedly, any judgment on whether the self-preferencing prohibition is infringed will rely on knowledge of the parameters used in the ranking process, which requires a certain degree of transparency from the platform provider, a point to which I return in Sect. 4.

3.3 *Favoring*

The identification of the types of conduct that, in the context of ranking, would infringe the self-preferencing prohibition is the most difficult part of the analysis required by Art. 6.5. Numerous interpretive challenges lie ahead. As this section makes clear, thinking practically about the identification of what constitutes favoring shows the limitations of an understanding of the DMA as a series of per-se, form-based prohibitions. The main issue faced when dealing with the notion of favoring is indeed whether rankings which statistically favor first-party products or offers, but which are based on ranking parameters that are also consumer-serving should be caught by the prohibition. To answer this question, some type of

[108] P2B Regulation, Recital 27.

[109] *Ibid.*

[110] Ranking Transparency Guidelines, para 17.

[111] Ranking Transparency Guidelines, para 22.

engagement with how a ranking algorithm can benefit consumers and business users will be needed.

Recital 52 DMA states that favoring is 'any form of differentiated or preferential treatment in ranking [by the gatekeeper]… in favor of products or services it offers itself or through a business user which it controls.' This statement presents a difficulty because ranking is by definition a process that institutes hierarchy: it assigns relative prominence by giving different weight to different parameters. By way of provocation, ranking is, in essence, discriminatory. So, what does the prohibition of favoring in the context of ranking really aims to capture?

Some forms of conduct intuitively fall into the prohibition: having ranking parameters that apply to all third-party users of a platform but not to first-party offers by the gatekeeper, as they are selectively disapplied or modified for the gatekeeper's own products, would no doubt run into the prohibition. For example, imagine that an e-commerce platform ranks the offers based on two simple parameters, price and number of reviews for the product, but it always reserves the first three positions to first party offers, no matter what the position that they would achieve in the ranking. This is an easy case: it is a form of differentiated treatment in ranking, which must fall into the prohibition. Based on the overall functioning of the DMA, there cannot be any space for the gatekeeper to argue that such a conduct is efficient or otherwise justified.[112] Similarly, in all cases in which it would be impossible for a third-party offer to obtain placement on top of the ranking or in a visually prominent section of the consumer interface, the favoring would be substantiated, as also in cases where the gatekeeper's offers are shown through more visible fonts, colors, or other visual features.

Another element of relative clarity is that the prohibition covers both direct and indirect favoring. In most cases the self-preferencing will be direct, namely the Gatekeeper favors directly its own products and offers in ranking. But gatekeepers may also engage in indirect self-preferencing, by favoring some third-party offers as a way to favor some of its own services. As unveiled by the Italian NCA, this is what Amazon did by downgrading in its rankings vis a vis consumers the offers of those business users which did not purchase some of its ancillary services.[113] Despite doubts raised in the scholarship,[114] this type of favoring seems to fall squarely within the prohibition: there is no indication that the favoring needs to be direct, the type of harm to consumers and business users appears the same (consumers get a biased representation of the offer and business users are deprived of their contribution to

---

[112] After a lively debate on the drafting phase, the DMA clearly contains no efficiency defense for the conduct rules or the gatekeeper designation. For some of that debate see Reyna (2021).

[113] Through these practices as unveiled by the Italian NCA Amazon case, gatekeepers like Amazon favor their logistics (warehousing and delivery) services. See Autoritá Garante della Concorrenza e del Mercato (Italian Competition Authority), Decision of 30 November 2021, Case A 528 – *FBA Amazon*. For a conceptualization of these forms of self-preferencing as hybrid differentiation see Graef (2020).

[114] Peitz (2022, 2023).

the platform). Furthermore, some of the precedents in 102 enforcement on which the prohibition is plausibly based addressed exactly this type of conduct.[115]

The key difficulty concerning the notion of favoring is how to deal with ranking rules that are uniformly applied, and where prominent positions are in theory accessible to all offers, but which still end up favoring, statistically, the products or offers of/by the gatekeeper. There is significant uncertainty concerning what the prohibition aims to catch in these more complex cases. Where a ranking systematically favors the products or offers of the gatekeeper, there would seem to be a strong indication that there is favoring. But what if the ranking parameters which systematically favor the gatekeeper are also parameters that serve the best interest of consumers, as it may be the case, for example, when the ranking is based on an impartial assessment of the quality of the product by the gatekeeper and the gatekeeper genuinely scores higher in terms of quality? The DMA offers no explicit answer to this question. But the answer we give to this question is very consequential, because it will fundamentally impact the ability of gatekeepers to escape the prohibition in cases of ranking algorithms that may give, statistically, an advantage to the gatekeepers' offers or results, but which are also good for consumers and/or business users.

Intuitively, it cannot be the case that every time a gatekeeper shows its product on top of a list of offers it runs into the prohibition. It must be possible, for first party offers and products, to obtain a prominent placement on the ranking. In turn, it clearly should not be possible for the gatekeeper to escape the prohibition by simply showing that the ranking parameters are uniformly applied: a ranking can be designed, and uniformly applied, to favor first party offers, even if the ranking parameters appear, on their face, neutral and objective.

In the case of rankings that are applied uniformly but which favor offers or products by the gatekeeper statistically more often, at least three scenarios can be envisioned: (1) rankings which rely on parameters that are designed to (or chosen based on experience because they) favor first party results, and do not also serve some interests of consumers and/or business users; (2) rankings which rely on parameters designed to (or chosen based on experience because they) serve some interest of consumers and/or business users, but which end up inadvertedly favoring first-party products or offers ; (3) rankings which rely on parameters that are designed to (or chosen based on experience because they) favor first party results, but which can also be shown to serve consumers and business users. While there is no doubt that the prohibition covers scenario 1, a judgment on the treatment of scenarios 2 and 3 is more difficult.

One possible solution would be to say that any statistical favoring of the gatekeeper's own products or offers above a certain threshold infringes the prohibition. Such a solution would demand of the gatekeeper a modification of the ranking parameters every time there is evidence that, statistically, the gatekeeper's own products are favored, for example by coming on top of the list too often. This

[115] Autoritá Garante della Concorrenza e del Mercato , Case A 528 – *FBA Amazon.*

solution would outlaw all three scenarios above. While such a solution may have some economic backing,[116] it would be a costly solution: very intrusive of the gatekeeper's business freedom and insensitive to the benefits that end users may accrue, for example, from integration of products and offers by the gatekeeper. This solution would also catch cases in which the algorithm is consumer (or business user) serving, so cases in which the platform is run in the best interest of its users. While such a solution may be maximizing contestability on the platform, it may do so at the expenses of consumers. Furthermore, it would outlaw rankings where the gatekeeper does not pursue platform bias, and the so-called conflict of interest which animates the prohibition does not materialize. All in all, such a solution would seat uneasily with the overall goals of the DMA which is generally interested in preserving the advantages that consumers may accrue from integrated ecosystems.

A more appealing and nuanced solution, which this contribution aims to defend, would be to say that self-preferencing catches ranking systems that statistically favor first party results, whether deliberately or not, but only insofar as the platform cannot show that the rankings are also serving consumers or business users. In the deliberation of what is consumer or business serving, the thinking process of the platform in the design of the algorithm comes to matter. This approach is appealing because it does away with the distinction between deliberate and statistical self-preferencing, a distinction which would be very hard to navigate, but, in line with the indications of the Ranking Transparency Guidelines, is not insensitive to the 'thinking process' of the platform in the design of the algorithm: the reasons why a certain parameter was adopted do carry some weight.

Under such solution, scenario 1 is outlawed, while scenarios 2 and 3 do not run into the prohibition. It is worth stressing that, in keeping with how DMA prohibitions are framed, this solution would require a statement that scenarios 2 and 3 do not constitute self-preferencing, and not that the self-preferencing is somewhat justified. If the statistically more frequent prominence of first party results can be explained away, for example because the platform is able to show that it is still acting in the interest of business users and consumers, there is no favoring. To illustrate, as per the Ranking Transparency Guidelines, a platform provider may show that the design of the algorithm 'was driven by a desire to ensure that consumers found goods or services that were local, cheap, of high quality'.[117] If this is the case, the fact that the gatekeeper has the best offer according to these parameters should be inconsequential. This means that gatekeepers must be allowed to show that the

[116] There is evidence that the ranking in a visible position alone, irrespective of whether it is a better match with what consumers want, increases the likelihood of clicks. See Glick et al. (2014). This is also observed by the Commission in Google Shopping which concluded that generic results generated significant traffic to a website when they were ranked within the first three to five results on the first general results page ('above the fold'), internet users paying little or no attention to subsequent results, which often did not appear directly on the screen. The Commission added that the first 10 results received approximately 95% of internet users' clicks. See Case T-612/17, *Google v. Commission*, para 65.

[117] Ranking Transparency Guidelines, para 42.

prominent positioning obtained by their products or offers is not the product of favoring but of consumer- serving features of the algorithm. To be sure, any such standard can only work if the disclosures by the gatekeepers are high-quality and the monitoring by the Commission robust.[118] The precise standard to be applied would need to be further specified, possibly through guidance by the Commission or through enforcement, but this overall direction seems desirable.

Several features of the DMA militate in favor of the solution here proposed. First, on substance, the emphasis on fair, transparent and non-discriminatory ranking and the *renvoi* to the Ranking Transparency Guidelines, suggests that the judgment on what constitutes self-preferencing depends on analysis of the parameters of the ranking. As mentioned, while a full disclosure of the algorithm is not required, platforms must be able to describe the main parameters and the reasons for choosing them—the thought process behind their adoption. This suggests that the said thought process has weight in whether the self-preferencing prohibition is materialized. Secondly this solution seems congruent with the overall goals of the DMA in relation to self-preferencing: as discussed above, a key concern in relation to self-preferencing is that a conflict of interest exists whereby the gatekeeper runs the platform in the interest of its own products or offers, and to the detriment of consumers and business users. And this is not the case in scenarios 2 and 3. Specific attention to consumer choice and the diversity of products/offers may need to be demanded, a point to which I return in the next section.

Yet, to engage in the above type of analysis in the context of the DMA may be contentious, because on its face it contradicts two of the fundamental policy choices described as defining features of the DMA. First, as mentioned, the DMA is a list of *per-se*, *form-based*, prohibitions. Secondly, no efficiency defense is available in the DMA. Concerning the first objection, I concede that the type of analysis I propose seats uneasily with a description of the self-preferencing rule as form based. But this brings me to question the said qualification, rather than the proposed solution. The DMA self-preferencing rule is form-based only in a very superficial way. True, the rule aspires to outlaw conduct that is defined by reference to its form and not its effects, in the interest of an easier monitoring of practices that have revealed their harmfulness thanks to the scrutiny they were subjected to in other regulatory fields, chiefly competition law. But as the above discussion shows, any identification of the outlawed conduct through its form is at most an aspiration. Whether favoring exists will depend in most cases on the parameters chosen to govern the ranking and the reasons why they were chosen. In such a context, as the next Sect. 4 further explores, it may be difficult to even construe the rule as an on/off prohibition which is either infringed or not. Such type of rule may in practice mostly work as a standard for the monitoring of the quality of ranking algorithms, aimed at limiting the amount of favoring in ranking, rather than sanctioning violations. I return to and expand upon this point.

[118] Crémer et al. (2023a).

Concerning the second objection, it is worth mentioning that the DMA does indeed exclude efficiency justifications or other justifications of objective necessity. Even if it does not do so explicitly in relation to the conduct rules, this feature of the DMA is amply emphasized in scholarly commentary and emerges clearly from the debates that have surrounded the adoption of the DMA.[119] Nonetheless, the type of analysis I propose is not an efficiency justification akin to article 101(3) TFEU or as judicially accepted in the context of 102 TFEU, nor it brings back the application of Art. 6.5 to a full effect analysis. As mentioned, the analysis stays focused on identifying the practices that incur in the prohibition. The said identification unavoidably engages with fact-dense discussions about the logic of ranking parameters and the design of the user interface. But, in the analysis propose, the dis-uniform application of ranking parameters in favor of the gatekeeper can never be justified as efficient, as such conduct is undoubtedly a form of self-preferencing. True, I propose to allow gatekeepers to bring evidence that the statistical favoring of their offers is due to parameters that are uniformly applied and consumer-serving, but this should not require proof that the working of the parameters is efficient or that it enhances consumer welfare. In turn I think it would be artificial to outlaw the language of efficiency if this is necessary or useful to show why a certain ranking parameter is good for consumers or business users. To identify a precise standard of what constitutes a consumer-serving ranking is beyond the scope of this contribution, and possibly cannot be done in the abstract.

4 Enforcement and Practical Challenges: The DMA and Self-Preferencing

The previous sub-section has offered a preliminary answer to what is perhaps the most contentious question in relation to the self-preferencing prohibition. Should the prominence that a gatekeeper is able to obtain because it scores better at parameters that are consumer-serving, objective, and uniformly applied be outlawed? My answer to this question has been negative. I argued that platforms should be able to show, also through disclosures such as illustrated in the ranking transparency guidelines, that their ranking parameters are adopted in the interest of (and/or end up serving) consumers or business users. My answer and the distinctions I have introduced, however, have so far largely ignored the practical constraints faced by enforcers and their limited knowledge of how ranking by platforms works. I have so far presented simplified scenarios about how the ranking algorithms are designed

[119] The possibility of relying on efficiency and objective justifications is mentioned in recital 10 DMA, as a specificity of EU competition law, from which the DMA is distinct, and which in turn it does not intend to jeopardize. Recital 23 further states, in the context of gatekeeper designation, but arguably by wishing to make a more general statement, that 'any justification on economic grounds seeking to enter into market definition or to demonstrate efficiencies deriving from a specific type of behavior by the undertaking providing core platform services should be discarded'.

and implemented, but more complex scenarios will be the norm rather than the exception.

Rankings are typically the product of the complex interaction of a long list of parameters, which are periodically modified, and that consumers themselves can alter. Furthermore, different forms of ranking often coexist at the same time. As clarified by the Guidelines on Ranking Transparency, 'providers of online intermediation services may, for example, combine ordered lists of search results with paid ranking results and editorial features such as recommendations, all in a single, seamless interface. Or they may differentiate such ordered lists by, for example, using different markings, annotations or headings, at different positions on the page (i.e. regardless of the 'position' of the products or services concerned in the list).'[120] In such scenarios, assessing whether a ranking parameter is uniformly applied may be difficult, let alone identifying what each parameter is about, as well as the relative weight of different parameters.

This reveals that even if it aspired to simplify enforcement through form-based rules, the enforcement of the DMA, including the self-preferencing prohibition, is likely to be very evidence heavy. In this context, even if it were to be possible to devise a standard for self-preferencing which would allow to give weight to consumer (or business user) serving features of the algorithm, while not amounting to a full blown efficiency defense, and in turn not making the identification of favoring dependent on the effects of a raking algorithm, it may be difficult to apply this standard in practice. While it may be surprising, this finding is congruent with the experience gathered in enforcing other areas where EU law resorts to per-se prohibitions—e.g. the identification of what constitutes a restriction by object in the law of article 101, which has steadily grown in complexity.[121]

Two more features of how vertically integrated platforms have been shown to work further complicate the picture. One is the existence of self-learning algorithms, for which the gatekeeper may not always be in the position to explain why a certain ranking is shown to consumers. The second factor concerns the amount of data on the activity of business users on the platform that gatekeepers have been collecting and are able to collect. This data concerns for example, which products sell well on the platform; based on which input consumers are shown certain offers; and why they value them. The ability of gatekeepers to collect such data places them in the privileged position to tamper with the ranking parameters and design them in ways that may seem neutral and even consumer-serving but are in fact aimed at ensuring that first party offers are awarded prominence. Furthermore, even where the algorithms were to be designed in good faith and genuinely aimed at serving the best interests of consumers, the gatekeeper may be infinitely more skillful in

[120] Ranking Transparency Guidelines, para 37.

[121] The trend is complex, but a good illustration of it can be observed in Case C-307/18, *Generics (UK) Ltd and Others v CMA*, ECLI:EU:C:2020:52, para 103 (pro-competitive effects of an agreement may be taken into account at the moment of identifying a restriction of competition by object insofar as they may call into question the characterization of the violation as such).

designing products or framing offers that allow them to gain prominence even on neutral and consumer-serving rankings. The DMA contains separate prohibitions aimed at limiting the collection of data from business users and the uses thereof by gatekeepers.[122] But such provisions may be working less than perfectly, especially in early phases of implementation. Hence the large amount of data about consumers and business users that gatekeepers hold must be a consideration in the application of article 6.5.

It is plausibly also due to awareness of the above difficulties, that EU legislators have set up DMA enforcement as collaborative. Indeed, if identification of a potential infringement relies on disclosures of the main parameters used by the ranking algorithm, and compliance on modifications of those parameters, it must be the case that enforcement is collaborative. Collaborative enforcement relies on disclosures of information and compliance strategies designed by the gatekeeper itself. This would ideally be underpinned by some degree of internalization by the gatekeepers of the goals of the DMA.[123]

As mentioned, such collaborative enforcement is a precise policy choice which is quite explicit in the DMA. Art. 11 provides that the designated gatekeepers must report to the Commission about the measures they intend to implement to ensure compliance with the substantive provisions of the DMA.[124] Any enforcement by the Commission will rely on such mandatory reporting, and the scholarship has forcefully emphasized the essential role of these documents for the success of the DMA.[125] Furthermore, pursuant to Art. 11.2, the gatekeepers should provide a non-confidential summary of the compliance reports which the Commission will make publicly available on its website. At the time of writing such reports have not been published yet, but their publication will provide essential material to further refine description of the functioning of the DMA and the self-preferencing rule.

As clarified by recital 68 of the DMA, the non-confidential summary should be clear and comprehensible while considering the legitimate interests of gatekeepers in protecting business secrets and other confidential information. 'This non-confidential publication should enable third parties to assess whether the gatekeepers comply with the obligations' of the DMA.[126] Based on these statements concerning the role of third parties, it has been proposed that the gatekeepers engage in some form of self-market-testing, whereby a proposed compliance solution is put out to the input of third parties and modified pursuant to it even before being presented to the Commission.[127] That such a development would be welcomed in the logic of the DMA seems confirmed by the emphasis on the need to make the com-

[122] See for example DMA Art. 6.2; Art. 6.10.

[123] Svetiev (2020); Crémer et al. (2023a).

[124] DMA, recital 68.

[125] Crémer et al. (2023a).

[126] DMA, Recital 68.

[127] Vanessa Turner, observations at online workshop *DMA & Self-Preferencing*, *supra* footnote 94.

pliance reports easily accessible to small and medium enterprises (SMEs), that are likely some of the third parties whose input would be most valued by the Commission, as well as potentially open to feedback from researchers.[128]

At the time of writing, at least some of the designated gatekeepers are communicating publicly about their strategies to comply with the DMA: Google and Apple have for example recently published blog posts detailing how they intend to alter their products and services in the EU.[129] While less explicit, in the model of enforcement foreshadowed by the DMA the identified gatekeepers take on a key role of self-monitoring also beyond the presentation of the compliance reports. For example, pursuant to Article 28, gatekeepers must institute a compliance function composed of at least one compliance officer, with some guarantees of independence from management. In turn the Commission is trying to build up expertise to be a reliable interlocutor: it has sought to diversify the expertise within its staff by hiring engineers and computer scientists in preparation for enforcement of the DMA.[130]

Given the above constraints in the application of article 6.5, coupled with the collaborative enforcement model clearly espoused by the DMA, it is likely that the enforcement of the self-preferencing prohibition will look different than what my discussion of the more doctrinal issues in Sect. 3 may have suggested. Enforcement will likely not proceed through the identification of prohibited self-preferencing practices and their gradual outlawing by the Commission, possibly challenged in subsequent litigation. Most plausibly, monitoring of compliance with Art. 6.5 will focus on proxies that reduce the risk of self-preferencing: for example, the gatekeeper may need to be able to show that an equally attractive offer to the one of the gatekeepers is also able to obtain prominence.

Since working on the detail of the ranking parameters may be prohibitively complex, design choices, and specifically choices about how the user interface is designed might come to help. The remedies designed by companies in response to some of the Commission 102 investigations may provide helpful examples. Think, for example, of Amazon who has offered to provide a second buy box where meaningfully differentiated offers by a competing provider are also prominently shown.[131] Think also of the remedy which emerged from the Google shopping case pursuant to which Google agreed to auction access to its Google shopping case on an equal

[128] See on this also Crémer et al. (2023a).

[129] Oliver Bethel, *An update on our preparations for the DMA*, January 17, 2024, https://blog.google/around-the-globe/google-europe/an-update-on-our-preparations-for-the-dma/. See also Apple, Press Release, *Apple announces changes to iOS, Safari, and the App Store in the European Union*, January 25, 2024. https://www.apple.com/newsroom/2024/01/apple-announces-changes-to-ios-safari-and-the-app-store-in-the-european-union/.

[130] European Commission, *Sneak peek: how the Commission will enforce the DSA & DMA - Blog of Commissioner Thierry Breton*, 5 July 2022, https://ec.europa.eu/commission/presscorner/detail/en/statement_22_4327. See Deutsch (2024).

[131] Commission Decision of 20.12.2022, Cases AT.40462 – *Amazon Marketplace* and AT.40703 – *Amazon Buy Box.*

footing.[132] Ultimately, in line with a trend described also in the evolution of EU competition law,[133] the enforcement of the DMA blurs the distinction between infringement detection and remedial design. Remedies are designed collaborative in ways that minimize the effects of potential harmful conduct and seek to prevent the emerge of future ones, in a context in which assessing conclusively whether self-preferencing has materialized or not may be too difficult. In such context, the unilateral design of remedies by the Commission and the imposition of fines are likely to be infrequent.

These observations bring us back to our discussion of the goals of the DMA. As aptly emphasized by Kuenzler, the remedies used to restore competition in the digital economy are often about product design as a feature of product quality,[134] and more specifically, in relation to rankings, about the ranking parameters and the design of the consumer interface. From this perspective, the self-preferencing prohibition can be conceptualized as a quality standard for rankings by gatekeepers.[135]

This suggests an interpretation of the prohibition as mainly geared to ensuring that the platform is run in the best interest of consumers. And the said best interest, in zero price markets, is likely to coincide with consumers being shown an unbiased selection of the offers present on the platform. The quality of the platform is here strictly linked to the variety of products consumers are shown and their quality. In turn a quality platform, as one that does not engage in self-preferencing, is one that adequately rewards the economic contribution of third party business users to the platform and its ecosystems, which is one of the key concerns of the DMA.[136] As observed by Kuenzler, Through this implicit emphasis on product quality, the DMA acknowledges that not all problems faced by consumers in the digital economy can be solved through exit, which more traditional competition law, both ordoliberal and consumer-welfare oriented, tends to assume.[137] The DMA aspires instead to assist consumers by insisting they have a say in the design of the products they consume, in continuity with a trend already emerging in EU competition law.[138] As discussed in Sect. 2, designing products in the interest of consumers maintains the platform competitive and in the long run may create opportunities for disruption by incumbent operators on the platform which may vertically integrate.

---

[132] Gerardin (2020).

[133] Svetiev (2020).

[134] Kuenzler (2019, 2020).

[135] Such an emphasis on product quality is also in line with calls for a stronger emphasis of the consumer protection features which are built within the DMA. See Turner and Reyna (2022).

[136] DMA, Recital 33.

[137] Kuenzler (2023).

[138] Kuenzler (2020, 2023).

5 Conclusions

This chapter described the self-preferencing prohibition under the DMA and brought into focus the main interpretative questions which are likely to emerge in its application. The first part of the chapter has provided some answers to the said questions. It has argued that the issue of whether two products are separate may become contentious, but its role may plausibly be marginalized given the overall goals of the DMA. It has further argued that the notion of ranking constitutes a clear limit to an overbroad interpretation of the prohibition. Ranking serves to distinguish the types of self-preferencing that the DMA aims to prohibit *ex ante* from other forms of self-preferencing that will still need to be investigated under article 102 or which may be prohibited by other DMA provisions. As such, the context of ranking should work as a real constraint in the identification of the outlawed conduct. Finally, in relation to the identification of what self-preferencing proper is, the chapter has advocated an interpretation that allows gatekeepers to show that their rankings which may statistically favor first party offers are still designed and/or operated in the best interest of consumers or business users—they are, in other words, users serving.

The chapter has however acknowledged some of the practical constraints in the operationalization of the provision. These have mostly to do with our constrained understanding of the ranking algorithms that would substantiate self-preferencing. When coupled with the collaborative form of enforcement espoused by the DMA, the said constrains prefigure a rather different functionality for article 6.5 than the discussion of the first part of the chapter may have suggested. The dominant discourse around the DMA describes it as a collection of *per se* form-based prohibitions thanks to which the Commission, freed from the need to engage with the economic-dense effects analysis demanded by EU competition law, will be able to discipline gatekeepers—on the model of what is perhaps an outdated but still deeply engrained vision of competition law as working through the identification of rule-violations, the assigning of responsibility, and deterrence through fines. In turn, a more granular engagement with one of the key conduct rules of the DMA, like the self-preferencing prohibition of 6.5 is, has revealed a different type of functioning for the DMA. The self-preferencing rule of article 6.5 is likely to work not so much as a form-base prohibition, but as a quality standard for designing ranking algorithms that avoid as much favoring as possible. On such vision, the precise contour of what constitutes self-preferencing will emerge through collaborative enforcement and cannot be fixated in advance. More fundamentally, the identification of a rule infringement may not matter so much as the moments of violation identification and remedial design are growingly blurred.

The above observations offer a competing story about the role of the DMA in the governance of digital platforms and its relationship to competition law. True, the DMA's impulse is plausibly to formalize the prohibition of forms of conduct that competition authorities had already certified as harmful, by overcoming the uncertainty concerning the identification of a theory of harm and the effects of the conduct. But the DMA is also responsive to novel concerns about product quality, variety, and entrepreneurship that traditional competition enforcement has tended to marginalize. In response to these concerns, the DMA calls the gatekeepers to constant self-monitoring, destabilization, and revision of their practices. This ensures that the quality of the platform, and here specifically its rankings, is monitored in the interest of consumers, which in turn preserves opportunities for business users to thrive on the platform and, ultimately, on the long, run contest its role. The competing story about the DMA I here presented through a focus on Art. 6.5 can be a starting point for developing a new normative imagination for governing the digital economy, which will in turn further guide interpretation of the self-preferencing prohibition, as well as the DMA more broadly.

References

Auer D (2021) Case Closed: Google Wins for Now. Truth on the Market. November 19, 2021. https://truthonthemarket.com/2021/11/19/case-closed-google-wins-for-now/

Balki B, Bugrahan S (2020) TCA's preliminary inquiry into Google's Shopping Unit Bidding Mechanism. Kluwer Competition Law Blog. https://competitionlawblog.kluwercompetitionlaw.com/2020/02/27/tcas-preliminary-inquiry-into-googles-shopping-unit-bidding-mechanism/

Baumol WJ (1982) Contestable markets: an uprising in the theory of industry structure. Am Econ Rev 72:1–15

Bourreau M, De Streel A (2019) Digital conglomerates and EU competition policy. https://perso.telecom-paristech.fr/bourreau/papers/Digital_Conglomerates.pdf

Bouzoraa Y (2022) Between substance and autonomy: finding legal certainty in Google Shopping. J Eur Compet Law Pract 13:144–153

Cabral L, Haucap J, Parker G, Petropoulos G, Valletti T, Van Alstyne M (2021) The EU Digital Markets Act: a report from a panel of economic experts. Luxembourg

Cafaggi F, Iamiceli P (2018) Unfair trading practices in the business-to-business retail supply chain. Publications Office of the European Union, Luxembourg. https://doi.org/10.2760/946607

Caffarra C, Scott Morton F (2021) How will the Digital Markets Act regulate big tech? Promarket 11 January 2021. https://www.promarket.org/2021/01/11/digital-markets-act-obligations-big-tech-uk-dmu/. Accessed 11 Feb 2024

Caffarra C, Etro F, Latham O, Scott Morton F (2020) Designing regulation for digital platforms: why economists need to work on business models. VOXEU/CEPR, 04 June 2020. https://voxeu.org/article/designing-regulation-digital-platforms

Caminade J, Carvajal J, Knittel CR (2022) An economic analysis of the self-preferencing debate. Competition 32:30–43

CNNum Conseil National du Numerique (2014) Platform neutrality: building an open and sustainable digital environment. Opinion n°. 2014-2. https://cnnumerique.fr/files/uploads/2014/06/PlatformNeutrality_VA.pdf

Cohen J (2019) Between truth and power. The legal constructions of informational capitalism. Oxford University Press, Oxford

Crémer J, de Montjoye Y, Schweitzer H (2019) Competition policy for the digital era. European Commission, Directorate-General for Competition, Publications Office. https://data.europa.eu/doi/10.2763/407537

Crémer J, Dinielli D, Heidhues P, Kimmelman G, Monti G, Podszun R, Schnitzer M, Scott Morton F, de Streel A (2023a) Enforcing the Digital Markets Act: institutional choices, compliance, and antitrust. J Antitrust Enforce 11:315–349. https://doi.org/10.1093/jaenfo/jnad004

Crémer J, Crawford GS, Dinielli D, Fletcher A, Heidhues P, Schnitzer M, Scott Morton FM (2023b) Fairness and contestability in the Digital Markets Act. Yale J Regul 40:973–1012
de la Mano M, Meunier V, Stenimachitis A, Hegyesi ZM (2021) The Digital Markets Act: back to the "form-based" future? Compass Lexecon. https://www.compasslexecon.com/wp-content/uploads/2021/06/The-DMA-Back-to-the-Form-Based-Future.pdf. (Study commissioned by Google)
de Streel A (2020) Should digital antitrust be Ordoliberal? Foreword. Concurrences 1:2–4
de Streel A, Larouche P (2021) The European Digital Markets Act Proposal: how to improve a regulatory revolution. Concurrences 2:46–63
Deutsch J (2024) Europe passed new tech rules. That was the easy part. Bloomber, 2 August 2022. https://www.bloomberg.com/news/newsletters/2022-08-02/europe-will-face-challenges-enforcing-new-tech-bills-dma-and-dsa
Deutscher E (2021) Google Shopping and the quest for a legal test for self-preferencing under Article 102 TFEU. Eur Pap 6:1345–1361
Digital Competition Expert Panel (2019) Unlocking digital competition. https://assets.publishing.service.gov.uk/media/5c88150ee5274a230219c35f/unlocking_digital_competition_furman_review_web.pdf
Eben M (2018) Fining Google: a missed opportunity for legal certainty? Eur Compet J 14:129–151
Etro F (2022) The economics of Amazon. https://doi.org/10.2139/ssrn.4307213
Ezrachi A (2017) Sponge. J Antitrust Enforce 5:49–75. https://doi.org/10.1093/jaenfo/jnw011
Franck J-U, Peitz M (2021) Market definition in the platform economy. Camb Yearb Eur Leg Stud 23:91–127
Gerardin D (2020) Taming the big tech platforms: DG COMP's remedy problem (as illustrated by the Google saga). The Platform Law Blog 23 November 2020. https://theplatformlaw.blog/2020/11/23/taming-the-big-tech-platforms-dg-comps-remedy-problem-as-illustrated-by-the-google-saga/
Glick M, Richards G, Sapozhnikov M, Seabright P (2014) How does ranking affect user choice in online search? Rev Ind Organ 45:99–119
Graef I (2020) Hybrid differentiation and competition beyond markets. Competition Policy International (CPI) Antitrust Chronicle June 2020(II):1-8§
Hagiu A, Teh T-H, Wright J (2022) Should platforms be allowed to sell on their own marketplaces? Rand J Econ 53:297–327
Hornung P (2023) The ecosystem concept, the DMA, and Section 19a GWB. J Antitrust Enforce jnad049. https://doi.org/10.1093/jaenfo/jnad049
Iacobucci E, Ducci F (2018) The Google search case in Europe: tying and the single monopoly profit theorem in two-sided markets. Eur J Law Econ 47:15–42
Ibanez Colomo P (2020) Self-preferencing: yet another epithet in need of limiting principles. World Compet 43:417–446
Jablonowska A, Tagiuri G (2023) Rescuing transparency in the digital economy: in search of a common notion in EU consumer and data protection law, yead005. https://doi.org/10.1093/yel/yead005
Jacobides MG, Lianos I (2021) Ecosystems and competition law in theory and practice. Ind Corp Change 30:1199–1229
Kaufman AC (2019) Elizabeth Warren On Breaking Up Amazon: 'You Don't Get To Be The Umpire And Have A Team'. 22 April 2019. https://www.huffpost.com/entry/elizabeth-warren-tech-amazon_n_5cbe6120e4b00b3e70ce32b8
Kerber W (2021) Taming tech giants with a per se rules approach? The digital markets act from the "rules vs. standard" perspective. Concurrences Review 3-2021
Khan L (2017) Amazon's antitrust paradox. Yale Law J 126:710–805
Khan L (2019) The separation of commerce and platform. Columbia Law Rev 119:973–1098
Kuenzler A (2019) Advancing quality competition in big data markets. J Compet Law Econ 15:500–537
Kuenzler A (2020) Direct consumer influence - the missing strategy to integrate data privacy preferences into the market. Yearb Eur Law 39:423–458

Kuenzler A (2022) Competition law as a catalyst for collective market governance: gauging the discursive benefits of intensified administrative action. Yearb Eur Law 41:252–278

Kuenzler A (2023) Third-generation competition law. J Antitrust Enforce 11:133–141. https://doi.org/10.1093/jaenfo/jnac035

Motta M (2023) Self-preferencing and foreclosure in digital markets: theories of harm for abuse cases. J Ind Organ 90:102974

Mukherjee S, Yun Chee F (2023) Meta appeals against EU gatekeeper status for Messenger, Marketplace. Reuters, November 15 2023. https://www.reuters.com/technology/meta-appeals-against-eu-gatekeeper-status-messenger-marketplace-2023-11-15/

Nadler J, Cicilline DN (2020) Investigation of competition in digital markets. House of Representatives, Subcommittee on Antitrust, Commercial, and Administrative Law of the Committee on the Judiciary, Majority Staff Report and Recommendations. https://www.govinfo.gov/content/pkg/CPRT-117HPRT47832/pdf/CPRT-117HPRT47832.pdf

Neves IF (2023) The Digital Markets Act: in search of a level playing field? Kluwer Competition Law Blog. March 13, 2023. https://competitionlawblog.kluwercompetitionlaw.com/2023/03/13/the-digital-markets-act-in-search-of-a-level-playing-field/

Nicas J, Collins J (2019) How Apple's Apps Topped Rivals in the App Store It Controls. The New York Times, 9 September 2019. https://www.nytimes.com/interactive/2019/09/09/technology/apple-app-store-competition.html

Nicas J, Griffith E (2021) Apple and epic head to court over their slices of the App Pie. The New York Times, May 2, 2021. https://www.nytimes.com/2021/05/02/technology/apple-epic-lawsuit-app-fees.html

Padilla J, Perkins J, Piccolo S (2022) Self-preferencing in markets with vertically integrated gatekeeper platforms 70:371–395

Pasquale F (2015) The Black Box Society: the secret algorithms that control money and information. Harvard University Press, Cambridge

Peitz M (2022) The prohibition of self-preferencing in the DMA. Cerre Issue Paper. https://cerre.eu/wp-content/uploads/2022/11/DMA_SelfPreferencing.pdf

Peitz M (2023) How to apply the self-preferencing prohibition in the DMA. J Eur Compet Law Pract 14:301–315

Petit N (2021) The Proposed Digital Markets Act (DMA): a legal and policy review. J Eur Compet Law Pract 12:529–541. https://doi.org/10.1093/jeclap/lpab062

Reimers I, Waldfogel I (2023) A framework for detection, measurement, and welfare analysis of platform bias. National Bureau of Economic Research, Working Paper 31766. https://www.nber.org/papers/w31766

Reyna A (2021) Why the DMA is much more than competition law (and should not be treated as such). Chillin'Competition. https://chillingcompetition.com/

Svetiev Y (2020) Experimentalist competition law and the regulation of markets. Hart Publishing, Oxford

Tan M, Wilkinson G, Gambarin M (2022) Open up your algorithm - or else: the DMA's not-so-final view on self-preferencing. Frontier Economics. https://www.frontier-economics.com/uk/en/news-and-insights/articles/article-i9387-open-up-your-algorithm-or-else/

Turner V, Reyna A (2022) BEUC recommendations for the Trilogue Negotiations on the Proposed Digital Markets Act, DMA. https://www.beuc.eu/sites/default/files/publications/beuc-x-2022-004_beuc_recommendations_for_the_trilogue_negotiations_on_the_proposed_dma.pdf

Vezzoso S (2022) The first New Brandeisian decision in Europe?: Insights from the Utah Statement. Concurrences 2:70–77

Woersdoerfer M (2023) The Digital Markets Act and EU competition policy: a critical ordoliberal evaluation. Philos Manag 22:149–171

Wytt AC (2023) The Digital Markets Act: Regulating the Wild West. Common Mark Law Rev 60:625–666

Digital Markets Act: A Promise for a Fairer Digital Environment or a Failed Experiment?

Thomas Papadopoulos and Louiza Kofina

Abstract "*For the first time he perceived that if you want to keep a secret, you must also hide it from yourself*", George Orwell wrote in his novel "*1984*". While the novel was written 60 plus years ago, it perfectly describes the digitalized society of today, with consumers being at severe risk of falling prey to the artificial temptation of digital consumerism. Tech giants as governors of the digital ecosystem are pulling the strings on businesses and consumers, resulting to the creation of an imbalanced competitive environment. Consumer data fuels the digital economy by allowing tech giants to increase their dominance to the detriment of competition and privacy. The Digital Markets Act was introduced as a tool of reversing these negative impacts. Our legal analysis will shed light on the role of the Digital Markets Act on ensuring a level playing field for all digital businesses regardless of their power and size, by also identifying its impact on empowering the privacy of consumers.

1 Introduction

The digital revolution that was started at least a decade ago set the foundations for the establishment of the new Datafied Society,[1] where at least every aspect of the everyday life of citizens is extensively turned into machine-readable data.[2] The digital transformation of our world provides innumerable new opportunities for small businesses and start-ups to access larger and previously restricted geographical

[1] Manganelli and Nicita (2022), pp. 2, 5.

[2] Schäfer and van Es (2017), p. 16.

T. Papadopoulos (✉) · L. Kofina
University of Cyprus, Department of Law, Nicosia, Cyprus
e-mail: papadopoulos.thomas@ucy.ac.cy; kofina.louiza@ucy.ac.cy

D. V. Popović, R. Kulms (eds.), *Repositioning Platforms in Digital Market Law*, European Union and its Neighbours in a Globalized World 15,
https://doi.org/10.1007/978-3-031-69678-7_9

markets,[3] while an unlimited source of innovative products and services[4] are provided to netizens. Digital ecosystems are comprised of multi-sided markets where online service providers act as gateways between other businesses and consumers,[5] allowing the interconnection of consumers and businesses from distinct groups. Nevertheless, digitalization is rapidly changing the competition game.[6]

Digital markets are considered as highly concentrated or even quasi-monopolistic,[7] since a limited number of companies, the well-known GAFAM,[8] are increasingly acting as gateways between businesses and consumers, resulting to the creation of entry barriers for new entrants to the market, and consumer lock-in effects.[9]Acting as the new governors of the digital capitalism,[10] having the power and financial freedom[11] to shape or re-shape digital markets so as to align with their own interests, tech giants create "*winner takes all*"[12] phenomena to the detriment of competition and privacy. Tech giants utilise data harvesting techniques, with profiling to be the most common one, allowing them to gather unlimited volumes of personal data,[13] resulting to the creation of locked markets where consumers cannot easily switch to a service provider that matches their preferences, having also a negative impact to their personal data and privacy.[14] While it can be argued that such practices of collecting unlimited volumes of data are simply a by-product of the digital life, and this is the correct way for digital markets to operate, *how much privacy consumers are willing to "trade" for enjoying the full benefits of the digital ecosystem?*

The admission that "*the world's most valuable resource is no longer oil, but data*"[15] demands a new approach for the antitrust regulatory framework. An overgrowing momentum to regulate tech giants is evident worldwide as an effort of governments to regain control over digital markets, allowing also consumers to reclaim access to their personal data.[16] The most recent example of such regulatory effort is the adoption on a European level of the Digital Markets Act.[17] Applying the tools of competition law in digital markets proved inadequate to properly deal with all potential risks (Sect. 2). The need to restore the "*fair and contestable*" nature of

---

[3] Akman (2022), p. 5.

[4] Bagnoli (2021), pp. 134, 140; Manganelli and Nicita (2022), pp. 35, 36.

[5] Manganelli and Nicita (2022), p. 7.

[6] Nazzini (2022).

[7] Manganelli and Nicita (2022), p. 138; Bagnoli (2021), pp. 138, 139.

[8] GAFAM: Alphabet (Google), Amazon, Apple, Meta (Facebook), and Microsoft.

[9] Akman (2022), p. 5; Manganelli and Nicita (2022), pp. 20, 21; Bagnoli (2021), p. 137.

[10] Bradford (2023); Kira (2023); Bagnoli (2021), p. 149; Lianos (2022).

[11] Manganelli and Nicita (2022), p. 9.

[12] Bagnoli (2021), p. 137; Cabral et al. (2021), p. 6.

[13] Bradford (2023) and Kira (2023).

[14] EDPS (2021), p. 9.

[15] The Economist (2017); Koponen and Mangiaracina (2013), p. 186; Mahari et al. (2021), p. 55.

[16] Manganelli and Nicita (2022), p. 1; Bradford (2023); Streel and Larouche (2021), p. 46.

[17] Hereinafter to be referred to as the "*Act*".

digital markets resulted in the adoption of a series of prohibitions against gatekeepers through the adoption of the Act, the leading players of digital markets, enabling smaller businesses to compete with them in much more fairer terms (Sect. 3). Personal data are considered as a valuable source for competing in digital markets, yet it is questionable if the provisions of the General Data Protection Regulation[18] may effectively be applied in parallel with the relevant requirements of the Act (Sect. 4). On this basis, we shall review the radical changes introduced by the new regulatory framework of the Act in an effort to shed light on the question of whether it can regulate tech giants to the benefit of effective competition and safeguarding the interests and rights of the consumer.

2 Setting the Foundations for a Change

2.1 Failures of the Past as Lessons of Today

While the European Union has gained a reputation of a regulatory superpower with worldwide impact,[19] empirical evidence indicated its failure[20] to effectively enforce its regulatory superpowers.[21] Tools of competition law were proved inadequate to address the lack of contestability and privacy in digital ecosystems,[22] resulting in an emerging discussion on the need of adopting a complete different and ad hoc solution.[23] The provisions of competition law cannot properly and fully take into account the unique characteristics of the zero-priced digital markets,[24] while the concept of "*relevant markets*" needs to be adjusted to the digital reality.[25] The need for regulatory intervention was more than evident, so as to enable the creation of viable competitive structures, the limitation of entry barriers to potential competitors and the promotion of innovative products and services for the benefit of consumers. A crucial regulatory challenge lies on the rapid evolution of the technological innovation and the risks that any effort for a regulatory intervention might become outdated.[26] At the same time, balancing needs to be achieved between the intention of limiting anti-competitive practices and promoting innovation so as to diminish the risk of

[18] Hereinafter to be referred to as the "*GDPR*".

[19] Bradford (2023); Bagnoli (2021), p. 153.

[20] Manganelli and Nicita (2022), pp. 18, 19; Nazzini (2022); Akman (2022), p. 25; Cabral et al. (2021), p. 3; Petit (2021), p. 530; Di Porto et al. (2021), p. 91; Bostoen (2023), p. 271.

[21] Bradford (2023); Cabral et al. (2021), p. 6.

[22] Streel and Larouche (2021), p. 46; Akman (2022), p. 5; Witt (2023), pp. 4–6; Blažo (2023), p. 63; Streel and Alexiadis (2023), p. 100.

[23] Podszun (2022), p. 1; Malheiro (2023); Ezrachi and Maurice (2022).

[24] Kira (2023); Manganelli and Nicita (2022), p. 139.

[25] Manganelli and Nicita (2022), p. 139; Nazzini (2022).

[26] Kira (2023); Manganelli and Nicita (2022), p. 7.

opposite results like hindering the entrance of business innovators to digital markets. Therefore, a flexible solution[27] needs to be introduced, allowing for adaptability based on the overgrowing transformation of digital markets.

As part of the vision of the European Union's strategy, "*A Europe fit for the digital age*",[28] the Digital Markets Act (Regulation (EU) 2022/1925[29]) came into force in November 2022,[30] aiming "*to contribute to the proper functioning of the internal market, and ensuring for all businesses, contestable and fair markets in the digital sector*",[31] allowing also businesses and consumers to gain the full benefits of the digital economy.[32] Contestability focuses on the structural features of the digital markets aiming at decreasing entry barriers for new competition and allowing at the same time multi-homing, while fairness is relevant with the conduct of the operators of digital markets.[33] The Act promises that start-ups and small businesses will have the opportunity to participate with more fair terms in the digital ecosystem, while consumers will have a larger variety of options for services and products, allowing them to freely choose the ones that match their preferences, including privacy choices, and easily switching to alternative solutions.[34] The Act is considered by the majority of academia as a legal "*revolution*".[35] European Union acts once again, as a pioneer in setting the path for regulating digital markets worldwide and practically intervening on how business models of the wealthiest entities of the world are set, and eventually how they offer and provide their services and products to individuals.[36] Big Tech businesses offering their goods and services to European citizens will be required to abide with the new set of rules, allowing European law to become global law.[37] Are all these for real or is this merely an ambitious experiment of the European Union? Will it be practically feasible for the new set of rules to effectively address the challenges[38] posed on competition and safeguarding of netizens privacy, or tech giants are actually too "*big*" to be regulated?[39]

---

[27] Akman (2022), p. 18; Kira (2023).

[28] Pop et al. (2022).

[29] Regulation (EU) 2022/1925 of the European Parliament and of the Council of 14 September 2022 on contestable and fair markets in the digital sector and amending Directives (EU) 2019/1937 and (EU) 2020/1828 (Digital Markets Act) OJ L 265, 12.10.2022, pp. 1–66.

[30] Podszun (2022), p. 1.

[31] Article 1 (1) of the Act, Privacy International (2022); Akman (2022), p. 6; Colomo (2021), p. 563; Bagnoli (2021), p. 153; Cabral et al. (2021), p. 12; Streel and Larouche (2021), p. 46.

[32] Bagnoli (2021), p. 137; Streel and Larouche (2021), p. 47.

[33] Akman (2022), p. 22; Pop (2022); Hoffman (2023), pp. 18–19.

[34] Pop (2022).

[35] Lundqvist (2021).

[36] Akman (2022), p. 1.

[37] Article 1 (2) of the Act and Di Porto et al. (2021), p. 85.

[38] Kira (2023).

[39] Bradford (2023).

2.2 A 360-degrees Shift for the Regulator

The Act has a complementary role to the enforcement of competition law as secondary law,[40] applying without prejudice to Articles 101 and 102 TFEU,[41] by addressing unfair practices that either fall outside the existing competition rules, or that cannot be as effectively addressed by these rules.[42] A novelty of the Act is the ex-ante effect of its rules,[43] meaning that they are automatically applicable to the "*gatekeepers*" of a "*core platform service*".[44] Specifically, as an entity-based Regulation,[45] its prohibitions and obligations are applied once a business entity is designated as a gatekeeper of a core platform service, without having to proceed with an analysis of the relevant market, or a finding of an anti-competitive conduct, as required under competition law.[46] The Act brings together a restricted group of business entities, mostly US-based companies, based on their size and financial position,[47] aiming to restore fair competition in digital markets.

An entity qualifies as a gatekeeper if it satisfies three (3) qualitative criteria, as follows (i) *has a significant impact on the internal market*, (ii) *operates as a core platform service which is an important gateway for business users to reach end users* and (iii) *enjoys an entrenched and durable position in its operations*.[48] It may be presumed though, that a business entity satisfies the said criteria, if it meets specific quantitative thresholds connected with its turnover.[49] A business entity satisfying the quantitative criteria shall notify the Commission within two (2) months of the thresholds being reached,[50] however, it is entitled to dispute the gatekeeper presumption by presenting evidence showing that the qualitative criteria are not satisfied.[51] The Commission is entitled to designate a business as a gatekeeper in cases where the qualitative criteria are met, but not all of the quantitative criteria,[52] following a market investigation and taking into consideration other quantitative factors including the number of business users utilizing the core platform service to reach consumers and the number of consumers. Companies are prohibited from performing any re-arrangement of their services or their structure so as to avoid

---

40 Streel and Larouche (2021), p. 47; Petit (2021), p. 529.

41 Recital, para 10 of the Act.

42 EDPS (2021), pp. 3, 7; Streel and Larouche (2021), p. 47; Chiarella (2023), p. 52.

43 Akman (2022), p. 16; Geradin (2021), p. 7.

44 Akman (2022), p. 9; Cabral et al. (2021), p. 9.

45 Akman (2022), p. 19; Petit (2021), p. 530.

46 Malheiro (2023); Colomo (2021), p. 566; Petit (2021), p. 530; Bostoen (2023), p. 273.

47 Akman (2022), pp. 18, 24; Cabral et al. (2021), p. 6.

48 Article 3 (1) of the Act and Petit (2021), p. 533.

49 Article 3 (2) of the Act and Podszun (2022), p. 1.

50 Article 3 (3) of the Act.

51 Article 3 (5) of the Act and Streel et al. (2021), p. 9.

52 Articles 3 (8), 15 and 17 of the Act.

falling within the quantitative thresholds,[53] and under such a scenario the Commission may still proceed with designating them as "*gatekeepers*" subjecting them to the set of rules of the Act.[54] The Commission is also entitled to designate a business entity as gatekeeper even where it does not yet enjoy an entrenched and durable position in its operations, but which will foreseeably enjoy in the near future.[55] The differences between gatekeepers of different digital markets are irrelevant for the purposes of defining a gatekeeper.[56]

Gatekeepers are defined as the entities providing core platform services.[57] Core platform services include a closed-list of ten digital services,[58] including online search engines, online social networking services or web browsers. A business entity may be considered as a gatekeeper for the provision of online social networking services, but not for the provision of online intermediation services.[59] It seems that the Commission accepts that a business may diversify its core platform services based on the purpose for which such services are used by either the consumers or other businesses, even where the users of the relevant services are the same or the services belong to the same category and type of core platform services.[60]

There were arguments indicating that once a business entity is designated as a gatekeeper for a core platform service, the Commission will be responsible for evaluating whether the other core platform services offered by the designated entity should be subject to the scope of the Act or not.[61] The methodology for the designation of gatekeepers as well as the criteria to be assessed need to be clarified and further interpreted, allowing legal certainty and transparency during relevant market investigations.[62] The ambiguity in the letter of the Act may have opposite results allowing tech giants to easily challenge a "*gatekeeper*" designation for specific core platform services,[63] suggesting that such services serve different purposes of businesses or consumers. Designated gatekeepers can also present arguments demonstrating that exceptionally due to the manner in which the relevant core platform service operates, they do not meet the three (3) qualitative criteria of the Act,[64] a scenario that may end up to the Court of Justice of the EU,[65] setting in risk the objectives of contestability, fairness, legal certainty and speed of enforcement. The

---

[53] Article 13 of the Act and Streel and Alexiadis (2023), p. 108.

[54] Malheiro (2023), p. 6.

[55] Article 17 (4) of the Act.

[56] Ambroziak (2022), p. 22.

[57] Article 2 (1) of the Act.

[58] Article 2 (2) of the Act.

[59] Feasey (2022).

[60] Annex A of the Act.

[61] Feasey (2022).

[62] Akman (2022), p. 7; Petit (2021), p. 534; Di Porto et al. (2021), p. 92; Geradin (2021), pp. 12, 14.

[63] Feasey (2022).

[64] Article 3 (5) of the Act.

[65] Akman (2022), p. 8.

effectiveness of the landmark legal tool is in risk due to the ambiguity existing in its letter,[66] which may allow businesses to easily escape the "*walled gardens*"[67] of the Act.

On September 2023, the Commission proceeded with the designation of six gatekeepers, capturing the American GAFAM[68] and Chinese ByteDance, while identifying a total of twenty-two core platform services.[69] Additionally, four market investigations were initiated aiming to review the arguments presented by Microsoft and Apple that although they meet the quantitative criteria, certain of their core platform services do not satisfy the qualitative criteria of the Act. The formal designation represents the first formal measures taken by the Commission under the Act, where it was clarified that a business may be designated as a gatekeeper for several core platform services.

2.3 A Series of Dos and Don'ts

Gatekeepers shall comply with specific prohibitions, the so-called "*commandments of Vestager and Breton*",[70] which relate with the use and access to data and the relationship between businesses with gatekeepers and consumers,[71] aiming at neutralising the competitive benefits of gatekeepers. The significant anti-competitive cases raised during the last ten years at European level provided the tools for implementing the series of Dos and Don'ts for gatekeepers.[72] Article 5 sets out a black list of self-executing obligations, while Article 6 includes a grey-list of semi self-executing requirements.[73] The difference between the two articles lies on the fact that the obligations of Article 6 are "*susceptible of being further specified following a regulatory dialogue*" between the gatekeeper and the Commission.[74] Article 7 of the Act introduces an interoperability obligation for interpersonal communications services. The direct effect of the prohibitions raised under Article 6 is questionable due to their very nature that require further interpretation.[75] While, the intention of the Act is to intervene and regulate the conduct of tech giants, the overgrowing development of the digital business models demand the presence of a regulatory tool that allows it to adapt based on the identifying needs.

[66] Carugati (2023).

[67] EDPS (2021), p. 13.

[68] Cabral et al. (2021), p. 9.

[69] Press Release Brussels (2023).

[70] Streel and Larouche (2021), p. 50.

[71] Manganelli and Nicita (2022), pp. 153–154.

[72] Ambroziak (2022), pp. 23–28.

[73] Streel and Larouche (2021), p. 50.

[74] Akman (2022), p. 13; Cabral et al. (2021), p. 10.

[75] Petit (2021), pp. 539, 540.

The Commission is entitled to proceed with adding or modifying the obligations by performing a relevant market analysis and adopting a relevant delegated act.[76] In practice, this may allow the Commission to keep a close watch to any new potential practices that may hinder competition in digital markets, allowing it to update the applicable legal framework in place so as to adjust to the new technological reality. However, this process might become too time-consuming, with scholars to suggest the adoption of a rule that will enable the Commission to take instead interim measures allowing the restriction of the presumed anti-competitive conduct, while conducting a market investigation.[77] Additionally, the prohibitions of the Act raise significant legal ambiguity to what gatekeepers can and cannot do, calling in question their direct and self-executing nature.[78] Further interpretation and clarifications are required[79] for clarifying the restrictions, setting not only a higher-than-expected level of compliance for gatekeepers,[80] but also making the monitoring work of the Commission much harder.

3 Fairness & Contestability in Digital Markets

3.1 Business User: The "Leading Actor" of the Act

Undoubtedly, business users have a leading role within the Act, setting a burden to gatekeepers to act or to refrain from acting with a specific manner, so as to compete with them on fairer terms. As part of such effort, gatekeepers cannot prevent other businesses from offering the same services or goods to consumers at prices or market conditions different from those offered by the gatekeepers,[81] while at the same time gatekeepers shall refrain from adopting practices requiring from businesses to subscribe to, or register with, any further core platform services, as a pre-condition for them to be able to use, access, sign up for or registering with any of the core platform services offered by the latter.[82] The Commission confirmed that access to ranking, query, click and view data may result in excluding potential competition in digital markets,[83] and as a result the prohibition of self-preferencing practices was

[76] Article 12 of the Act, Ambroziak (2022), p. 23; Podszun (2022), p. 2; Streel and Alexiadis (2023), p. 109.

[77] Podszun et al. (2021), p. 4; Streel et al. (2021), pp. 35, 36.

[78] Podszun et al. (2021), p. 1; Streel and Alexiadis (2023), p. 105.

[79] Crémer et al. (2023), p. 3.

[80] Akman (2022), pp. 25, 26; Manganelli and Nicita (2022), p. 160.

[81] Article 5 (3) of the Act.

[82] Article 5 (8) of the Act.

[83] Recital 61 of the Act.

introduced requiring from gatekeepers to apply transparent, fair and non-discriminatory conditions when ranking services or goods.[84]

Any form of different or preferential treatment through legal, commercial or technical means,[85] of ranking on the core platform service is strictly prohibited. Inspiration for the inclusion of the self-preferencing prohibition in the bible of the Act derived from the well-known *Google Shopping*[86] case, where the General Court of the EU concluded that Google abused its dominant position by favoring its own comparison-shopping service over competing comparison-shopping services. Competition law provides the tools for dominant entities to suggest objective justifications aiming to declare inapplicable the Article 102 TFEU by justifying the identified anti-competitive conduct. Nevertheless, it appears that the self-preferencing prohibition of the Act does not allow the provision of objective justifications,[87] adopting a stricter approach against gatekeepers by not allowing them to justify their interests in favoring their own or affiliated interests, in a manner that negatively impacts fair competition and reduces consumer welfare. Guidance for assessing self-preferencing cases can be drawn from Regulation (EU) 2019 / 1150 on the promotion of fairness and transparency for business users of online intermediation services.[88] It was argued however, that algorithms are mostly utilized by gatekeepers for the adoption of self-preferencing techniques, and that since gatekeepers are not required to disclose the algorithms used for their business activities, this makes the mission of detecting or identifying self-preferencing even harder for the Commission.

Businesses offering online search engines shall be provided with access on fair, reasonable and non-discriminatory terms—FRAND terms—to ranking, query, click and view data in relation to free and paid search generated by end users on gatekeepers' online search engines.[89] The gatekeeper shall ensure that adequate measures are taken for the safeguarding of personal data of consumers, allowing for the anonymization of search data where such include personal data and ensuring a low risk of their re-identification for ensuring compliance with the GDPR (General Data Protection Regulation).[90] True anonymization can be very hard.[91] On the other side, search engines businesses are required to ensure that the data they obtained from gatekeepers do no comprise of any personal data so as not having any risk of

[84] Article 6 (5) of the Act and Arcelin (2023), pp. 323–324.

[85] Recital, para 52 of the Act.

[86] Case T-612/17 *Google LLC, formerly Google Inc. and Alphabet, Inc. v European Commission* not yet published (Court Reports - general).

[87] Cabral et al. (2021), p. 13; Bostoen (2023), p. 294; Blažo (2023), p. 68; Bostoen (2023), p. 286.

[88] Recital, para 52 of the Act.

[89] Article 6 (11) of the Act.

[90] Recital, para 61 of the Act. Regulation (EU) 2016/679 of the European Parliament and of the Council of 27 April 2016 on the protection of natural persons with regard to the processing of personal data and on the free movement of such data, and repealing Directive 95/46/EC (General Data Protection Regulation) OJ L 119, 4.5.2016, pp. 1–88.

[91] Kerrigan (2022), p. 169.

infringing the GDPR.[92] Additionally, businesses are entitled to a fair, reasonable, and non-discriminatory access to the gatekeepers' software application stores, online search engines and online social networking services.[93] *But what FRAND terms a gatekeeper may adopt so as to ensure compliance with the provisions of the Act?* By considering that FRAND terms cannot be easily and duly understood in IT or antitrust areas of laws,[94] their inclusion in the letter of the Act raises questions on the practical implementation of the obligations by gatekeepers.

The Act recognizes that interoperability constitutes a crucial tool enabling the promotion of innovation and the empowerment of competition.[95] It is defined as the "*ability to exchange information and mutually use the information which has been exchanged through interfaces or other solutions, so that all elements of hardware or software work with other hardware and software and with users in all the ways in which they are intended to function*".[96] Gatekeepers providing interpersonal communication services shall allow a horizontal interoperability, enabling as an example, a Viber user to communicate with a WhatsApp user, or an Android user to send an online message to an iPhone user. In particular, basic functionalities are required to become interoperable, including end-to-end text messaging between end users and sharing of images or voice messages. Undoubtedly, interoperability enhances consumer choice and allows for the promotion of innovation, however, the safeguarding of consumers' personal data is at risk.

3.2 "Killer" Acquisitions vs. the Act

Mergers and acquisitions of start-ups or small players by the tech giant constitutes a common phenomenon in digital markets, which can entrench monopolies by limiting new competition entering the market.[97] These are known as "*killer*" acquisitions, since their main strategy is to "*buy-or-bury*"[98] against existing or potential competitors, allowing tech giants to reinforce their dominance. GAFAM acquired more than 900 companies[99] since their foundation, the majority of which remained outside of the radar of competition authorities as being below the applicable size thresholds. The Act introduced a crucial reporting obligation of gatekeepers requiring them to report any intended concentration that involve other providers of core

[92] Article 6 of the GDPR.

[93] Article 6 (12) of the Act.

[94] Jordan and Sokol (2023), p. 109.

[95] Privacy International (2022); Kerber and Schweitzer (2017), p. 39.

[96] Article 2(29) of the Act.

[97] Cabral et al. (2021).

[98] OECD (2023), p. 17.

[99] Gugler et al. (2023), p. 2.

platform services or other services of the digital sector.[100] Nevertheless, there are not many hopes that this rule will be a game changer.

The joint governments of Germany, France and the Netherlands issued in 2021 a paper setting out their suggestions to enhance the rules of the back then proposal of the Act.[101] In respect to mergers, their suggestion was to strengthen and speed up merger control since the reporting of mergers and concentrations to the Commission without subjecting such mergers to a full investigation of their legality under the applicable competition legal framework of Regulation (EC) No. 139/2004 was considered inadequate.[102] Their suggestions lie on setting clear and legally certain thresholds for mergers by gatekeepers with relatively low turnover, but with high value, and amending the substantive test to effectively tackle cases of potential "*killer*" acquisitions something that is not achieved by the current approach of the antitrust review of acquisitions.[103] Moreover, it was argued that the Act fails to take into proper consideration the limitations in the Commission's market monitoring, detection and investigation capacity towards digital acquisitions.[104]

3.3 *Weak Enforcement?*

The European Commission is responsible for ensuring a proper implementation of the requirements from gatekeepers, as the single enforcer of the Act.[105] Monitoring of compliance with the requirements of the Act might involve the exercise of the investigative powers of the Commission,[106] including an investigation of complaints received by consumers or business users against a specific gatekeeper,[107] an assessment of the results of an investigation performed by a national competition authority,[108] or a review of the compliance report submitted by gatekeepers.[109] In respect to the compliance report, within a period of six months from the gatekeepers' designation, gatekeepers need to submit a report to the Commission indicating the measures they implemented so as to ensure compliance with the requirements of

[100] Article 14 of the Act.

[101] Friends of an effective Digital Markets Act (2021).

[102] Caffarra and Morton (2021a).

[103] Mahari et al. (2021), p. 56; Jordan and Sokol (2023), p. 111.

[104] European Court of Auditors (2020).

[105] Article 26 of the Act and Crémer et al. (2023), p. 2.

[106] Article 20 (2) of the Act.

[107] Article 27 of the Act.

[108] Article 38 of the Act.

[109] Article 11 of the Act.

the Act,[110] with gatekeepers having the burden to prove their compliance.[111] Cases of non-compliance with the obligations of the Act will result in the adoption of an implementing act by the Commission setting out its finding of non-compliance,[112] and the Commission may impose a fine of not exceeding 10% of the total worldwide turnover in the preceding financial year for failure to comply with the requirements of the Act.[113] Where the case of non-compliance is related with a repeated violation of the Act, then a fine up to 20% of the total worldwide turnover of the gatekeeper may be imposed.[114]

Many have stressed the risk arising due to the full concentration of enforcement powers of the provisions of the Act on the Commission.[115] Other third parties, including private independent bodies, consumer organizations, or even the Member States should have a role to the enforcement of the Act. There were arguments indicating that such independent bodies are closer to the consumer, having also developed technical and legal expertise for better understanding the malpractices utilized by businesses in the digital ecosystem.[116] Nicolas Petit argued that the letter of the Act provides two possibilities of decentralization.[117] First, it appears that the Act allows Member States to subject tech giants to stricter competition rules,[118] while the direct effect of the Act as a Regulation will allow national courts to ask preliminary references to the Court of Justice of the EU connected with the application of the provisions of the Act, enabling an indirect cooperation between national and European bodies. The Act does not explicitly indicate how a potential conflict with national rules of Member States can be addressed.[119] Such a conflict might be decided in favor of the Act on the basis of the principle of supremacy of EU law.

The Act develops a cooperation mechanism between the Commission and national competition rules connected with the exchange of information through the European Competition Network.[120] Additionally, it is indicated that a national competition authority may initiate investigations on gatekeepers based on national competition law provided that it informs the Commission accordingly. A recent example of the implementation of national rules that may be considered as connected with the activities of gatekeepers, was the application of the German Competition

[110] Directorate-General for Competition, Directorate-General for Communications Networks, Content and Technology (2023).

[111] Crémer et al. (2023), p. 7.

[112] Article 29 of the Act.

[113] Article 30 (1) of the Act.

[114] Article 30 (2) of the Act.

[115] Podszun et al. (2021), pp. 8, 9; Witt (2023), p. 33.

[116] Privacy International (2022); Monti (2021), p. 6.

[117] Petit (2021), pp. 539, 540; Witt (2023), p. 26.

[118] Recital, para 10 of the Act.

[119] Petit (2021), pp. 539, 540.

[120] Article 38 of the Act.

Authority of Section 19a GWB[121] against Google. This provision allows the designation of an undertaking as of paramount significance for competition across markets, and the German Competition Authority may prohibit such undertaking from acting in a specific manner. The German Competition Authority accepted certain commitments presented by Google for enhancing competition and also allowing the empowerment of consumers' personal data, since it restricts Google from combining personal data collected from third sources, unless consent is given.[122] While Mr. Mundt, the president of the Authority, emphasized the active collaboration between the national competition authority and the Commission during the proceedings, it appears that the Authority failed to duly comply with the current framework of the Act, since it did not notify the Commission of its intention to launch an investigation against gatekeepers based on national laws.[123] The Act pursues different legal interests than those pursued by competition law,[124] therefore, it needs to be applied without prejudice to the rules of anti-competitive conduct.[125]

While the Act pursues the objective to ensure that markets where gatekeepers are present are and remain contestable and fair, competition law intents to the enhancement of undistorted competition on the market.[126] A conduct might trigger simultaneously the ex-ante provisions of the Act, and the ex-post tools of competition law, resulting to an overlapping.[127] This raises the concern of whether the overlapping will breach the principle of *"ne bis in idem"*, the right not to be tried or punished twice for the same offence.[128] "*Friends of an Effective Digital Markets Act*" team of France, Germany and the Netherlands stressed that competition enforcement and the Act must complement, and not weaken each other.[129] Significant guidance to this matter can be drawn from two recent cases of the Court of Justice of the EU, in its decisions on *bpost SA v Autorité belge de la concurrence*[130] and *Bundeswettbewerbsbehörde v Nordzucker.*[131] It was confirmed that there is no breach of the principle of *"ne bis in idem"* in cases where the two distinct set of rules pursue different objectives, and a set of procedures requirements are satisfied, including the two cases are brought close to each other in time and the "*doubleness*" of the cases does not create an unnecessary burden for the concerned person. The latter can be considered as satisfied if the concerned party can foresee the parallel

[121] Baschenhof (2021), p. 140.

[122] Press Releases from the Bundeskartellamt (2023).

[123] Article 38 (2) of the Act & 55. Martínez (2023).

[124] Recital, para 11 of the Act.

[125] Recital, para 10 of the Act.

[126] Recital, para 11 of the Act.

[127] Crémer et al. (2023), p. 20; Monti (2021), p. 14.

[128] Article 50 of EU Charter of Fundamental Rights.

[129] Crémer et al. (2023), pp. 30, 31.

[130] Case C-117/20 *bpost SA v Autorité belge de la concurrence* not yet published (Court Reports - general).

[131] Case C-151/20 *Bundeswettbewerbsbehörde v Nordzucker AG and Others* not yet published (Court Reports - general).

application of the two distinct set of rules. While the first condition of different objectives is satisfied in the case of potential application of the Act and the anti-competitive provisions, a concern was raised by academia for cases where antitrust proceedings were initiated before the Act was set in force, where someone can easily suggest that the concerned undertaking could not be in the position to foresee the parallel application of the two different set of rules. To overcome the potential infringement of the principle, it was suggested that the investigation for the antitrust case to be performed for the period before the obligations of the Act kicked-off, allowing a parallel application of both set of rules for past and future conduct at the same time.[132]

4 Safeguarding of Privacy

4.1 Privacy Concerns

The Act complements the existing level of protection provided under the GDPR, clarifying that gatekeepers shall comply with the provisions of the Act in line also with the set of rules on personal data and privacy,[133] by considering that the *"data protection and privacy interests of end users are relevant to any assessment of potential negative effects of the observed practice of gatekeepers to collect and accumulate large amounts of data from end users*".[134] The intention of the Act is to enable consumers to regain control over their data so as to decide which to share with the tech giants, and to enhance transparency on how tech giants use their data.[135] The proposed harmonious co-existence of the distinct set of rules may be proved to be a fallacy, since there might be cases where an overlapping of obligations might occur or conflicts of obligations might arise.

Each of the legal instruments have a different scope and serve distinct purposes.[136] Businesses have the leading role within the Act which aims at restoring the fairness in digital markets, while consumers are in the very heart of the GDPR, having the intention to protect individuals' right to protection of their personal data. An overlapping of the obligations of the Act and the GDPR arises that seems to create a high burden for gatekeepers of managing to achieve compliance with both set of rules. Particularly, gatekeepers are prohibited from processing consumers' data for specific purposes, unless consumers have been presented with a specific choice, and their consent was provided.[137] Moreover, gatekeepers are required to grant other

[132] Crémer et al. (2023), p. 21.

[133] European Commission (2020b), p. 5, Recital para 12 of the Act and Privacy International (2022).

[134] Recital para 72 of the Act and EDPS (2021), p. 7.

[135] Pop et al. (2022).

[136] Geradin et al. (2022), p. 2; Podszun (2021), p. 200.

[137] Article 5 (2) of the Act.

businesses with access to their data, including personal data of the users of their services,[138] provide effective data portability to consumers,[139] as well as access to ranking, query, client and view data of its users, including personal data.[140] In addition, and within six months following the designation of a business entity as a gatekeeper, the gatekeeper shall submit an independently audited description of any techniques used for profiling of consumers, and such the report shall be forwarded by the Commission to the European Data Protection Board.[141] The lack of explicit reference for a potential collaboration between the Commission and Data Protection Authorities may be considered as a missed opportunity for allowing the solving of any inconsistencies or even conflicts arising between the application of the two distinct sets of rules.

First, data sharing obligations may raise significant concerns. While the intention of the GDPR is to restrict any unnecessary sharing of personal data between third parties, the Act intends at enhancing data sharing so as to allow small players to compete in a fairer digital environment.[142] Nevertheless, providing access to data in a GDPR-compliant manner poses a regulatory and technical challenge for gatekeepers. The need to safeguard personal data,[143] or confidentiality of trade secrets or even intellectual property rights can be used as an excuse for gatekeepers of not complying with the provisions of the Act.[144] The purpose limitation principle of the GDPR provides that personal data need to be collected for "*specified, explicit and legitimate purposes and not further processed in a manner incompatible with those purposes*".[145] As a result, a gatekeeper may refuse to share personal data with its competitors on the basis that such a transfer will be incompatible with the purpose for which the personal data were originally collected by the gatekeeper, and as a processing activity could have not been foreseen and predicted by the individuals.[146] On the other hand, if the gatekeeper shares personal data of its users with its competitors as it is required to be performed under the Act, then if a consumer elect to exercise the right to be forgotten, the gatekeeper will be required to notify an indefinite number of recipients of the data about their obligation to erase the consumers' data "*without undue delay*".

[138] Article 6 (10) of the Act.

[139] Article 6 (9) of the Act.

[140] Article 6 (11) of the Act.

[141] Article 15 of the Act.

[142] Feasey and Streel (2020), pp. 26–29.

[143] Baschenhof (2021), p. 118.

[144] Lundqvist (2021).

[145] Article 5 (1) (b) of the GDPR.

[146] Article 29 Data Protection Working Party (2013), pp. 26, 37; Demircan (2022), pp. 155, 156.

4.2 Consent: A Pseydo-Solution

Gatekeepers are prohibited from proceeding with certain practices involving the processing of personal data of consumers, including processing for the purpose of providing online advertising services, or combining the personal data of consumers from other sources like other services offered by the service platform.[147] The Act recognizes that any of the referred prohibited actions can take place only where the consumers have been presented with a specific choice and provided their consent for such processing of their personal data. This prohibition aims at empowering the right to personal data by allowing individuals to decide and have a choice on how and whom may share their personal data, enhancing also the contestability of digital markets by allowing businesses to compete with gatekeepers on much fairer terms.[148] Additionally, gatekeepers shall provide businesses with "*effective, high-quality, continuous and real-time access to, and use of, data*", and where such data include personal data, such access shall be provided only where the "*data are directly connected with the use effectuated by the end users in respect of the products or services offered by the relevant business user through the relevant core platform service*" and "*when the end users opt in to such sharing by giving their consent*".[149] This requirement aims at allowing data sharing between competitors by enabling small players operating on larger platforms to access data that are essential for them operating in digital markets.[150] Moreover, the Act prohibits the mandatory subscription of consumers to additional core platform services of the gatekeeper, as a condition for being able to use, access, sign up for or registering with any of that gatekeeper's core platform services.[151] It is considered that this prohibition mitigates competition concerns arising from compulsory "*bundling of services*"[152] and single consent buttons, while, at the same time, it enhances indirectly the safeguards to data protection and privacy.[153]

Mr. Mundt stressed as part of the proceedings against Google that "*Without the voluntary and informed consent of the user, the data from Google and third-party services may no longer be used or even merged in separately provided Google services. We have ensured that Google will provide a separate choice in the future.*" However, the concept of "*consent*" as a lawful basis for the processing of personal data under the GDPR is highly debatable due to the malpractices that the majority of data controllers follow when requesting consumers' consent for specific processing activities.[154] Consent must be freely given, specific, informed and unam-

---

[147] Article 5 (2) of the Act and Wolfgang (2022), p. 15.

[148] Caffarra and Morton (2021b).

[149] Article 6 (10) of the Act.

[150] Weigl et al. (2023), p. 4; Mahari et al. (2021), p. 55.

[151] Article 5 (8) of the Act.

[152] Feasey and Streel (2020), p. 64.

[153] EDPS (2021), para 26.

[154] Pop et al. (2022).

biguous. A 33-page Guidelines on consent have been issued by the European Data Protection Board,[155] as an effort to shed some light to this controversial legal basis of the GDPR. The European Data Protection Supervisor (EDPS) in its recommendation for the Proposal of the Act suggested that the Act needs to be amended so as to include an obligation for the gatekeepers to provide a user-friendly solution for consent management, allowing consumers to easily provide, modify or even withdrawing their consent,[156] while it was further argued that additional obligations need to be introduced enabling the rule of Article 5 (a) of the Act to become more precise.[157] The practical implementation[158] of the presentation of such user-friendly and valid consent banner to consumers allowing gatekeepers to comply with their obligations both under the Act and the GDPR leaves room for interpretation, where additionally the concept of "*specific choice*" remains undefined.[159] Certain stakeholders argued that the final wording of the Article, and specifically, the part indicating the prohibition for "*process, for the purpose of providing online advertising services*",[160]is problematic, since it implies that online advertising is based on a single data processing purpose, while consumers data can be collected from various ad targeting processing activities of the same gatekeeper. This enables gatekeepers to combine all data collected from its various business activities by relying on an all-encompassing, single button consent.[161] *Having obtained consent from consumers will result in regaining the control over their personal data and review how much of their personal data are being processed, combined or cross-used by gatekeepers?*[162]

While it seems that a burdensome procedure is created,[163] where gatekeepers are required to collect valid consent from specifically each affected consumer, experience shows that gatekeepers implement unnecessary complex, long and difficult to understand privacy policies or terms and conditions. It can be argued that the letter of Article 5 (2) of the Act creates a high burden for gatekeepers to overcome, requiring them to prove that a valid consent was provided by consumers for the specific processing activities, limiting at the same time the number of cases where a single button consent practice will be followed. A valid consent practically means that a clear and explicit explanation is provided to consumers on how their personal data will be processed, and consumers consent specifically for any intended use.[164] Consumers are found themselves in a position where they are forced to accept rules

[155] EDPB (2020).

[156] EDPS (2021), p. 10.

[157] Podszun (2021), p. 203.

[158] Apostle and Rose (2022).

[159] Podszun (2021), p. 198.

[160] Article 5 (2) (a) of the Act.

[161] European Publishers Council and Digital Content Next (2022).

[162] Pop et al. (2022).

[163] Geradin et al. (2022), p. 8.

[164] EDPB (2020), p. 15.

that are not for their benefit and they are easily being tricked to provide their consent for a bundle of processing activities.[165] The concept of *"consent fatigue"*[166] has been used by many data protection professionals as an excuse of not using consent as a legal basis for processing personal data.[167] Specifically, consent shifts the risks to the individual, while the individual is not in the position to properly assess all risks derived from the concerned processing activities, due to the immediate benefits to be enjoyed once consent is given. Let us take the example of cookies banners that we come across during our web browsing, and the easiness of how quickly we provide our consent, without even bothering to duly read or understand how our underlying personal data is used by the data controllers. Yet, the Commission chooses to incorporate the lawful basis of consent so as to allow gatekeepers from justifying the relevant processing, combination, cross-using or sharing of personal data, having the risk of being a further formalistic obstacle with little impact for users.[168]

The prohibition of combining personal data from other sources unless consent is provided derives as many have argued[169] from the experience gained by the European Union through the well-known German antitrust case of Meta. Meta was processing not only the personal data provided directly from the users of the social media service, but also personal data collected from the profiles its users had with the Meta group entities. Users of Meta were informed about the combination activity through the user agreement which was required to be agreed so as for consumers to be able to use the social network. The Court of Justice of the EU highlighted in this case that the dominant position of the data controller may affect the freedom of choice of the user, who might be unable to refuse or withdraw consent without detriment. Such a dominant position may create a clear imbalance between the parties which will favour the imposition of conditions that are not strictly required for the performance of the contract between the dominant company and the user.[170] Hence, users' consent in phenomena of "*take it or leave it*", practically mean no consent at all.[171] It appears that granting of a GDPR-compliant consent in the digital ecosystem may become a utopian dream rather than a realistic scenario.

Gatekeepers are part of multi-sided markets, where a significant number of transactions and trades are performed at the same time. An increasing number of businesses may claim access to the exclusive data sets of gatekeepers, requiring that consumers will be specifically informed about the types of data that will be shared, the identities of the recipients, as well as the purposes for which such recipients will process the personal data. If consumers refuse to provide their consent, they will be

[165] Chirita (2018), pp. 172–175.

[166] Pop et al. (2022).

[167] Moerel and Prins (2016), pp. 27, 34; Demircan (2022), pp. 152, 153.

[168] Podszun (2021), p. 199.

[169] Baschenhof (2021), p. 12; Caffarra and Morton (2021b); Crémer et al. (2023), p. 14.

[170] Case C-252/21, *Meta Platforms and Others (Conditions générales d'utilisation d'un réseau social)* not yet published (Court Reports - general), paras 148–150.

[171] Geradin et al. (2022), pp. 8, 9.

simply restricted from using the goods or services of the tech giants,[172] while a withdrawal of consent[173] will demand an immediate suspension of the concerned processing activities from gatekeepers or the suspension of data sharing. Reliance on the lawful basis of consent so as to empower fair and contestable digital markets is indisputably problematic, since withdrawal of consent which can occur at any time, practically allows gatekeepers to deny sharing personal data with their competitors, resulting in "*boostering*" the closed digital markets instead of "*opening*" digital competition. While the Act recognises that where there is no consent or a withdrawal of consent takes place, gatekeepers shall offer them a less personalised but equivalent alternative experience of its services,[174] there is no consensus of what such less personalised but equivalent alternative means.[175]

It is questionable whether consent as a mechanism for justifying the relevant processing activities of the Act is adequate to silence any competition concerns.[176] *Will the fair competition being promoted if the majority of the users of the Meta platform consent to their combination of their personal data with other sources, while some other refuse such combination?* Inge Graef emphasised that the effectiveness of the remedy of consent in promoting competition is completely depended on individual users' choices,[177] hence falling short in achieving the goal of fair and contestable markets. She continues by suggesting the replacement of consent with the lawful basis of "*necessary for the performance of a contract*", clarifying that the combination of data with the sole purpose of increasing personalisation or profiling of consumers should fall outside of the notion of "*performance of a contract*".[178]

4.3 The Duality of Data Portability

The Act recognizes that gatekeepers are benefiting from the huge amounts of data they collect while providing core platform services,[179] hence and in order to limit cases of "*closed digital markets*" where consumers do not have the opportunity to switch to alternative providers, it introduced the requirement to provide consumers with "*effective portability of data provided by the end user or generated through the activity of the end user*".[180] This obligation seems to complement the right to data

[172] Bagnoli (2021), p. 139.
[173] Article 7 (3) of the GDPR.
[174] Recital para 36 of the Act and Caffarra and Morton (2021b).
[175] Podszun (2021), p. 198.
[176] Graef (2021).
[177] Graef (2021).
[178] Graef (2021)
[179] Recital para 59 of the Act.
[180] Article 6 (9) of the Act.

portability under the GDPR,[181] which sets out the right of data subject of receiving her personal data which she has provided to a data controller, or of transferring such to another data controller. The suggestion that the data portability right under the GDPR and the data portability obligation under the Act are "*two sides of the same coin*" cannot be verified,[182] since in practice, the Act provides for a far broader concept of data portability compared with that of the GDPR.[183]

First, the data protection right pursues the "*further strengthening of the data subject's control over her personal data*",[184]while the obligation of the Act intends to maintain fair and contestable digital markets. While someone can argue that the exercise of the GDPR right might allow the empowerment of contestable markets since data subjects will have the opportunity to switch to alternative service providers that are aligned with their preferences, GDPR does not pursue any objectives related with the promotion of competition.[185] Second, a significant distinction is observed regarding the scope of data covered under both overlapping concepts. The right to data portability refers solely to the portability of personal data, therefore and as per the Guidelines of Working Party 29, "*any data that is anonymous or does not concern the data subject*" do not fall within the scope of the GDPR.[186] Specifically, it covers only personal data that were provided by the data subject to the controller including data observed from the activities of the data subject,[187] by virtue of the use of a service or device, clarifying also, that the category of "*observed data*" did not include data actively created by the controller itself. Unlike the GDPR right, the obligation of the Act seems to cover portability of both personal and non-personal data,[188] including not only data provided by the end user, but also data that were generated through the activity of the end user, and independently created by the controller itself.

Moreover, an undisputed difference derives from the exercise of the data portability under the GDPR compared with the Act. The data portability right covers only personal data processed on a basis of consent, or a contract. This restriction is not part of the obligation of data portability under the Act, allowing the porting of data processed under additional lawful bases, including legitimate interests and lawful obligation.[189] Aside from the aforesaid, it seems that gatekeepers will be required to satisfy different conditions so as to be in line with the obligations raised on each legal instrument. Particularly, the Act provides that gatekeepers shall provide effective portability "*free of charge*", while the GDPR allows the imposition of a

[181] Article 20 of the GDPR & Recital para 59 of the Act.

[182] Geradin et al. (2022).

[183] Baschenhof (2021), pp. 114, 115; Feasey and Streel (2020), pp. 45, 46.

[184] Recital 68 of the GDPR.

[185] Geradin et al. (2022), p. 4.

[186] Article 29 Data Protection Working Party (2017), p. 9.

[187] Article 29 Data Protection Working Party (2017), pp. 9, 10.

[188] Article 6 (9) of the Act.

[189] Geradin et al. (2022), p. 5.

reasonable fee where it can be demonstrated that the requests are manifestly unfounded or excessing, "*in particular because of their repetitive character*".[190] Moreover, and while controllers shall directly transmit personal data to another controller, where this is technically feasible,[191] without having to adopt or maintain processing systems that are technically compatible,[192] the Act requires from gatekeepers to "*ensure, by means of appropriate and high-quality technical measures*"[193] the undisturbed and continuous porting of data.

The above raises the question on how in practice gatekeepers can pursue compliance with their data portability obligations arising under both of the legal instruments. The Article 29 Working Party emphasized that where a specific European or Member State law in another field provides for some form of data portability, then such specific framework needs to be taken into consideration when applying the GDPR data portability. However, in cases where it is clear that the intention of the data subject is not to exercise its data portability right, but to exercise any relevant rights deriving from other sectorial legal framework, then the GDPR won't be applied to such request.[194] The practical conflicts arising raise concerns that consumers might still suffer from lock-in effects.[195]

The Commission acknowledged back in 2020 that the full potential of the right to data portability was not fully unlocked, recognizing that the Commission would explore how the preparation of the Digital Services Act package will enhance data portability.[196] Three years later, the Commission discussions are concentrated on the need to enhance the right to data portability under the GDPR through the adoption of a Data Act,[197] which aims to shift the control over personal data from service providers to the data subject, allowing the latter to decide on whether they will share personal data to third parties.[198] Admitting that overlapping and potential conflicts of both legal instruments might in practice have opposite results, a panel of economic experts recommended that instead of transferring personal data from gatekeepers to other business users, businesses shall be granted with in-situ rights to access end user data while such data remain in the infrastructure of the gatekeeper.[199]

[190] Article 29 Data Protection Working Party (2017), p. 15.

[191] Article 20 (2) of the GDPR.

[192] Recital para 68 of the GDPR.

[193] Recital para 59 of the Act.

[194] Article 29 Data Protection Working Party (2017), pp. 7, 8.

[195] Manganelli and Nicita (2022), p. 149.

[196] European Commission (2020a) Data protection as a pillar of citizens' empowerment and the EU's approach to the digital transition - two years of application of the General Data Protection Regulation https://eur-lex.europa.eu/legal-content/EN/TXT/PDF/?uri=CELEX:52020DC0264, pp. 8, 9.

[197] European Commission (2023).

[198] Braeken et al. (2023).

[199] Cabral et al. (2021), p. 22; Weigl et al. (2023), pp. 3–6, 7.

5 Conclusion

The adoption of the Digital Markets Act can be considered as a bold decision by the Commission, targeting to regulate the tech giants of the digital economy. It has a great potential to impact the behaviour of tech giants, allowing consumers to benefit from the full potential of the digital ecosystem, and diminishing entry barriers for new competition. Nevertheless, its success is greatly linked with the requirement of providing clarification on its letter, so as not to allow any room for conflicting interpretations. The issuance of guidelines or clear rulebooks by the Commission and the active collaboration with other third parties, including national competition authorities or courts and independent organisations, may enhance efforts to build a consensus to the interpretation of the Act.

Nevertheless, the Act may be considered as a conservative legal instrument which its proper application is restricted due to the reliance on highly debatable concepts, including GDPR-compliance consent and data portability. Consumers as victims of the digital economy are "*forced*" to share their personal data with the tech giants, without even realising it in most cases, so as to gain access to the innumerable benefits of the digital ecosystem. Without realising the true value of personal data, and by simply ticking a box for showing our agreement with the extensive and unrestricted use of our data by tech giants, we unintentionally contribute to the empowerment of the dominance of tech giants. The asymmetry in the relationship between gatekeepers and consumers may be reduced by requiring gatekeepers to be held accountable exhaustively for their actual processing activities. This may be achieved by enhancing the notification or reporting obligations of the tech giants, requiring them to provide details and clarifications about the manner in which they collect, including the use of algorithms, or use the personal data. Additionally, an active collaboration shall be established between the Commission and the EDPS allowing the search of potential solutions in cases of conflicts arising due to the overlapping of the GDPR with the Act.

The Act is undoubtedly a complex legal instrument that demands an active collaboration of European and national parties so as to overcome the barrier of overgrowing technological innovation and allowing the experiment of the Commission to be successful.

References

Akman P (2022) Regulating competition in digital platform markets: a critical assessment of the framework and approach of the EU Digital Markets Act. Eur Law Rev 47:1–30

Ambroziak A (2022) EU's perspective on the functioning of giant online platforms in the digital economy. In: Dąbrowski DL, Suska M (eds) The European Union Digital Single Market, 1st edn. Routledge, pp 5–34

Apostle J, Rose M (2022) The EU's Digital Markets Act: what does it mean for businesses and data privacy? https://www.orrick.com/en/Insights/2022/11/The-EUs-Digital-Markets-Act-What-Does-It-Mean-for-Businesses-and-Data-Privacy
Arcelin L (2023) Solidarity and competition: a (re)conciliation on the digital market. In: Castets-Renard C, Eunard J (eds) Artificial intelligence law, between sectoral rules and comprehensive regime comparative law, 1st edn. Bruylant, pp 307–335
Article 29 Data Protection Working Party (2013) Opinion 03/2013 on purpose limitation
Article 29 Data Protection Working Party (2017) Guidelines on the right to data portability
Bagnoli V (2021) Designing competition policy in digital markets for developing economies: how the EU can contribute with the Digital Markets Act and Digital Services Act. RDC 9:133–158
Baschenhof P (2021) The Digital Markets Act (DMA): a procompetitive recalibration of data relations? J Law Technol Policy 2022(1):101–154
Blažo O (2023) Efficiencies under the Digital Markets Act – is there space for the rule of reason? Acta Universitatis Carolinae Iuridica 68(2):53–70
Bostoen F (2023) Understanding the Digital Markets Act. Antitrust Bulletin, Tilburg Law School Research Paper 68(2):263–306. https://doi.org/10.2139/ssrn.4440819
Bradford A (2023) What is at stake if antitrust regulation fails? Network Law Review
Braeken B, Versteeg J, Berg D (2023) Big data, the Digital Markets Act and the Data Act: the growing importance of data in competition law. https://bureaubrandeis.com/big-data-the-digital-markets-act-and-the-data-act-the-growing-importance-of-data-in-competition-law/?lang=en
Cabral L, Haucap J, Parker G, Petropoulos G, Valletti T, Alstyn VM (2021) The EU Digital Markets Act a report from a panel of economic experts. Publications Office of the European Union 1:30. https://doi.org/10.2760/139337, JRC122910
Caffarra C, Morton FS (2021a) How will the Digital Markets Act regulate big tech? https://www.promarket.org/2021/01/11/digital-markets-act-obligations-big-tech-uk-dmu/
Caffarra C, Morton FS (2021b) The European Commission Digital Markets Act: a translation. https://voxeu.org/article/european-commission-digital-markets-act-translation
Carugati (2023) The difficulty of designating gatekeepers under the EU Digital Markets Act. Blog Spot. https://www.bruegel.org/blog-post/difficulty-designating-gatekeepers-under-eu-digital-markets-act
Chiarella ML (2023) Digital Markets Act (DMA) and Digital Services Act (DSA): new rules for the EU digital environment. Athens J Law 9(1):33–58
Chirita AD (2018) The rise of big data and the loss of privacy. In: Bakhoum M, Gallego BC, Mackenrodt M-O, Surblytė-Namavičienė G (eds) Personal data in competition, consumer protection and IP law. Springer
Colomo IP (2021) The Draft Digital Markets Act: a legal and institutional analysis. J Eur Compet Law Pract 12(7):561–575
Crémer J, Dinielli D, Heidhues P, Kimmelman G, Monti G, Podszun R, Schnitzer M, Morton FS, Streel A (2023) Enforcing the Digital Markets Act: institutional choices, compliance, and antitrust. J Antitrust Enforce. https://doi.org/10.1093/jaenfo/jnad004
Demircan M (2022) The DMA and the GDPR: making sense of data accumulation, cross-use and data sharing provisions. Forthcoming, IFIP Advances in Information and Communication Technology, Springer. https://doi.org/10.2139/ssrn.4297229
Di Porto F, Grote T, Volpi G, Invernizzi R (2021) I see something you don't see, a computational analysis of the Digital Services Act and the Digital Markets Act. Stanford Comput Antitrust 6:84–116
Directorate-General for Competition, Directorate-General for Communications Networks, Content and Technology (2023) Commission publishes template for compliance report under the Digital Markets Act. https://digital-markets-act.ec.europa.eu/template-compliance-report-under-digital-markets-act-published-2023-10-09_en
EDPB (2020) Guidelines 05/2020 on consent under Regulation 2016/679
EDPS (2021) Opinion 2/2021 on the Proposal for a Digital Markets Act. Available via EDPS website. https://edps.europa.eu/system/files/2021-02/21-02-10-opinion_on_digital_markets_act_en.pdf

European Commission (2020a) Data protection as a pillar of citizens' empowerment and the EU's approach to the digital transition - two years of application of the General Data Protection Regulation. eur-lex.europa.eu/legal-content/EN/TXT/PDF/?uri=CELEX:52020DC0264
European Commission (2020b) Proposal for a REGULATION OF THE EUROPEAN PARLIAMENT AND OF THE COUNCIL on contestable and fair markets in the digital sector (Digital Markets Act) COM(2020) 842 final
European Court of Auditors (2020) Special Report - The Commission's EU merger control and antitrust proceedings: a need to scale up market oversight. https://www.eca.europa.eu/Lists/ECADocuments/SR20_24/SR_Competition_policy_EN.pdf
European Publishers Council, Digital Content Next (2022) Statement on the DMA EPC & DCN statement on the DMA (epceurope.eu)
European Commission (2023) Press Corner, Data Act - Questions and Answers
Ezrachi A, Maurice E (2022) The darker sides of digital platform innovation. Network Law Review
Feasey R (2022) Note on designation of gatekeepers in the Digital Market Act. Centre on Regulation in Europe 1–11
Feasey R, Streel A (2020) Data sharing for digital markets contestability towards a governance framework. Centre on Regulation in Europe
Friends of an effective Digital Markets Act (2021) Non-paper: Strengthening the Digital Markets Act and Its Enforcement. pdf (overheid.nl)
Geradin D (2021) What is a digital gatekeeper? Which platforms should be captured by the EC Proposal for a Digital Market Act? 1–20. https://doi.org/10.2139/ssrn.3788152
Geradin D, Bania K, Karanikioti T (2022) The interplay between the Digital Markets Act and the General Data Protection Regulation. https://doi.org/10.2139/ssrn.4203907
Graef I (2021) Why end-user consent cannot keep markets contestable - a suggestion for strengthening the limits on personal data combination in the proposed Digital Markets Act. VerfBlog, 2021/9/02. https://verfassungsblog.de/power-dsa-dma-08/
Gugler K, Szücs F, Wohak U (2023) Start-up acquisitions, venture capital and innovation: a comparative study of Google, Apple, Facebook, Amazon and Microsoft. WU Vienna University of Economics and Business. Department of Economics Working Paper Series No. 340
Hoffman L (2023) Fairness in the Digital Markets Act. Eur Pap 8(1):17–23
Jordan B, Sokol DD (2023) Data valuation and law. Southern California Law Review, Forthcoming, 101–125
Kerber W, Schweitzer H (2017) Interoperability in the digital economy. JIPITEC 9:39–58
Kerrigan C (2022) Artificial intelligence, law and regulation, 1st edn. Edward Elgar Publishing
Kira B (2023) Rethinking regulation for dynamic digital ecosystems. Network Law Review
Koponen J, Mangiaracina A (2013) No free lunch: personal data and privacy in EU competition law 9(2):183–195
Lianos I (2022) Mind the (institutional) gap: digital economy, competition law and the toolkit approach. Network Law Review
Lundqvist B (2021) The Proposed Digital Markets Act and access to data: a revolution, or not? IIC 52:239–241. https://doi.org/10.1007/s40319-021-01026-0
Mahari R, Lera SC, Pentland A (2021) Time for a new antitrust era: refocusing antitrust law to invigorate competition in the 21st century. Stanford Computational Antitrust
Malheiro A (2023) The EU Digital Markets Act: a one-of-a-kind regulation. Network Law Review
Manganelli A, Nicita A (2022) Regulating digital markets, the European approach. Palgrave Macmillan
Martínez AR (2023) The Appropriation of Article 5(2) DMA: Google's Commitments under Section 19a of the German Competition Act. Kluwer Competition Law Blog. https://competitionlawblog.kluwercompetitionlaw.com/2023/10/09/the-appropriation-of-article-52-dma-googles-commitments-under-section-19a-of-the-german-competition-act/
Moerel L, Prins C (2016) Privacy for the Homo Digitalis: Proposal for a New Regulatory Framework for Data Protection in the Light of Big Data and the Internet of Things. https://doi.org/10.2139/ssrn.2784123

Monti G (2021) The Digital Markets Act – institutional design and suggestions for improvement. TILEC Discussion Paper, 1–18. https://doi.org/10.2139/ssrn.3797730
Nazzini R (2022) Mergers in the digital economy. Network Law Review
Organisation for Economic Co-operation and Development (OECD), Directorate for Financial and Enterprise Affairs Competition Committee (2023), Theories of Harm for Digital Mergers – Summaries of contributions, DAF/COMP/WD(2023)70
Petit N (2021) The Proposed Digital Markets Act (DMA): a legal and policy review. J Eur Compet Law Pract 7(12):529–541
Podszun R (2021) Should gatekeepers be allowed to combine data? - Ideas for Art. 5(a) of the Draft Digital Markets Act. https://doi.org/10.2139/ssrn.3860030
Podszun R (2022) From competition law to platform regulation – regulatory choices for the Digital Markets Act. Economics 17:1–13. https://doi.org/10.1515/econ-2022-0037
Podszun R, Bongartz P, Langenstein S (2021) Proposals on how to improve the Digital Markets Act. https://doi.org/10.2139/ssrn.3788571
Pop F, Bezemer J, Grant L (2022) The Digital Markets Act: more choice and improved data protection for users? EIPA. https://www.eipa.eu/blog/the-digital-markets-act-more-choice-and-improved-data-protection-for-users/
Press Release Brussels (2023) Digital Markets Act: Commission designates six gatekeepers. Available at European Commission. https://ec.europa.eu/commission/presscorner/detail/en/IP_23_4328
Press Releases from the Bundeskartellamt (2023) Bundeskartellamt gives users of Google services better control over their data. https://www.bundeskartellamt.de/SharedDocs/Meldung/EN/Pressemitteilungen/2023/05_10_2023_Google_Data.html?nn=3591286
Privacy International (2022) Recommendations for the trilogue on the Digital Markets Act. https://privacyinternational.org/advocacy/4754/recommendations-trilogue-digital-markets-act
Schäfer MT, van Es K (eds) (2017) The Datafied Society, Studying Culture through Data Schäfer and Es (2017)
Streel A, Alexiadis P (2023) The European way to regulate big tech: the EU's Digital Markets Act. In: Vicente DM, Vasconcelos Casimiro S, Chen C (eds) The legal challenges of the Fourth Industrial Revolution, The European Union's Digital Strategy, pp 91–125
Streel A, Larouche P (2021) The European Digital Markets Act proposal: how to improve a regulatory revolution. Concurrences 2:46–63
Streel A, Feasey R, Krämer J, Monti G (2021) Recommendations Paper, Making the Digital Markets Act more resilient and effective. Centre on Regulation in Europe
The Economist (2017) The world's most valuable resource is no longer oil, but data, The data economy demands a new approach to antitrust rules. Available via the Economist website. https://www.economist.com/leaders/2017/05/06/the-worlds-most-valuable-resource-is-no-longer-oil-but-data. Accessed 15 Feb 2021
Weigl L, Barbereau T, Sedlmeir J, Zavolokina L (2023) Mediating the tension between data sharing and privacy: the case of DMA and GDPR. Zurich Open Repository and Archive
Witt CA (2023) The Digital Markets Act – regulating the Wild West. Forthcoming Common Market Law Review 60(3):1–43
Wolfgang K (2022) Taming tech giants: the neglected interplay between competition law and data protection (privacy) law. Antitrust Bull 67(2):1–28

Re-orientating Digital Platform Regulation in the US and Australia: Treading Water or Experimenting?

Yane Svetiev

Abstract This paper analyses the re-orientation of digital platform regulation in the United States and Australia, including through legislative proposals to deal with platform power as well as enforcement cases against digital platforms. It argues that new initiatives to address platform power in these jurisdictions follow a common emergent template, involving measures focused on identifying conduct violations for platforms specifically designated on the basis of structural criteria including market share, size and concentration. The paper argues that such initiatives are unlikely to provide a magic bullet for addressing the problem of the concentration of economic or political power by the digital behemoths. This is because the emergent regulatory templates are not sensitive to the root causes of the emergence of digital platforms as a model of production and exchange, nor do they seek to address the remedial problems of traditional legal competition enforcement. More promising approaches would seek to resolve specific problems that arise in the platform ecology, for both collaborating firms and final users, through innovative remedial design based on the experimentalist disciplines of monitoring and recursive adjustment.

1 Introduction

As the various contributions in this volume illustrate, there has been a worldwide intense and growing focus on the regulation of digital platforms. This focus is producing a broad-based re-orientation of existing market regulatory tools, which may

This paper benefited from discussions at the workshop organized by the University of Belgrade Faculty of Law. I acknowledge the able research assistance of Ignat Kozlov, although the usual disclaimer applies.

Y. Svetiev (✉)
University of Sydney Law School, Sydney, NSW, Australia
e-mail: yane.svetiev@sydney.edu.au

D. V. Popović, R. Kulms (eds.), *Repositioning Platforms in Digital Market Law*, European Union and its Neighbours in a Globalized World 15,
https://doi.org/10.1007/978-3-031-69678-7_10

be regarded as a precursor to the emergence of a specialised digital markets law. The push towards specialist digital markets rules and regulatory instruments has been observed not only in the major jurisdictions and template setters, such as the United States, the European Union, and to some extent, the United Kingdom, but also in many 'follower' jurisdictions, including Australia, Canada, China, Japan, South Korea, and others.

In several jurisdictions examined in this volume, including the United States and Australia, the push to regulate digital platforms has had both a political and a technocratic impetus. In particular, over the past decade or so, regulatory and competition experts have argued that existing enforcement tools are ineffective in the digital world, calling for new rules and mechanisms. To support such arguments and to propose new mechanisms, expert reports have been commissioned in various jurisdictions.[1] In Australia, the Australian Competition and Consumer Commission (ACCC) has been undertaking a longer-term Digital Platforms Services Inquiry (DPSI) since 2020, which has recommended various novel instruments of digital market regulation, some of which have been adopted already.[2]

Importantly, the diagnosis of the problems identified by competition authorities or competition experts across different jurisdictions is broadly similar. Enforcers and experts have argued that there are specific features of digital platforms that make them fall in the interstices of existing regulatory frameworks and analytical tools for competition enforcement. As a result, the enforcement procedures and remedies in competition law and other market regulation, such as for example consumer law, may be ineffective in the digital environment.

Given such alignment in the diagnosis, it is perhaps unsurprising to observe considerable similarity in the proposed solutions across jurisdictions, which typically converge on the imposition of 'ex-ante' obligations. Such obligations are triggered by structural features of the concentrated markets in which digital platforms operate, but they target specific conduct formulated around familiar antitrust categories, and often even without specific requirements to prove negative effects of the impugned conduct. This re-orientation (back) towards structure and conduct apparently aims to compensate for an increasing inability of technocratic analytical tools to reliably predict anti-competitive effects in the highly dynamic environments in which digital platforms operate. This latter observation has also led to a re-examination of the broad-based consensus around consumer welfare as the appropriate standard for antitrust intervention.[3]

Given the foregoing trends, discussed also in other chapters, this contribution focuses on the evolution of digital markets law in the United States and Australia. In

[1] See Crémer et al. (2019), Furman et al. (2019), for an analysis of these reports see Kerber (2019) and Lancieri and Sakowski (2021).

[2] Australian Competition and Consumer Commission (September 2022). The ongoing inquiry outputs are available at https://www.accc.gov.au/inquiries-and-consultations/digital-platform-services-inquiry-2020-25.

[3] For an outline of the debate for and against retaining the consumer welfare standard, see Melamed and Petit (2019).

the United States, there has been a push towards a reorientation in platform regulation from both sides of politics. Both Republicans (including former President Trump) and Democrats (including through specific measures promulgated by the Biden's administration) have signalled greater political appetite for more ambitious control of platform power. This bipartisan interest can be attributed to a growing recognition of the substantial influence that digital platforms have on the political process, even though the two sides of politics have differing diagnoses of the nature and source of the problems associated with digital platforms.

The political interest in regulating digital platforms in the US also has a technocratic face, with the emergence of a group of scholars who have argued for more activist and ambitious enforcement of the antitrust laws in that country, including specifically against digital platforms.[4] Such scholars have been labelled as Neo-Brandeisian, given their support for the use of antitrust for the broader deconcentration of economic power vested in platforms, recalling Louis Brandeis' views as an antitrust enforcer before his appointment to the US Supreme Court.[5] As we will see, however, notwithstanding more ambitious political and technocratic projects for reorientation of digital markets law and the appointment of Neo-Brandeis thinkers to key antitrust enforcement posts in the US Department of Justice (DoJ) and Federal Trade Commission (FTC), the reality of the results achieved, even after almost 4 years in the Biden Administration, is more modest.

Australia, by contrast, has generally been a "rule-follower" in many areas of market regulation.[6] The Australian approach to competition law—ever since the implementation of the Trade Practices Act of 1974, subsequently restyled as the Competition and Consumer Act of 2010 ('CCA')—has been to codify the knowledge gained from other jurisdictions and Australian enforcement efforts,[7] into detailed textual rules comprehensively defining prohibited conduct, which can be applied by judges in a more legalistic way. To provide a safety-valve, in addition to rule-based statutory violations, the Australian CCA provides special procedures for administrative bodies, such as the ACCC and the Australian Competition Tribunal, to consider and balance positive or negative effects of impugned conduct on the broader public interest, mainly through technocratic cost-benefit methodologies.[8]

Following that tradition, the ACCC's longer term inquiry into digital platforms and services has made numerous law reform recommendations. The original impetus for the regulatory inquiry was also political, arising from concerns about the possible deleterious effects on quality journalism and reporting, particularly in regional Australia, of the sharing of news and news captions via digital platforms. This original impetus for the inquiry led to one unique mechanism for the control of

[4] See Wu (2018) and Khan (2017, 2018).

[5] Brandeis' papers were collected and are available in Fraenkel and Lewis (1935) Curse of Bigness: Miscellaneous Papers of Louis D. Brandeis, which title is explicitly adopted by Tim Wu.

[6] Lavenex et al. (2021) (defining rule-making, rule-taking and rule-promoting jurisdictions).

[7] Dawson et al. (2003), pp. 125–126.

[8] Svetiev (2023).

digital platform power in the use and dissemination of news content. In this respect, Australia was a pioneer in implementing a news media bargaining code, through legislation that essentially imposes a bargaining framework between the digital platforms and news media content providers.[9] The code follows an Australian regulatory tradition of bargaining obligations between commercial parties, subject to penalty defaults in the absence of commercial agreement.[10] Experience with the implementation of the code has triggered similar regulatory efforts elsewhere.

Following on the original report on digital platforms and the news media, the ACCC's inquiry went onto investigate the more traditional mechanisms of competition law enforcement, as a tool to control the market power by digital platforms more broady. In the fifth interim report of its DPSI, published in September 2022,[11] the ACCC proposed a set of specific mechanisms for the regulation of digital platforms. These proposals are largely similar, albeit with some local variation, to the proposals that have been considered or implemented in the United Kingdom and the European Union, as well as legislative proposals considered in the United States.

The main argument in this contribution is that the measures considered or implemented in both the United States and Australia (as with those of other jurisdictions), are unlikely to provide a silver bullet in the control of the power of digital platforms (however such power and its negative consequences are defined). This is because such proposals respond to the (structure and conduct) symptoms of digital platform power, without necessarily investigating its root cause. Such root cause analysis, in turn, requires consideration of the reasons for the emergence of the platform as a business model, as well as the specific features of platform production. Arguably, the new digital markets regulatory templates and proposals are too closely wedded to familiar pre-existing models and tools of competition law and ex-ante regulation or they propose possibly unworkable hybrids.[12] Most importantly, the proposals in different jurisdictions do not adequately address the problem of remedies, as one of the most significant shortcomings of antitrust enforcement more generally, which is particularly acute in the digital context.[13] As a result, any remedies implemented under the emergent digital markets law are neither going to produce a broad deconcentration of digital platforms (as the Neo-Brandeisians suggest), nor are they likely to resolve specific problems in platform production (as envisaged in experimentalist conceptions of competition law).[14]

Section 2 of this paper will examine the emergence of the platform as a form of production and distribution, as well as the distinguishing it from the other models of production that have profoundly influenced earlier regulatory and antitrust paradigms. Investigating the reasons for the emergence of the platform business model

[9] See *Competition and Consumer Act 2010*, pt IVBA.

[10] Svetiev (2023) [12.170]-[12.180].

[11] Australian Competition and Consumer Commission (Sept 2022).

[12] C.f. Moreno Belloso and Petit (2023).

[13] Pitofsky (2002), pp. 169, 173–174.

[14] See Svetiev (2007, 2020).

may be essential to identify the root causes of the problems that are presented by digital platforms and a precondition to speculating about possible regulatory solutions and their likely efficacy. Such analysis also requires an examination of the alternative mechanisms (pre-existing and new) through which the platform production problems can be solved. As is evident from other contributions in this book, digital markets law spills over much beyond the traditional fields of competition law and ex ante market regulation to affect areas as seemingly distant as constitutional and private law.

Section 3 will examine recently proposed and implemented measures in the United States and Australia to regulate digital platforms. As mentioned above, such measures largely follow an emergent model of platform regulation focused on practices that have been identified as suspicious because they could result in the entrenchment of platform power, including by gobbling up neighbouring markets. Enforcing these new rules depends on the ease with which enforcement agencies (or private plaintiffs) can detect and prove conduct, such as self-preferencing, in the digital environment. These proposals also seem to skirt around the problem that many, if not most, users might prefer a centralized model of governing their digital life at the expense of marginal (or possibly even more significant) improvements in functionality through multiple choices in platforms or platform services. If this is true, the spectre of large digital private behemoths is indeed a serious one, exacerbating the political problem of platform concentration, unless the platforms can be democratized from within (something that does not seem to be contemplated by any current proposals).

This would suggest that there is currently no promising model for disentrenching digital platform power through conventional tools of competition law. One hope rests with the idea of deterrence of anticompetitive platform conduct through the *prospect* of high fines. Such deterrence might operate atmospherically in an environment of uncertainty ie, even if no jurisdiction is able to adequately define what conduct precisely amounts to a violation. Another possibility is that litigation could be used by enforcers to distract currently dominant incumbent platforms.[15] Apart from a potentially vain hope that such residual, if imprecise, deterrence strategies might hit the target, the alternative is to focus on the resolution of problems in platform production and to overcome the tendency for platforms to default to anticompetitive strategies even when such strategies do not promote even the platforms' own longer term interests. Such problem-solving remedies may come from smaller experiments, in which enforcers, private parties, and courts seek workarounds to the obstacles in traditional enforcement. The efficacy of such experiments in providing responses to the platform problem largely depends on the courts' (as well as agencies' and defendants') willingness to be creative in their conception of the role and

[15] It has been suggested by some that the litigation against Microsoft in the early 2000s distracted the company and allowed for the growth and dominance of Google, see Streitfeld and Wyatt (26 April 2012) U.S. escalates Google case by hiring noted outside lawyer. New York Times. Available via https://www.nytimes.com/2012/04/27/technology/google-antitrust-inquiry-advances.html. But see also Cass (2013), p. 185.

format of antitrust remedies. As such, we may still be riding the wave of antitrust that commenced with the Microsoft litigation and yet to resolve the remedial problems that this litigation uncovered.[16]

2 The Platform as a Business Model: Root Cause Analysis and Regulatory Responses

The focus in this part of the paper is the digital platform as a business model and the identification of the root causes of the problem of platform power. To highlight key features of the platform model, it may be useful to begin with the characteristics identified in the reports on digital platforms by competition authorities or commissioned experts. These reports have sought to identify the features of *digital* platforms that enable them to escape competition law disciplines, while at the same time allowing them to entrench their market power over time.

In Australia, the Ministerial direction for the ACCC to conduct its review of digital platforms and services[17] identified digital platform services to include internet search engine, social media, online private messaging, digital content aggregation platform, media referral and electronic marketplace services.[18] In the Final Report of its original digital platforms inquiry, the ACCC emphasised the multi-sided nature of digital platforms, defining them as 'applications that serve multiple groups of users at once, providing value to each group based on the presence of other users.'[19]

The ACCC's 2022 Interim Report identified a range of features common to digital platforms that generate concerns about the entrenchment of platform power through anticompetitive conduct. A key problem identified by the ACCC, similar to reports in other jurisdictions, arises from the combination of economies of scale and network effects in the provision of platform services.[20] The economies of scale are attributable to a high fixed investment cost needed to provide the service, particularly in a world where most such services are nominally provided for free, while the marginal cost of providing the to additional users is negligible.[21] The network effects, in their direct form, are familiar from the telephone network in which the service is more valuable to a single user the more users are connected to it. This leads to the tipping point problem whereby beyond a certain number of users the network might tend towards a monopoly, unless multihoming is possible.[22] With

[16] Svetiev (2007).

[17] The Digital Platform Inquiry (DPI) (for the final report, see Australian Competition and Consumer Commission (2019)); Digital Advertising Services Inquiry (DASI) (for final report, see Australian Competition and Consumer Commission (2021)).

[18] Frydenberg, *Competition and Consumer (Price Inquiry—Digital Platforms) Direction 2020* (10 February 2020) s 4.

[19] See Australian Competition and Consumer Commission (2019), p. 41.

[20] Australian Competition and Consumer Commission (Sept 2022), pp. 6–7.

[21] Ibid p. 33, see also Australian Competition and Consumer Commission (2019), pp. 73, 79.

[22] Australian Competition and Consumer Commission (Sept 2022), p. 33.

multi-sided digital platforms that bring together different types of users, there is the additional problem of indirect network effects, whereby having more users on one side of the platform makes the network more valuable also for users on another side of the multi sided platform. As such, a dominant platform attracts more users, more advertisers, as well as more suppliers writing applications for that platform.

According to many agencies and competition experts, the above features of digital platforms create the risk of their long-term entrenchment. One reason for this is because the main competitive forces that could disentrench such platforms may tend to come from neighbouring or adjacent services to the core platform service. However, such threats can easily be neutralised through mergers or other (less direct) forms of integration by the platform into adjacent services, such as bundling, tying as well as withdrawal of cooperation with existing providers. Such practices of platform predation are identified as problematic by many agencies around the world. According to the ACCC, while they are widespread, entrenched and systematic in many platforms, they cannot easily be addressed through traditional competition enforcement.[23]

I would argue that the above set of commonly identified characteristics of digital platforms are the *symptoms* of digital platform power. However, to be able to diagnose the problem and propose a solution, it is also necessary to ask the further question about the *root cause* that gives rise to the platform production business model, including its digital variant. Another way to reframe the same question is to ask: why are digital platforms becoming a dominant form of production and distribution in markets and are there any (preferable) alternatives?

For understanding the alternatives to platforms, it may be useful to begin with some observed alternative models of production, distribution and exchange.[24] One alternative to platforms is fully decentralised forms of production combined with (principally) market-based exchange. This is the market-based production and exchange paradigm consistent with Adam Smith's metaphor of the invisible steering hand of competitive markets: a production ecology involving many relatively small traders, none of whom have significant market power. For that reason, they are subject to the competitive discipline of market exchange and the ability of their customers to easily switch their custom elsewhere. It is worth recalling that, while Adam Smith was acutely concerned about the problem of monopoly in markets, in his time the most likely source of monopoly were the political or legal barriers to the freedom to participate in economic exchange imposed in the pre-market (feudal) political and economic order.[25]

Another alternative to platform production is the vertically integrated corporation that was said to dominate production over the course of much of the twentieth

---

[23] ACCC (2023) Submission to senate standing committee on economics - inquiry into the influence of international digital platforms p. 2; ACCC (11 Nov 2022); ACCC calls for new competition and consumer laws for digital platforms. Web page. Available via https://www.accc.gov.au/media-release/accc-calls-for-new-competition-and-consumer-laws-for-digital-platforms.

[24] In the spirit of Williamson (1973).

[25] Gill (2023).

century. The vertically integrated corporation was hierarchical, combining multiple complementary divisions into a single organisation, and ruling them with, what Alfred Chandler termed, the "visible hand" of managerialism.[26] The vertically integrated corporation was said to generate transactional efficiencies in the process of production, including improving interoperability in the supply chain or among complementary products and services, controlling opportunism in relationships involving asset specificity, and allowing for the exploitation of economies of scale through mass production of products for consumer markets.[27] Those efficiencies in transactions, production and distribution could deliver benefits for consumers. Whether efficiencies of size and integration would also deliver the happy outcome of lower consumer prices necessarily depended on the degree of competitive pressure forcing the corporation to pass efficiencies onto consumers, instead of absorbing them as additional profits.

The first and second waves of antitrust enforcement and doctrines, at least in the United States, could be seen to reflect an appreciation of the benefits of the foregoing forms of industrial organisation, production and exchange. As such, the first wave antitrust doctrines focused on ensuring the freedom of individual trader decision making. The suspiciousness towards cross-firm restraints on the freedom to act, particularly with respect to price as the key conduit of market information, are consistent with the perceived benefits of a decentralised production model (as well as being consonant with values such as freedom and opportunity). Such a vision of deconcentrated markets could deliver the happy outcomes of small firm size and effective discipline through absence of market power, which was also seen to preserve economic opportunity and be democracy enforcing.[28]

The second wave of antitrust was principally driven by Chicago school thinkers, but it was based on a broad economic consensus shared also by the Harvard school.[29] The Chicago antitrust scholarship aimed to get courts to adjust the strict rules of prohibition, so as to recognise that both firm size and cross firm restraints could play a useful economic function and were not to be seen as inherently suspect or anticompetitive. The recognition of the efficiency benefits and pro-competitive effects of size or inter-firm restraints raised the prospect of more complex balancing of effects in antitrust decision-making, which courts may or may not have been able to conduct. The scholarly prescription for dealing with that problem was a more abstemious competition law, which should not be suspicious of business conduct and should be more concerned with false positive findings of violation, as opposed to false negatives.[30]

26 Chandler (1977).

27 This is the insight of the transactions cost scholarship on the use of alternative forms of production. See Williamson (1973) and Coase (1937).

28 Svetiev (2007).

29 For discussion of the overlap between the Chicago and Harvard perspectives on US antitrust, see Kovacic (2007).

30 Easterbrook (1984).

The slow transition from the first to the second wave of antitrust demonstrates that the courts' limited ability to translate emergent knowledge about different production models and market effects into competition decision-making can produce two forms of overshooting.[31] The first arises where old rules (based on prior understanding of business models and their effects) continue to be adhered to, well-past their use by date, even once the underlying production environment has moved on. The second arises where once, with considerable delay, new insights about business models are incorporated into legal doctrines, such doctrines are applied across the board without much attempt to distinguish the contexts in which the new insights are applicable from those where prior understandings may still be relevant. Such overshooting reflects the fact that courts are institutionally not well-adapted to understanding the evolution of business models to tailor doctrines to such evolution.

Arguably, one way to pinpoint the root causes of the platform business model, and the problems it gives rise to, is to understand possible reasons for the (re-emergence) of non-integrated models of production as an alternative to the vertically integrated hierarchical multi-divisional firm. This issue is the subject of a different and vast literature, which I have discussed and recounted elsewhere.[32] It is probably not possible to provide a comprehensive account of the drivers of this transformation in the forms of industrial organisation, but we can pinpoint a few possible salient drivers, based on the literatures that identified the governance problems of the vertically-integrated corporation, as well as the scholarships identifying the benefits of disintegrated platform production and the scope conditions for such disintegration.

First, scholars of the hierarchical business organisation pointed out that effective hierarchical control of large corporate bureaucracies is, by no means, an easy task.[33] In fact, the greater the distance between management and subordinates, many of whom have specialised (divisional) knowledge, the more difficult it is for management to effectively assign tasks and supervise subordinates' performance in large corporations. Thus, paradoxically, whereas the hierarchical firm was supposed to deliver organisational efficiencies through bringing multiple functionalities and divisions under a single roof, employing command and control mechanisms, it also created significant agency problems and inefficiencies. Thus, the need to better supervise the performance of various divisions of the corporation, including to cut the costs of their operation (due to slack or agency problems), could create pressures for devolution within the corporation.

Secondly, to the extent that the corporate bureaucracy relies on the breaking down of tasks into component processes and the development of rules that can guide subordinates and enable supervisors to oversee their performance, such processes create inherent inflexibility in the operation of integrated business organisations.[34]

[31] Pitofsky (2008).

[32] See Svetiev (2007).

[33] See generally Miller (1992).

[34] See generally Sabel (2006).

As a result, corporate bureaucracies are likely to be less agile to respond to changing conditions in their operating environment. The rigidity of rules and procedures also implies that integrated corporations may become less capable of innovating. Operating within organisational strictures and bureaucratic procedures, most employees (as well as managers) become good at one particular component of the overall task of the organisation, making it more difficult for them to imagine altogether different ways of doing those tasks (or running the overall corporate operations). It follows that the pressure to be able to innovate and respond to innovative competitors may also create further pressures for devolution and collaboration with different partners as opposed to relying on vertical in-house integration.

Finally, given the broader context of liberalisation of market entry in different industries nationally,[35] combined with the opening up of markets transnationally, corporations had greater access to other potential collaborators at different levels of the supply chain. In other words, just as corporate bureaucracies might have faced pressures to either cut costs or to become better at innovating, or both, they might also have had a greater choice of external supply chain partners to work with. This combination of both need and availability provide some background conditions for the vertically integrated firm to devolve towards more decentralised and collaborative production.[36]

However, in the same way that governing the integrated corporation is no easy task, nor is the coordination of decentralised production with multiple partners. The firm that operates as a central node of a larger network of collaborators, such as an original equipment manufacturer (OEM), must be able to select appropriate and capable suppliers, maintain relationships with such suppliers, while also maintaining sufficient innovative capability in the network (which is undermined by stability in network membership[37]). It must also ensure that the component parts sourced from different suppliers seamlessly interoperate with each other, so that it can deliver a functional final product or service to satisfy market demand.[38]

Generalising the platform for networked production, a multi-sided platform may be understood as a model of production that brings together different specialisations, who may be otherwise independent of each other, to generate an output useful to (different groups of) users.[39] It provides functionalities for network production, such as a language for collaboration (interoperability)[40] and a regime for assessing the capability, probity and reliability of independent collaborators for the purposes of delivering final products or services to users,[41] as well as (potentially) accessing

35 Svetiev (2016).

36 As such, functional (say competitive or cost) pressures might have played some role in the transformation, without necessarily providing the full story. Compare Granovetter (1985).

37 Schrank and Whitford (2011).

38 See, e.g. Ray and Jones (2006).

39 Compare Hagiu and Wright (2015).

40 Wegner (1996).

41 Gilson et al. (2009), p. 431.

user feedback about the quality and usefulness of that product or service to be recursively fed into the networked production process.[42]

As is evident from the above brief recount of the literature, a platform need not be digital. Any OEM that operates as a central or core node in a network of specialised firms at different levels of the supply chain, provides a platform for collaborative or networked production.[43] This would include hardware OEMs, such as aircraft manufacturers Boeing and Airbus,[44] or complex machinery producer John Deere,[45] so long as they do not produce all their component parts for the final product in house, but source them externally. While platforms need not be digital (in the sense that a platform OEM often has physical production and produces a physical product), it goes without saying that the use of information and communication technologies (ICTs) makes it much easier for firms to organise decentralised and devolved modes of production across different industries.[46] ICTs ensure that orders, requirements and specifications can be communicated across organisational boundaries much more easily and speedily, with less room for mistake and delay. Such technologies also make it easier to assess the capability (including both quality and accuracy) of collaborators, as well as their reliability (including timeliness) in delivering components.[47] The deep enmeshment—and mutual observability—allowed by ICTs may allow collaborators to deliver the benefits of collaboration and interoperability, while maintaining organisational separation.[48]

In light of the foregoing, it is unsurprising that the literatures on business organisation as well as the legal structures that support such organisation, outline diverse modalities for production through collaboration across organisational boundaries. For example, business devolution can be pursued through a firm outsourcing component parts or non-core activities to an external supplier, where it is the outsourcing partner that is expected to ensure efficiencies in delivering the component product or service, by economising on costs through better supervising its own employees and suppliers, while (potentially) being better able to innovate.[49] Disintegration can also be based on contracting for joint innovation. Such contracting frameworks ensure that OEMs, such as John Deere or Boeing, or large pharmaceutical firms, such as Pfizer or Glaxo, have access to multiple capable collaborators and suppliers of novel technologies or complementary functionalities, which collaborators remain at the leading edge of their own component or process or technology, while also controlling for opportunistic hold up problems arising in close collaborations.[50]

---

[42] Von Hippel (2005).

[43] Schmidt and Foss (2023).

[44] Rossetti and Choi (2005).

[45] Bernstein (2015).

[46] See, e.g. Fransman (2010).

[47] Mokudai et al. (2021); Herrigel et al. (2013).

[48] C.f. Gasser and Palfrey (2007).

[49] See, e.g. Weeks and Feeny (2008).

[50] Gilson et al. (2009).

To the extent that the disintegration in production is an observable phenomenon, the economy is replete with platforms, which provide infrastructure and mechanisms for collaborative and networked production. Notably, such platforms are an aspect of the *deconcentration* of production and, generally, perhaps for that reason, most OEMs have not been viewed as appropriate candidates for special regulation or antitrust enforcement. Moreover, ICTs and the digital revolution may be among the key enablers of such disintegration and deconcentration of production.

This set of observations necessarily leads us to the question: what, if anything, is special about digital platforms? Such platforms also provide infrastructures for collaborative decentralised production and exchange. They also bring together different groups of producers and users with different interests and specialisations, through the deployment of ICTs. Why should digital platforms present special concerns about concentration, monopolisation and entrenchment in ways that other platforms do not?

One possible answer to those questions may arise from the fact that the inputs and productive capabilities of the different collaborators delivering digital products and services on digital platforms are not so distinct. For all participants in the digital platform supply chain, data (or information) are the relevant input, while coding is the relevant production technique. In the absence of distinct production inputs, resources and capabilities for firms at different levels of the supply chain, the lines between different lines of activity and service delivery are porous to the point of being inexistent. Given that platform production relies on intimate and relatively seamless exchange of information among collaborators,[51] which is increasingly processed in nonhuman ways through machine learning and artificial intelligence, we may even speculate that the distinction between activities *within* or *across* organisational boundaries, as well as the distinction between *horizontal* and *vertical* relationships, becomes very difficult to sustain.

Arguably, it is this last feature of digital production that may give rise to the *special* concerns about the entrenchment of (extant) digital platforms as the intermediaries and conduits: not only of digital commerce, but also of the digital public sphere. This aspect of digital platforms, more so than other platforms, may enable them to commoditize and devalue their collaborators developing adjacent functionalities.[52] The non-specific nature of the inputs and production capabilities in digital platforms means that a platform (that benefits from collaborating with many different firms and users) can potentially extend its reach to every facet of economic and even political life, which may account for concerns about the platforms' voraciousness or expansiveness. An added problem arises from the fact that the centralisation of information has obvious benefits for users, while also creating significant, and potentially catastrophic, risks.[53]

Those concerns about digital platforms, and the economic, political and rights consequences of digital concentration, are exacerbated by a further concern that the

---

[51] See, e.g. Jennejohn (2016).

[52] Svetiev (2007) but see also Khan (2017).

[53] See, e.g. Orgad and Reijers (2021); Mac Síthigh and Siems (2019).

usual market based or private law mechanisms that may ordinarily be relied upon to attenuate the exercise of power and inefficient integration by platforms may be ineffective.[54]

One possible control mechanism on platform expansionism through integration into adjacent fields might be the market mechanism, whereby the platform owner wishes to maintain the attractiveness of its platform to users and collaborating firms by ensuring an open ecosystem of collaborators that optimise functionality and variety.[55] After all, as we discussed above, it may be precisely the inefficiencies of integrated corporate bureaucracies that trigger devolution towards platforms.

As I have highlighted in the context of the Microsoft litigation,[56] we cannot necessarily rely on the platform owner to be a good steward for the optimal integration to maintainthe platform's attractiveness for several reasons. First, as Farrell and Weiser have explained,[57] uncertainty about the future competitive and regulatory landscape may drive the platform owner towards expansionist conduct by devaluing the investments of collaborating firms. This is because such firms present potential threats to the platform itself, particularly given the non-specific nature of the technology inputs and production processes in the digital ecology. Secondly, an even more fundamental problem stems from the fact that in the digital production ecology, combining seamless data sharing and technological surveillance, there might not be much practical difference between working with a collaborator formally in a separate business organisation as opposed to one that is within the boundaries of the platforms itself. To the extent that decentralised production could cope with the managerial dilemmas of the corporate bureaucracy, data exchange and surveillance may provide mechanisms to address such problems within as much as outside the organisation.[58]

The market-based mechanism through which to solve the problem of inefficient platform integration also harnesses the autonomy of collaborating firms and users to decide which platform they deal with, and either exit platforms that engage in predatory integration or voice their concerns and seek to negotiate better terms.[59]

The emergent consensus in scholarly and agency reflections on this problem is that the mechanisms of exit or voice are deeply weakened for both collaborating firms and users vis-à-vis the so-called 'gatekeeper' digital platforms. To be able to exercise the option of exit, users or collaborating firms need to have (i) multiple choices of platforms to deal with (including not to be locked into particular platforms) which offer meaningful alternatives and (ii) the ability to meaningfully choose among such alternatives by distinguishing the practices of different platforms and their effects on the quality of service provided or on the levels of data

[54] Svetiev (2007), see also Bostoen and Petit (2023).

[55] Farrell and Weiser (2003).

[56] Svetiev (2007).

[57] Farrell and Weiser (2003).

[58] See, e.g. Aloisi and De Stefano (2022); Aloisi and Gramano (2019).

[59] Hirschman (1970).

acquisition and retention as the consideration paid by users for the free use of platform services. In other words, where the relevant metric for choosing is not simply the price paid relative to easily observable product quality, as for many garden-variety goods or services, it is much more difficult for collaborating firms or users to exert discipline through exit even if they had multiple platforms to choose from offering meaningfully different options.

An even more fundamental barrier to effective exit by users, already alluded to, is the possibility that in a world of increasing complexity and digital surveillance, there may be perceived benefits for users from centralising information and data flows, as opposed to dealing with multiple (including new) providers. In other words, the marginal benefits of increased innovation and functionality for most users might be perceived as small compared to the marginal costs of increased complexity and data fragmentation. Arguably, the most hopeful avenues of enhancing user autonomy in a digital world rely on machine learning and artificial intelligence.[60] This observation, in turn, only reagitates the question of who owns, operates and oversees such digital and computational mechanisms that may potentially subvert the autonomy of users as well as enhancing it.

We may posit that collaborating firms would be better informed, compared to final users, to be able to effectively exercise exit options so as to discipline platforms, but this might not be the case either.[61] First, many such firms are much smaller and less capable to either effectively distinguish different platform models and practices or be able to exit. Secondly, the venture capital model of financing digital start-ups depends upon such start-ups being bought out by one of the dominant platforms as the main return on the original investment.[62] The venture financing model may drive most start-ups to position themselves so they can sell their business to a digital platform (such as Google or Facebook) at an appropriate moment in the evolution of their application. This implies that new application developers are to some degree locked into collaborating with particular platforms, and it may also mean that their strategic objectives will rarely extend to being the "new" Google or Facebook or Amazon.

Similar constraints affect the ability of users and collaborating firms to exercise effective voice through bargaining for better terms of engagement with digital platforms that intermediate among various groups. Consumer and small business law will rarely be sufficiently tailored to play a substitute for voice.[63] If regulation is to enhance users and collaborating firms' exercise of effective voice in their dealings with digital platforms, this requires not only enhancing their ability to understand and compare different terms of dealing and service, so as to enhance their bargaining *efficacy*, but also enhancing their bargaining *power*, potentially through novel tools for individual or collective bargaining.[64]

---

[60] See, e.g. Lippi et al. (2020). Such tools can also be used to assist enforcement agencies. See Schrepel (2021).

[61] Svetiev (2007).

[62] See Appadurai and Alexander (2020).

[63] Bostoen and Petit (2023).

[64] For a growing interest on the topic of collective bargaining, beyond its deployment in the context of workplace negotiations, see Estlund and Liebman (2021); Paul et al. (2022); see generally

What are the implications of the foregoing discussion for the regulation of digital platforms? As with other business models, it is precisely the advantages of the platform model of production and exchange and of the use digital technologies, that may both give rise to the ubiquity of digital platforms and also generate the problems of platform power. In particular, the use of ICTs allows closer and more intimate collaboration between firms, which creates risks of predatory platform integration while erasing the boundaries between the productive capabilities of different firms along the supply chain. Regulating conduct through rules of prohibition and threats of divestiture are unlikely to be effective regulatory strategies in such an ecology; the more promising avenue may be a search for enhancing the autonomy and power (including collective power) of counterparties.

3 In Search of Models for Regulating Digital Platforms: US and Australia

While some of the discussion in the previous section may be regarded as speculative, I argue it illustrates the kind of root-cause thinking that is necessary to properly diagnose the scope of the platform problem and to outline the range of potentially productive responses to address it. It would seem that regulatory solutions to the above diagnosis could fall within three broad categories: (i) measures to enhance the ability of users and collaborating firms to exercise either voice or exit; (ii) instruments directly regulating the conduct of digital platforms to prevent inherently pernicious practices (assuming that such practices can be identified); (iii) broad based mechanisms for deconcentration of the platform ecology in the hope that it would be possible to create multiple viable (smaller?) intermediaries *and* that such a digital ecology will deliver tangible *net* public interest benefits.

In this part we will examine some reforms ventilated in the United States and Australia to understand which of the above three categories they fall into and to speculate about their likely effectiveness in addressing some of the root causes of the digital platform problems identified above. Foreshadowing some key findings, despite the fact that Neo-Brandeisians have assumed key enforcement posts in the United States, and some interest in this project in Australia,[65] neither jurisdiction has implemented any broad deconcentration instruments. Arguably, in light of the above discussion, it is not entirely clear at the conceptual level what deconcentration means in the fluid digital ecology of non-specialised production assets and capabilities. It is also not clear at the practical level through what kinds of remedies or instruments such deconcentration may be achieved.[66] In that respect, emergent

Paul (2023).

[65] Varan (2022).

[66] While spin-off by Facebook of WhatsApp and Instagram has been contemplated in the US, the viability of this remedy may be contested. See Hovenkamp (2023).

ideas about digital constitutionalism as an alternative format for controlling power, including private power, may offer a way forward, though to provide concrete solutions this discipline must move beyond high-level principles and concepts,[67] towards tangible institutional mechanisms for allocating decisional and balancing rights.[68]

As we will see, most of the responses and proposals in both jurisdictions fall in the second category outlined above, which appears to be consistent with the emergent international consensus discussed by other contributors in this book. One exception is the Australian experiment of implementing a code aimed at enhancing the power of news media organisations vis-à-vis digital platforms, which taps into Australia's tradition of employing mechanisms that enhance bargaining power and efficacy of small players both within and beyond labour law.

3.1 USA

The United States has been at the forefront of developments in antitrust law over the course of the past century and has provided rules and enforcement procedures emulated in the rest of the world. It has also been a source of intellectual leadership with the Harvard, Chicago and post-Chicago schools having influence on doctrine and practice well beyond the US. Apart from antitrust, the US approach to regulation of natural monopolies in the networked regulated markets, such as telecommunications and energy, has arguably provided a model emulated by many jurisdictions for market regulation of newly liberalised markets since the 1990s.[69]

For such reasons, the Neo-Brandeisian movement in the United States was seen as a potential new tectonic shift in the orientation of antitrust enforcement, particularly as it relates to digital platforms. The election of a Democratic president led to the appointment of some prominent Neo-Brandeisianians in key enforcement posts. This expectation was amplified by an apparent by-partisan legislative interest in reigning in such platforms in that country. On the Republican side of politics, such interest was motivated by the perception of left-leaning bias in many of these platforms. On the Democratic side of politics, it was the perception that the dissemination of fake news on many digital platforms had disproportionate and consequential effects on the outcomes of elections. As a result, at least five bills discussed below have been introduced in the US Congress with the aim of addressing specific types of conduct of digital platforms.[70]

The Augmenting Compatibility and Competition by Enabling Services Switching (ACCESS) Act and the Platform Competition and Opportunity Act (PCOA) are

[67] E.g. Suzor (2018); De Gregorio (2022).

[68] C.f. Paul (2020).

[69] Svetiev (2016).

[70] For a more detailed discussion of the several bills as well as the arguments for and against, see Chin (2022).

both bipartisan bills that were introduced on 11 June 2021. The ACCESS Act would require platforms to guarantee minimum standards of interoperability, as well as data portability between different digital platforms. It would thus facilitate users' ability to transfer their data to a competitor platform. It is targeted at platforms with a threshold number of users and annual sales deemed by the DoJ or FTC to be "covered platforms", although it appears that its main target is Facebook. The aim would be to reduce the impact of network effects that advantage incumbent digital platforms.[71] Further, the PCOA is based on the premise that digital platforms have engaged in killer acquisitions that have allowed the platforms to eliminate potential competitors before these grow large enough to effectively compete with the platform. It aims to make certain acquisitions by dominant online platforms unlawful. The platforms affected would be Alphabet, Amazon, Apple and Meta. The PCOA would shift the burden of proof by requiring any dominant platform proposing a merger or acquisition to prove that the proposed acquisition would not cause anti-competitive effects.

The Ending Platform Monopolies Act (EPMA) is a bipartisan bill introduced on 24 June 2021. It would prevent large platforms (those with at least 50 million monthly active U.S. users and a market cap of $600 billion or more) from owning or operating a marketplace while also simultaneously operating in that marketplace. It would affect app stores, ad exchanges and music or video services by separating out the vertical ownership of multiple businesses and imposing fines.

The Open App Markets Act (OAMA) is another bipartisan bill introduced on 11 August 2021. Its aim is "[t]o promote competition and reduce gatekeeper power in the app economy, increase choice, improve quality, and reduce costs for consumers."[72] It seeks to ensure that operators of mobile app stores allow "sideloading", meaning the transfer of files or data to applications from web sources that are not specifically approved by the vendor of the app store, and by preventing those vendors from (self-)privileging their inhouse applications in searches. It targets app stores with more than 50 million users and would therefore only apply to the Apple App Store and the Android Google Play Store. While it clearly aims to prevent Apple and Google from engaging in self-preferencing in operating their app stores, it has been criticised for being arbitrary, having potentially negative impacts on security and safety, and being designed to help competitors rather than consumers.[73]

Finally, the American Choice and Innovation Online Act (ACIOA) is a bipartisan bill introduced on 6 November 2021. It also addresses self-preferencing by prohibiting large online platforms such as Amazon, Apple and Google from giving preference to their own products on their platforms, unfairly limiting the availability of competing products from other businesses or discriminating in the application or enforcement of the platforms terms of service among similarly situated users. Part of the motivation for the ACIOA is the fact that Alphabet ranks its own services, e.g.

[71] See Chin (2022), p. 5.

[72] *Open App Markets Act*, S.2710, 117 Cong. (2022).

[73] Radic (2022).

Google Flights and YouTube, above competing third-party websites in Google Search results.[74] The bill would designate such conduct as unlawful or discriminatory. It has been argued that this law could also have adverse impacts on user privacy and security, as it could stop platforms from installing spam filters and malware protection or imposing privacy or security rules for third-party businesses.[75]

Given the vicissitudes of US politics and its legislative processes, the prospects of any of the above bills garnering sufficient support in both houses of the US Congress is fairly slim.[76] Most of the proposed measures against self-preferencing and favouring portability and interoperability are similar to structure-oriented measures targeting specific conduct that have been considered or implemented in other jurisdictions, including the EU, UK and Australia.

Given the limited prospects for legislative change in that country, of greater consequence was the appointment by President Biden of several prominent members of the Neo-Brandeisian school of thought to leading position in the antitrust enforcement agencies. This included Jonathan Kanter's appointment as assistant attorney general for the Department of Justice Antitrust Division, Lina Khan's appointment as Chair of the FTC (both of them confirmed with support across both parties), as well as the appointment of Tim Wu, the author of *The Curse of Bigness: Antitrust in the New Gilded Age*,[77] a sort of Neo-Brandeis manifesto, as Special Assistant to the President for Technology and Competition Policy. As a member of the Biden administration, Wu was responsible for helping to author the antitrust-focused Executive Order 14036, which instructed the FTC and DoJ to "enforce the antitrust laws vigorously" with a nod to divestitures by noting "that the law allows them to challenge prior bad mergers that past administrations did not previously challenge".[78] The Executive Order also created a White House Competition Council to coordinate pro-competition efforts, as well as introducing a range of individual measures to increase competition in specific sectors.

Following such appointments, the DoJ and FTC filed several prominent antitrust cases targeting the digital behemoths, including Google, Amazon and Facebook, some of which are discussed below.

On 20 October 2020, the US DoJ and several States filed a complaint seeking 'to restrain Google from unlawfully maintaining monopolies in the market for general search services, search advertising, and general search text advertising in the United States through anticompetitive and exclusionary practices, and to remedy the effects

---

[74] As such, the concerns are similar to that of the European Commission's *Google Shopping* decisions, in which the efficacy of the remedy has been deeply contested. See Svetiev (2020).

[75] Chin (2022), pp. 2–3.

[76] Holland (7 Oct 2022) Experts torn on impact of antitrust bills passed by house. TechTarget. Available via https://www.techtarget.com/searchcio/news/252525883/Experts-torn-on-impact-of-antitrust-bills-passed-by-House.

[77] See Wu (2018).

[78] President [Joseph Biden]. Executive Order 14036: Executive Order on Promoting Competition in the American Economy, 9 July 2021. Federal Register. vol. 86 no 132 36987–36999.

of this conduct.'[79] It is alleged that Google maintains monopolies in search and advertising markets and has violated US antitrust laws through anticompetitive practices such as exclusionary agreements and tying agreements with device manufacturers, major US wireless carriers, and internet browser developers, to secure default status for its search engine. It is alleged that as a result of these practices, Google has a nearly 90 percent share of all general-search engine queries in the US and even more so on mobile devices. Through such exclusionary contracts, competitors are said to be denied vital distribution, scale and product recognition. For example, Google is alleged to pay device manufacturers and others to have Google as the default search engine. In addition, Google has agreements with device makers to preinstall certain Google applications to have access to its other products.

The complaint noted that Google was using the same practices that it claimed were anti-competitive when Microsoft was engaging in them.[80] The lawsuit alleges that Google has harmed consumers by reducing the quality of general search services (including dimensions such as privacy, data protection, and the use of consumer data), lessening choice in general search services, and reducing innovation.[81] The DoJ sought various loosely specified remedies, including for the Court to enjoin Google from continuing to engage in these practices. In August 2024, the DoJ prevailed in establishing Google's antitrust violations at first instance, but the question of the remedy was not yet resolved.

Another lawsuit was commenced by the DoJ against Google on 24 January 2023, also supported by several states, alleging that Google has engaged in anticompetitive practices in the advertising technology (ad tech) market, including:

- by neutralising or eliminating competitors through acquisitions, including acquisitions that had not been opposed by the antitrust agencies, such as the 2007 acquisition of DoubleClick (providing the industry-leading publisher ad server) and the 2011 acquisition of its nascent competitor AdMeld (which had described itself as "the largest, independent practitioner of RTB [Real Time Bidding] behind Google");
- by positioning itself as buyer, seller and auctioneer of digital display advertising; and by using its dominance in the market to force website publishers and advertisers to use its products, while disrupting their ability to use competing products.[82]

According to the complaint, when Google's competitors responded through developing innovative new approaches (e.g. 'yield management functionality' and 'head bidding'), Google responded by acquiring and extinguishing any competitive threats. As a result, Google is now said to control the technology used by nearly

---

[79] Department of Justice's Complaint filed on 20 October 2020 in the District Court for the district of Columbia, *United States of America v Google LLC* (Case No.: 1:20-cv-03010), p. 2.

[80] Ibid p. 6.

[81] Ibid p. 53.

[82] Department of Justice's Complaint filed on 24 January 2023 in the District Court for the Eastern District of Virginia, *United States of America v Google LCC* (Case No.: 1:23-cv-00108).

every major website publisher to offer advertising space, allegedly providing the only realistic option for web-publishers. Google's anticompetitive behaviour is alleged to have raised barriers to entry to artificially high levels, forced key competitors to abandon the market and dissuaded potential competitors from joining the market, forcing website creators to earn less and advertisers to pay more than they would in a more competitive market.

The DoJ has sought to bring the alleged anticompetitive effects back to a consumer theory of harm, arguing that Google's conduct has ultimately harmed consumers whereby publishers make less money from advertisements, and therefore fewer of them are able to offer their content without subscriptions or paywalls.[83] According to the *Washington Post*, Publishers and Google's tech rivals, including the News Media Alliance, have applauded the DoJ's decision to bring the lawsuit.[84] Notably, on the remedial front, the request for relief is again reasonably vague: apart from declarations and injunctions to stop the anticompetitive conduct, the DoJ is also seeking damages and orders of (unspecified) divestiture.

In a case brought in November 2023, the FTC alleges that Amazon is setting prices at an artificially high level by not allowing sellers to offer their products on competing platforms for a lower price.[85] In particular, Amazon is said to engage in punitive and coercive tactics to punish sellers who sell on other markets at a discount. As a result, the FTC alleged that Amazon is acting unlawfully in two markets: the online superstore market that serves shoppers and the market for online marketplace services purchased by sellers. Its exclusionary conduct is allegedly designed to maintain a monopoly position even in the face of declining quality of service, by preventing competitors from entering, emerging and growing in light of significant barriers to entry because of scale economies, the cost of switching (from Amazon) and network effects.

Importantly, just as with the DoJ's litigation against Google, the FTC complaint alleges several forms of consumer harm resulting of the conduct, arising because Amazon

- replaced relevant, "organic" search results with advertisements while increasing junk ads thereby worsening the customer experience;
- biased Amazon's search results to preference Amazon's products when other products may be of better quality;
- charged costly fees on sellers who must rely on Amazon to stay in business, with sellers paying close to 50% of total revenues to Amazon, in turn increasing final prices for consumers both on and off Amazon.

[83] Commentators have observed that the DoJ's case is conventional and does not rely on any novel or untested theories, such as those propounded by the Neo-Brandeisians, see Mehra (2023).

[84] Zakrezewski et al. (24 Jan 2023) Justice Department sues Google over dominance in online advertising. Washington Post. Available via https://www.washingtonpost.com/technology/2023/01/24/doj-google-lawsuit-ads/.

[85] See the Federal Trade Commission's Complaint filed on 2 November 2023 in the District Court for the Western District of Washington, *Federal Trade Commission v Amazon.com, Inc* (Case No.: 2:23-cv-01495-JHC).

As those of the DoJ against Google, the prayer for relief by the FTC is both broad and vague. It seeks for Amazon to be permanently enjoined from engaging in its unlawful conduct or similar conduct, but also any conduct with the same or similar purpose and effect, together with structural and monetary relief. As such, the FTC has attempted to future proof the remedial injunction, although it is not clear whether a court will accede to enjoining conduct that has not (yet) been found to violate the antitrust laws.

Considering the analysis presented earlier, it is worth highlighting several points about these cases against Google and Amazon. First, as commentators have pointed out, these cases are litigated under existing antitrust doctrines as established by the US courts and agencies without seeking to push the boundaries with any novel legal or economic theories of harm.[86] The theories of harm are based on establishing the existence of monopoly power protected by barriers to entry, as well as engagement in exclusionary conduct such as acquisitions and tying, which have been described as having a 'long pedigree' in US antitrust. In other words, the complaints invoke standard forms of wrongful conduct under US law and are rooted in the consumer welfare paradigm. As such, they are described as 'fairly orthodox' albeit in a novel factual context, reflecting the recognition that US courts are unlikely to engage in a sudden wholesale reorientation of antitrust doctrines.[87]

To establish an antitrust violation in such cases, the US agencies work within the balancing framework (applied to both joint and unilateral conduct) established by the DC Circuit in the seminal *Microsoft* case of the third wave of antitrust, where the court held:

> First, to be condemned as exclusionary, a monopolist's act must have an "anticompetitive effect." That is, it must harm the competitive process and thereby harm consumers. In contrast, harm to one or more competitors will not suffice. ...
>
> Second, the plaintiff ... must demonstrate that the monopolist's conduct indeed has the requisite anticompetitive effect.
>
> Third, if a plaintiff successfully establishes a prima facie case ... by demonstrating anticompetitive effect, then the monopolist may proffer a 'procompetitive justification' for its conduct. ... If the monopolist asserts a procompetitive justification ... that its conduct is indeed a form of competition on the merits because it involves, for example, greater efficiency or enhanced consumer appeal ... then the burden shifts back to the plaintiff to rebut that claim. ...
>
> Fourth, if the monopolist's procompetitive justification stands unrebutted, then the plaintiff must demonstrate that the anticompetitive harm of the conduct outweighs the procompetitive benefit.[88]

---

[86] Mehra (2023).

[87] In fact, the agencies thus far have had limited success in cases against digital platform mergers. See *Federal Trade Commission v Microsoft Corp.* (Case No.: 3:23-cv-02880-JSC, Northern District of California). For comment see Gray and Santesteban (2023).

[88] *United States v Microsoft Corp.* 253 F.3d 34, 58-59 (DC Cir, 2001).

This framework for analysis has generally been applauded as providing considerable flexibility, in that it allows the court to consider both pro- and anti-competitive effects of the conduct and balance them.[89] However, in the context of digital platforms, the balancing framework presents several difficulties for the enforcement agency or a private plaintiff. In particular, the need to demonstrate anticompetitive effects (including specifically for consumers) may be difficult where the harmful effects may occur in the future and the extent of such harms may depend on the evolution of market dynamics. Establishing that the net balance of effects of platform conduct would be negative is arguably made more challenging by the US Supreme Court's decision in *Ohio v American Express Co.*[90] In that case, in the context of a payment card network, the Court held that "due to indirect network effects" in both directions, a payment card platform "cannot raise prices on one side without risking a feedback loop of declining demand" on the other side of the double-sided market.[91] As such, it was held that "courts must include both sides of the platform" in defining the market for purposes of assessing anticompetitive effects.

Some have argued that this "may be the worst antitrust decision in many decades."[92] It has been suggested that a "separate markets approach allows more precise measurement of competitive conditions", which can differ between the two sides of the market.[93] By contrast, "aggregation of distinct groups of consumers into a single market impairs … granular assessment of competitive realities".[94]

Notwithstanding such criticism, the decision provides a precedent at the apex of US judicial hierarchy. It illustrates the difficulties faced by US antitrust agencies in engineering a wholesale revolution in the antitrust law as it applies to digital platforms through the ordinary route of litigation before the courts, where the pre-existing doctrines are sticky and act as a barrier to new knowledge and novel thinking.

The limits of the litigated approach are also reflected in the very generic requests for relief in the complaints filed by the DoJ and FTC against Google and Amazon. Apart from general prayers for injunctive relief and penalties, the complaints seem also to envisage structural relief (such as through divestiture), though without hinting as to what kinds of divestitures would be feasible to achieve improvements in competitive conditions or in the platform ecology more broadly.[95]

The foregoing comparison suggests that several lessons of the DoJ's litigation against Microsoft in 2003 should be instructive for the US enforcement agencies, but that they may have been forgotten. First, one key reason that the DoJ ultimately

[89] Fox (2002).

[90] 575 S. Ct. 2274 (2018).

[91] Ibid 12.

[92] Salop et al. (2022), p. 883.

[93] Salop et al. (2022); see also Katz and Sallet (2018).

[94] Salop et al. (2022), p. 901.

[95] See Hovenkamp (2023).

prevailed in the Microsoft litigation at first instance and on appeal was the fact that for many of the allegations of exclusionary conduct, Microsoft did not provide plausible pro-competitive justifications supported by evidence (probably in the expectation that consumer harm could not be established for products, such as the internet browser, that were offered for free). As commentators have noted, companies such as Google, Facebook and Amazon, may have learned from that experience and it is unlikely that they would be caught off-guard in this round of litigation.[96] Secondly, notwithstanding the DoJ's comprehensive win on the liability issue in Microsoft, the remedial formulation in that case proved to be a significant stumbling block,[97] that ultimately brought Microsoft and the DoJ back to the negotiating table. Structural relief through the separation of Microsoft's Windows operating system, and its applications (such as Microsoft Office) was one of the remedies contemplated.[98] However, given that the inputs, processes and capabilities for producing the operating system and applications for that system were not distinct, both the technological and organisational boundaries between the different functionalities were not that clear either. In such a production context, it was not obvious that maintaining structural separation between two corporate entities would be either easy or meaningful. As a matter of fact, it was precisely the indistinct boundaries between different products and production processes that allowed Microsoft to commingle the code of the operating system and the browser as a form of technological tying.

This discussion takes us back to the earlier point about the conceptual and practical difficulties for any policy based on deconcentration in the digital production ecology. One takeaway is that even an order of structural divestuture in such a context would not be a surgical one-off remedy that would unleash competitive rivalry, but one that would require ongoing supervision, monitoring and revision as envisaged in experimentalist models of competition regulation.[99] The problem of fashioning, monitoring and revising remedies is something that the US antitrust agencies will have to grapple with even where they prevail in the above cases against the digital behemoths, such as in the Google search case. In that context, it is worth recalling that the US agencies, just as the competition authorities in the EU,[100] have much greater flexibility to fashion remedial mechanisms focused on specific problems and risks of harm through consent decrees and negotiated remedies. The outcomes of such existing decrees could provide a better indication of the extent and mechanisms through which platform regulation is being re-oriented in the Neo-Brandeisian enforcement era.[101]

---

[96] Greene (30 March 2011) Has Google learned Microsoft's antitrust lessons? CNET. Available via https://www.cnet.com/tech/services-and-software/has-google-learned-microsofts-antitrust-lessons/.

[97] Shelanski and Sidak (2001).

[98] Page and Lopatka (2007).

[99] Svetiev (2020).

[100] Svetiev (2014).

[101] Williams et al. (2023); Murray (2023).

3.2 Australia

Australia's efforts to reform and strengthen digital platform regulation, both through enforcement and legislative changes, have thus far been fairly modest. As discussed above, Australia is generally a follower in market regulation and tends to adopt—through local codification—templates from other jurisdictions including the UK, EU or the US. As such, Australia tends to approach law reform with caution and with the aim of textual comprehensiveness.

With respect to digital platforms, several reform options have been examined through the inquiries, mentioned earlier and conducted under the auspices of the ACCC, which have focused on different problems presented by digital platform power to recommend legislative changes to the Parliament. The ACCC's inquiries began in 2017 when the Government instructed the regulator to study the "impact of online search engines, social media and digital content aggregators on competition in the media and advertising services markets."[102] The original inquiry had a political trigger arising in the context of proposed legal reforms to Australia's cross-media ownership rules. These rules, with a long pedigree, had been implemented to deal with Australia's concentrated media landscape, by limiting common ownership of different types of media outlets. As such, rather than having a narrow (price-oriented) consumer welfare goal, these rules were designed to ensure continued viewpoint diversity in the local media as a necessary pre-condition for democratic political contest.

Legislative reforms of these rules had been contemplated by successive governments. Ultimately, the widely changing media landscape triggered by the increase in the variety of news sources distributed through the Internet allowed the (then centre-right) government to propose a relaxation of the cross-media ownership rules. In return for support for these legislative changes in the Senate, the Government undertook to direct the ACCC to conduct an inquiry into the effects of digital platform news distribution on the variety and quality of news sources and to recommend necessary legislative changes.[103]

The ACCC's 2019 report found that dissemination of news via different digital platforms had a negative effect on the quality and diversity in news reporting, specifically through "reduced production of particular types of news and journalism, including local government and local court reporting" seen to be "important for the healthy functioning of the democratic process".[104] Such journalism had historically been funded by advertisements in local media outlets and, according to the ACCC, no alternative business model had emerged to provide adequate returns for such journalism.[105] The ACCC further found that there was a bargaining power imbalance in the relationship between digital platforms and news organisations in negoti-

---

[102] Australian Competition and Consumer Commission (2019), p. 4.

[103] Flew and Wilding (2021).

[104] ACCC (2019), p. 1.

[105] Ibid.

ating the share of advertising revenue (generated by digital platforms through disseminating news) that should go to the organisations that create such news. More specifically, it found that even if such news content contributes to the advertising revenue generated by digital platforms, news media organisations generating content were unable to negotiate an appropriate share of that revenue.[106]

The ACCC's report led to the legislation of the News Media Bargaining Code. The Code requires designated digital platforms to share sufficient revenue with Australian publishers of news content. It seeks to achieve this goal through a mandatory code of conduct aimed at addressing the bargaining power imbalance in negotiations between news organisations and digital platforms that disseminate their news.

Given that the root cause of the problem was not necessarily any specific conduct by the digital platforms, with dissemination of news or snippets by digital platforms often bringing about benefits to the creators of news content, the proposed solution did not involve conduct restrictions. Instead, the problem identified was the fair distribution of the advertising revenue, which was said to be skewed towards the digital platforms given their disproportionate bargaining power.

In addressing the problem, the Code does not entail any price regulation either. It does not regulate the revenue shares as between the parties, but requires designated digital platforms and registered news businesses to engage in good faith bargaining over the appropriate share (or distribution) of advertising revenue. To rebalance the bargaining power as between the parties, the Code provides for compulsory arbitration as a penalty default.[107] Specifically, if the parties do not reach a (commercially negotiated) agreement about the remuneration for covered news content made available on designated digital platforms (ie, the apparently preferred option), the regime defaults to compulsory arbitration. To further incentivise the parties to negotiate reasonably, should the arbitration alternative be triggered, the arbitral panel is directed to select one from the two final offers made by the bargaining parties.

This model of platform regulation appears to identify a specific problem, whereby the dissemination of news through digital platforms has a negative impact on funding the creation of a specific type of news content. It proposes a tailored solution to the problem, which incidentally seeks to eschew either a regulatory or political actor engaging in price-determination as between collaborating parties in the platform ecology. Instead, the threat of arbitration acts as a penalty default to encourage parties to negotiate a mutually acceptable commercial solution and to make plausible and reasonable proposals in those negotiations, given that ultimately it is one of the parties' final offers that would be selected by the arbitral panel.

While generally not regulating conduct, the Code does require designated platforms to provide registered news business corporations with advance notification of any *planned* changes to any of their algorithms or internal practices that would have

---

[106] Ibid p. 206.

[107] Baker and Krawiec (2004), p. 663.

a significant effect on covered news content.[108] This intervention should further aid news organisations in effectively bargaining for a fair share of the revenue by addressing information asymmetry. It seeks to enhance the bargaining autonomy and power of upstream news organisations, rather than regulate the ability of platforms to change their algorithms or other commercial strategies.

The former Chair of the ACCC, Rod Sims, has argued that the Code "has been successful in achieving" the narrow objective to which it had been targeted.[109] Scholars have been less sanguine, suggesting that the effects of the Code have been more heterogeneous, with only some Australian news media businesses managing to strike deals with platforms such as Google and Meta.[110] At the same time, it has been argued that the operation of the Code (largely as a background threat, rather than through actual designation of platforms or arbitrated outcomes) "has resulted in significant funding being directed to Australian newsrooms and the employment of more journalists" and has the support of news media organisations, including those who have not managed to secure deals.[111] The main threat to the viability of the code is identified as the highly dynamic digital ecology and the changing nature of the commercial practices and business models pursued by the platforms themselves, as well as by news organisations, which necessitates on-going review of the operation of the Code and its outcomes.[112]

The 2023 review of the operation of the Code revealed that it had facilitated 23 agreements between Google and news publishers, and 13 agreements between Meta (as owner of Facebook and Instagram) and news publishers. The report recommended granting the ACCC information gathering powers to reveal more details about the otherwise secret deals struck as between platforms and news organisations, as a mechanism that can potentially further rebalance the bargaining power between the two negotiating parties.[113]

The ACCC's digital platforms inquiry went on to consider other problems and limitations in the regulation of platform power through competition law, along the lines of similar reviews conducted in other jurisdictions. In respect of the enforcement of traditional competition law against digital platforms in Australia, it is worth noting (as many of the submissions to the ACCC inquiry did) that the ACCC has pursued few cases against digital platforms, compared to other jurisdictions around the world (including comparable jurisdictions such as Japan or South Korea). The ACCC's approach seems to reflect a degree of modesty on the part of the Australian enforcer about the extent to which a relatively small jurisdiction, such as Australia, can impose its own preferred solutions on large digital platforms operating through global business practices. As such, the ACCC's occasional interventions have

[108] *Competition and Consumer Act 2010* s 52S.

[109] Sims (2022).

[110] Bossio and Barnet (2023).

[111] Ibid pp. 622–623.

[112] Ibid pp. 623–624.

[113] Treasury, Australian Government (2022).

impugned conduct that has a specifically local dimension or salience for local users, including pursuant to its consumer protection mandate.

For example, some actions by the ACCC have focused on data collection, retention or sharing practices by digital platforms and the appropriate disclosure to users. A 2020 action assailed Google for misleading and deceptive conduct under the Australian Consumer Law based on the way in which Google used personal data for targeted advertising to users.[114] Similarly, an action for misleading and deceptive conduct was pursued against Facebook for the use of personal data of Australian users in the aftermath of the Cambridge Analytica scandal.[115]

A case that illustrates the limited ability of the Australian enforcer to impose its own preferred solutions for platform conduct that has broader global implications is the outcome of the ACCC's review of Google's proposed acquisition of Fitbit Inc. (Fitbit). Both merging parties were global US-based companies, and they originally sought informal clearance for the merger from the ACCC in light of their Australian operations. The ACCC's preliminary assessment raised two competition concerns arising due to Google's role as a key intermediary with a leading position in collection of consumer data. The ACCC was concerned that the acquisition of Fitbit would lead to the anticompetitive aggregation of data with Google obtaining access to Fitbit's health and fitness data relevant to services in several markets, including data-related health services and online targeted display advertising. Precisely because of its platform position, Google's ownership of key inputs for wearables (including Maps and the Android operating system) would mean that integration into the health wearables segment through ownership of Fitbit could result in foreclosure by Google of rival wearables manufactures through the familiar self-preferencing practices.[116]

Originally, Google offered remedial undertakings to obtain the ACCC's blessing for the merger, but these were rejected by the ACCC following public consultation. However, despite not having the ACCC's clearance, Google proceeded with its acquisition of Fitbit in January 2021, with the merger consummation providing the basis for an ACCC enforcement investigation. Following the completion of the transaction, the ACCC also commenced a misleading and deceptive conduct action against Fitbit for providing misleading information to Australian consumers about their right to obtain a replacement of a faulty device, which was inconsistent with the consumer guarantees under the Australian Consumer Law.[117]

---

[114] *Australian Competition and Consumer Commission v Google LLC (No 4)* [2022] FCA 942.

[115] This case is ongoing. In 2022, the Full Court of the Federal Court rejected Facebook's appeal with respect to a procedural question in the case, see *Facebook Inc v Australian Information Commissioner* (2022) 289 FCR 217; [2022] FCAFC 9.

[116] See Australian Competition and Consumer Commission (28 June 2020) Statement of Issues: Google LLC Proposed Acquisition of Fitbit Inc. Available at https://www.accc.gov.au/system/files/public-registers/documents/Google%20Fitbit%20-%20Statement%20of%20Issues%20-%2018%20June%202020.pdf.

[117] Australian Competition and Consumer Commission (24 October 2022) Fitbit in court over statements to consumers on faulty devices. ACCC. Available at https://www.accc.gov.au/media-release/

There have been also a relatively small number of private actions under Australia's competition law, whereby smaller firms collaborating with the digital platforms have complained about conduct which appears to abuse the platform's gatekeeper or intermediary position by withdrawing cooperation or self-preferencing.

Unlockd Ltd v Google Asia Pacific Pte Ltd,[118] provides a good illustration of the challenges faced by small firms that are dependent on continued collaboration with digital platforms to reach their customers. In that case, Unlockd Ltd, an Australian company, produced an app that allowed a user to opt into watching advertising on their phones, for which they were rewarded with credits that could be used to buy other credits, such as for mobile phone usage or frequent flyers points.

Unlockd had developed and sold its app through the Android PlayStore. Google decided that the app was outside its AdMob and Google Play terms and conditions, governing how advertising is presented to Android users. It indicated that the Unlockd app would be removed from the Google Play store. As the app worked only on Android devices, this would leave Unlockd without a way to sell and reach potential users. In the Australian Federal Court, Moshinky J granted an interim injunction that prevented Google from terminating or suspending Unlockd's access to the Google Play Store and Google AdMob services. The court recognised the dependence of Unlockd on continued access to Google's PlayStore to be able to commercialise its application. However, for a small firm such as Unlockd, the litigation process was too long and costly to be able to prevail on the merits. Eventually Unlockd went into administration,[119] and the competition matter never proceeded to a resolution on the merits.

In a trial on the merits for misuse of market power under s 46 of the CCA, Unlockd would have faced the difficulty in assessing the effects of the termination, as it would have been difficult to identify the precise market in which Unlockd competed and it does not seem likely that Google would have sought to leverage itself into that market in any event. Potentially, Unlockd could have argued that Google was trying to snuff out a nascent rival which could have undermined its market power in digital advertising, but this argument faces the challenge that Unlockd clearly was not a significant player or threat at the time of the termination of the relationship by Google (if ever).[120]

A similar case has been pursued by Epic Games against Apple, based on Apple's insistence that the game be distributed only via the Apple Appstore and using Apple's payment system for within-app purchases. This Australian litigation proceeded in parallel to similar litigation in the US,[121] relying on alleged violations of

fitbit-in-court-over-statements-to-consumers-on-faulty-devices.

[118] *Unlockd Ltd v Google Asia Pacific Pte Ltd* [2018] FCA 826.

[119] *Re Unlockd Ltd (administrators apptd)* [2018] VSC 345, [1].

[120] See Svetiev (2023) [8.430].

[121] It is worth noting that Epic is pursuing parallel actions, based on similar theories of violation and harm, against both Apple and Google, in the US as elsewhere, see DeGeurin (2023) The curious case of Epic Games: how the developer beat Google but not Apple. The Guardian. Available via https://www.theguardian.com/technology/2023/dec/16/epic-games-antitrust-google-apple.

the Australian competition provisions. The Full Federal Court of Australia, on appeal, overturned a stay in proceedings based on the parties' commercial agreement (prepared by Apple) which had stipulated an exclusive jurisdiction (in California) for any disputes as between the parties. The Court's decision was based, inter alia, on the fact that "serious issues of public policy" with far reaching implications for Australian consumers were to be ventilated as part of the dispute, which may be seen to rebalance to some extent the bargaining position of the parties.[122] The case on the substance is, as such, still ongoing.

The experiences in the foregoing cases against digital platforms are, to some extent, reflected in the ACCC's fifth interim report in its Digital Platform Services inquiry released in 2022, which also recommended regulatory reforms. As a prelude to its law reform recommendations, the ACCC argued that traditional enforcement of competition law is unlikely to provide an adequate response to the control of digital platform power for several reasons, including:[123]

- the analytical tools used in competition enforcement, such as definition of markets (in which power and effects are evaluated) perform poorly in digital markets where services are provided for free, reductions in quality cannot be easily measured and the boundaries between markets are difficult to draw as they also shift continuously in response to technological and preference changes;
- the evidence required to demonstrate likely negative effects on competition and consumer welfare would often be unavailable at the time of litigation in highly dynamic markets, making it very difficult to establishing an effects-based violation in a legal proceeding with the requisite standard of proof;
- the long duration of court enforcement proceedings for competition law violations implies that determinations and remedies arrive too late to reverse any anticompetitive effects or to provide any deterrence in dynamic market environments;
- the limits of traditional competition law remedies, particularly where the scope of a remedy is limited by the court's violation findings, imply that antitrust defendants can easily re-design their anticompetitive conduct or refocus it on different segments in the platform ecology.

Consequently, the ACCC proposed the legislative elaboration of specific digital service-oriented mandatory codes of conduct. The proposal appears clearly inspired by the EU and UK regulatory models recently implemented and discussed by other contributors, as well as the bills before the US Congress discussed above. As in those other templates, the specific conduct obligations proposed would operate separately and in addition to competition law rules, though they would attach to specifically identified platform *services* (rather than the platforms themselves as in other jurisdictions). The fact that the conduct obligations are formulated around specific

[122] *Epic Games, Inc v Apple Inc* (2021) 286 FCR 105; [2021] FCAFC 122.

[123] See Australian Competition and Consumer Commission (Sept 2022), pp. 48–51. Notably, these are precisely some of thereasons to pursue experimentalist forms of enforcement in digital markets. See Svetiev (2020).

services in the digital sphere is justified by the objective to make those obligations better tailored to the specific kinds of concerns about harm for specific services.[124] As in the other jurisdictions, for a platform to be subject to these conduct obligations, it has to be specifically designated by reference to a combination of quantitative and qualitative criteria related to market structure and indicators of firm size and dominance.

Rather than seeking to encourage directly negotiated solutions between firms in the digital ecology, as does the News Media Bargaining Code, the proposed mandatory service-specific conduct obligations for digital platforms would be implemented within the traditional law enforcement paradigm. The mandatory codes would define service-specific conduct obligations for platforms, allowing an enforcer to pursue violations of those obligations. However, the ACCC believes that such enforcement would be more agile because the conduct obligations would be more clearly defined (compared to the more generic competition violations in the statute), making it easier to detect and establish violations by the platforms (compared to purpose or effects-based competition violations). Further, the ACCC is of the view that these obligations could be more flexibly defined, and *re-defined*, in light of experience, by the ACCC in close consultation with market stakeholders. It appears that remedies would be based on traditional civil penalties, which would aim to provide appropriate deterrence for platforms not to engage in the prohibited conduct.

4 Conclusion

The analysis in this paper suggests that the platform wave of antitrust started with the *Microsoft* cases in both the United States and the European Union,[125] although it may be that the lessons of those cases and their remedial problems have not been learned in the ongoing reorientation of digital platform law.[126] The Microsoft litigation(s) illustrated the indeterminacy of the effects of conduct that might broadly be characterised as platform predation. The cases in both the US and EU also illustrated the acute problem of fashioning effective remedies, including through finding modalities to influence corporate decision making, away from defaulting to (apparently) anti-competitive strategies under conditions of uncertainty, even when such strategies are not necessarily in the longer-term interests of an incumbent platform. This last point implies that platform owners (or managers) may not be good stew-

[124] Thus, for example, an application store service may give rise to different kinds of anticompetitive conduct compared to a search engine. This probably reflects the Australian legislator's aim for textual specificity.

[125] Svetiev (2007). See *Microsoft Corp. v. Commission* (2007; T-201/04) and *United States of America v. Microsoft Corporation* (2001) 253 F.3d 34.

[126] Lopatka and Page (2022) argue that Google is engaging in the same anticompetitive practices that it accused Microsoft of in the early 2000s.

ards of the platform ecology in ways that would be consistent not only with the public interest, but also with the platform's strategic interests. At the same time, neither exit nor voice by users or collaborating firms operating in the platform ecology provides effective disciplines on platform decision-making either. This also diminishes the hope that competitive constraint is exercised by other similar platforms, given the observed and growing overlap in the activities of different platforms, and their rivalry for user attention, even if they may be seen to provide different kinds of digital services.[127] The effectiveness of such discipline depends on consumers (or users) being able to compare and choose among meaningfully different offerings, which may be a tall order in an increasingly confounding digital environment. As a result, the platform effects on the political process become an even more significant concern. Their ability to muddy the political waters anticipates a dystopic outcome that platforms escape any kind of control (public or private) because there are no actors with sufficient knowledge to exercise effective discipline.

I have argued that the re-orientation of digital platform law has led to the diffusion of common templates across different jurisdictions, all of which aim to control specifically defined conduct (typically through self-preferencing and other forms of leveraging or foreclosure) by designated digital platforms (typically based on their size and structural characteristics of their operations). These templates seek to identify the species of conduct that have been pursued in existing antitrust actions, generalise them into a broader genus of conduct and apply them to large and strategically significant platforms. They also aim to make it easier for enforcers to prevail vis-à-vis digital platforms by either changing the presumptions or the burden of proof, more specifically defining prohibited conduct and removing requirements to prove negative effects on consumers or on competition in dynamic contexts. Such templates are diffusing despite the absence of much evidence that they are likely to provide an effective response to the specific problems posed by digital platforms.

The key argument of this paper is that the ongoing reorientation of digital markets law is not supported by a root-cause analysis of the drivers that give rise to the platform model of production and the specific problems arising in digital industrial organisation. If some of the postulates about the behaviour of users or collaborating firms in a digital platform's ecology are correct, it is not clear at all whether either the regulatory approaches followed by most jurisdictions or even the neo-Brandeisian deconcentration project are going to deliver any tangible benefits to the market. The litigated cases in the US against the tech platforms are proceeding around familiar antitrust categories. Ultimately, even where the US agencies prevail in the litigation, as in the Google search case, the crucial question will be the design of remedial relief. There is currently no indication of what kind of behavioural restrictions, divestiture or deconcentration would be appropriate in the digital platform ecology on non-specific inputs and production capabilities or assets. Even a structural remedy will require monitoring and adjustment, as envisaged in experimentalist enforcement models. Thus, to the extent that the increased focus on digital markets law by

[127] Petit (2020).

policy-makers and regulators is going to produce any novel experiments that successfully respond to the problems in inter-firm collaboration or user protection, they are more likely to come from enforcers and firms developing innovative and recursive remedial workarounds to overcome the limits of traditional legal enforcement.

References

Aloisi A, De Stefano V (2022) Your boss is an algorithm: artificial intelligence, platform work and labour. Hart Publishing, Oxford

Aloisi A, Gramano E (2019) Artificial intelligence is watching you at work: digital surveillance, employee monitoring, and regulatory issues in the EU context. Comp Labor Law Policy J 41:95–121

Appadurai A, Alexander N (2020) Failure. Polity Press, Cambridge

Australian Competition and Consumer Commission (2019) Digital platforms inquiry final report. https://www.accc.gov.au/about-us/publications/digital-platforms-inquiry-final-report

Australian Competition and Consumer Commission (2021) Digital advertising services inquiry final report. https://www.accc.gov.au/about-us/publications/digital-advertising-services-inquiry-final-report. Accessed 10 Dec 2023

Australian Competition and Consumer Commission (Sept 2022) Digital platform services inquiry interim report no. 5. <https://www.accc.gov.au/about-us/publications/serial-publications/digital-platform-services-inquiry-2020-2025/digital-platform-services-inquiry-september-2022-interim-report-regulatory-reform>

Baker S, Krawiec KD (2004) The penalty default canon. George Wash Law Rev 72:663

Bernstein L (2015) Beyond relational contracts: social capital and network governance in procurement contracts. J Leg Anal 7:561–621

Bossio D, Barnet B (2023) The news media bargaining code: impacts on Australian journalism one year on. Policy & Internet. https://doi.org/10.1002/poi3.361

Bostoen F, Petit N (2023) Platforms' treacherous turn. https://doi.org/10.2139/ssrn.4664056

Cass RA (2013) Antitrust for high-tech and low: regulation, innovation, and risk. Econ Policy 9:169–200

Chandler A (1977) The visible hand: the managerial revolution in American business. Belknap Press, Cambridge

Chin C (2022) Breaking down the arguments for and against U.S. antitrust legislation. Centre for Strategic & International Studies. https://www.csis.org/analysis/breaking-down-arguments-and-against-us-antitrust-legislation

Coase RH (1937) The nature of the firm. Economica 4:386–405

Crémer J, de Montjoye Y-A, Schweitzer H (2019) Competition policy for the digital era. Publication Office of the European Union, Luxembourg

Dawson D, Segal J, Rendall C (2003) Review of the competition provisions of the Trade Practices Act. The Commission, Canberra

De Gregorio G (2022) Digital constitutionalism across the Atlantic. GlobCon 11:297–324

Easterbrook FH (1984) The limits of antitrust. Tex Law Rev 63:1–40

Estlund C, Liebman WB (2021) Collective bargaining beyond employment in the United States. Comp Labor Law Policy J 42:371

Farrell J, Weiser PJ (2003) Modularity, vertical integration, and open access policies: towards a convergence of antitrust and regulation in the internet age. Harv J Law Technol 17:85

Flew T, Wilding D (2021) The turn to regulation in digital communication: the ACCC's digital platforms inquiry and Australian media policy. Media Cult Soc 43:48–65. https://doi.org/10.1177/01634437209260

Fox EM (2002) What is harm to competition? Exclusionary practices and anticompetitive effect. Antitrust Law J 70:371–411
Fransman M (2010) The new ICT ecosystem: implications for policy and regulation. Cambridge University Press, Cambridge
Furman J, Coyle D, Fletcher A et al (2019) Unlocking digital competition: report from the Digital Competition Expert Panel. HM Treasury, London
Gasser U, Palfrey J (2007) Breaking down digital barriers: when and how ICT Interoperability drives innovation. Research Publication, Berkman Center for Internet & Society
Gill F (2023) Work and social justice. Bristol University Press, Bristol
Gilson RJ, Sabel CF, Scott RE (2009) Contracting for innovation: vertical disintegration and inter-firm collaboration. Columb Law Rev 109:431–502
Granovetter M (1985) Economic action and social structure: the problem of embeddedness. Am J Sociol 91:481–510
Gray J, Santesteban C (2023) The FTC needs to focus arguments on technological transitions after high-profile losses. In: Promarket. https://www.promarket.org/2023/09/22/ftc-needs-to-focus-arguments-on-technological-transitions-after-high-profile-losses/
Hagiu A, Wright J (2015) Multi-sided platforms. Int J Ind Organ 43:162–174
Herrigel G, Wittke V, Voskamp U (2013) The process of Chinese manufacturering upgrading: transitioning from unilateral to recursive mutual learning relations. Glob Strategy J 3:109–125
Hirschman AO (1970) Exit, voice and loyalty: responses to decline in firms, organizations, and states. Harvard University Press, Cambridge
Hovenkamp H (2023) Structural antitrust relief against digital platforms. University of Penn, Institute for Law & Economic Research Paper No 23 - 44. https://doi.org/10.2139/ssrn.4616175
Jennejohn M (2016) The private order of innovation networks. Stan Law Rev 68:281–366
Katz M, Sallet J (2018) Multisided platforms and antitrust enforcement. Yale Law J 127:1–31
Kerber W (2019) Updating competition policy for the digital economy? An analysis of recent reports in Germany, UK, EU, and Australia. Available at SSRN: https://doi.org/10.2139/ssrn.3469624
Khan L (2017) Amazon's antitrust paradox. Yale Law J 126:710–805
Khan L (2018) The new Brandeis movement: America's antimonopoly debate. J Eur Comp Law Pract 9:131–132
Kovacic WE (2007) The intellectual DNA of modern U.S. competition law for dominant firm conduct: the Chicago/Harvard double helix. Columb Bus Law Rev 2007:1–80
Lancieri F, Sakowski P (2021) Competition in digital markets: a review of expert reports. Stan J Law Bus Fin 26:65–170
Lavenex S, Serrano O, Büthe T (2021) Power transitions and the rise of the regulatory state: global market governance in flux. Regul Gov 15:445–471
Lippi M, Contissa G, Jablonowska A et al (2020) The force awakens: artificial intelligence for consumer law. J Artif Intell Res 67:169–190
Lopatka JE, Page WE (2022) The Microsoft litigation's lessons for United States v. Google. Univ Miami Law Rev 77:319–387
Mac Síthigh D, Siems M (2019) The Chinese social credit system: a model for other countries? Mod Law Rev 82:1034–1071
Mehra S (2023) The DoJ's adtech suit against Google is anything but unconventional. In: Promarket. https://www.promarket.org/2023/03/09/doj-adtech-suit-against-google-is-anything-but-unconventional/
Melamed AD, Petit N (2019) The misguided assault on the consumer welfare standard in the age of platform markets. Rev Ind Organ 54:741–774
Miller GJ (1992) Managerial dilemmas: the political economy of hierarchy. Cambridge University Press, Cambridge
Mokudai T, Schröder M, Müller M et al (2021) Digital technologies as lean augmentation: a preliminary study of Japanese automotive manufacturers. Int J Automot Technol Manag 21:228–249

Moreno Belloso N, Petit N (2023) The EU Digital Markets Act (DMA): a competition hand in a regulatory glove. Eur Law Rev 38:391
Murray (2023) "Shadow" settlements and the Tunney Act. In: Competition Policy International. Available via PYMNTS. https://www.pymnts.com/cpi_posts/shadow-settlements-and-the-tunney-act/#:~:text=The%20premise%20of%20these%20%E2%80%9Cshadow%E2%80%9D%20criticisms%20is%20that%20the%20antitrust,that%20the%20premise%20is%20flawed
Orgad L, Reijers W (2021) How to make the perfect citizen? Lessons from China's social credit system. Vanderbilt J Transnatl Law 54:1087–1121
Page WH, Lopatka JE (2007) The Microsoft case: antitrust, high technology, and consumer welfare. University of Chicago Press, Chicago
Paul S (2020) Antitrust as allocator of coordination rights. UCLA Law Rev 67:378
Paul S (2023) On firms. Univ Chic Law Rev 90:579–622
Paul S, McGaughey E, McCrystal S (eds) (2022) The Cambridge handbook of labor in competition law. Cambridge University Press, Cambridge
Petit N (2020) Big tech & the digital economy: the moligopoly scenario. Oxford University Press, Oxford
Pitofsky R (2002) Antitrust at the turn of the twenty-first century: the matter of remedies. Geo Law J 91:169–181
Pitofsky (ed) (2008) How the Chicago school overshot the mark: the effect of conservative economic analysis on U.S. antitrust. Oxford University Press, Oxford
Radic L (2022) 7 Big Questions about the Open App Markets Act. In: Truth on the Market. https://truthonthemarket.com/2022/11/01/7-big-questions-about-the-open-app-markets-act/
Ray SR, Jones AT (2006) Manufacturing interoperability. J Intell Manuf 17:681–688
Rossetti C, Choi TY (2005) On the dark side of strategic sourcing: experiences from the aerospace industry. Acad Manage Perspectives 19:46–60
Sabel CF (2006) A real-time revolution in routines. In: Heckscher CC, Adler PS (eds) The firm as a collaborative community. Oxford University Press, Oxford; New York, pp 106–156
Salop SC, Francis D, Sillman L et al (2021–2022) Rebuilding platform antitrust: moving on from *Ohio v. American Express*. Antitrust Law J 84:883–931
Schmidt J, Foss N (2023) Modularity, adaptation problems, and the governance and problem-solving capabilities of core firms in ecosystems. J Manage. https://doi.org/10.1177/01492063231215023
Schrank A, Whitford J (2011) The anatomy of network failure. Social Theory 29:151–177
Schrepel T (2021) Computational antitrust: an introduction and research agenda. Stan Comput Antitrust 1:1
Shelanski HA, Sidak JG (2001) Antitrust divestiture in network industries. Univ Chic Law Rev 68:1–99
Sims R (2022) The logic behind Australia's news media bargaining code. In VoxEU. Centre for Economic Policy Research (CEPR). https://cepr.org/voxeu/columns/logic-behind-australias-news-media-bargaining-code
Suzor N (2018) Digital constitutionalism: using the rule of law to evaluate the legitimacy of governance by platforms. SM+S 4. https://doi.org/10.1177/2056305118787812
Svetiev Y (2007) Antitrust governance: the new wave of antitrust. Loy Univ Chic Law J 38:593–694
Svetiev Y (2014) Settling or learning: commitment decisions as a competition enforcement paradigm. Yearb Eur Law 33:466–500
Svetiev Y (2016) The EU's private law in the regulated sectors: competitive market handmaiden or institutional platform? Eur Law J 22:659–680
Svetiev Y (2020) Experimentalist competition law and the regulation of markets. Hart Publishing, Oxford
Svetiev Y (2023) Corones' competition law in Australia, 8th edn. Thomson Reuters, Sydney
Treasury, Australian Government (2022) News media and digital platforms mandatory bargaining code: the code's first year of operation. Available at: https://treasury.gov.au/publication/p2022-343549

Varan A (2022) Addressing misuse of market power by large scale data driven digital platforms: a Neo Brandeis approach to competition issues in Australia. Aust Bus Law Rev 50:173–204

Von Hippel E (2005) Democratizing innovation. MIT Press, Cambridge

Weeks MR, Feeny D (2008) Outsourcing: from cost management to innovation and business value. Calif Manage Rev 50:127–146

Wegner P (1996) Interoperability. ACM Comput Surv 28:285–287

Williams C, Lee T, Marquiss N (2023) Room for agreement? Antitrust merger consent decrees policy and practice under the Biden administration. In: Competition Policy International. Available via PYMNTS. https://www.pymnts.com/cpi_posts/room-for-agreement-antitrust-merger-consent-decrees-policy-and-practice-under-the-biden-administration/#_ftn1

Williamson OE (1973) Markets and hierarchies: some elementary considerations. Am Econ Rev 63:316–325

Wu T (2018) The curse of bigness: antitrust in the new gilded age. Columbia Global Reports, New York

MIX
Papier aus verantwortungsvollen Quellen
Paper from responsible sources
FSC® C105338

If you have any concerns about our products,
you can contact us on
ProductSafety@springernature.com

In case Publisher is established outside the EU,
the EU authorized representative is:
Springer Nature Customer Service Center GmbH
Europaplatz 3, 69115 Heidelberg, Germany

Printed by Libri Plureos GmbH
in Hamburg, Germany